MAGILL'S
SURVEY
OF
WORLD
LITERATURE

MAGILL'S SURVEY OF WORLD LITERATURE

Volume 3

Golding–Kipling

Edited by
FRANK N. MAGILL

Marshall Cavendish Corporation
New York • London • Toronto • Sydney • Singapore

Published By
Marshall Cavendish Corporation
2415 Jerusalem Avenue
P.O. Box 587
North Bellmore, New York 11710
United States of America

Library of Congress Cataloging-in-Publication Data
Magill's survey of world literature. Edited by Frank N. Magill.
          p. cm.
   Includes bibliographical references and index.
   1. Literature—History and criticism. 2. Literature—Stories, plots, etc. 3. Literature—Bio-bibliography. 4. Authors—Biography—Dictionaries. I. Magill, Frank Northen, 1907-
PN523.M29 1992
809—dc20
ISBN 1-85435-482-5 (set)   92-11198
ISBN 1-85435-485-X (volume 3)   CIP

Second Printing

PRINTED IN THE UNITED STATES OF AMERICA

CONTENTS

MAGILL'S SURVEY OF WORLD LITERATURE

MAGILL'S
SURVEY
OF
WORLD
LITERATURE

WILLIAM GOLDING

Born: St. Columb Minor, Cornwall, England
September 19, 1911
Died: Perranarworthal, England
June, 1993

Principal Literary Achievement

Golding's novels explore the dark side of the human psyche. His *Lord of the Flies* became a classic fictive study in the dark side of human nature.

Biography

William Gerald Golding was born on September 19, 1911, in St. Columb Minor in Cornwall, England. His father was an extremely well-educated schoolmaster, and his mother was a strong-minded suffragette. Golding grew up in the family home at Marlborough. When he left to enter Brasenose College, Oxford, he had planned to study science, but he later decided to study English literature instead. After graduating, he worked for a while in a London theater group, writing, acting, and producing. In 1939, however, he married and then followed in his father's footsteps, becoming a schoolmaster at Bishop Wordsworth's School in Salisbury. He left Bishop Wordsworth's to serve in the Royal Navy during World War II. He saw action at sea as a lieutenant on a rocket launcher and was very affected by seeing the violence of which people were capable. He returned to the school in 1945 and taught there until 1961.

As a child, Golding had been fascinated with words, and as an adult he tried his hand at writing, but with little early success. A small volume, *Poems* (1934), was published when he was twenty-three, but Golding decided he was not a poet. During the early years of his teaching career, he wrote several novels that he himself described as being too derivative, too much like works that had already been written. Publishers were not interested in these works, either. Trying a new tactic, Golding wrote *Lord of the Flies* (1954). For this novel, he adopted an unusual perspective that he then altered at the end, and he used his experience with small boys to explore the dark side of humanity, which the war had brought to his attention. This time, Golding was more pleased with his efforts, but twenty-one publishers rejected the novel before Faber and Faber published it in 1954. Thus, Golding was forty-three when his literary career began to flourish.

A fairly regular stream of novels followed: *The Inheritors* (1955), *Pincher Martin* (1956; first published in the United States as *The Two Deaths of Christopher Mar-*

tin,) Free Fall (1959), and *The Spire* (1964). In addition, he published a collection of essays and book reviews, *The Hot Gates and Other Occasional Pieces* (1965). By 1964, Golding was enjoying the respect of scholars, a widening audience, and financial security. He left Bishop Wordsworth's in 1961 and, after a year as writer-in-residence at Hollins College in Virginia, devoted himself solely to writing.

With the publication of *The Pyramid* (1967), Golding's reputation suffered a slight decline. Critics gave its linked episodes and light social satire mixed reviews. The publication of three novellas in *The Scorpion God: Three Short Novels* (1971) did nothing to recoup Golding's reputational losses, nor did the twelve-year hiatus before *Darkness Visible* was published in 1979. That novel, however, attracted favorable critical attention and won for Golding the James Tait Black Memorial Prize in 1979. Golding's reputation was on the rise again. *Rites of Passage*, the first novel of The Sea Trilogy, followed in 1980, winning the Booker Prize and garnering much praise for Golding's parody of eighteenth century prose and for his adaptation of the tradition of sea journals. Golding also won the Booker Prize for his collection of essays, *A Moving Target*, published in 1982. In 1983, Golding was awarded the Nobel Prize in Literature; he was knighted in 1986.

Before Golding completed The Sea Trilogy, three other books appeared: *A Moving Target* (1982); *The Paper Men* (1984), a novel dismissed by most critics as the autobiographical musings of a cranky author who both craved and rejected critical attention; and *An Egyptian Journal* (1985), an account of a trip to Egypt in the winter of 1984. The publication of *Close Quarters* in 1987 and *Fire Down Below* in 1989, however, completed The Sea Trilogy and confirmed the critical praise received for *Rites of Passage*. The trilogy firmly reestablished Golding as a major novelist of the twentieth century.

Analysis

Critics have called Golding an allegorist, a fabulist, and a mythmaker. Of the three terms, Golding prefers mythmaker, and when he was awarded the Nobel Prize the citation acknowledged the mythic quality of his work, his ability to illuminate the condition of humankind by means of a concrete story.

In framing the concrete stories, Golding often draws on literary precedents, both specific works and genres. For *Lord of the Flies* Golding turns to the genre of boys' adventure stories and to R. M. Ballantyne's *The Coral Island* (1858), in particular. Yet where Ballantyne's boys, stranded on a desert island, have a jolly time and live harmoniously, Golding's boys become little savages. So Golding turns the literary precedent on its head, using it only as a starting place for his own unique view.

Golding also draws on his interests and his biography in his works. For example, Golding grew up near the sea, served in the navy, and has written essays on the pleasure and pain of sailing his own boat. Thus, in The Sea Trilogy, Golding is able to describe accurately the tensions of shipboard proximity, the moods of the ocean, and the nautical minutiae with which the crew must be concerned.

Golding has said that although he is, by nature, an optimist, he hopes that a defective logic makes him a pessimist. This view in many ways sums up the themes that play in his novels. In other words, his logic and objective observation reveal the dark side of human nature that people prefer to deny or ignore. There may be hope, some reason for optimism, however, if that dark side can be laid bare and acknowledged, for humankind has the potential for good as well as for evil.

The exploration of the dark side of humanity is a major thematic focus in virtually every novel, and Golding has been criticized as limiting himself to this one dimension. Even as he explores human depravity, however, Golding implies or asserts a second theme: the value of self-awareness and love as the means of coping with this inherent evil. In some works, such as *Lord of the Flies*, mostly depravity is shown. In *Darkness Visible*, however, the potential for good is explored more fully. The protagonist, Matty Windrave, devotes himself to the powers of good and saves one character from his evil impulses.

These two major themes in Golding's work are reinforced by some elements of his style and other characteristics of his novels. Often Golding creates remote or confined settings: a desert island in *Lord of the Flies*, a rock in the middle of the ocean in *Pincher Martin*, or the microcosm of the ship in The Sea Trilogy. In these settings, the characters may act out the evil that civilization keeps in bounds or be forced to look inside themselves to see the darkness lurking there. A restricted point of view forces readers to see from a particular, sometimes unfamiliar, perspective. In addition, Golding may suddenly change that perspective at the end of a novel, forcing the reader to see the situation anew.

Golding has been charged with obscurity, but whatever obscurity exists in his work serves a thematic purpose. He creates a fictional world seen with new eyes from unusual perspectives. The degree to which readers experience a connection between the fictional world and the world they inhabit is the degree to which Golding succeeds as a mythmaker.

LORD OF THE FLIES

First published: 1954
Type of work: Novel

> British schoolboys stranded on an island exhibit savagery that was suppressed in the supposedly civilized, war-torn world they left behind.

Lord of the Flies opens with schoolboys wandering out of the jungle, into which their plane has crashed, and onto the beach of a remote island. In this isolated setting, the boys first try to maintain a veneer of civilization, but they soon shed it to exhibit the evil that is inborn. Golding tells the story from the boys' perspective until the final few pages, where he then alters the perspective to enlarge the context. Little boys are not the only ones who have savagery at their core; the grown-ups do as well.

The first two boys to emerge, Ralph, an easygoing but fairly responsible boy, and Piggy, a thinker who is fat and asthmatic, gather the rest of the boys by sounding a conch shell. At their first assembly, the boys recognize the need for some rules: "After all, we're not savages. We're English." They elect Ralph chief and make Jack the leader of the boys who will hunt for food and keep a signal fire going.

Before long, the boys' immaturity and irresponsibility are clear and are a source of frustration to Ralph and Piggy. After building a couple of shelters, the boys would rather swim and roll rocks than work. The hunters would rather hunt than follow through on their other job of keeping a signal fire going. As a result, they miss the chance to signal a passing ship.

Immaturity and irresponsibility soon give way to violence and fear-inspired frenzy as the last vestiges of the veneer of civilization disappear. For Jack the early fun of hunting becomes a compulsion to track down and kill. He teaches his hunters to circle and close in on their prey, and in the circle the boys become bloodthirsty savages.

Fear works to intensify the power of the mob. Some of the little boys are afraid of a "beastie," and their fear spreads to all the boys. Only one boy, Simon, has the insight to know that the beast is inside them and the savagery they have always suppressed is what they should fear. Seeing something move among the rocks, the boys conclude that they have found the beast and are terrified. Only Simon has the courage to investigate. He finds a dead aviator, his parachute lines entangled in the rocks. Exhausted from his search and sick at what he has found, Simon crawls down the mountain, arriving on the beach to find himself in the middle of a circle of madly dancing, paint-smeared boys. In a blind frenzy, somehow thinking Simon is the beast crawling toward them, they kill him.

Although Piggy refers to Simon's death as an accident, Ralph knows it was murder and says he is scared "of us." Like Simon, Ralph knows the beast is within; he becomes the next scapegoat. The circle is closing on Ralph when the boys are rescued by officers from a cruiser. The perspective changes immediately. One officer remarks, "Fun and games." He asks Ralph jokingly, "Having a war or something? . . . Nobody killed, I hope? Any dead bodies?" The reader knows, as Ralph does, the awful truth of two dead bodies. The officer's naïveté reinforces the irony of the whole novel. The boys come out of a world at war. They land in an idyllic spot where their basic needs are met and where they can escape the carnage of the adult world. Since evil is within them, however, they, too, war on one another. They return, finally, to a world at war because escape from the island is not escape from evil. Evil is in the hearts of people.

PINCHER MARTIN

First published: 1956
Type of work: Novel

A self-centered man, stranded alone on what seems to be a rock in the middle of the ocean, faces the dark center of his being as he struggles to evade the nothingness of death.

Pincher Martin (first published in the United States as *The Two Deaths of Christopher Martin*) depicts one man's ferocious struggle against the nothingness, the loss of identity that death brings. Typically, Golding places the main character in a remote setting, where he is forced to take a long, hard look at himself. Also typically, what the character sees is a darkness at his core. A quintessentially self-centered person, Martin realizes that in his life he did whatever was necessary to come out on top or to have his own way. In death, however, he is fighting the one force that will erase all that he is and has. Thus he fights it with all his strength.

Seemingly the only survivor of a torpedoed ship, Martin is in fact alive only inside his own head. That is where his struggle takes place, but he imagines the battle raging on a rock in the middle of the ocean, a rock he has created from the memory of one of his own teeth.

Appropriate to the focus of the story, Golding tells virtually the whole story from Martin's perspective. Initially, Golding elicits sympathy for Martin by describing in detail the horror of his near drowning. Once Martin reaches the rock, he admonishes himself to think, to use his intellect and reason to survive. Admiration grows for this man who can keep his wits about him and devise shelter and find water and food. Yet since the story is being told from inside Martin's mind, he also returns to memories that reveal a self-centeredness at the core of his being. Thus Golding moves to a familiar theme, the revelation of the darkness and depravity in the heart of humanity.

Using Martin's memories and repeated images of eating, Golding slowly paints a picture of an unscrupulous, cruel man who nevertheless once felt moved by a love that was his one chance to experience something other than self-satisfaction. Martin remembers all the people he "ate": a nameless woman and a young boy whom he used sexually and tossed aside, the producer whose wife he seduced. More specifically he remembers Nathaniel, whom Martin loved for some reason that he cannot understand. He also hated him because Nat had obtained without apparent effort what Pincher could not get by force: Nat had peace of mind and also had Mary. For Martin, hate was stronger than love, so he raped Mary and tried to kill Nat.

All the images of eating converge into one symbol, the Chinese box. Martin recounts that the Chinese bury a fish in a tin box. Maggots eat the fish first and then each other until there is one maggot left, a rare dish. The sound of a spade knocking on the side of the box as it is dug up is like the sound of thunder. Pincher Martin lives his whole life trying to be the last successful maggot. When he realizes that the rock is only his tooth, imagined out of his effort to hang onto his identity, the only thing he has, he hears thunder and knows that the black lightning of God is coming for him. When the black lightning comes, he will be eaten.

After the lightning takes Martin's center, the perspective must change, for Pincher Martin no longer exists, even in his own mind. The end of the novel relates a conversation between the man who discovered Martin's body washed ashore and the officer who identifies and removes the body. The former wonders if Martin suffered; the latter tells him Martin never had time to kick his seaboots off. From Martin's perspective, however, the power of the imagination at the moment of death and his self-centeredness have extended his agony.

DARKNESS VISIBLE

First published: 1979
Type of work: Novel

A deformed and unlikely savior appears in the modern wasteland, bringing a message of spiritual power and love to its inhabitants.

Darkness Visible, by its title, conveys Golding's central preoccupation, that of making the darkness within visible through fiction. This novel focuses on the spiritual darkness of the modern world and its accompanying loss of love. The urban wasteland is represented by Greenfield, an English village once aptly named but currently suffering all the ills of urbanization, such as pollution, noise, and overcrowding. Two overlapping tales show that the people who live there are also suffering. For them, love is either distorted or absent; the old rituals have either died or lost their power to put people in touch with the divine.

The story begins in war-ravaged London, where the central character, Matty Windrave, emerges in flames like a burning bush from one of the fires. This child survives but is extremely deformed and without any family. He is shuttled from place to place, his distorted features making people uncomfortable. They see only the outside and do not value his kindness, honesty, or hard work. Although Matty craves love, he is rebuffed or used at every turn.

His teacher, Mr. Pedigree, likes handsome young boys and sits Matty almost behind a cabinet. Pedigree's perversity leads him to ask favorite boys to his rooms under the guise of helping them with their lessons. When he is warned by the headmaster about these meetings, Pedigree uses Matty to screen himself. Knowing that no one would think he had ulterior motives for inviting such an ugly child, he asks Matty to come to his rooms. The current favorite cannot deal with his rejection and falls to his death, which ultimately leads to Pedigree's imprisonment. Pedigree tells

Matty it is all his fault. Matty believes him. He thinks Pedigree is a friend he betrayed and resolves to make amends.

To those who reject him, Matty looks inhuman, but he is perhaps more than human. Unlike others who have lost touch with the spiritual world, Matty communicates with angels who help him in his quest to answer questions about who he is and what his mission is. Matty knows that the old rituals have lost their power, so he creates his own or endures new versions of the old ones. He memorizes and recites Bible passages, walks in chains through a swamp in self-baptism, and suffers a mock crucifixion. He knows he may be perceived as mad but feels that he needs the rituals to cleanse himself of his perceived sin, ward off evil, and gain the more-than-human power he will need for his mission of salvation.

The second story focuses on Sophy Stanhope, one of twin girls who grow up in Greenfield. Unlike Matty, Sophy and her sister, Toni, are beautiful. They are objects of attention and affection for everyone except their father, from whom they want love. Sophy's frustration comes out in violent, destructive impulses. Like Matty, she is in touch with mysterious forces, but she taps into them for evil purposes. Her first experience involves sensing and acting on the synchronous moment when a small duck swimming by can be killed by a large stone thrown into the water. Also like Matty, Sophy craves love. She has a family, but in her part of the wasteland world, family love is a joke. Her mother has abandoned the family, and her father consorts with a series of "aunties." Sophy's own love life involves an undercurrent of risk, violence, or manipulation.

The paths of the characters converge after they are grown up or have grown old. Matty's mission is to guard the messianic child that his angels tell him will be the new representative of divine power on earth. Sophy plots with others to kidnap the same child, the ransom and the evil adventure appealing to her. When Sophy's cohorts bomb the school where the child lives, Matty whirls through the fire to save him, becoming the burnt offering the angels have told him he must become.

Matty must also save Pedigree from himself. An old man who preys on children in the park, Pedigree knows that his compulsion will one day lead him to murder a child to keep him from telling. Nevertheless, he cannot stop himself. Pedigree is in the park waiting for his next boy to come close when he has a vision. The dead Matty approaches to take away the brightly colored ball that Pedigree uses to entice the boys. As Pedigree clutches the ball to his chest, it becomes his beating heart; when Matty pulls it from him, his heart stops and he dies. Yet Pedigree dies with insight. It is he who realizes that Matty was the only person who loved him and that love is what all people are searching for whether they call it sex, money, or power. Thus Matty is vindicated and evil thwarted at the end of the novel by the power of love and a higher, inexplicable power with which Matty was in tune.

THE SEA TRILOGY

First published: *Rites of Passage*, 1980; *Close Quarters*, 1987; *Fire Down Below*, 1989
Type of work: Novels

In the journals chronicling his voyage to Australia, Edmund Talbot comments on fellow passengers, the crew, and shipboard events while revealing his own maturation.

Rites of Passage, Close Quarters, and *Fire Down Below* comprise Golding's The Sea Trilogy. The focus of the trilogy, taken as a whole, is Edmund Talbot's maturation. Showing Talbot from his departure as a young upstart, sure of preferment and success, to his reflections as an old man, the novels allow Talbot to demonstrate his growth as a human being. Using the literary genre of the sea journal, Golding allows Talbot to speak for himself. Talbot's eighteenth century prose and his insistence on learning sailors' jargon lend authenticity to his record of the physical journey, while the content and tone of his journals reveal the results of his psychological journey and growth. In particular, his maturity is revealed in his record of his relationships with the other passengers and the crew and in his comments about himself.

In *Rites of Passage*, Talbot is a snob, easily impressed by titles, fine clothing, or fancy manners. He holds himself aloof and seems quite self-satisfied, certain of his intellect, his talents, and his future success. Any insecurity is revealed in the obsequious tone he sometimes adopts in his journal, which is written for his benefactor and godfather in England. He is very much concerned with being witty and painting a favorable picture of himself on the voyage.

As part of his commentary, Talbot introduces the other people on board. The passengers include Zenobia Brocklebank, an older woman attempting to seem younger and more socially prominent than her condition warrants; her father, who resorts to drink; Mr. Prettiman, a rationalist; Miss Granham, a spinster dismissed by Talbot as cold and unattractive; and Reverend Colley, an earnest but overzealous clergyman. The crew includes Captain Anderson, chief officer and strongly anticlergy; Billy Rogers, a handsome sailor who becomes Colley's shame; Mr. Summers, a lowborn officer with highborn qualities; and Wheeler, servant to Talbot.

The central event of this first novel is the death of Colley. Talbot finds Colley a ridiculous figure for much of the novel, and it is clear why Colley becomes the butt of jokes. A practical joke played by the sailors as part of the rites of crossing the equator is carried too far, however, and Colley simply wills himself to die of shame. After reading the letter that Colley left behind, Talbot must take a second look at the man. In addition, Talbot examines his own role in Colley's death, sensing that blaming the sailors is too easy. In this way, Talbot takes the first major step toward maturity. Examination of cruelty and blame—and the evil in human nature that prompts such tormenting—also allies *Rites of Passage* with earlier Golding novels.

With *Close Quarters*, Talbot begins a new journal. This one is to be written for himself rather than his patron, so he is freed from the necessity of banter and afforded the opportunity for introspection. In this novel, Talbot is less snobbish and displays an improved sense of humor. Still bristly when teased by being called "Lord Talbot," he can sometimes laugh at himself. Primarily, though, he matures in his relationships and has his courage tested. With one exception, his focus shifts somewhat from the passengers to the crew as the decrepit condition of the ship becomes significant.

When the ship is becalmed beside the *Alcyone*, Talbot finds new interests. In particular he falls in love with Marion Chumley, the ward of the captain of the *Alcyone*. His infatuation at first seems ridiculous, but his intentions are honorable and he remains true through their subsequent separation. In addition, he has a new officer to observe. Lieutenant Benet is sent to Talbot's ship in order to end an affair on board the *Alcyone*.

A risk taker, Benet is soon in conflict with Mr. Summers, who conservatively calculates the odds before acting. Their disagreements with each other and with Captain Anderson about how to handle the ship's broken mast afford Talbot an opportunity to admire the discipline of the ship's social order, particularly the way Summers yields to it despite his frustration at having to carry out orders with which he disagrees. As Talbot becomes better acquainted with Summers, his admiration and their friendship develop. It is a mark of Talbot's maturity that their friendship can survive a falling out.

Once the mast breaks, all aboard are in grave danger, and Talbot records their ways of facing impending death. One drinks, another prefers a quick, self-inflicted gunshot to longer suffering, and some retain their dignity. Talbot is among the latter despite his very real fear. In *Close Quarters*, Talbot is tested in love, friendship, and courage and is not found wanting.

Fire Down Below further demonstrates Talbot's maturation as he continues to learn to look beneath surface appearances to find true worth. The novel also returns to the theme of accountability, touched on in *Rites of Passage*. As Talbot's friendship with Summers is renewed and grows, Talbot sees clearly the qualities that make Summers superior to an officer who trades solely on his good family ties. Talbot appreciates Summers' kindness and concern, even for little things like helping to relieve the itch of being salty all the time. He recognizes Summers' sensitivity, his allowing Talbot to stand the night watch to avoid being in the cabin where Wheeler, Talbot's servant, committed suicide. Talbot also reforms his opinion of Miss Granham, now Mrs. Prettiman, appreciating her strength and intelligence. Talbot is more willing to learn from others about the practicalities of what to wear to be comfortable for months at sea or about social philosophy, which he discusses with the Prettimans.

If Talbot's character is in better shape in *Fire Down Below*, the ship is in worse shape. It survives a terrible storm and an encounter with an iceberg, but the foremast is shifting, slowing the ship's progress. Benet proposes running a hot metal bolt through the foremast, and Anderson agrees. The ship moves faster, but Summers alone acknowledges the danger that the mast will be smoldering on the inside. The ship safely reaches port, and Summers' loyalty seems to be rewarded when he is given command of the ship. In fact, Anderson and Benet have simply walked away from the responsibility for what they have done. When the ship catches fire and sinks, it is Summers who dies on board.

Events move swiftly once the ship reaches Sydney. Talbot's fortunes are reversed and then reversed again. When his patron dies, he must adjust to being penniless. Then when he finds he has been left a seat in Parliament, he is able to marry Marion and return to England. It is to Talbot's credit that he can accept his misfortune and rejoice in his good fortune. He has developed an equanimity he lacked when he first set out.

At the end of *Fire Down Below* Talbot speaks not to himself in his journal but, as an old man, to an audience of "dear readers." Looking back over his life, Talbot has some regrets that he turned down the adventure of setting off with the Prettimans to build a new world in Australia and instead chose the safer path of life as a member of Parliament. His final assessment, however, is that while his life has not been without disappointment or sorrow, it has been a good one. The self-satisfied narrator of *Rites of Passage* has become, by the end of the trilogy, simply satisfied.

Summary

As a mythmaker, William Golding writes stories that illuminate a truth about human nature. He sometimes creates those stories by presenting literary precedents in new ways and sometimes supplies the concrete details by drawing on his own experiences and interests. The truth he most often reveals is the existence of a depravity most humans would like to ignore or deny. The pessimism of such a focus is sometimes balanced by the possibility that self-awareness empowers goodness in people. In those novels that present both the darkness and the potential light, Golding's pessimistic logic and optimistic nature merge.

Bibliography

Babb, Howard S. *The Novels of William Golding*. Columbus: Ohio State University Press, 1970.

Biles, Jack I. *Talk: Conversations with William Golding*. New York: Harcourt Brace Jovanovich, 1970.

Biles, Jack I., and Robert Evans, eds. *William Golding: Some Critical Considerations*. Lexington: University Press of Kentucky, 1978.

Carey, John, ed. *William Golding: The Man and His Books. A Tribute on His Seventy-fifth Birthday*. Boston: Faber, 1986.

Cromptom, Don. *A View from the Spire: William Golding's Later Novels*. New York: Basil Blackwell, 1985.

Hodson, Leighton. *William Golding.* Edinburgh, Scotland: Oliver & Boyd, 1969.

Johnston, Arnold. *Of Earth and Darkness: The Novels of William Golding.* Columbia: University of Missouri Press, 1980.

Kinkead-Weekes, Mark, and Ian Gregor. *William Golding: A Critical Study.* New York: Harcourt, Brace & World, 1967.

Subbarao, V. V. *William Golding: A Study.* New York: Envoy Press, 1987.

Tiger, Virginia. *William Golding: The Dark Fields of Discovery.* London: Calder and Boyars, 1974.

Rebecca Kelly

OLIVER GOLDSMITH

Born: Pallas, County Longford(?), Ireland
November 10, 1728 or 1730
Died: London, England
April 4, 1774

Principal Literary Achievement

Goldsmith was a superb and highly versatile author. His humorous writings exhibited grace and charm with an awareness of the blessings and sorrows of life.

Biography

Oliver Goldsmith's life divides into almost equal segments. The first half is poorly understood. The second, beginning in 1756 with his arrival in London, is well documented. Goldsmith's birth is shrouded in some mystery. It is believed that he was born on November 10, 1728 or 1730, at his parents' home at Pallas, County Longford, Ireland. The uncertainty arises because the year next to Goldsmith's recorded birth was ripped out of the family Bible. He was the fourth child and second son of Charles Goldsmith, a leisure-loving curate who rose slowly in the Anglican church, and Ann Jones Goldsmith. Shortly after Oliver's birth, the family moved to Lissoy, where Charles became curate-in-charge of the parish at Kilkenny West.

At school, Oliver Goldsmith was a careless student, but never an unintelligent one. He was good in Latin and translated some of Vergil into English verse. This early taste for versification deepened in his youth, when he had the opportunity to hear professional storytellers and entertainers. Their lively tales increased his interest in romantic writing. Goldsmith's mother recognized his interest in, and devotion to, poetry and music from his early childhood. When he was older, she insisted, in spite of a grave financial condition, that he be educated as had his father and older brother. With financial backing from an adoring uncle, the decision was made for Goldsmith to attend Trinity College at Dublin in 1745. He was to enter as a sizar, or "poor scholar." Sizars swept the floors, were subjected to an embarrassing dress code requirement, and waited on others in return for room, board, and tuition fees. Goldsmith disliked his situation, wanting to quit school. Fortunately, his uncle encouraged him to continue, pointing out that Sir Isaac Newton had once been a sizar at Trinity.

Goldsmith was graduated from Trinity College in 1750 with a B.A. degree. Over the next two years, he worked as a tutor, failed in his efforts to be ordained in the Anglican church because of his age, and seriously considered emigrating to America

Edwin sc.

OLIVER GOLDSMITH, M.B.

or studying law in Dublin. He finally did neither, entering the University of Edinburgh in 1752 to study medicine. After two years, he still had not received a degree. In 1754, Goldsmith traveled to the University of Leyden in Holland to continue his medical studies. He then spent a year or so traveling throughout Europe. He arrived in Dover, England, on February 1, 1756. For several years, he worked at a variety of positions, including apothecary's assistant, physician, proofreader at a printing house, and usher at a boys' school. He also launched his literary career in 1757 by contributing articles to the *Monthly Review*, a practice that continued until his death. In the next few years, he continued writing and published *An Enquiry into the Present State of Polite Learning in Europe* (1759). He also produced *The Memoirs of a Protestant* (1758), an English translation of Jean Marteilhé's *Mémoires d'un Protestant* (1757), and essays to the *Critical Review, Bee, Busy Body, Weekly Magazine, Royal Magazine, British Magazine,* and *Lady's Magazine.* For the next two years, 1760 to 1761, he wrote his famous "Chinese Letters" for *The Public Ledger,* which were published in book form in *The Citizen of the World* (1762). He became known as "Dr. Goldsmith" at this time and became friends with such writers as Thomas Percy, Tobias Smollett, Edmund Burke, and, most importantly, Samuel Johnson.

Goldsmith became a prolific writer during the last fifteen years of his life. Hardly a year passed when he did not publish several works. Also, his versatility was, and still is, astonishing. Goldsmith wrote essays, translations, plays, novels, and poems. He also contributed paid hack work for publisher John Newbery. Goldsmith was always plagued by poverty. He was also jealous by nature, particularly of other writers. His most successful works were often spurred by others' success. Some good examples are the novel *The Vicar of Wakefield* (1766), in a genre that he normally despised, and two plays for the theater, including his masterpiece *She Stoops to Conquer: Or, the Mistakes of a Night* (1773).

In 1772, he became seriously ill with a bladder infection. Ailments would continue to haunt him until his death. Remarkably, his literary output did not decrease but remained constant. In fact, his productivity increased in the months preceding his demise. It was as if he knew that the end was near. A number of his works were unfinished, or published posthumously. On March 25, 1774, he became sick with kidney trouble. At the time, he was staying at the Temple in London. Ignoring the advice of several doctors, Goldsmith insisted on medicating himself by taking Dr. James's Fever Powders. The patent medicine had brought him relief in the past, but this time it induced severe fits of diarrhea and vomiting. Goldsmith refused to stop the medication. The symptoms worsened. In London on Monday, April 4, 1774, he went into violent convulsions and, after ninety minutes of agony, died. Five days later, Goldsmith was buried in an unmarked grave at the Temple Churchyard. The eulogies on his passing were effusive. Johnson wrote a Latin epitaph that was placed in the Poets' Corner at Westminster Abbey.

Analysis

Washington Irving wrote of Goldsmith that his genius "flowered early, but was late in bringing its fruit to maturity." Yet what an abundance poured forth during the last fifteen years of Goldsmith's life. Numerous studies have examined his separate contributions as essayist, novelist, dramatist, biographer, philosopher, and poet.

Goldsmith's literary career was launched in the April, 1757, issue of the *Monthly Review*, but his first important work did not appear until two years later with the publication of his first book, *An Enquiry into the Present State of Polite Learning in Europe*. The author published it anonymously, and for good reason, since he was aiming at the decline of learning in general. Goldsmith's work was self-serving. It allowed him to attack his enemies, particularly the pedantic critics who judged English literature by classic Greek or Latin standards. Needless to say, he raised a hornet's nest of criticism and received the serious literary attention that he craved. Goldsmith is difficult to categorize as a writer because he wrote so well on so many topics and in so many genres. William Hazlitt said of him:

> Goldsmith, both in verse and prose, was one of the most delightful writers in the language. His verse flows like a limpid stream. His ease is quite unconscious. Everything in him is spontaneous, unstudied, yet elegant, harmonious, graceful, nearly faultless.

Goldsmith was not a radical thinker like Jean-Jacques Rousseau but infused his work with moderation, sensibility, and irony. In his essays, he denounced the evils of capital punishment, cruelty to animals, excessive gambling; he noted the stupidity of revenge, the negative effects of luxurious living, and he made sensible suggestions about children's education. He had strong feelings about the prevalence of sentimental comedy, which he despised and tried to destroy by bringing back boisterous humor to the English stage.

In verse, Goldsmith was certainly skilled. He could pen poetical epistles, prologues, epilogues, and ballads, as well as more conventional poems. His versifying was always spontaneous, humorous, and it reflected dignity. Goldsmith's poetry could demonstrate strength, as well. In *The Traveller: Or, A Prospect of Society* (1764) and *The Deserted Village* (1770), he employed the similar theme of a man isolated from others, longing for his home. Goldsmith's use of a narrator in these poems also appears in *The Vicar of Wakefield*. He engaged the device of speaking directly to the reader so that the Vicar could comment on the criminal code and penal system. Yet, such is his artistry that the character always remains a true literary creation.

Poverty fueled Goldsmith's genius. All his life, he struggled to survive. It was only his writing that kept him out of the poorhouse or debtors' prison. The lack of financial resources helps explain why he was so prolific. To be blunt, Goldsmith was also a hack writer. Johnson says of Goldsmith that he was always able to adorn the most menial labor. Publishers often requested certain types of work, which may explain his versatility and why he never stayed with one genre for long. It was not uncommon for him to write in several genres at the same time. In 1766, for example, he published *The Vicar of Wakefield* and *A Concise History of Philosophy and Philosophers*, which was an English translation of Jean Henri Samuel Formey's *Histoire abrégée de la philosophie* (1760). He also composed *Poems for Young Ladies in Three*

Parts: Devotional, Moral, and Entertaining (1767) and began his first comedy, *The Good-Natured Man* (1768).

A worse criticism of Goldsmith, besides the serious charge of hack writer, is that he often plagiarized others. The accusation was first leveled at him in 1759, when he became sole contributor to the *Bee*, a weekly magazine whose pages he had to fill. Week after week, he wrote a number of essays, many of which were lifted from volume 5 of the French *Encyclopédie*. Goldsmith never defended his practice, justifying it as hack work, not literature. Even his famous series of "Chinese Letters" was lifted or adapted from several other sources, particularly *Lettres Chinoises* (1739-1740) by Jean Baptist de Boyer, Marquis D'Argens. In his lengthy two volume *An History of England in a Series of Letters from a Nobleman to His Son* (1764), Goldsmith borrowed heavily from Voltaire, Paul Rapin de Thoyras, Smollett, and Burke. He freely admitted "borrowing" the character Croaker in his play *The Good-Natured Man* from Johnson's *The Rambler*. He stole ideas, characters, words, and paragraphs from others throughout his career.

Goldsmith was no saint. He was highly irritable, possessing a mercurial temperament, envied other writers, gambled heavily, drank too much, borrowed money that he could not repay, lied to his friends and relatives, was often dishonest in his business dealings, and demonstrated a parasitic dependence on other writers. Yet, Goldsmith recognized his shortcomings and his absurd behavior. In the end, he triumphed over his imperfections. He became a warmhearted individual who gave freely of himself, always kept his integrity when it mattered, refused to write or dedicate work for people whom he did not respect, and always made his plagiarized borrowings more distinguished than the original. In short, he was a genius whose work revealed wisdom, seasoned judgment, and good humor. These attributes are best exemplified in two of his most famous works: *The Vicar of Wakefield* and *She Stoops to Conquer*.

THE VICAR OF WAKEFIELD

First published: 1766
Type of work: Novel

This charming, comical, romantic tale features a pastoral setting and is about a simple vicar experiencing a series of family misfortunes.

The Vicar of Wakefield, although published in March, 1766, was actually written years earlier. Scholarly evidence suggests that Goldsmith began writing the novel in 1760 and probably finished it in 1765. Mysterious stories surround the composition, sale, and publication of the work. One such tale concerns the venerable Samuel Johnson. According to his biographer, James Boswell, Johnson was summoned for immediate assistance by Goldsmith. It seems that Goldsmith was behind in his rent, and his landlady had had him arrested. Johnson quieted the much disturbed writer, learned of an unpublished novel, and sold a one-third share to a bookseller. Goldsmith discharged the debts and eventually sold the remaining shares.

The work in question is strongly believed to be *The Vicar of Wakefield*. Why did he write it? Speculation suggests that Goldsmith wrote the novel because he was consumed with jealousy by the publication, in January, 1760, of *The Life and Opinions of Tristram Shandy, Gent.* (1759-1767) by Laurence Sterne. Though Goldsmith professed a long dislike for the novel, the celebrity status enjoyed by Sterne may have motivated the still little-known Goldsmith to match his rival's success. Much has been made of the autobiographical elements to be found in *The Vicar of Wakefield*, including its faulty plot structure, the narrative technique employed, and the sentimental reversal-of-fortune conclusion. He uses the vicar, the delightful creation of Dr. Charles Primrose, as the novel's narrator and through the character voices many of his own ideas and experiences.

The Vicar of Wakefield falls neatly into two equal segments. The first is humorous, a comically ironic idyll. The second is romantic, underscored by a series of unrelieved disasters that befall the Primroses. Most critics believe that the second section is superior. The novel's central theme, that innocence can become contemptible in the face of evil or worldly wisdom, while never fully articulated by Goldsmith, supports the whole work. The vicar and his family are simple, innocent folk enjoying a pleasant, pastoral existence until they come into contact with reality. Their very virtues are turned on them as they suffer one disaster after another. Goldsmith reveals that the overthrow of their innocence is replaced by wisdom and compassion.

Perhaps that is why *The Vicar of Wakefield* achieved immediate popularity that increased substantially following Goldsmith's death. During the nineteenth century, for example, the novel enjoyed at least two editions a year. It has been translated into many languages. The reason for its success may be that the novel can be interpreted in many different ways. It exudes irresistible charm and ebullience, demonstrating Goldsmith's genius and absurdity. *The Vicar of Wakefield* remains one of the most popular books from the eighteenth century. The only other work by Goldsmith to match it in continuing popularity is his play *She Stoops to Conquer* (1773).

SHE STOOPS TO CONQUER

First produced: 1773 (first published, 1773)
Type of work: Play

This delightful comedy revolves around two youthful couples pursuing romantic intrigue against a background of deception, error, and the machinations of several eccentric characters.

She Stoops to Conquer: Or, the Mistakes of a Night was an immediate success for Goldsmith, his last literary triumph. The opening night audience, at Covent Garden on March 15, 1773, roared its continued approval. Five days following the premiere, every copy of the published version of the play was sold. Yet the circumstances surrounding the production of the play were marked by enormous difficulty for Goldsmith because the theater manager anticipated certain failure. Goldsmith finished writing the comedy in September, 1771. He took it to George Colman, manager of the Covent Garden, who repeatedly postponed producing it. It was only through the firm intervention of Johnson that Colman reluctantly agreed to stage it. (Goldsmith inscribed the published work to Johnson.) The script was much revised and altered during the weeks of rehearsal. Several of the leading actors refused to appear in it and were replaced. Yet the play's approval was such a complete success that Colman was severely criticized for his delay.

Looking back, it is difficult to comprehend Colman's reluctance to stage the comedy. *She Stoops to Conquer* was Goldsmith's second play. (Five years earlier at Covent Garden, Colman produced Goldsmith's first effort, *The Good-Natured Man* (1768), also well received by the public.) The problem stemmed from the fact that Goldsmith's views on comedy were different from prevailing taste. He had taken aim on the whole genre. In a piece published early in 1773 entitled "Essay on the Theatre: Or, A Comparison Between Sentimental and Laughing Comedy," he had bemoaned the prevailing taste of audiences for "sentimental comedy," which he called a bastard form of tragedy. In its place, Goldsmith proposed a new comic genre to be called "laughing comedy." The new form of comedy, as his two plays aptly demonstrated, eliminated moralizing, false appeals to sentimentality, and extraneous song and dance and concentrated instead on mirth, the exposure of human follies, utilizing characters from middle and lower classes and dialogue that was easy and natural. The general aim was laughter.

She Stoops to Conquer is a perfect example of Goldsmith's theories. The play opens with two gentlemen from London looking for the home of Mr. Hardcastle. They are tricked into thinking that the home is an inn and conduct themselves accordingly. One of the young men is there to woo young Kate Hardcastle. Kate pretends to be a barmaid until the hero declares his love for her. The Londoners behave boorishly to all concerned, and the nonstop frolic escalates rapidly. *She Stoops to Conquer* contains vital energy, many farcical elements, and amusing irony. Goldsmith's major theme is exploring the follies of blindness that all humans commit. After poking fun at all the characters, the playwright ends the comedy on a note of discovery. The hero, for example, finds himself and discovers the meaning of true love, marrying the perfect woman for him.

About a year after its premiere, dramatist Goldsmith died. *She Stoops to Conquer* endured, however, to become one of the most frequently produced plays of the English repertoire. Hardly a year passes in America that it is not staged by some professional, community, or university theater company. It has also been produced several times for television.

Summary

Oliver Goldsmith is one of the great writers of the eighteenth century, ranking with Jonathan Swift, Alexander Pope, and Samuel Johnson. He was certainly the master comedian of his age. His versatility in producing important poems, dramas, novels, and essays is without peer.

Goldsmith always remained a puzzle to his contemporaries. He was a difficult personality for them to comprehend. After his death, however, he assumed legendary proportions. Over the centuries, many anecdotes and recollections of the man have been offered, including countless books and shorter works. Perhaps Johnson wrote it best in his Latin inscription on Goldsmith's memorial in the Poets' Corner in Westminster Abbey: "in genius lofty, lively, versatile; in style weighty, clear, engaging."

Bibliography

Bloom, Harold. *Oliver Goldsmith*. New York: Chelsea, 1987.

Irving, Washington. *Oliver Goldsmith, A Biography; Biography of the Late Margaret Miller Davidson*. Edited by Elsie Lee West. Boston: Twayne, 1978.

Jeffares, A. Norman. *Oliver Goldsmith*. London: Longmans, 1959.

Kirk, Clara M. *Oliver Goldsmith*. New York: Twayne, 1967.

Quintana, Ricardo. *Oliver Goldsmith: A Georgian Study*. New York: Macmillan, 1967.

Rosseau, G. S., ed. *Goldsmith: The Critical Heritage*. London: Routledge & Kegan Paul, 1974.

Sells, Arthur Lytton. *Oliver Goldsmith: His Life and Works*. New York: Barnes & Noble Books, 1974.

Swarbrick, Andrew, ed. *The Art of Oliver Goldsmith*. London: Vision Press, 1984.

Wardle, Ralph M. *Oliver Goldsmith*. Lawrence: University of Kansas Press, 1957.

Woods, Samuel H., Jr., ed. *Oliver Goldsmith: A Reference Guide*. Boston: G. K. Hall, 1982.

Terry Theodore

NADINE GORDIMER

Born: Springs, Transvaal, South Africa
November 20, 1923

Principal Literary Achievement

Recipient of the 1991 Nobel Prize in Literature, Gordimer is noted for her vivid portrayals of human lives under apartheid.

Biography

Nadine Gordimer was born in Springs, a small gold-mining town in South Africa, on November 20, 1923. Her maternal grandfather emigrated from Europe to South Africa in the 1890's to go prospecting for diamonds. Her Lithuania-born Jewish father, who was also a part of the white colonial expansion in the early 1900's, started out as a watch repairer for mine workers and eventually owned a jeweler's shop. The circumstances of Gordimer's white middle-class upbringing provoked her understanding of the racial stratification in South African society.

One of two daughters, Gordimer had little formal education. As a very young girl, she took great pleasure in dancing until the age of ten, when she had persistent fainting spells. The condition was diagnosed as a rapid heartbeat caused by an enlarged thyroid gland. Forced to forgo dancing and participate in less strenuous activities, Gordimer recalls feeling considerably deprived during her childhood. She learned to channel her energies into reading and writing.

Gordimer had begun writing at the age of nine, and at the age of thirteen she published her first literary effort in a children's magazine. Because of the medical diagnosis, her mother was able to take young Nadine out of school, an act that caused Gordimer (in later years) to resent her mother. For an entire year, at the age of eleven, Gordimer stayed at home and read. Among her readings, Upton Sinclair's *The Jungle* (1906) affected her nascent social and political sensibilities. Her education was resumed with the hiring of private tutors. Most of her formative years, then, were isolated from other children and spent largely in the company of adults. From observing and listening to others, Gordimer was already collecting an arsenal of material for her writing.

By the age of fifteen, Gordimer had her first short story published in a magazine. At the age of twenty-one, she attended the University of Witwatersrand but left after a year. Nevertheless, this brief period at the university left a deep impression on her developing political consciousness. It was the first time that she mixed with blacks

771

and was able to observe for herself their terrible plight in South Africa. At the university, Gordimer mingled with blacks as "equals," as people engaged with the world of ideas. Still, from her early reading of Sinclair's novel about America's unjust labor practices, she was able to compare the situation of blacks in South Africa. She perceived that they were denied an education, exploited economically, and summarily dehumanized by a white minority government.

Gordimer's assessment of her hometown, especially in the light of her time at the university, is particularly harsh. Growing up in the Transvaal region of South Africa, she was frequently bored by what she perceived as trivial or practical matters of existence. She believes that her life changed completely in her early twenties, when she became intellectually stimulated by the events in the world and in her country. Although she did not participate actively in politics, she began to take what she considered a liberal humanist approach to the injustices visited upon the black population. In the 1940's, leftist movements, communist discussion groups, and black national movements were not yet banned by the white government, and the flurry of political activities attracted Gordimer's interest and attention. She was concentrating intensely on her writing at this time and had not yet incorporated these political observations into her work.

In 1949—the same year the White National Party officially came into power— Gordimer published a book of short stories, *Face to Face*, in Johannesburg, South Africa. She was twenty-six at the time. That was followed by a collection entitled *The Soft Voice of the Serpent and Other Stories* (1952), which was published in New York and London. Stories also began appearing in *The New Yorker* and journals such as *The Virginia Quarterly Review* and *The Yale Review*. She observes that politics and the devastating effects of apartheid on all South Africans have played a significant role in her development as a writer, but that "I was writing before politics impinged itself upon my consciousness."

Her first novel, *The Lying Days*, appeared in 1953, and there are specific autobiographical overtones. The main character, Helen Shaw, also undergoes a transformation in her political awareness at the university. Helen leaves her sheltered home life to discover a world populated with whites and blacks. Her first confrontation with issues of life and death occurs after she befriends several students who are committed to social change. Unlike Gordimer, however, who has stayed in South Africa to confront the conflicts directly, Helen departs from the country at the end of the novel. Although Helen is wiser and more sensitive to the turmoil in her country, her decision to leave contrasts sharply with the author's determination to produce change by staying.

In the next forty years of her writing career, Gordimer's many novels and short stories focused increasingly on the effects of apartheid. The kinds of changes her different characters experience reflect the modifications of her country. Like people in real life, her characters endure the joys and hardships that social and political changes bring. Her fifth novel, *A Guest of Honour* (1970), won the James Tait Black Memorial Prize, and her sixth novel, *The Conservationist* (1974), was awarded the

Booker Prize, a CNA Literary Award, and the Grand Aigle d'Or (a French international award). Gordimer's fictional work is substantially supplemented by her many pieces of nonfictional writing and her public interviews. In 1988, Stephen Clingman collected and published several from this wide array of writings in *The Essential Gesture: Writing, Politics, and Places.*

In 1990, Gordimer joined the African National Congress (ANC), an organization led by Nelson Mandela (who had been released the previous year from a twenty-eight-year imprisonment) that opposes the rule of a white minority government. That same year, South Africa began the process of dismantling apartheid. After more than fifty years of literary production Gordimer was awarded the Nobel Prize in Literature in 1991. The Nobel Foundation praised *The Conservationist, Burger's Daughter,* and *July's People* (1981) as the masterpieces of her career. Only years before, several of her novels had been officially banned in South Africa for their political content.

Analysis

Gordimer is often praised for her unsentimental portrayals of human lives under apartheid. She has emphasized repeatedly that "the real influence of politics on my writing is the influence of politics on people." In her novels, as Gordimer herself becomes increasingly aware of and indignant about the political apparatus of her country, each character experiences a transformation that reflects the changes in South Africa. All of Gordimer's characters are situated in the context of a political system where the nation's economic and judicial power is concentrated in and exercised by a minority racial group. She portrays the entire spectrum of lives—blacks and whites—oppressed by a racist regime.

In her fiction, Gordimer begins to hold South Africa accountable for the suppression and eradication of a majority of its people. Even those characters who strive to be as apolitical as possible are directly affected. As an example, a character in *A Guest of Honour*, Rebecca, proclaims her general ignorance in matters of politics. In the novel Rebecca falls in love with Colonel Bray, a white administrator who supports black liberation, and who dies violently; the remainder of the novel expresses Rebecca's disorientation and her feelings of dispossession as she wanders in London, unable to forget the politically motivated events leading to her lover's death.

Sometimes her characters openly express an apathetic stance, but even they are deeply affected at a personal level. In her second novel, *A World of Strangers* (1958), the main character is young, white, and upper-crust. Toby Hood moves from one social circle to another without much concern for social or political causes. Toby's lack of care for the politics in South Africa comes to an abrupt halt when his black friend Steven Sitole is hunted down by the police in a fatal car chase. Only then does Toby begin to recognize the inequities created by the color of someone's skin. After identifying Steven's body—much to the surprise of the white policemen, who view the friendship as an anomaly in South Africa—Toby begins to confront his own relationship to his country. Shortly after another friend, Anna, is arrested for subversive activity against the government, Toby makes the decision to leave South Africa.

Like the character Helen in *The Lying Days*, Toby realizes the shallowness of his own life and begins to find the terms for his own existence. Because the characters are so entrenched in their personal situations, it is difficult for them to be openly or even deeply concerned about the lives of other people. Like her early characters, who begin to take at least a humanist approach to the atrocities of apartheid, Gordimer herself observed that the relationship of politics to people was not so apparent to her in the beginning either, and that the realization came to her slowly. Having grown up in an insular, white, middle-class household, Gordimer began to shape her own awareness about the conflicts in South Africa only through reading about other people's pain in a variety of literature.

Her next novel, *Occasion for Loving* (1963), shows several characters who live without social consciousness and responsibility. The lives of the Stillwell family and their friends are empty and without much virtue; they move carelessly in and out of relationships and appear unmoved by the catastrophes that occur in the background. This novel ends a decisive phase in Gordimer's work, where she begins to move away from issues such as ignorance and indifference and toward events that require the individual to take some form of direct action against apartheid.

Yet if the apathy and momentary flashes of recognition are discouraging to Gordimer, they do not dissuade her from representing fully the people who suffer and endure in a system of apartheid. In *The Late Bourgeois World* (1966), Gordimer begins to experiment with different narrative strategies in order to capture as fully as possible the complexities of human lives in the grip of an oppressive regime. The main character, Liz Van Den Sandt, seems to begin where Helen Shaw might have continued years later had she returned to South Africa. In a novel that encompasses the events of a single day, Liz first learns of her ex-husband's death as the story opens. In the course of the day, which includes her breaking the news to their son at the boarding school, Liz memorializes the death of her politically active ex-husband. In untangling some mysteries of life and death, she decides that the meaning of life in South Africa includes becoming active and responsible. At the end Liz meets with a former ally of the "cause" and is incited to take subversive political action against apartheid.

The Late Bourgeois World marks a definite turning point in the way that Gordimer writes about the influence of politics on people. Until then, and in the short stories of the 1950's and 1960's, Gordimer emphasized the course of individual human lives, focusing on their personal joys and pains. As Gordimer's own political consciousness grew, she found the novel form more difficult to write because her worldviews had grown considerably.

One complaint that uninitiated readers have about Gordimer's later novels concerns the difficulty of identifying who is narrating or speaking about the events. As in the various forces that make up and affect the political situation in South Africa, Gordimer's narrative strategies reflect the complexities of human relationships. Specifically, because blacks and whites are completely segregated and any attempts to assemble are considered subversive to the central government, Gordimer's novels mirror this reality without oversimplifying the devastating consequences.

Both blacks and whites are represented in a variety of situations. In *A Guest of Honour*, the former administrator (who is white) has been invited to return to a liberated Africa in order to reform its educational system. Colonel Bray's observations of the effects of revolution reveal his sensitivity to the injustices that apartheid has inflicted upon the country. As the novel progresses, the reader experiences Bray's split allegiance to the two new black leaders as well as to white South Africa. In *The Conservationist*, the white landowner treats his help with great indifference and arrogance; after all, he is the boss. Although Mehring owns the land (the veld, as the landscape in South Africa is called), he does not understand it in the way the black natives do. Through a series of unusual events and natural catastrophes, Mehring slowly loses first the control of the land and then the land itself. By the novel's end, Mehring may be dead, and the ambiguity of this event is displaced by the one that closes the novel: The blacks are burying one of their own in their land.

Like *The Conservationist, Burger's Daughter* employs a multiperspective narration. At times, the reader appears to be inside the head of the main character and at other times to be watching that character involved in some objective situation. At times, the narrative perspective appears to be in the first person while at other times it appears omniscient. While these approaches may appear unusual, they are in fact consistent with the complicated situations that Gordimer represents in her fiction. For example, when Rosa Burger remembers the past, she thinks of herself as "another" person, one who used to do or say certain things. When she is seen waiting outside the prison at the age of fourteen, the narrative must capture the fact that "she" is being watched by someone else. Later, when her activities are directly under police surveillance, it is reasonable to expect the narrative to tell what was observed about her. If Rosa remembers a conversation she had with a former lover, she indicates that it was "I" who said or felt these things.

Gordimer begins to take greater liberties at finding different forms to capture the essence of the vastness and complexities of those living under apartheid and to express precisely the events that are private and public. In both *July's People* and *A Sport of Nature* (1987), she casts the events in the future, after a revolution to liberate Africa might already have occurred. Progressively, her novels have a more specific political orientation that is directed toward some agenda or course of action. In *My Son's Story* (1990), she continues to deal with the impact that political events have on the process and outcome of all human relationships.

THE CONSERVATIONIST

First published: 1974
Type of work: Novel

In the wake of political change and natural catastrophes in South Africa, a white landowner loses everything.

The Conservationist was held by the South African Censorship Board for ten weeks before it was finally released to the public. The novel, which tells the story of a white landowner named Mehring whose farm is run by black natives, begins with the discovery of a dead African found on Mehring's land. At the end, after a careless burial by white policemen exposes the body, the native is given a proper burial by the blacks who work Mehring's farm. The story's last sentence summarizes the spirit of the novel: "They had put him away to rest, at last; he had come back. He took possession of this earth, theirs; one of them." In an interview in *The Paris Review* in 1983, Gordimer explained that the African battle cry, "mayibuye," means "Africa, come back"; it is also the slogan of the ANC. The "coming back" refers to the return of the dead in the novel as well as to the theme that blacks will someday reclaim Africa as their own.

In combining the resurrection theme with a political one, Gordimer conveys a larger message that deals with life and death under apartheid. The image of the dead African permeates the other events in the novel and serves as a constant reminder of the shallowness of the character Mehring, who owns and rules a piece of Africa without understanding the land or the natives who inhabit it. In this respect, Mehring is like the living dead who unnaturally impose their values on those who are forced to exist under apartheid.

Mehring's actions are completely detached from those of the Africans in the novel. His activities include driving his Mercedes into town to attend parties or other social gatherings, where he is seen in a variety of situations that reveal his dissatisfaction with his life. By contrast, the Africans are represented in ritual events that strengthen their tie to the land: There are dances, the community's slaughter of a calf, a kind of Christmas party, and, most important, the burial of the dead African at the novel's end. While Mehring appears bored or has unpropitious sexual encounters, the Africans are actively engaged with their work, even with the menial tasks that will keep the farm running. Mehring's personal relationships are also disparate ones. He has lost contact with his son, and his mistress Antonia becomes increasingly disconnected from him. Meanwhile the Africans are portrayed in situations that suggest the strength of their community. Jacobus, the farm's foreman, is the mediator between Mehring and the land and is the first to inform the owner of the dead body. It is also Jacobus who brings the Africans together to bury the dead and call for the return of Africa.

If Mehring is to symbolize the decline of the white ruling class, Gordimer achieves this message with the amazing storm that literally sweeps Mehring off his land. In his last scene in the novel, Mehring is fleeing from the farm (after the African's dead body is washed up from the storm) when he spots and picks up a colored woman hitchhiker; they drive to a deserted cyanide mine dump. The scene ends ambiguously with the presence of a third person who may be a coconspirator with the colored girl, and the culmination of the encounter appears as a prelude to Mehring's demise.

The novel frequently shifts perspectives to achieve the full effects of the events. Sometimes Mehring is speaking of events in the present; at other times he is reflecting upon or remembering some other event. At still other times in the novel, there appears to be a completely detached observer who is recounting events. The shifts set a swift pace to events that are otherwise stagnant in development. They also capture the distinct events as they occur. For example, in the scenes where the Africans are involved in communal or ritual activities, it would be unrealistic for Mehring to narrate the fullness of the events, since he is never present at any of their affairs. Similarly, it is impossible for any of the Africans to narrate Mehring's activities and thoughts, since these people do not seem to possess the language skills to do so convincingly.

The Conservationist contains the author's vision that blacks will someday reclaim Africa. In the 1970's, when the novel appeared, the Black Power movement had been gaining momentum. Blacks argued that they must speak their cause on their own behalf and must first return to the traditions and roots of Africa in order to do so. Furthermore, in the liberation of Africa from white rule, it was unfortunate but essential that whites become fully dispossessed. Only in an ultimate and absolute return of the land to those who first inhabited it could liberation be complete. When the novel closes, Mehring's fate is unspecified but nevertheless certain, and the Africans are totally engaged with the forces that constitute life and death.

BURGER'S DAUGHTER

First published: 1979
Type of work: Novel

A young woman comes to personal and political terms with the meaning of the life and death of her father.

Burger's Daughter expresses well the author's contention that "fiction is a way of exploring possibilities present but undreamt of in the living of a single life." The novel is the evolution of Rosa Burger's awareness and understanding of the forces that make up the life of her politically active family. It also chronicles the fictitious life of Lionel Burger, a white member of the Communist Party, and the activities that reflect the historical development of South African politics from the 1920's to the

1970's. Through the lives of the father and the daughter, Gordimer explores the possibilities present to the Burger family and shows the choices that they make.

One of the novel's main themes concerns the degree to which an individual is expected to make a political commitment to the life of the republic. Initially, in Rosa's case, the choice to go against apartheid is in fact the legacy from her family rather than from anything resembling a personal decision. In the course of the novel, Rosa retraces the steps of her family's past, as she also understands the real and devastating effects of a segregated society. She makes a series of difficult choices that land her in a South African prison at the novel's end.

The novel begins with Rosa at the age of fourteen, as she waits alongside others who have come to bring supplies and messages to imprisoned loved ones. She is seen in a schoolgirl's uniform carrying a quilt and a hot-water bottle for her mother who is in prison. The narrative shifts from this third-person perspective to the voice of Rosa herself as she recounts that event from girlhood as well as the many others that shape her life.

The tone of the first-person perspective is self-analytical, as it reflects upon the personal experiences. There is the scene of her brother's death by drowning; her mother's death by multiple sclerosis; the intense love relationship with a man named Conrad; the imprisonment and death of her father; the first time she leaves South Africa and politics to spend a yearlong respite in Paris with Madame Bagnelli (Katya), her father's first wife; and finally, the events that lead to her own decision to be involved with politics after all.

Against the background of her family's history lies that of South Africa. Two major events are reported in *Burger's Daughter* that lend factual veracity to the fictional story: the Sharpeville shootings of 1960, preceding Lionel's final arrest, and the Soweto Riots of 1976. In her remembrances of the events, Rosa addresses her thoughts to her past lover Conrad as well as to Madame Bagnelli. Only at the end of the novel does Rosa address her dead father, admonishing him as well as herself for the choices made in their lifetimes.

Among Rosa's many encounters and experiences, perhaps the most striking one is the phone call she receives one night from Baasie, years after they played together as children in the Burger household. He reproaches her for what he perceives as her capitalizing on her father's name without understanding the real plight of blacks in South Africa. As a dispossessed black, Baasie refers to a political rally at which he spotted her and condemns her patronage of the black cause. Rosa is literally sickened by the encounter with this disembodied voice from her past, but it nevertheless encourages her to take some form of political action.

Like *The Conservationist*, *Burger's Daughter* is told with multiple points of view in the narrative. Although the bulk of the novel is told from Rosa's perspective, other perspectives are operating in the novel as well. There is an objective voice that fills in the gaps of the Burger family's history as well as South Africa's political history, and there appears to be another objective perspective told by someone who is particularly familiar with Rosa's life and compassionately reports the facts. When Rosa is under surveillance, reports of her activities appear in an "official" capacity.

All of these combined narrative strategies produce a full presentation of Rosa's life as it is constituted by her family and her country. The novel also addresses the issue of individual identity in two contexts: Can the individual be truly autonomous, or is the individual always the object of historical forces over which he or she has very little final control? Rosa is not unduly oppressed by these concerns, and her narrative is particularly balanced in the way it presents the possibilities available to her under the circumstances.

Thrust at birth into the hotbed of political concerns, Rosa discovers that her father's legacy does not necessarily preclude her individual actions and choices. In the end, she determines that being Burger's daughter means respecting her father's choices as well as finding the terms for her own existence.

JULY'S PEOPLE

First published: 1981
Type of work: Novel

This work focuses on the plight of a white family during a successful period of black liberation.

July's People is set in a time and place when the African effort to liberate blacks from white rule has successfully taken place. The entire country has become a battleground; the novel focuses on the plight of the Smaleses, an enlightened white middle-class family.

Bamford and Maureen Smales are "rescued" from deterioration by their servant, July, who takes them and their children into his native village. On the way there, July is seen literally caring for them, and it is obvious to the reader that he has not entirely abandoned his socialized role as a servant to white people. The Smaleses are uncomfortable with the shifting situation as they discover their increasing dependence on July. The novel's epigraph is an emblem of what the reader might expect in the course of events. Gordimer quotes from *Quaderni del carcere* (1948-1951, 6 volumes; partial translation as *Selections from the Prison Notebooks of Antonio Gramsci*, 1971): "The old is dying and the new cannot be born; in this interregnum there arises a great diversity of morbid symptoms." Africa is experiencing a change, and both blacks and whites are caught in the "interregnum," in the midst of change itself.

Gordimer, however, does not simplify the political implications. In other words, she does not advocate a view that white liberals such as the Smaleses must necessarily be excluded from black liberation. Neither does she cast an approving eye on the transition to black South African rule. Both groups experience pains in the transition; the new cannot yet be born in the middle of all the changes. Everyone is thrust into chaos and uncertainty; all social roles are shifting and changing.

If the lack of a concrete political agenda is a major issue in the novel, it also turns everything upside down for all the people. For one thing, sexual roles are confused. Bam, who had been the head of the household, is emasculated by relying on his former servant to save him and his family. Subsequently, he becomes figuratively, then literally, impotent, since he progressively loses his ability to relate to Maureen in any marital way. Much of the perspective of events is seen through Maureen's experiences. She comes to see more clearly the lines drawn to differentiate race, class, and gender. More specifically, she understands that the lines allow for cultural oppression at many levels. Like many white South Africans who inherited their place in the country from generations of black oppression, however, Maureen does not know how to make a radical change in her own daily way of being.

July himself responds to the changes by acting in the most pragmatic way: He takes care of the white people as he has always done and, given the situation, takes the logical step of bringing them to his village. There, July has them meet the chief, whose main concern is to solicit Bam's aid in combating the Russians and Cubans, whom the chief considers to be worse enemies than the white South Africans. The old relationship between July and the Smaleses takes on a new, but hardly radical, dimension as the white family becomes divested of their former "authority." Because July has always lived in the city and taken care of the Smaleses, the transposition to the village does not in fact change his role very much—July is *still* taking care of the family. Only now, July answers to the authority of the chief.

The novel raises the question of who should properly rule Africa—the whites who have profited from the suppression of blacks, or the blacks who have failed to adapt to the industrial growth of the country? Gordimer projects a vision of the future, one that is filled with many complex considerations, and appears uneasy about making a prophetic statement. In essence, South Africa is always undergoing political and social turmoil, since its policy of apartheid displaces all people at all levels.

July's people, then, are both the blacks and the whites who constitute Africa. In this novel, however, there do not appear to be any heroes who will rescue the entire nation.

CITY LOVERS *and* COUNTRY LOVERS

First published: 1956
Type of work: Short stories

Two pairs of lovers suffer the consequences of opposing South African law.

Originally published as "Town and Country Lovers," the two short stories "City Lovers" and "Country Lovers" are paired stories that reveal the devastating personal effects of racial segregation. The Prohibition of Mixed Marriages Act of 1949 and the Immorality Act of 1950 were laws passed by the white government to prevent miscegenation in any form. In "City Lovers," Dr. Franz-Josef von Leinsdorf is a foreign geologist who becomes sexually involved with a colored shopgirl. The girl, who is appropriately unnamed to indicate her lack of social status, becomes little more than the object of the doctor's sexual and domestic needs. The two are arrested, and their transgression is made public. In "Country Lovers," a white boy and a black girl grow up together and become teenage lovers. Although the girl, Thebedi, marries a black man she soon gives birth to a child that was no doubt fathered by Paulus, her white lover. At the story's end, the child is dead and the parents stand trial, but insufficient evidence fails to convict either parent for the violation of law.

Both stories are told in a straightforward manner and tone, but the emotional impact of the events is strongly suggested. In the compact form of a short story, Gordimer effectively captures the impact of South African laws upon individual lives.

Summary

In illuminating the horror and devastation of South African politics, Nadine Gordimer's writings are brilliant expositions of the way that human lives endure in the face of adversity. As Stephen Clingman writes in his introduction to a collection of her essays, Gordimer is the interpreter par excellence of her country. Significantly, Gordimer has lived in South Africa all of her life and has accumulated a lifetime of observations and experiences to make her characters and situations appear real even to those who will never know what it means to live under apartheid. For a writer whose work is filled with political situations, Gordimer strives to represent as fully, honestly, and intelligently as possible the entire spectrum of experiences.

Bibliography

Boyers, Robert, et al. "An Interview with Nadine Gordimer." *Salmagundi* 62 (Winter, 1984): 3-31.

Clingman, Stephen. *The Novels of Nadine Gordimer: History from the Inside.* London: Allen & Unwin, 1986.

Cooke, John. *The Novels of Nadine Gordimer: Private Lives/Public Landscapes.* Baton Rouge: Louisiana State University Press, 1985.

Gray, Stephen. "An Interview with Nadine Gordimer." *Contemporary Literature* 22 (Summer, 1981): 263-271.

Hurwitt, Jannika. "The Art of Fiction LXXVII: Nadine Gordimer." *The Paris Review* 88 (1983): 82-127.

JanMohamed, Abdul R. "Nadine Gordimer: The Degeneration of the Great South African Lie." In *Manichaean Aesthetics: The Politics of Literature in Colonial Africa.* Amherst: University of Massachusetts Press, 1983.

Wade, Michael. *Nadine Gordimer.* London: Evans Bros., 1978.

Cynthia Wong

GÜNTER GRASS

Born: Danzig (now Gdańsk), Poland
October 16, 1927

Principal Literary Achievement

Considered one of the most important figures in post-World War II German literature, Grass is known for a controversial combination of art and politics in his fiction.

Biography

Günter Wilhelm Grass was born a Catholic in Danzig (now Gdańsk), Poland, on October 16, 1927, the son of a German shopkeeper and his wife, who was Kashubian, or Slavic. Grass's racially mixed ancestry appears frequently in his written work. From 1933 to 1944, Grass attended school in Danzig and became a member of the Hitler Youth movement. He was drafted into the German army in 1944 at the age of seventeen, was wounded in the Russian advance, and was taken prisoner by the Americans. In his novel *Kopfgeburten: Oder, Die Deutschen sterben aus* (1980; *Headbirths: Or, The Germans Are Dying Out*, 1982), Grass himself acknowledges that had he been born ten years earlier, he would have "developed unswervingly into a convinced National Socialist" (Nazi). Grass did not question the Nazi philosophy until he was taken, as a reeducation measure after the war, to visit the concentration camp at Dachau. After his release in 1946, Grass held many jobs: farm worker, potash miner, stonemason's apprentice. In 1947, he moved to Düsseldorf to study art, painting, and sculpture. He also was a drummer in jazz bands. The details of these various occupations and enterprises frequently occur in his work.

In 1951 and 1952, Grass toured Italy and France. In 1954, he married the Swiss ballerina Anna Schwarz. In 1955, after moving to Berlin, Grass joined the literary organization Gruppe 47 (Group 47), whose authors read aloud and criticized one another's works-in-progress. In 1957, Grass read from his first novel *Die Blechtrommel* (1959; *The Tin Drum*, 1961). The members of Gruppe 47 saw great artistic promise in Grass; in 1958, he was awarded the Gruppe 47 prize, the stipend of which helped finance a trip to Poland to complete research for *The Tin Drum*. Grass, now the father of twin boys, Franz and Raoul, born in 1957, became famous with the publication of his first novel. The Bremen Senate refused to award their literary prize for the novel, but it received the Berlin Critics' Prize. Praised as innovative and daring, condemned as blasphemous and obscene, *The Tin Drum* set the stage for critical

reception of Grass's future novels as well. During this time, he continued to write lyric poetry and drama, in addition to beginning work on his next novels.

In 1961, the year of his daughter Laura's birth, the novel *Katz und Maus* (1961; *Cat and Mouse*, 1963) appeared, followed in 1963 by the novel *Hundejahre* (1963; *Dog Years*, 1965). These two works were later published, along with *The Tin Drum*, as the Danzig Trilogy, since all three take place in Grass's birthplace of Danzig. At this time, he developed tuberculosis; he also became actively involved in politics, which penetrates his fictional work. In 1963, he was elected to the Berlin Academy of Art.

Grass began to travel extensively in 1964, making several trips to the United States, while continuing to produce drama, ballets, essays, and poetry. His son Bruno was born in 1965. In 1966, with *Die Plebejer proben den Aufstand* (1966; *The Plebeians Rehearse the Uprising*, 1966), Grass achieved solid dramatic success. He was awarded several prizes, and he prepared a novel and dramatic version of the same material: *Örtlich betäubt* (1969; *Local Anesthetic*, 1970) and *Davor* (1969; partial translation as *Uptight*, 1970; complete translation as *Max: A Play by Günter Grass*, 1972). The novel *Local Anesthetic* was a success in the United States. Grass and the novel were featured in *Time* magazine, April 13, 1970. He became increasingly politically active from 1969 to 1972, giving numerous campaign speeches, and in 1972 he published *Aus dem Tagebuch einer Schnecke* (1972; *From the Diary of a Snail*, 1973). Though fictional and supposedly his diary as a political campaigner, *From the Diary of a Snail* is addressed to his children as a lesson in history and gives Grass's political views as well as a private picture of Grass and his family.

In 1974, though he continued to travel abroad and to write numerous editorials, speeches, poems, and essays, Grass returned more of his attention to fictional art, producing, in 1977, *Der Butt* (1977; *The Flounder*, 1978), dedicated to his daughter, Helena. *The Flounder* was so widely acclaimed that, in 1978, he was able to endow a literary award in the name of one of his admired teachers, administered by the Berlin Academy of Art. In 1977, Grass also participated actively in the film production of his novel *The Tin Drum*, with director Volker Schlöndorff. Though he had earlier dismissed friends' concerns about the state of his marriage, he and his wife Anna were divorced in 1978. The following year he married Berlin organist Ute Ehrhardt Grunert. They traveled extensively, with Schlöndorff and his wife Margarethe von Trotta, to Asia and the Far East. In 1979, when the film *The Tin Drum* appeared, it won the Golden Palm award at Cannes and the Academy Award for Best Foreign Film.

In 1979, Grass also published *Das Treffen in Telgte* (1979; *The Meeting in Telgte*, 1981), which, like *The Flounder*, joins history and fiction. Autobiography and fiction are joined in *Headbirths*. In this work, as in *From the Diary of a Snail*, Grass allows more glimpses into his personal life, detailing his travels with Grunert and the Schlöndorffs, while also detailing the travels of fictional characters. He continued his travels and published several more works: essays, poems, an index of etchings and lithographs. In 1986, he published *Die Rättin* (1986; *The Rat*, 1987), in which his earlier fictional characters are reunited.

Analysis

History and objects are almost an obsession with Grass. Most of his fiction is driven by the momentous events of history, and Grass employs objects, and extended metaphors with these objects, until they become symbols of that history. (He is both praised and condemned for his use of minute details in his novels. This mass of detail contributes to the bulk of most of his works. When he employs less detail, as in *Cat and Mouse* and *Headbirths*, the works are significantly shorter.) World War II is the overwhelming background in many of Grass's works: *The Tin Drum, Cat and Mouse*, and *Dog Years*, for example; while *The Flounder* tackles the entire history of the human race, especially the history of males and females. The tin drum, in the novel of the same name, serves as the symbol of Germany's military aggression, as well as other human violence. In *Cat and Mouse*, the character Mahlke has an Adam's apple "like a mouse," and the narrator is "the cat" intent on (and successful at) destroying Mahlke the mouse. Other historical symbols of destruction abound in this novel, including a sunken minesweeper and a stolen Iron Cross. In *Dog Years*, scarecrows, dogs, and ballerinas are only a few of the objects that become symbols of destruction, violence, and (at times) rebirth. In *The Flounder*, a talking fish becomes the guiding intelligence throughout humankind's violent history and continual rebeginning.

Another hallmark of Grass's fiction is the point of view: shifting, unpredictable, self-aware. Many of his narrators are unreliable, shifting between first and third person in telling their own tales, changing their minds, telling different versions of the same events. Oskar, of *The Tin Drum*, begins his story with the line, "Granted: I am an inmate of a mental hospital," and he shifts constantly between "I" and "he, Oskar," sometimes within the same sentence. The three narrators in *Dog Years* contradict one another. The first-person narrator of *The Flounder* is a different male during each period of history, as well as the contemporary man in the tale; the "I" in this novel is a different version of each of his male predecessors while, at the same time, encompassing all of these ancestors. In his later works, *From the Diary of a Snail* and *Headbirths*, Grass himself becomes the narrator, and he is a narrator who constantly interrupts his own story to rearrange things or to change his mind.

Many of Grass's narrators are highly self-aware artists and storytellers. *The Tin Drum*'s Oskar says, "I have just reread the last paragraph. . . . Oskar's pen . . . has managed . . . to lie." Pilenz, the narrator of *Cat and Mouse*, says of himself and Mahlke, "Even if we were both invented, I should have to write." *Dog Years* opens with the lines, "You tell. No, you. Or you." *Local Anesthetic* opens with, "I told my dentist all this." Grass's narrators know that they are creating art: They debate the merits of doing so; they mock their audience; they despair of their ability to create the best art possible. Grass's characters also frequently appear in several of his novels. Oskar drums his way into *Cat and Mouse, Dog Years,* and *The Rat*. These appearances of the same characters in different novels shift the point of view back to the author himself, and to Günter Grass as the storyteller, creating art.

Religious and political themes dominate Grass's work. Indeed, religion and politics are inseparable from the fiction. After a visit to the Church of the Sacred Heart, in *The Tin Drum*, Oskar insists that he is more Jesus than Jesus because the plaster statue is unable to play Oskar's tin drum. Mahlke of *Cat and Mouse* worships the Virgin Mary and builds shrines to her. The historical politics of World War II are pervasive in *The Tin Drum, Cat and Mouse,* and *Dog Years.* The politics of religion throughout history are woven into the structure of *The Flounder,* and contemporary politics appear when the flounder is put on trial for giving men (and not women) advice. *From the Diary of a Snail* and *Headbirths* both continue this discursive weaving of art, politics, and religion.

THE TIN DRUM

First published: *Die Blechtrommel,* 1959 (English translation, 1961)
Type of work: Novel

Against the backdrop of the rise of Nazism, World War II, and Germany's collapse, the self-made dwarf Oskar Matzerath narrates his life story.

The Tin Drum opens with the line, "Granted: I am an inmate of a mental hospital," thus setting the stage for its unreliable narrator, Oskar Matzerath, who tells varying versions of his story throughout the book. Oskar begins his life story with his Kashubian grandmother Anna Bronski and her improbable impregnation by Joseph Koljaiczek, who eludes police by hiding under Anna's four skirts as she sits in a potato field. This fantastic conception is only one of the "miraculous" events that occur in the novel. The importance of history is evident in Oskar's concern with the ancestry details.

Anna Bronski's daughter Agnes grows up into a lovely woman, falls in love with her beautiful cousin Jan Bronski, but marries the German Alfred Matzerath, whom she nurses during the war. Throughout the first part of the novel, Agnes is torn between these two men, just as the Poles are torn between Germany and Poland, and Oskar continually speculates on the true nature of his parentage, unable to decide which of the two men is his real father. When Oskar is born, clairaudient and with his mental development completed at birth, Alfred Matzerath promises that Oskar shall inherit the grocery when he grows up. Preferring his mother's promise of a tin drum on his third birthday, and entranced by the sound of a moth beating its wings against a 60-watt light bulb, Oskar decides to stay: "Besides, the midwife had already cut my umbilical cord." That is a pattern with Oskar: Whenever possible, Oskar chooses childhood pursuits over adult responsibilities; whenever possible, he claims responsibility for actions that have already occurred or that he could not have controlled.

On his third birthday, Oskar does indeed receive his drum, and, disgusted with the world of adults, with its deception and sordidness, including his mother's ongoing affair with her cousin Jan, Oskar decides that he will not become an adult: He throws himself down the cellar stairs in order to have an explanation for his having stopped growing at the age of three. Throughout book 1, Oskar drums his way through the increasingly sordid Danzig environs, paralleling the rise of National Socialism. Germany's increasing aggression mirrors the deteriorating personal moral standards of the characters. Oskar's tin drum serves as an extended metaphor not only for Germany's military aggression but also for all human violence, as well as for Oskar's refusal to grow up.

Book 2 parallels World War II. The attack on the Polish post office makes a partisan martyr out of Oskar's "presumptive father" Jan Bronski. In this book, Oskar's association with violence and immorality increases, though he does not actually commit the crimes himself (a defense that, historically, has often been claimed by accused Nazi war criminals). Oskar travels with the dwarf Bebra, whom he met in book 1, who is now part of Joseph Goebbel's Nazi propaganda machine. In Nazi uniform, Oskar tours Paris and other occupied territories, playing his drum and breaking glass for the German soldiers with his voice. Oskar's disillusionment with the Church in general, and with Catholicism in particular, which began in book 1, continues until Oskar decides that he himself is Jesus. Oskar/Jesus leads a gang of juvenile delinquents, called the Dusters, inspiring them to commit ever greater crimes. After the gang is betrayed, Oskar/Jesus is put on trial but found innocent because of his age. This trial foreshadows the trial in book 3, in which Oskar is found guilty and placed in a mental institution. The violence and destruction of book 2 increases, resulting in Alfred Matzerath's death. At Matzerath's funeral, Oskar is hit in the head by a rock, throws himself into Matzerath's grave, and decides to grow, to begin a responsible, adult life.

Book 3 is the reconstruction of Oskar's life, just as it is the rebuilding of Poland, Europe, and Germany after the war. Oskar's fascination with women continues. In book 1, his mother was the object of his interest. Book 2 gave him Maria, until she was unfaithful; then he turned to the midget Roswitha. In book 3, Oskar is fascinated with Sister Dorothea, whom he never sees and with whose murder he is charged. The details of Grass's various postwar occupations appear here: Oskar becomes an apprentice stonemason and a jazz drummer. Oskar becomes a wealthy recording star by taking old people, through his drumming, back to their childhoods. Oskar spends most of book 3 ruminating about the events in books 1 and 2. Book 3 is considered, almost unanimously by the critics, to be less effective than the earlier parts of the novel, perhaps because Grass tries, unsuccessfully, to show Oskar's (Germany's) survival despite his having become deformed during his growth spurt, perhaps because Grass lacked the necessary distance to present his material objectively. The film version of *The Tin Drum* did not include book 3, ending with Oskar's beginning to grow and leaving his birthplace of Danzig. The novel ends with a children's rhyme about the Black Witch, a line to which Oskar has repeatedly referred throughout the novel: "Here's the black, wicked Witch./ Ha! ha! ha!"

HEADBIRTHS

First published: *Kopfgeburten*, 1980 (English translation, 1982)
Type of work: Novel/autobiography

Grass's own political thoughts are interwoven with the travels of Harm and Dörte Peters, who are indecisive about having a child.

In *Headbirths*, Grass becomes the narrator of his own novel, a technique that he used in *From the Diary of a Snail*. Though not a novel in the traditional sense, *Headbirths* presents the story of a German couple, Harm and Dörte Peters, who, even as they travel through Asia, are unable to get away from the political upheavals at home and who are unable to decide whether to have a baby of their own. This decision is the source of the title: The only births are "head births," and at this rate, writes Grass, the German race will die out. Grass also ponders a world populated with as many Germans as there are Chinese, for example, and puts Harm and Dörte, at the end of the novel, in their old Volkswagen in the midst of a huge crowd of Turkish, Indian, Chinese, and African children, still unable to decide on a child of their own.

Headbirths explores one of Grass's major interests: the making of art, and the relationship of artist, art, and audience. In this novel, Grass writes that Harm and Dörte disagree with him on certain issues, so that Grass is "forced" to change his original ideas. His other major interest, politics, also is an integral part of this book. Grass presents not only his own political views but also Harm and Dörte arguing about the upcoming political election at home. Sometimes Grass and Dörte "agree" with each other, and Grass writes that he and Dörte attend press conferences together, a plot point that blurs the line between art and reality. Though Grass actually did travel to Asia, *Headbirths* is more about his political and theoretical ruminations than about the actual travels. Harm and Dörte, though sometimes shown visiting fertility temples, or indirectly presented arguing about politics or the "Yes-to-baby/No-to-baby" question, are never fully developed as characters. Rather, they serve as a springboard for Grass to present his political views and concerns.

Summary

The fiction of Günter Grass is a fantastic blend of minute (often grotesque) details, incisive satire, macabre humor, and political commentary. His longer novels are sometimes flawed in their latter sections; his shorter novels are occasionally flawed by his lack of objectivity or by his failure to develop characters adequately. Grass's body of work, however, presents one of the most powerful visions of post-World War II Europe and Germany. His style and meticulous attention to detail make him a unique and vital representative of German literature.

Bibliography

Cunliffe, W. Gordon. *Günter Grass*. New York: Twayne, 1969.

Grass, Günter. *On Writing and Politics, 1967-1983*. Translated by Ralph Manheim. New York: Harcourt Brace Jovanovich, 1984.

Hayman, Ronald. *Günter Grass*. London: Methuen, 1985.

Keele, Alan Frank. *Understanding Günter Grass*. Columbia: University of South Carolina Press, 1988.

Lawson, Richard H. *Günter Grass*. New York: Frederick Ungar, 1985.

Miles, Keith. *Günter Grass*. New York: Barnes & Noble Books, 1975.

O'Neill, Patrick, ed. *Critical Essays on Günter Grass*. Boston: G. K. Hall, 1987.

Reddick, John. *The Danzig Trilogy of Günter Grass: A Study of "The Tin Drum," "Cat and Mouse," and "Dog Years."* New York: Harcourt Brace Jovanovich, 1974.

Sherri Szeman

ROBERT GRAVES

Born: Wimbledon, England
July 24, 1895
Died: Deyá, Majorca, Spain
December 7, 1985

Principal Literary Achievement

Recognized as one of the technical masters of English verse, Graves believed that true poetry must be literally inspired by the Muse of ancient myth.

Biography

Robert Ranke Graves was born July 24, 1895, at Wimbledon, near London, England. His father, Alfred Percival Graves, a minor poet and Gaelic scholar, had remarried late in life to Amalie von Ranke; through his mother, Robert Graves was related to the distinguished German historian Leopold von Ranke. There were eventually nine children in the Graves family, including Robert, and the household was a fairly typical, late-Victorian establishment, dedicated to maintaining the conventions of society, especially those of religion. Until his teenage years, Robert, in particular, was a devoutly religious boy with a particular fastidiousness about sexual matters and an aversion to any rituals or beliefs that deviated from the strictest tenets of reformed Protestantism.

From 1910 until 1914, Graves attended Charterhouse, one of the famous English public schools. His stay at Charterhouse was generally unpleasant for several reasons. He was repulsed by the general air of homosexual affections that permeated the place but, at the same time, inadvertently encouraged such interests, as Graves himself later recognized and admitted in his autobiography, *Goodbye to All That* (1929).

Graves was also a scholarship student, which exposed him to the cruel and snobbish mockery of his classmates. As the relationship between Great Britain and Germany steadily deteriorated during this time, Graves was further tormented because of his German middle name. Finally, he was ridiculed because of his desire to write poetry. It was practicing this talent, however, that helped make Charterhouse bearable for Graves and attracted the notice of Edward Marsh, a patron of the prevailing "Georgian School" of English poetry. Marsh encouraged Graves in his efforts and introduced him to other writers, helping to prepare the way for Graves's first book of poems, *Over the Brazier* (1916).

Before this appeared, however, Graves had embarked on the most traumatic expe-

rience of his life, service in the trenches during World War I. Intensely patriotic, Graves had enlisted in 1914 at the outbreak of the war, joining the Royal Welch Fusiliers, one of the most notable units in the British army. Sent to France as an officer when only nineteen years old, Graves experienced the horrors, frustrations, and insanity of modern warfare. In 1916, he was severely wounded and listed as dead. His unexpected return to his family was, at least for Graves, a literal resurrection that forever marked his thinking and poetry. The war wounded Graves psychologically as well as physically. He found himself unable to face strangers, incapable of holding a regular job, and a victim of nightmares and unexplainable fears. His poetry, which had been light and lyrical, took on deeper and more brooding tones; throughout his career, he would return in various fashions to his experience in battle, in particular his wounding and "death."

After a long period of recuperation, Graves was married in January, 1918, to Nancy Nicholson. Only eighteen, Nicholson had strongly held feminist convictions; she demanded that the marriage vows be rewritten to excise references to obedience and that any daughters take her surname. Graves agreed to these requests, an early sign of what was to become first a recognition and then an exaltation of the role of the female in human life and artistic creation. Eventually the Graves-Nicholson marriage would produce four children.

After living in a cottage on the estate of the poet John Masefield, failing as a shopkeeper, and experiencing great financial want, Graves returned to school, taking his degree at St. John's College, Oxford. He continued to write poetry all during this time and between 1920 and 1925 published a volume of poems each year. He also met a number of prominent persons, among them T. E. Lawrence, better known as Lawrence of Arabia, the philosopher Bertrand Russell, and the poet and novelist Thomas Hardy.

In 1926, these friends helped Graves obtain the post of professor of English literature at the new Egyptian University at Cairo. Accompanying Graves and his wife was their new friend, the American poet Laura Riding, who was to exert a powerful influence on Graves's personal and poetic life. After only one year, the trio returned to England as severe domestic disputes strained the Graves's marriage; in 1929, Graves left his wife for Riding and moved to Deyá, Majorca, a small island off the coast of Spain. Graves would make Majorca his home for the rest of his life, leaving it only for brief periods or when forced away by war.

During the next ten years, Graves was deeply influenced by Riding's theories of composition and inspiration, especially the belief in the essentially feminine nature of creativity. Graves would later personify this principle as the White Goddess, whom he identified with the Muse of classical mythology. In 1939, however, while he was in the United States because of World War II, the Graves-Riding relationship dissolved, and each of them found another companion. Graves married Beryl Hodge, the ex-wife of one of his best friends. In 1946, the couple moved to Majorca.

After that, Graves's personal life remained fairly settled, and the controversies and excitements he caused were artistic and intellectual. He had already scored one of his few truly popular successes with his novel *I, Claudius* (1934), a fictional account of the early Roman emperors. While researching Greek myths for another historical novel, *The Golden Fleece* (1944; also known as *Hercules, My Shipmate*, 1945), Graves was struck by a new and radically different view of these ancient stories. Rejecting the traditional interpretations, Graves saw the myths as distorted but still decipherable links to an older, more universal religion that worshiped an all-powerful moon goddess. This figure, the White Goddess, was also present, Graves maintained, in Celtic and northern European folklore and poetry. Graves claimed additional evidence for his theories from the works of anthropologists, such as *The Golden Bough* (1890-1915), by Sir James Frazer. The presence of the White Goddess, the only true Muse of poetry and for whom Graves claimed a literal existence, remained Graves's central theme for the rest of his life.

Graves's theories were not without critics, and later works also drew attacks, especially those that challenged traditional Christianity, such as *The Nazarene Gospel Restored* (1953), or disputed ancient Jewish beliefs, as did *Hebrew Myths: The Book of Genesis* (1964). Graves defended his iconoclastic theories with skill and learning in numerous books and in his lectures at schools and colleges throughout the world, from the Massachusetts Institute of Technology to Trinity College, Dublin. From 1961 through 1966, he was professor of poetry at Oxford.

It was as an original poet, however, that Graves made his most individual and lasting mark. The body of his poetic work is unmatched among twentieth century writers for lyrical intensity and technical skill. Avoiding obscurity for its own sake, forsaking experimentation for traditional disciplines of meter and rhyme, Graves pursued the craft of poetry more as a sacred calling than as a career. When he died in Dejá, Majorca, Spain, on December 7, 1985, he left behind achievements that made him one of the truly indispensable writers of his time.

Analysis

Graves is best known as one of the most accomplished lyric poets of the twentieth century, but his highly individualistic and often controversial scholarship won for him almost equal, and certainly more fiercely contested, notice. He was also an excellent author of historical fiction, and his short stories and essays rank among the best produced in his time; several works, such as *I, Claudius* and the story "The Shout," have been recognized as modern classics.

Graves's poetry was part of the grand procession of English verse, emphasizing the use of rhyme, regular meter, and definite, often traditional structure. Although his career overlapped those of poets such as T. S. Eliot and Ezra Pound, Graves disdained their innovative, nonconventional forms and techniques. Graves believed, as did Edgar Allan Poe, that a long poem was impossible because inspiration could not sustain itself for more than brief stretches; therefore, he never attempted anything on the order of Eliot's *The Waste Land* (1922) or Pound's *Cantos* (1925-1972). Graves further thought that deliberate obscurity in poetry was a fault, so his verse does not have the enigmatic complexity of some of Eliot's lines or the recondite cultural references that Pound sometimes inserted into his lines. In short, Graves believed in and practiced clarity, technical mastery, and an absolute devotion to what he considered the true themes of poetry.

These themes inevitably revolved around the love of man and woman, and Graves is rightly regarded as one of the twentieth century's greatest love poets. Because of his peculiar beliefs about the nature of his inspiration, however, Graves's love poetry contains dimensions that are lacking in other authors. For Graves, the relationship between the poet and his lover echoed a more ancient and enduring situation, that between the White Goddess and the sacrificial king who died only to be reborn with the onset of spring. This goddess was symbolized, if not actually embodied, in a mortal woman, thus inspiring poets. What their poems celebrated, however, was greater than a single woman or individual love affairs; it was the universal and immortal goddess herself. All true poems, Graves insisted, told some aspect of this ancient tale. It was in this sense that he wrote, in "To Juan at the Winter Solstice," that "there is one story and one story only."

A Graves poem, then, is generally a brief vision of an aspect of this immortal and recurring story, peopled by contemporary characters, perhaps, but always referring, even if implicitly, to the underlying myth. In this sense, Graves's personal system of philosophy-mythology invites comparison with that erected by William Butler Yeats, whose book *A Vision* (1925) provided the scaffolding and explanation for the themes, symbols, and meanings of his (Yeats's) poetry. In both cases readers can, and often have, rejected the theories behind the poetry in favor of the poems themselves. So great are the powers of these two poets, and so enduring are their poems, that this is possible.

Still, in both cases the reader can find more to appreciate and consider by knowing the theories and, in the case of Graves, can find considerable enjoyment in the way those theories are presented. *The White Goddess: A Historical Grammar of Poetic Myth* (1948), his lengthy and polemical presentation of his ideas, is a remarkable book. Rejecting much of traditional historical, literary, and anthropological writings, Graves boldly turns Greek myths upside down, rewrites the development of Western poetry, and scorches his opponents with fierce and learned sarcasm. The Greek god Apollo, for example, was not for Graves the true patron of the arts but only an impostor who had ousted the goddess by fraud, force, and deceit. That was a typical Graves's interpretation, delightful to read, and, because of Graves's learning, impossible to dismiss out of hand.

Had Graves been only a poet, he would have commanded his place in literary history. If mythology and cultural studies had been his main thrust, he would still have to be reckoned with as a quirky but important figure. Should he be considered solely for his autobiography, *Goodbye to All That*, he would rank among the foremost of modern writers to tell his own story and that of his entire generation. He was a far more versatile talent, however, as his many outstanding novels, stories, essays, and occasional pieces demonstrate. The list of Graves's works is long, and there seems to be no genre that he did not attempt, and few in which he did not excel.

In his own eyes, however, Graves was always a poet. In the religious sense, poetry was his vocation, his calling. It was a mystery to which he had been summoned by the goddess, to whom he owed all of his allegiance and dedicated all of his talents. Never was a goddess better served.

GOODBYE TO ALL THAT

First published: 1929
Type of work: Autobiography

Graves recounts his childhood and youth and his devastating experiences as a soldier in World War I.

As Graves recalls in *Goodbye to All That*, he grew up in a household that stressed the time-honored virtues of Christianity, patriotism, and progress. Along with millions of other young Englishmen, he found that these virtues were severely shaken, if not totally destroyed, by the nightmare of World War I. Unlike most of his contemporaries, however, Graves was a brilliant writer, and his classic autobiography is an account of both his own personal experiences and the end of innocence for an entire generation and nation.

Although the book covers all Graves's life up to the time he wrote it, the work is primarily a memoir of his service in the Royal Welch Fusiliers, one of the most respected regiments in the British army. After a brief account of his family life and a rapid but thorough review of his education at Charterhouse, Graves thrusts the reader directly into the experiences of modern warfare. These are by turns stirring, boring, horrifying, heroic in brief moments and brutal for long stretches. The battlefield of World War I was not a glamorous place or an arena for storybook heroism; it was a nasty, death-filled place. The Western Front was a morass of death and mud where huge armies grappled without seeming purpose or hope of victory.

As a young lieutenant being sent into battle, Graves had a life expectancy on the front lines of just about three months; he lasted for two years. He was then severely wounded and reported as dead. For more than a week, his friends and family back in England believed that Graves had, in fact, died. His unexpected recovery and the delayed notification to his family constitute the "resurrection," which is one of the central passages of *Goodbye to All That*. The experience clearly had a deep and lasting influence on Graves both as a man and as a poet.

The war scarred Graves and nearly broke his spirit. That this should be so is hardly remarkable, and the reader of *Goodbye to All That* will find example after example of stupidity and callousness from higher officers, government officials, the popular press, and even the general public. On the one hand, Graves was rightly proud of his unit, the Royal Welch Fusiliers, and its men. Without false sentiment or vainglory, he presents an affectionate and moving portrait of a distinguished and honored regiment, skilled at its tasks and as brave as modern soldiers can be. On the other hand, Graves felt nothing but contempt for the commanders who wasted such brave men in criminally stupid fashion. Frontal attacks on entrenched positions, pointlessly enduring endless bombardments that blasted men into bloody fragments, repeated encounters with the horrors of gas warfare and trench combat—these were inflicted on the Fusiliers by the Allied high command, not the German enemy. Graves never got over that fact. Had he not been wounded, he might have gone totally insane; as it was, he suffered a severe mental setback and did not recover for many years after the war. In one sense, in his hatred for British hypocrisy, Graves never did recover, nor did he ever wish to recover.

Goodbye to All That, then, is more than an autobiography. It is also an explanation of Graves as a man and as a poet, setting forth what he believes and why he believes it. Having been transformed by his wartime experiences, Graves felt compelled to chart those changes and present them. His book, as the title implies, is also a farewell to England and English life. In one sense, it is literally a farewell, for when *Goodbye to All That* was published, Graves left England for Majorca with Laura Riding. Although he and Riding would separate in 1939, Graves would remain in Majorca for the rest of his life; although he made occasional visits to Great Britain, he never again considered it his home.

In another sense, Graves was saying goodbye to a way of life that had been destroyed by war and time. His childhood and youth had been spent in another age, a time when the world seemed certain, the future was bright, and men and women lived orderly, confident lives. Nothing of that remained after the war. Uncertainty, fear, and doubt reigned, and all the promises of religion and politics had been revealed as nothing more than hollow, cynical words to fool the masses. Not without a sense of regret at lost innocence, Graves also said goodbye to all that he had known in his youth.

THE WHITE GODDESS

First published: 1948
Type of work: Literary and mythological criticism

Graves traces all true poetry back to an ancient religion of the three-part moon goddess, the truths of which have now largely been lost.

The White Goddess eventually had its source in Graves's first popular success in fiction with the novel *I, Claudius* (1934), an account of the first four Roman emperors. He followed this with a sequel, *Claudius the God and His Wife Messalina* (1934). While researching material for another novel set in ancient times, *The Golden Fleece* (1944; also known as *Hercules, My Shipmate*, 1945), Graves was seized by a revelation of what he believed to have been the true structure and nature of all ancient poetry and, indeed, of all real poetry to modern times. This vision was expanded, with recondite references to Celtic, northern European, and Mediterranean myths and prehistory, to form the basis for his most notable and controversial work of criticism, *The White Goddess*.

The book is subtitled *A Historical Grammar of Poetic Myth*, and in it Graves presents a highly detailed account of what true poetry is, what constitutes its unvarying themes, and how these themes have been used by all real poets for thousands of years. Although Graves indulges in numerous digressions, his main points can be briefly summarized.

Until the end of the Bronze Age, roughly 1000 B.C., a single religion had held sway in most of the world from northern India to the British Island; that is, in those areas where the Indo-European language was established. This religion consisted of worship of the three-part, or tripartite, goddess, who, because of her mutable nature, was most commonly associated with the moon; her phases were those of Maiden, Wife and Mother, and Crone. In these three guises, the universal goddess presided over all birth, growth, and death. Two gods attended the goddess: the god of the spring, or waxing year, who was ritually slain at midsummer and supplanted by his rival, the god of the waning year, who ruled until the winter solstice. At that time, the god of the waxing year was resurrected through the power of the goddess, and the cycle began once more. This cosmic story was repeated in human society and individual human lives, and it was the task of the true poet to celebrate this mystery; the poet succeeded only to the extent that he accepted the power of the goddess and was granted her inspiration.

Graves maintained that this goddess worship, which formed the essential basis for all real property, was violently disrupted and then displaced by invaders from the Middle East, worshipers of a supreme male god, who usurped the rightful place of the goddess. This process occurred in several stages, beginning with the advent of the classical Greek pantheon of gods dominated by Zeus and culminating with the spread of patriarchal Christianity throughout Europe. The worship of the goddess, and therefore the practice of true poetry, was effectively outlawed. Where it persisted, it did so either under hidden forms, such as those practiced by the Welsh bards, or as a debased and only partially correct memory. Modern poets still manage to exist, Graves maintained, and to be inspired by the White Goddess as a muse, but they do so largely unconsciously and often in defiance of accepted social and critical conventions.

The White Goddess is a work packed with references to a wide range of historical, anthropological, and mythological studies, including Sir James Frazer's *The Golden Bough* (1890-1915). Drawing upon Frazer's illuminating study of the truths behind myths, Graves added his own interpretations of traditions ranging from the obscure, such as the ancient Welsh poem "The Battle of the Trees," to the familiar, as in the book of Revelation from the Bible. All of these provide evidence, Graves insists, to support his thesis.

Such arguments by Graves are one reason *The White Goddess* has been so controversial since its publication. By positing a single, unified goddess worship that extended through Indo-European culture, Graves is inverting or contradicting much of traditional scholarship. His interpretation of Greek myths in support of his theory has been attacked as idiosyncratic at best, simply wrong at worst, and his subsequent account of these stories, *The Greek Myths* (1955), was attacked by many critics on these grounds.

A second reason for the controversy surrounding *The White Goddess* was that Graves presented his work not simply as a historical or critical study but as a literal and truthful account of the continuing source of true poetry. Graves does not use the triple goddess as a metaphor; rather, she is an actual deity. Worshiped before the coming of the patriarchal invaders, she inspired poets; known only dimly and by chance inspiration now, she is still the only real Muse of true poems in the contemporary world. Such a belief seems to many in the modern world perverse, yet it is the position that Graves forcefully and learnedly argued in *The White Goddess* and which he maintained in the body of his poetic work.

The White Goddess thus joins the ranks of those works of English literature that cannot be satisfactorily classified. Along with Robert Burton's *The Anatomy of Melancholy* (1621), Thomas Carlyle's *Sartor Resartus* (1833-1834), William Butler Yeats's *A Vision* (1925), and James Joyce's *Finnegans Wake* (1939), it is an achievement that has inspired admiration, condemnation, and continued debate among its readers.

ULYSSES

First published: 1933
Type of work: Poem

The wandering Greek hero of Homeric legend must always be with a woman because of his devotion to the eternal goddess.

As Graves demonstrates in "Ulysses," he was, above all else, one of the greatest poets of the twentieth century. His lyrical gifts were extraordinary and his technical mastery of verse form, rhyme, and rhythm were unrivaled. Unlike many other poets of the modern era, Graves did not engage in free verse, idiosyncratic form, or unusual styles. He worked within the traditions of English poetry, almost always using a specific pattern of rhyme and a regular meter to frame his message. This message varies, but more often than not it is a variant of his central theme, the concept of the three-part goddess and the true poet's devotion to her. Since the goddess often appears in the guise of a mortal woman, Graves is predominantly a love poet, and his lyrics celebrate the possibility of enduring affection between man and woman. Graves was not, however, without his sardonic side. The gulf between deity and daily life was all too obvious for Graves, and even the most heroic of men, such as Ulysses, could be blind to the truths offered by the goddess. Such is the case in this poem that has the hero's name.

Ulysses is fated to need women but never truly understand them; at the same time, he is secretly terrified by the changeable nature of women. He comprehends enough to recognize the mutable nature of the goddess who appears sometimes as a virgin, a loving wife, a seductive temptress, and even as an implacable, natural force. The mythological Ulysses encountered all of these in his return from the Trojan War, and Graves's poem is a compressed litany of this journey. Ulysses meets the goddess as the sorceress Circe, in the form of the Symplegades, or clashing rocks, and as the Sirens, destroyers of ships and men. The goddess also takes her form in Ulysses' chaste wife, Penelope, who waits for him for twenty years while he is fighting on the plains of Asia and then trying to return home. What Ulysses senses, without consciously realizing it, is that all of these women are the same and are versions, avatars, of the White Goddess. What he does accept is that he needs them and that without them he is incomplete.

TO JUAN AT THE WINTER SOLSTICE

First published: 1945
Type of work: Poem

The only true theme for an authentic poet is the recurring myth of the White Goddess and her powers.

The rule of the triple goddess, which Graves explains in his book *The White Goddess*, finds its most trenchant and beautiful exposition in "To Juan at the Winter Solstice." The Juan of the poem may be the poet's own son or it may equally well be Don Juan, the famous lover of many beautiful women and thus a worshiper of the goddess in her many aspects. To whomever it is addressed, the poem is both an invocation of the Muse of true poetry and an example of the mysteries she performs.

"There is one story and one story only," Graves says in his opening line, and by the time the poem concludes he has shown that the various aspects of the myth of the goddess encompass all the truths that humankind can know or poets can relate. In doing this, Graves recapitulates his arguments from *The White Goddess*, showing how the Welsh tree poems, the myth of the Zodiac, and the recurring legends of sacrificial kings are part of this single, powerful tale, the story of the goddess.

Graves moves, methodically but poetically, through these mutations. These are the subjects, he says, for a true poet: verses about the Zodiac, which is a representation of the goddess in her heavenly, seasonal aspect; poems about the god of the waxing year, who rules only to be sacrificed at midsummer, as "Royally then he barters life for life." On the other hand, the poet may turn inward, but still, if he is a true poet, his personal story will reflect the universal one.

In the end, Graves maintains, the one story that can be told is that of the goddess, her beauty, and her power:

> Her brow was creamy as the crested wave,
> Her sea-grey eyes were wild
> But nothing promised that was not performed.

THE PERSIAN VERSION

First published: 1945
Type of work: Poem

This poem is an account of the battle of Marathon from the losing side.

Graves admitted that "at times the satiric left hand of poetry displaces the lyric right hand," and "The Persian Version" is a poem written with his left hand but one that also contains a hint of the real pain and suffering he endured in World War I, when so many pointless and useless Allied defeats and deaths were reported to the gullible public as great victories or examples of British fortitude. As he showed in *Goodbye to All That*, Graves understood that the German public had been fed the same lies. Why should it have been different in ancient times?

This is the premise for "The Persian Version," where the famous battle of Marathon is put into its true—that is, Persian—perspective. For European history, Marathon was the first and perhaps greatest struggle of democracy against tyranny, the prototype of all subsequent battles for freedom. For the Persians, Graves's poem says, the event was only a minor event, a "trifling skirmish" upon which "truth-loving Persians" do not like to dwell; the implication here is that the Greeks have lied about the battle, an accusation often levied in wartime. Using terminology from the military, Graves calls Marathon "a mere reconnaissance in force" and notes, as any well-trained military spokesperson would be sure to add, that the ships involved were only "light craft detached from the main Persian fleet." In other words, Marathon was essentially a local, almost unnoticed event, not the world-shaking clash of legend.

"The Persian Version" is an ironic, even savage poem, which underscores the futility of warfare and the endless idiocies to which governments will go to wrest some shred of spurious victory from even the most obvious defeat, just as the Persians claim to be the victors in this encounter because, despite the losses and deaths, "All arms combined magnificently together." That is exactly the sort of bombast Graves read while his friends were being killed beside him in the trenches. In "The Persian Version," he made it a joke, but it is a joke with a serious, bitter center.

Summary

Robert Graves considered himself a poet. His other work, while done to the best of his ability, was either to support himself while he wrote his poems or to explain them. He felt chosen to compose relatively short poems of praise to a universal goddess whose existence almost all others denied and in a style that many had ceased to practice. Graves was thus a strange combination of Georgian English poet and Bronze Age Greek.

He accepted that largely self-created role and prospered artistically in it, writing some of the most beautiful and enduring poetry of the twentieth century. In his verse forms and patterns, Graves is often entirely conventional, while in his underlying themes he is enduringly ancient. Above all, he remains Robert Graves, and his poems are a lasting combination of all of these elements.

Bibliography

Canary, Robert H. *Robert Graves*. Boston: Twayne, 1980.

Day, Douglas. *Swifter than Reason: The Poetry and Criticism of Robert Graves*. Chapel Hill: University of North Carolina Press, 1963.

Graves, Richard Perceval. *Robert Graves: The Assault Heroic, 1895-1926*. New York: Viking Press, 1989.

_____. *Robert Graves: The Years with Laura, 1926-1940*. New York: Viking Press, 1990.

Seymour-Smith, Martin. *Robert Graves: His Life and Work*. New York: Holt, Rinehart and Winston, 1982.

Snipes, Katherine. *Robert Graves*. New York: Frederick Ungar, 1979.

Vickery, John B. *Robert Graves and the White Goddess*. Lincoln: University of Nebraska Press, 1972.

Michael Witkoski

GRAHAM GREENE

Born: Berkhamsted, England
October 2, 1904
Died: Vevey, Switzerland
April 3, 1991

Principal Literary Achievement
One of the greatest novelists of the twentieth century, Greene has also distinguished himself as the author of numerous short stories, plays, travel books, and film criticism.

Biography

Graham Greene, born in Berkhamsted, England, on October 2, 1904, was the fourth of six children. His father, Charles Henry Greene, was a history and classics master who, in 1910, became headmaster of Berkhamsted School.

As a highly sensitive, imaginative youth from a respected upper-middle-class family, Greene had the opportunity to develop more exotic emotional problems than are characteristic of children of the lower classes. When he first discovered that he could read, he hid this fact from his parents out of fear that they would then make him enter preparatory school. He began to live a covert life, secretly reading books about adventure and mystery of which his parents would not approve. As a child, Greene also developed inordinate fears of the dark, of birds and bats, of drowning, and of the footsteps of strangers. He developed recurrent nightmares about a witch who would lurk at night in the nursery at the linen cupboard.

In 1912, as he approached his eighth birthday, Graham Greene enrolled in Berkhamsted School. He was to spend the next ten years there, the last five of which proved to be a hellish confinement for him. Being the headmaster's son, he felt himself alienated from the other boys and was bewildered by his sense of divided loyalties. His filial devotion was constantly challenged by his desire to be accepted. He was never able to resolve these conflicting loyalties, and, to make matters worse, two schoolboys, Carter and Wheeler, sadistically exploited Greene's anxiety with cruel psychological precision. While Greene never disclosed the specfic details of their actions, Norman Sherry, in his biography of Greene, has shown that these two boys exercised a powerful control over Greene during a critical time in his development. Being more experienced in worldly matters, they took pleasure in attacking Greene's naïveté and trust. Carter not only tormented Greene for being the headmaster's son,

but also, after winning his confidence and discovering his secret dreams and desires, disabused Greene of many of his romantic and chivalric ideals. As the murderer of Greene's childhood and his arch betrayer, Carter would appear in many forms throughout Greene's stories and novels and become one of the powerful demons that Greene would spend his literary life attempting to exorcise. Years later Greene was to observe that every creative writer worth consideration is a victim, a man given over to an obsession.

By 1920, Greene had developed a manic-depressive and suicidal behavior that led his parents to send him to a psychoanalyst for treatment. The experience proved beneficial, and Greene began self-consciously to record and analyze his dreams and feelings. It was also during this period that he began to write short stories, the act of which served, perhaps unwittingly, to shape and to help control his fears and depressions.

In 1922, Greene entered Balliol College, Oxford, to study history. His academic career was not especially distinguished. He edited the Oxford *Outlook* and during his last year at the school published a volume of verse entitled *Babbling April* (1925), a work derivative of the style of Edna St. Vincent Millay.

In the autumn of the following year, in a confused state of intolerable boredom and sexual frustration, Greene took his older brother's revolver, slipped a bullet into the chamber, spun the barrel, placed the muzzle against his right ear, and pulled the trigger. The excitement of gambling with his own life rejuvenated him. During the next few months he played this dangerous game several more times. These adrenaline ecstasies soon abated, but his acute fear of boredom, and his penchant for dangerous acts that he hoped would curb that fear, remained with him for life. His later excursions into Africa, Mexico, and Vietnam during periods of bloody revolutions, for example, were largely motivated by the same dreadful feeling of emptiness in his life and became for him a new form of Russian roulette.

After he was graduated from Balliol, he began a career in journalism, working for the Nottingham *Journal* and then *The Times* in London. It was during this time that he met and proposed marriage to Vivien Dayrell-Browning, a Roman Catholic. In order to understand and appreciate better the religion of his future wife, Greene took instructions in the faith and became a Catholic in 1926. Having agreed to a monastic marriage, Greene married her the next year and apparently abided by this unusual agreement until his separation from her several decades later. In his spare time, he wrote his first novel, *The Man Within*, published in 1929. Stirred by its success, he devoted full time to writing novels, short stories, and book reviews. In 1930, he published *The Name of Action* and, in 1931, *Rumour at Nightfall*, two action novels. He finally achieved the notice he was seeking with the publication of *Stamboul Train: An Entertainment* (1932; published in the United States as *Orient Express: An Entertainment*, 1933). Based upon a rugged trip to Liberia during 1934-1935, Greene's travel book, *Journey Without Maps* (1936), reveals his attempt to return to a pure and innocent landscape. Significantly, Greene had long conceptualized Africa as being roughly the shape of the human heart.

During the next few years, Greene was sued by representatives of Shirley Temple over a caustic review that he wrote of her movie *Wee Willie Winkie* (1937). He also produced a thriller entitled *A Gun for Sale: An Entertainment* (1936; published in the United States as *This Gun For Hire: An Entertainment*). With the publication of *Brighton Rock* in 1938, critics discovered that Greene was a writer whose work contained explicitly Catholic themes. His most popular and most explicitly Catholic novel was *The Power and the Glory* (1940; reissued as *The Labyrinthine Ways*), published two years after he visited Mexico to report on the religious persecution in that country. Recruited into the Secret Service in 1941, Greene was sent to West Africa, where he wrote *The Ministry of Fear: An Entertainment* (1943), a melodrama filled with bizarre twists of plot. After World War II, in 1946, he began work on another major novel, *The Heart of the Matter* (1948), set in the West Africa he came to know so well. When motion-picture producer Alexander Korda wanted to make a film about the four-power occupation of Vienna, he sent Greene to that city to research the subject. The result was the film script for *The Third Man*, released in 1950. Starring Orson Welles and Joseph Cotton, the film has become a classic.

During the next ten years, Greene produced three more novels: *The End of the Affair* (1951), *The Quiet American* (1955), and *Our Man in Havana: An Entertainment* (1958), all of which were made into motion pictures. *The Quiet American* was especially upsetting to American reviewers because of its damning analysis of the United States' involvement in Vietnam during the early 1950's. Greene also wrote three plays during this period: *The Living Room* (1953), *The Potting Shed* (1957), and *The Complaisant Lover* (1959). The first two plays focused heavily upon Catholic themes, including the unfashionable belief in miracles.

In 1961, he published *A Burnt-Out Case*. Ostensibly about an architect who comes to an African leprosarium to escape the mindless adulation he has received in Europe, the novel is very autobiographical and suggests Greene's growing uneasiness with his faith. *The Comedians* (1966), his next novel, is set in Haiti during the bloody reign of Papa Doc Duvalier. The motion picture based on the novel is distinguished by its two stars: Richard Burton and Elizabeth Taylor. Greene also published two collections of short fiction during this time: *A Sense of Reality* (1963) and *May We Borrow Your Husband? and Other Comedies of the Sexual Life* (1967). Although overshadowed by his novels, his short stories are nevertheless quite powerful and worthy of careful attention.

In 1971, Greene published the first volume of his autobiography, *A Sort of Life*, which extends only to the 1930's. His 1980 *Ways of Escape* brings his life up to date. The focus in both books is upon his literary, rather than his personal, life. *The Honorary Consul*, published in 1973, was one of Greene's favorite novels, though critics have never ranked it among his very best works. *The Human Factor* (1978) is based upon the sensational defection to the Soviet Union of Kim Philby, Greene's former boss in the Secret Service.

With the publication of *Monsignor Quixote* in 1982, Greene compared Catholicism and Marxism by having the principals of the novel, a Spanish priest and a Communist ex-mayor, debate the relative merits of their beliefs. *Getting to Know the General: The Story of an Involvement* (1984) is Greene's reportorial hymn to his friend General Omar Torrijos of Panama. In 1985, *The Tenth Man* appeared. This novel is based upon an old manuscript by Greene that was discovered in the vaults of a Hollywood motion-picture company. Greene apparently had forgotten he had ever written it, but after it was discovered, he allowed it to be published. His last published novel, *The Captain and the Enemy*, published in 1988, is a slim work that lacks the fire and the complexity of his earlier fiction.

Having lived in Antibes for the last twenty-five years of his life, Greene managed from this outpost to remain a liberal gadfly, attacking in newsprint any and all countries that compromised his sense of justice and humanity. Many believed that he was never awarded the Nobel Prize in Literature because of his radical political views. He died on April 3, 1991, of an undisclosed blood disease, in a hospital in Vevey, Switzerland. His last publication, a collection of short stories uncannily entitled *The Last Word* (1990), appeared a few months before his death.

Analysis

Greene's exciting, fast-paced narratives have an illusive transparency about them, as if one can see and hear the characters and visualize their surroundings without the distractions of the author's presence or stylistic mannerisms. This authorial invisibility may derive from Greene's experience in writing film scripts and from the many years he spent in reviewing motion pictures. It is interesting to note, in this connection, how few of his novels are written from the first-person point of view, a perspective clearly unsuited to a motion-picture script.

Although many of his novels are based on topical events—whether in England, Mexico, Vietnam, or Haiti—Greene's personal involvement in those events as a reporter and as a student of human nature allows him the perspective of an insider. It is almost as if he would not ask his characters to do or think something that he himself had not done or thought. Life, to Greene, is a series of risks and moral choices; the dangers are betrayal, corruption, and failure. The central quest of his obsessed heroes is for the peace and innocence of their lost childhood, an adventure that is characterized by great tension and suffering, and one that often ends only in death.

Greene's fiction offers a unique vision of the world, a vision derived from his obsession with certain themes, characters, and events. Feeling that his childhood innocence was savaged at Berkhamsted School by the psychological bullies Carter and Wheeler, Greene became obsessed with the theme of lost childhood, a theme that dominates most of his novels and short fiction. Greene is like Samuel Taylor Coleridge's Ancient Mariner, who burns with a constant passion to tell the passerby his story; like the Mariner, he can hold his audience with the hypnotic eye of a true believer and weave his obsession into a compelling fiction. In fact, Greene acknowledged that his writing was a form of therapy that enabled him to escape the madness, melancholy, and panic inherent in the human condition.

Greene's obsessions and fascinations are many and evolve into themes focused on innocence, evil, pity, hatred, the isolated and hunted individual, betrayal, suicide, dreams, seedy and decadent surroundings ("Greeneland," as some critics call it), violence, carnal sexuality, and failure. His characters fall into four categories: the sinner, the innocent, the pious, and the humanist.

All of these obsessive figures, themes, and subjects are circumscribed by Greene's fatalistic and pessimistic vision of the world. There is little healthy humor or laughter in most of his novels, but rather a sense of inevitable failure, pain, and suffering. There may be a God in Greene's world, but the focus is almost always on the twisted world itself: its nightmarish oppression, its squalor, and its seeming hopelessness.

Greene's Catholicism and his obsessions supply much of the strength of his novels. They are the muscles that make the body of his fiction work, but they should not be viewed in isolation from the total performance, which concerns itself with the human condition and the fundamental theme of much great literature: the struggle of innocence against evil and the hope of redemption. Greene's fiction appeals to the reader's profound urge to avenge an imperfect world that has betrayed his or her own youthful fantasies and ideals.

BRIGHTON ROCK

First published: 1938
Type of work: Novel

The young leader of a gang of racetrack hoodlums finds his world disintegrating as he is relentlessly pursued by a self-righteous avenger.

Brighton Rock is the story of a seventeen-year-old brutal criminal named Pinkie Brown, who has recently assumed the leadership of a gang of racetrack hoodlums working out of Brighton, an English seaside resort. A man named Hale, an advertising agent who is in Brighton to promote his newspaper, has betrayed Kite, the former leader of the gang now run by Pinkie. Hale knows that Pinkie has recognized him and is planning revenge. The pursuit and murder of Hale are set against a background of fun-seeking holiday crowds, band music, flower gardens in bloom, and a warm summer sun.

While seeking refuge from his would-be killers, Hale takes up with a vulgar, sensual woman named Ida Arnold. After Hale is murdered, Ida takes it upon herself to seek revenge. In the meantime, Pinkie befriends a young waitress named Rose, whose knowledge of his gang's involvement in Hale's murder makes her a threat to his safety. He then marries her because he knows that a wife cannot testify against her husband in court. Ida, delighting in her role as detective and avenger, begins to focus more clearly on her suspects, harasses Rose, and begins to frighten Pinkie with her constant inquiries about Hale.

Pinkie panics and kills one of his fellow gang members whom he feels he can no longer trust. Then, in a desperate attempt to rid himself of Rose, who in his mind has come to represent the horrors of sexuality and entrapment, he lures her into a suicide pact with him. His plan is to let Rose take her own life, which, out of reckless love for Pinkie, she is willing to do, and then escape. After they drive to the coast to consummate the pact, Dallow, a member of Pinkie's gang, arrives to inform him that the police know who killed Hale and that there is no hope for any of them now. As Pinkie reaches for the bottle of vitriol, which he always carries with him, to hurl at Dallow, the acid flies back into his face. He runs screaming over the edge of an embankment and plunges to his death in the water below.

The novel ends on a note of terrible irony. Rose's only consolations are the possibility that she will have Pinkie's baby and will enjoy playing for the first time a gramophone recording that he had made for her earlier on the Brighton pier. He had told her that he had put something "loving" on the record; what he had actually said was, "God damn you, you little bitch, why can't you go back home forever and let me be?" The novel ends with Rose walking toward her room in the hope that Pinkie's love for her will be expressed and confirmed on the recording.

Pinkie Brown is the embodiment of depraved innocence. Greene visualizes Pinkie in realistic detail, but his metaphorical language elevates the young killer's character almost to the level of a morality play or a parable. On one level Pinkie may be a common thug from Brighton in the 1930's, but on another level he is a fallen angel, a tragicomic hero who, on an irrevocable course of self-destruction, transcends time and space.

The theme of lost or betrayed innocence is central to this novel. The neighborhood in which Pinkie was born and reared is called Paradise Piece and is now reduced to rubble. Pinkie's fear of sexuality is directly related to the theme of lost innocence. When he believes that he will soon be inextricably bound to Rose as her husband, he feels as if he were shut out from an Eden of ignorance.

Pinkie's only real choice in life is suicide. That is his only way of escape from human contacts and other people's emotions. Other people make Pinkie's world a hell, but at least he understands hell, whereas heaven is just a word to him. When they christened him, he asserts, the holy water did not work, and he never howled the devil out. His faith is in Satan, not in God.

THE POWER AND THE GLORY

First published: 1940
Type of work: Novel

During the persecution of Catholics in Mexico, a hunted, alcoholic Catholic priest overcomes his human failings to achieve martyrdom.

The setting of *The Power and the Glory* is Mexico during the late 1930's, when President Plutarco Elias Calles, in the name of revolution, was closing down the churches and murdering or exiling priests and practicing Catholics. The hero is an unnamed whiskey priest who is pursued through the countryside by an unnamed lieutenant. The fact that the protagonists are not named gives the novel the form of a parable. The priest represents a human, Christlike figure persecuted by the lieutenant, who embodies the ruthless, secular ideals of socialism.

In his continuous search for safety and food, the priest takes refuge in a barn owned by Captain Fellows, an English banana planter. His thirteen-year-old daughter, Coral, risks her and her family's safety in attending to the priest's needs during his stay. She stands in vivid contrast to the priest's own illegitimate daughter, Brigita. Coral is still an innocent and later appears to the priest in a comforting dream moments before he is executed. Brigita, on the other hand, despite her youth, has lost her innocence amid her squalid poverty. The priest is overcome by his guilt for having brought a hopeless child into the world and prays that God will take his faith and life in exchange for the salvation of his daughter. Along his travels the priest meets up with a mestizo, a grotesque Judas figure who leads the priest to his capture by the lieutenant. Awaiting execution in prison, the priest reveals a profound contrition for his sins, especially for the damage he has done to his child, and in his final moments selflessly prays for her redemption.

One of the little boys in the town, Luis, who earlier had admired the machismo of the lieutenant, now spits on him, the spittle landing on the lieutenant's revolver. Through this scene Greene suggests that the execution of the whiskey priest thus has a moral impact on the next generation. The novel concludes with a mysterious stranger knocking at the door of Luis' home. He identifies himself as a priest and Luis kisses his hand. The fugitive church, the reader is reassured, is still a vital presence and will survive the violence of socialist oppression.

The theme of the hunted man establishes an exciting and nightmarish atmosphere that makes this novel a first-class thriller. There is much more here, however, than a simple manhunt. Greene has created characters that are at once human and symbolic. The priest and the lieutenant embody the extreme dualism of the human spirit: godliness versus godlessness, love versus hatred, spirituality versus materialism, concern for the individual versus concern for the state. The symbiotic relationship between the two men is brought out after the priest's death, when the lieutenant feels that his vitality has been drained from him and that he no longer has a clear purpose in life.

THE MINISTRY OF FEAR

First published: 1943
Type of work: Novel

In war-torn London, an innocent man unwittingly finds himself hunted down by a network of spies.

Set in London during the height of the German Blitzkrieg, *The Ministry of Fear: An Entertainment* develops the theme of pity as an isolating and self-destructive force. The hero, Arthur Rowe, has poisoned his wife because he could not bear to watch her suffer from an incurable disease. Although the court finds him innocent of any crime, he nurses a powerful sense of guilt for his actions and continues to be driven by a disproportionate sense of responsibility for the suffering of those around him.

The novel opens with Rowe entering a local fair. He is drawn to the fair because it reminds him of his lost innocence. Despite the war raging around him, the fair affords him lush gardens and sweet smells from his childhood. Ironically, his attendance at the fair leads to his becoming a hunted man. He wins a cake that, unknown to him, contains a microfilm of secret naval plans placed there by a spy ring. When he returns home, one of the Nazi agents who constitute the Ministry of Fear visits him in an attempt to poison him. Recognizing the smell of the poison (the same one he used for his wife), Rowe realizes that someone wants to kill him for no apparent reason, turning his sense of reality into a Kafkaesque nightmare. Later, while Rowe is attending a séance, one of the guests is murdered with Rowe's knife and Willi Hilfe, a young Austrian relief worker (who pretends to be Rowe's friend but who actually masterminds the Nazi spy ring) advises Rowe to go underground. The murder, however, is merely a contrivance to drive Rowe into hiding. He is seriously injured when, upon opening a case supposedly containing books, a bomb goes off.

The second part of the novel finds Rowe a victim of amnesia from the bomb blast and a patient in a nursing home run by Dr. Forester, one of the spies. Through an act of crippling violence, Rowe, remembering nothing from his past, is ironically returned to a more innocent world. His amnesia allows him to enjoy an Arcadian existence for a time, unaware of the war in London, his murder trial, and his fugitive past.

When Rowe challenges Dr. Forester for his cruelty to one of the patients at the home, the doctor retaliates by revealing Rowe's real name and showing him a newspaper clipping of his murder trial. This sudden illumination marks the beginning of Rowe's rebirth and return to the sordid, complex world from which he enjoyed only a temporary retreat. He gradually puts the bits and pieces of his past back together again and moves closer to becoming a whole man. He still, however, does not know the details of his murder trial.

The novel ends with Rowe's confrontation of Willi Hilfe. After Rowe disarms him, Willi offers Rowe a deal: He will complete Rowe's memory about the death of his wife and turn over the microfilm in exchange for Rowe's revolver and a single bullet with which to commit suicide. Rowe refuses but Willi insists on revealing the details of Rowe's trial anyway. His curiosity satiated, Rowe feels himself a whole man once again and, in still another act of pity, allows Willi to commit suicide.

Rowe's anguish over the suffering of others leads him to become a sinister force of violence himself. His sense of pity leads to the murder of his wife and to the suicide of Willi Hilfe. He is hunted by the Ministry of Fear, the reader is told, because he loved, but Rowe misleads one here. His selfishness and quiet arrogance are the forces that actually motivate his most important actions and shape his emotional commitments to others. Thus the victim of the Ministry of Fear is actually the victim of his own pity, the most terrible passion Greene allows his characters.

THE HEART OF THE MATTER

First published: 1948
Type of work: Novel

A middle-aged police officer in British West Africa is driven to suicide in order to protect his wife and his mistress from suffering.

Major Scobie, the hero of *The Heart of the Matter*, is a middle-aged police officer in British West Africa. During his fifteen years of service he has acquired a reputation for unfailing integrity. His wife, Louise, is a nagging and restless woman who plans a holiday trip to South Africa to escape the languid, oppressive atmosphere of Sierra Leone and the embarrassment caused by her husband's failure to be promoted to commissioner. Scobie, whose love for her has long been replaced by an obsessive sense of pity and responsibility, borrows the money for her vacation from a Syrian smuggler and usurer named Yusef.

During his wife's absence Scobie falls in love with a nineteen-year-old girl named Helen Rolt, who has been widowed in a shipwreck off the coast. When Louise returns, Scobie still feels morally bound to live up to his private vow to see to it that she is always happy. Complicating matters further, Scobie writes Helen a letter reassuring her of his love for her. This letter winds up in the hands of Yusef, who blackmails Scobie into helping him smuggle some diamonds out of the country.

Shortly after her return home, Louise asks Scobie to go to Holy Communion with her. He goes to confession but cannot promise the priest that he will not see Helen again and so cannot be absolved of his sin. In order to ward off any suspicion of his adultery, however, he receives Communion in the state of mortal sin. He willingly risks his eternal damnation rather than inflict pain on Louise. At the same time, his love and sense of responsibility for Helen are so strong that he cannot bring himself to end the affair. He thus tells God that he will accept eternal damnation in exchange for the happiness of these two women.

Tormented by his religious hypocrisy and by the certain knowledge that his dilemma will lead him to inflict unnecessary pain on Louise or Helen, Scobie decides to commit suicide. Both women, he reasons, will forget him after his death and will regain their happiness. He studies the symptoms of angina pectoris so that his death may appear to be natural then poisons himself with tablets prescribed by his doctor for the pretended illness.

Scobie is a sympathetic figure, demanding the reader's pity and respect. His sense of pity and responsibility for the happiness of others, however, is excessive and demonstrates an almost monstrous pride that leads to his self-destruction. The reader feels sorry for Scobie because he cannot help himself. Watching his fall from grace is like watching the hero of a drama who, flawed by a critical blindness in his character, seeks peace and happiness but ironically and irrevocably brings upon himself and others pain, suffering, and death. The novel conveys a strong sense of fatalism as a chain of interlocking events combines with Scobie's obsessive personality to diminish his freedom and finally makes suicide the only means by which he can resolve his overwhelming dilemma.

During Scobie's last moments he begins a prayer to God that he fails to finish. The reader is inclined to believe that this tragic man, who has suffered deeply, will at last be awarded the peace of God, but Greene characteristically denies the reader the restful certainty of that conclusion. Strictly speaking, suicide is a mortal sin that cannot be repented, and thus, according to Catholic doctrine, Scobie's soul is damned to Hell. Afterward, Scobie's priest, Father Rank, points out that the Church does not know what goes on in a single human heart, thereby leaving the door open to the possibility that Scobie's final state of mind might have made his salvation possible.

Summary

Despite the variety of literary forms that Graham Greene explored, his greatness clearly lies in his fiction. Unlike writers of the 1920's and 1930's, he practically ignored the experimental novel. Rather, he followed the loose tradition of such diverse writers as Charles Dickens, Wilkie Collins, Robert Louis Stevenson, H. Rider Haggard, Joseph Conrad, and Marjorie Bowen.

Greene's main achievements in the novel are twofold. First, he is a master storyteller, one of the chief reasons for his popular success. Second, he has created a unique vision of the world, having turned his personal obsessions into universal works of art. Greene both lived and wrote on the dangerous edge of things, and in the world of his novels he has re-created the bittersweet conflict between the fascination of innocence and the hell-haunted drama of human existence. It is a surprising, suspenseful, frightening, and dark world that he has created, but it is above all a human place, peopled with sad and suffering men and women with a profound longing for peace, some of whom occasionally startle the reader with their compassion and love and childlike simplicity.

Bibliography

Allott, Kenneth, and Miriam Farris. *The Art of Graham Greene.* New York: Russell, 1963.

Atkins, John. *Graham Greene.* London: Calder and Boyars, 1966.

De Vitis, A. A. *Graham Greene.* Rev. ed. Boston: Twayne, 1986.

Kelly, Richard. *Graham Greene.* New York: Ungar, 1984.

Meyers, Jeffrey. *Graham Greene: A Revaluation.* London: Macmillan, 1990.

O'Prey, Paul. *A Reader's Guide to Graham Greene.* Worcester, England: Thames and Hudson, 1988.

Spurling, John. *Graham Greene.* London: Methuen, 1983.

Thomas, Brian. *An Underground Fate: The Idiom of Romance in the Later Novels of Graham Greene.* Athens: University of Georgia Press, 1988.

Richard Kelly

THE BROTHERS GRIMM

Jacob Grimm
Born: Hanau, Germany
January 4, 1785
Died: Berlin, Germany
September 20, 1863

Wilhelm Grimm
Born: Hanau, Germany
February 24, 1786
Died: Berlin, Germany
December 16, 1859

Principal Literary Achievement

Accomplished scholars of Teutonic folklore, linguistics, and philology, the Brothers Grimm gained literary immortality with their collection of German fairy tales.

Biography

Jacob Ludwig Carl Grimm was born on January 4, 1785, in Hanau, Germany. His brother, Wilhelm Carl Grimm, was born a year later on February 24, also in Hanau. Their parents were Philpp [Sic] Wilhelm Grimm, a German official, and Dorthea Zimmer Grimm. Jacob and Wilhelm were close all of their lives, lived together, worked as a team on certain projects, held professorships at the same universities, and contributed enormously to Germanic studies. Jacob was the dominant force, disciplined, with an appetite for tedious research. Wilhelm was frailer, warmer, more sociable, drawn to music and literature. Yet each had the generous, even temper needed to sustain a lifetime of collaboration.

As law students at the University of Marburg, they were influenced by Professor Friedrich Karl von Savigny. At a time when Napoleon I was conquering all of Europe, Jacob had a revelation of his and Wilhelm's life work while browsing in Savigny's library. From that time forward, the Grimms devoted themselves to resurrecting the German past in scholarship. They were inspired by patriotism, but a kind that looks back wistfully.

The brothers began editing medieval manuscripts. Their first publication of note, *Altdeutscher Meistergesang* (1811), was a series of essays on medieval German poetry.

The Grimms also began collecting folktales from friends and neighbors. Their next publication, a large assortment of these folktales, eventually put the Grimms on the literary map for good. It was *Kinder- und Hausmärchen* (1812-1815; *German Popular Stories*, 1823-1826), published in two volumes. These stories became known and loved in English as *Grimm's Fairy Tales*. Its publication was a landmark of the German Romantic movement, for within it was the voice of the common people given literary expression in enchanting stories. The book began a new era in folklore collecting, a respect for the story as told. Reviewers found it boorish, but it gained immediate public acceptance and was promptly translated. The book saw several editions in the Grimms' lifetimes alone.

After the Napoleonic Wars, Jacob found work in Cassel in the same library that employed Wilhelm. The output of the Grimms was enormous. Among their notable achievements was an exhaustive two-volume study of German legends, *Deutsche Sagen* (1816-1818); *The German Legends of the Brothers Grimm*, 1981), an account of proverbs as the basis of German law, *Deutsche Rechtsalterthümer* (1828), and an encyclopedic study of Teutonic mythology, *Deutsche Mythologie* (1835; *Teutonic Mythology*, 1880-1888). In 1819, Jacob Grimm published his German grammar, *Deutsche Grammatik* (1819-1837), a work that, in its second edition of four volumes, amazed the scholarly world. Jacob amassed a huge body of evidence to codify the consonant shifts in the Germanic family of languages from earliest times to the nineteenth century. The exact relationship of those shifts is called Grimm's law, and it established linguistics as a science.

When Wilhelm married Dorothea Wild in 1825, Jacob continued to live in the household amiably. Both brothers found positions at the University of Göttingen, with Jacob becoming head librarian and full professor in 1830 and Wilhelm receiving a professorship in 1835. When the Grimms signed a protest over the king of Hanover abolishing the constitution, they were fired. Both returned to Cassel. Then in 1840 they received professorships at the University of Berlin, which they held until their deaths. Their last great labor was on the first volume of a colossal thirty-two-volume German dictionary, the *Deutsches Wörterbuch* (1854-1961), which took four generations of scholars and more than one hundred years to finish. Wilhelm died in Berlin on December 16, 1859. Jacob died there on September 20, 1863.

Analysis

Grimm's Fairy Tales has a distinctive German flavor even in English translation. The settings are German: forests, castles, mountains, quaint villages, inns, and huts. The characters are old-fashioned German types: merchants, cobblers, tailors, millers, huntsmen, tramps, robbers, woodcutters, parsons, peasants, kings, queens, princes, and princesses. Even the supernatural beings have a Germanic coloring: witches, dwarves, giants, elves, nixies, and the devil. Yet this very seventeenth century German quality adds to the magic of the stories. If these stories were not so firmly grounded in their time and place, they would lose their essence, their ability to reveal the universals of human experience.

Stories that satirize stupidity and laziness are common to every culture that values practical intelligence and hard work. Tales such as "Clever Elsie," "Frederick and Catherine," "Wise People," and "Lazy Harry" show with some wit the folly of the stupid and the idle. Ridicule is a tool to make misfits conform, but when it is directed at characters in an amusing story, the point is made without the sting of personal venom.

There are many animal tales in *Grimm's Fairy Tales*, some of which are fables, tales with a moral. In "The Wolf and the Fox," the wolf's rampant gluttony leads to its destruction, while foresight saves the fox. In "The Cat and Mouse in Partnership," gluttony is symbolic of the greedy and powerful, who swallow the weak under the guise of benevolence. There are realistic stories, too, and these deal with cruelty to the helpless, which is always condemned. Tales such as "The Nail," "The Old Man and His Grandson," "The Poor Boy in the Grave," "Sharing Joy and Sorrow," and "The Bright Sun Brings It to Light," depict the hard, evil side of human nature unsoftened by fantasy. In fact, "The Bright Sun Brings It to Light" eerily foreshadows the Holocaust in a small way. Religious stories also form an important part of *Grimm's Fairy Tales*; "Mary's Child" is an outstanding example. There is a whole section devoted to these stories under the heading "The Children's Legends." Finally, there are nonsense tales, brief bits of humor told for sheer exuberance. "My Household" has cumulative nonsense, "The Louse and the Flea" contains nonsense on the theme of getting carried away, "The Ditmars Tale of Wonders" displays the nonsense of obvious absurdities, and "Fair Katrinelje and Pif-Paf-Poltrie" reveals the nonsense of the proposal ritual.

It is for the fairy tales, however, that the Grimms are remembered. In them, poetic fantasy and realistic detail blend in startling ways, as in dreams. Yet if these tales resemble dreams with their magic and wish-fulfillment, they are consciously crafted stories that follow the rules of the genre.

Fairy tales are meant to be recited or read aloud to children. One thing that a child wants is a good story. The plot must therefore be the main attraction. The story needs dramatic contrast: good versus evil, kindness versus cruelty, loyalty versus treachery. Further, the hero or heroine must have some purpose, such as winning a royal mate, helping others, undoing a spell. The plot also needs suspense, things that hinder the hero or heroine from achieving the goal. That is the reason for the pattern of three so common in fairy tales—three nights in a haunted castle, three riddles to be solved, three magic tasks. Three is the ideal number for building suspense: Four is too long, and two is too short, to hold a child's interest.

Magic is significant in fairy tales. There are magic helpers who assist the kind-hearted to reach their goals. Old women and gnomes furnish magic objects and advice. Talking animals, fish, birds, and insects perform the tasks that the hero or heroine finds impossible. Magic objects enable the hero to do specific feats that would otherwise be beyond him. Besides helpful magic, there is evil magic in fairy tales— spells that turn a human into a beast, spells that petrify a place, and spells used to dupe the trusting. To overcome evil magic, it takes patience and love.

Since everything in a fairy tale is subordinate to the plot, the characters are revealed by their acts and speech. The heroes and heroines lack complexity and often a name. Yet they usually have the qualities necessary to heroism, whether heroism in story or in real life. These are courage, generosity of spirit, and the persistence needed to overcome adversity. The wicked people in fairy tales and in life are proud, unhappy, envious, and mean. They cannot stand adversity and take nasty shortcuts to get what they want. Sooner or later, their treachery is exposed. Fairy tales are grounded in the basic qualities of human experience.

THE WATER OF LIFE

First published: "Das Wasser des Lebens," 1815 (English translation, 1826)
Type of work: Folklore

In seeking a cure for his father, the third of three sons finds his future wife and suffers the treachery of his older brothers.

"The Water of Life" is storytelling pared to the bone. The tale is so lucid and simple that it almost defies analysis. Situation, speech, and action blend in one flowing narrative. A king is dying. His three sons learn from an old man that the only way to save their father is to bring him the water of life. The dying king reluctantly gives one son after the other permission to seek the water.

When the two proud older brothers meet a dwarf who asks where they are going, they answer rudely, so the dwarf sends them up a ravine, where they become trapped. Arrogance itself is a trap, and the ravines are symbolic of the older brothers' hard pride that keeps them from progressing. When the third prince meets the dwarf, he answers politely and confesses that he does not know where the water of life is. The dwarf then tells him that the water is in an enchanted castle, and he gives the prince the three things that he needs to enter the castle: a wand to open the gate and two small loaves of bread to feed the guardian lions. The dwarf also warns him to leave the castle by midnight. The prince thanks him and leaves. The amount of information conveyed in a few sentences is amazing: The hero is revealed as courteous, humbly honest, and grateful.

Once inside the castle, the prince acts on his own initiative. He finds a hall with spellbound princes and removes their rings. He finds a sword and a loaf of bread that he takes. He finds a lovely princess, who wakes and kisses him. She says that they will be wed in a year and that her kingdom will be his. She also tells him where the water is and warns him that he will be imprisoned in the castle if he stays past midnight. He falls asleep, however, and barely awakens in time to fetch the water and escape, losing part of his heel as the gate slams shut. The events in the enchanted castle are vivid, mysterious, and dreamlike. Yet they work a change in the hero. He becomes both more affectionate and more effective. His one blind spot, however, is that he trusts his brothers.

Again he meets the dwarf, who tells him that the sword (the wand, magically transformed) can defeat many armies and that the supply of bread will never end. The prince asks about his brothers, and the dwarf releases them, warning the prince about their evil hearts. The brothers are joyfully reunited and travel home together, with the youngest telling of all that befell him. On the way, they find three sucessive kingdoms ravaged by war and famine. The prince saves each with his sword and bread. Before arriving home, the brothers undergo a sea journey in which the older brothers switch the water of life for sea water while the youngest sleeps. Sleep is a real danger in this tale.

The youngest son is accused of attempted poisoning after giving his father the salt water, while his brothers get the credit for rejuvenating the king. The king then orders his huntsman to execute his third son on a hunting trip. Yet the prince is so considerate of the huntsman's feelings that the huntsman tells him of the king's orders and, instead of killing him, exchanges clothes with the prince. The prince hides in the forest for a year. Meanwhile, the king repents his hasty act when three wagons of gold and jewels come for his third son from the three kingdoms that he had saved. When the huntsman tells the truth, the king grants his lost son amnesty.

The princess orders a golden road built to her castle and tells her servants to send away all who ride up by the side of the road, but to admit the one who rides down the middle. The older brothers ride to the side when they notice that the road is gold. The prince, however, never notices, his mind being full of the princess; he rides down the center to his bride, her kingdom, and his father's love. His wicked brothers set forth on the sea and are never heard from again.

The main symbols in the story almost speak for themselves. The wand and two small loaves of bread that admit the prince into the castle become, magically, the sword and loaf by which he saves three kingdoms. The water of life is balanced by the water of death (sea water). The golden road that leads to success must not be approached gingerly; it must be ridden down the center with all of one's being focused on the goal.

MARY'S CHILD

First published: "Marienkind," 1812 (English translation, 1823)
Type of work: Folklore

A young woman is cast out of heaven for her sins and must suffer repeated losses until she repents and confesses.

"Mary's Child" has three levels operating in perfect harmony. One is the story surface, the actual events and language; another is symbolic, with parallels in everyone's life; and the third is the spiritual level, eternity revealed through time.

Mary takes a starving woodcutter's baby girl to heaven to rear as her own. The infant is given the best of care and has angels for playmates. When the girl is fourteen, Mary goes on a long trip and leaves the keys to thirteen rooms in heaven with the girl, telling her that she may open every door but the thirteenth, which is forbidden. The girl opens a new door every day to find an apostle. On the thirteenth day, devoured by curiosity, she opens the forbidden door and sees the Trinity blazing in fire and glory. She gazes in awe and puts out her finger, which turns to gold. Suddenly, she is seized by panic, closes the door, and rushes to Mary, who knows immediately what has happened. Three times Mary asks the girl if she opened the forbidden door, and three times the girl denies it. Mary has no choice but to send her to earth. It is Original Sin repeated, but it is also the way that adolescence is experienced, as a loss of innocence and being cared for by adults. It marks the beginning of suffering as a constant part of the human makeup and the point at which one must accept the consequences of one's actions.

The girl is isolated from all human contact in a part of the forest surrounded by thorns. She tries to cry out but finds that she is mute. She must fend for herself, eating roots, nuts, and berries, and having only a hollow tree for shelter. She looks back on her life in heaven with longing. That is how things are out in the cold, harsh world of adolescence, where pain isolates one from everyone else.

The girl becomes a woman. Her clothes have dissolved in shreds, but she is covered by her long, golden hair. One spring, a king chases a roe into her area of forest and must hack through the thorns. He finds a beautiful, mute young woman, whom he takes home and marries. At this point, the courtship rite is stripped to its basics. A man chases a sleek, healthy animal into cover. If he persists in his hunt through the thorns of misunderstanding, jealousy, female contrariness, and pain, he will behold the one woman in the world for him, exactly as she is, naked and splendid. She, in turn, will behold a king.

In the following three years of marriage, the queen has two sons and a daughter. After the birth of each, Mary visits the queen and asks if she opened the forbidden door, and each time the queen denies it. Thereupon Mary takes the child to heaven, again leaving the queen mute. After the disappearance of each child, the king's councillors and subjects accuse the queen of cannibalism until the king can no longer ignore them. The queen is tried, convicted, and sentenced to burn at the stake. Her one sin, compounded by six lies, leads to death. Yet as the flames rise, her icy heart melts, and she cries out, "Yes, Mary, I did it." Mary then quenches the fire with rain, fully restores the queen's speech and three children, and blesses her with happiness. Mary herself points out the moral that forgiveness is gained only by repentance and confession. The real miracle is that God is humble enough to accept last-minute repentance.

Summary

The style of the Brothers Grimm tales is simple, appropriate for a child. The language is serious, dignified, and poetic. There is little description, a lot of action, and enough speech to make the narrative interesting. In some stories, a person or an animal will resort to verse at a crucial point. The openings and closings of the Grimms' fairy tales are ritualistic, pungent, and much more inventive than the stale "once upon a time" and "they lived happily ever after."

In selecting and arranging their folktales, the Grimms, and Wilhelm especially, showed balance, taste, and love. The result was wonderful.

Bibliography

Bettelheim, Bruno. *The Uses of Enchantment: The Meaning and Importance of Fairy Tales.* New York: Alfred A. Knopf, 1976.

Bottigheimer, Ruth B. *Grimms' Bad Girls and Bold Boys: The Moral and Social Vision of the Tales.* New Haven, Conn.: Yale University Press, 1987.

Campbell, Joseph. "Folkloristic Commentary." In *The Complete Grimm's Fairy Tales,* by Wilhelm and Jacob Grimm. New York: Pantheon Books, 1944.

Ellis, John M. *One Fairy Story Too Many: The Brothers Grimm and Their Tales.* Chicago: University of Chicago Press, 1983.

McGlathery, James M., ed. *The Brothers Grimm and Folktale.* Urbana: University of Illinois Press, 1988.

Sutherland, Zena, and May Hill Arbuthnot. *Children and Books.* 7th ed. Glenview, Ill.: Scott, Foresman, 1986.

Tatar, Maria. *The Hard Facts of the Grimms' Fairy Tales.* Princeton, N.J.: Princeton University Press, 1987.

Zipes, Jack David. *The Brothers Grimm: From Enchanted Forests to the Modern World.* New York: Routledge, Chapman & Hall, 1988.

James Weigel, Jr.

KNUT HAMSUN

Born: Lom, Norway
August 4, 1859
Died: Nørholm, Norway
February 19, 1952

Principal Literary Achievement

In addition to writing poetry and drama, Hamsun is recognized as an originator of the modern psychological novel and one of its most skilled practitioners.

Biography

Knut Hamsun was born Knut Pedersen on August 4, 1859, at the farm Garmotræet in the district of Lom, Norway. His father, Peder Pedersen, and mother, Tora Pedersen, were both of peasant stock. In 1863, Pedersen and his family moved to Hamarøy in Nordland, Norway, where they settled on the farm Hamsund, from which Hamsun later took the name by which he is known. Hamsun's early childhood was a happy time. At the age of nine, however, he was sent to live with his uncle, who owned Hamsund and to whom his parents were indebted. The boy worked hard and was harshly treated, but at the age of fourteen he was released and began working odd jobs.

The young Hamsun was familiar with both the popular writing of his time and some of its more valuable literature. Dreaming about becoming a writer, he published two short books while yet in his teens and was able to obtain the support of a wealthy merchant. He produced another manuscript and traveled to Copenhagen but was unable to find a publisher. He spent a difficult winter in the city of Christiania (later Oslo), Norway, and later spent several years in the United States, where he worked in a variety of jobs, read widely, and lectured to his compatriots on cultural and literary topics.

Hamsun's difficult times provided him with the material for his novel *Sult* (1890; *Hunger*, 1899), which gave him his literary breakthrough. Some lectures on the state of literature, held in 1891, further contributed to his fame; Hamsun argued in favor of the new psychological novel, of which *Hunger* was a groundbreaking example.

The 1890's were very productive years for Hamsun. He wrote such significant novels as *Mysterier* (1892; *Mysteries*, 1927), *Pan* (1894; English translation, 1920), and *Victoria* (1898; English translation, 1929), enjoyed an increasing reputation, and traveled much. He also wrote poetry and drama. In 1898, he married Bergljot Bech, whom

he had met the previous year and who inspired the beautiful love story *Victoria*. The couple were divorced in 1906.

During the next few years, Hamsun wrote a number of other novels that are not considered to be among his best. After his marriage to Marie Andersen in 1909, however, he turned away from focusing on the solitary mind and increased his attention to social relationships. One of these novels, a celebration of rural life entitled *Markens grøde* (1917; *Growth of the Soil*, 1920), garnered for him the Nobel Prize in Literature in 1920. The book, in which the author argues in favor of traditional values, tells about a man who goes into the woods of northern Norway, clears land for a farm, and rears a family in close contact with nature.

Growth of the Soil was inspired by Hamsun's life on his farm Skogheim in Hamarøy, northern Norway. He found himself too isolated there, however, and purchased the farm Nørholm in the far south, where he settled in the 1920's. Fearing that his creativity was failing, he began psychotherapy in 1926. The following year, he published his novel *Landstrykere* (1927; *Vagabonds*, 1930; also as *Wayfarers*, 1981), which is universally regarded as the finest book from the second half of his career. The first volume in a trilogy, it was followed by *August* (1930; English translation, 1931) and *Men livet lever* (1933; *The Road Leads On*, 1934). The trilogy tells about a dreamer and eccentric named August, who is both admired and criticized by the author. August possesses a priceless creative imagination, but he uses it mostly for schemes that bring trouble to those who know him.

By the time of the conclusion of the August trilogy, Hamsun was well into his seventies. He was not as intellectually keen and physically strong as he had been, and his hearing was failing. He published what was expected to be his final book, *Ringen sluttet* (1936; *The Ring Is Closed*, 1937), and he would probably have remained silent were it not for the political developments of the time. Hamsun had always admired Germany and German culture and had been rather contemptous of the British. He now allowed himself to become an admirer of Adolf Hitler and, when Germany invaded Norway, supported the collaborationists and urged Norwegian soldiers not to fight. After the war, he was brought to trial, convicted of treason, and heavily fined. As a defense, he published the moving memoir *På gjengrodde stier* (1949; *On Overgrown Paths*, 1967), lived quietly, and died on his farm in Nørholm, Norway, on February 19, 1952.

Analysis

As a young man, Hamsun keenly felt the difference between himself and those who possessed wealth and power in society. An outsider, he wanted to achieve social and material success, but he also valued the freedom of not having to fulfill the expectations of others. Many of his early protagonists have been placed in a similar position, in that they have to choose between, on the one hand, freedom and powerlessness, and, on the other, power and its accompanying ties.

Another characteristic of the young Hamsun was that he believed himself to be talented but unappreciated. This characteristic is also found in his heroes, many of whom are afflicted with an extreme self-absorption stemming from a lack of recognition.

Hamsun's early novels, such as *Hunger* and *Pan*, are inquiries into the minds of hypersensitive, gifted, and lonely individuals. In order to facilitate the exploration of the mind, these books make use of first-person narrators through whose narration the reader is given the illusion of having direct access to the psyches of the narrator-protagonists. These characters often seem to confirm or even celebrate their independence by outrageous acts, such as when the hero of *Hunger* deliberately eats until he vomits, when Nagel in *Mysteries* frightens the lowly character who is called the Midget, and when Glahn in *Pan* spits into the ear of the Finnish baron. Yet the same characters also strive to fit into their society, pursuing art, women of a higher social standing, or both. Each of these men also tries to climb socially through love. The ties of artistic success and respectability are definitely felt to be ties that bind, and so are the bonds of matrimony, but each of these outsider-protagonists are nevertheless in pursuit of them.

Hamsun's literary style changed dramatically as he moved into the second half of his career, and so did his thematic concerns. After achieving success, he was not as interested in the character of the lonely outsider as before, and he turned his attention to portraying the workings of social life. He also abandoned the first-person perspective in favor of third-person narration, employing omniscient narrators through which he could have access to the minds of all of his characters. He retained some interest in the exceptional individual, but his concern largely shifted to the social group. At the same time, the author became highly critical of many of the features of modern life, such as industrial production, women's liberation, and the labor movement.

These objections to modernity first came to the fore in the two novels *Børn av tiden* (1913; *Children of the Age*, 1924) and *Segelfoss by* (1915; *Segelfoss Town*, 1925), both of which have as their setting the town of Segelfoss in northern Norway. Through a portrayal of the gradual industrialization and modernization of the community, which grows from a few houses scattered around a flour mill into a small town, Hamsun analyzes the process by which the old and semifeudal social order vanishes and is replaced by the social and economic reality of the twentieth century. The author distrusts modern life with its lack of respect for authority, its money-based economy, and its system of education, through which talented young people degenerate into clergymen, doctors, and lawyers. Both of the novels have an engaging story line, interesting characters, and several humorous episodes, but the general tone is one of pessimism.

Hamsun's critique of modern life continues in *Growth of the Soil*, in which he creates a positive counterpart to the decaying society at Segelfoss. Isak Sellanraa, the protagonist, is a man without not only a past but also the cultural baggage of contemporary life. The novel tells about how he conquers the wilderness of northern Norway and builds a farm, rears a family, and passes his farm on to one of his sons. Sellanraa was named for an Old Testament patriarch; his values are hard work, patriotism, and the simple life. His is not an entirely paradisiacal existence, however, for civilization closes in on him in the form of a mining operation that goes bankrupt, and he loses part of his family to modern thinking. An important motif in the book is the author's anti-Americanism. Hamsun placed his story in northern Norway in order to show that there was no need for enterprising people to emigrate to the United States at the end of the book, Isak's oldest son has no way out but emigration, constituting a powerful indictment of the American way of life.

In the trilogy that consists of *Vagabonds*, *August*, and *the Road Leads On*, many of the themes of *Growth of the Soil* are continued. A tragic character named Edevart, who does not have the strength to resist the allure of the modern world, is corrupted and emigrates to the United States where he does not feel at home. Returning to Norway, he feels equally out of place, and the rootlessness extends itself to his relationship with women. His counterpart, August, on the other hand, is unsettled from the beginning; his ideology is completely in line with that of high capitalist industrialism, although his acts are those of a parasite. Other characters exemplify Hamsun's positive values but are given comparatively little space. The anti-American theme is continued in Hamsun's final novel, *The Ring Is Closed*, which is a dark and pessimistic book.

HUNGER

First published: *Sult*, 1890 (English translation, 1899)
Type of work: Novel

A budding writer starves in the capital city of Christiania (now Oslo), Norway.

Hunger, which was based on Hamsun's many unhappy experiences in Norway's capital city of Christiania, was one of the first modern psychological novels in world literature. Told in the first person, it is the story of a young writer of exceptional sensibility who, stripped of all of his property and without any reliable means of support, is about to perish from extreme hunger. The book contains little action in the traditional sense. With the exception of the story of a few attempts to secure employment and the account of a brief encounter with a lady of the middle class, the text consists almost exclusively of reports of the narrator's mental life during periods of starvation.

The experience of hunger was surely not uncommon among artists at the time, and the social consequences of hunger figure prominently in the naturalistic literature of the Scandinavian countries. The importance of *Hunger* lies not in its subject matter but rather in the manner in which the author deals with it, for his focus is on a portrayal of the strange workings of the mind while in an altered state resulting from the lack of nourishment. To this end, Hamsun uses a stream-of-consciousness technique through which the reader is given access both to the perceptions, moods, and strange ideas of the narrator and to his reflections on his own state of consciousness.

The narrator views himself as a completely committed artist, and his concern is both to prevent his hunger from negatively affecting those sensibilities that make him capable of producing art and to utilize his unpleasant experiences in his art. The narrator's tendency toward self-observation can be viewed both as a part of his artistic project, the gathering of material for a novel that he wants to write, and as a means of making certain that the needs of his body do not overcome his mental or artistic needs.

Little is learned about the narrator's past throughout the book, and only a few details concerning his identity are mentioned. These details do not even include the mention of his name, but it is clear that he is an individual who, in the past, has been somewhat better off economically; it is possible to deduce that he, like Hamsun himself, has worked in other occupations before devoting his life entirely to writing. The novel does show, however, that he is not exclusively concerned with examining his own mind for the purpose of his art. A mysterious young middle-class woman named Ylajali, to whom he is attracted, appears to have little artistic significance to him; his interest in her seems to originate in a concern for social position. The narrator's pursuit of Ylajali can be read as an alternative means to the kind of success that, so far, he has not been able to achieve through his art. That makes the narrator-protagonist of *Hunger* appear to be a practical man who, perhaps like his creator Hamsun, views art as a means of social advancement at least as much as an end in itself.

PAN

First published: *Pan*, 1894 (English translation, 1920)
Type of work: Novel

A young lieutenant experiences love and the dynamics of power during a summer in northern Norway.

Pan has a rather complex narrative structure. It is a first-person novel in which the main part of the story is told by the narrator-protagonist, Glahn, two years after the events that are being narrated took place. The main part is followed by an epilogue, also in the first person, in which the story of Glahn's death is told by an unnamed hunting companion.

The main story takes place in northern Norway during the summer months of the year 1855. Glahn, a lieutenant who has obtained leave from his commission, is living a rather primitive life as a hunter and fisherman in a cabin near the trading post Sirilund. He is tired of civilization, he says, and has left behind the norms of cultured society, being unable to get along well with cultivated people. In narrating his story, Glahn tells both about the external events of his life in a natural context and about his reflections on existence, and it is clear that he is trying to become an artist.

During visits to the trading post, Glahn becomes acquainted with Edvarda, the daughter of the trader Mack. Being attracted to her both because of her social position and for her own sake, he tries to win her, but Edvarda is emotionally unpredictable, and a love-hate relationship, in which they take turns torturing each other, develops. Glahn also enters into a sexual relationship with Eva, who, despite her marriage to the local blacksmith, is the lover of Edvarda's father, Mack, whom Glahn displaces. Attempting to play the role of the Greek god Pan, Glahn also seduces a young goatherd named Henriette.

Much of the story deals with the battle between Glahn and Mack over Eva, as well as with Glahn's attempts to get rid of two rivals in his relationship to Edvarda—the local doctor and a Finnish baron who is conducting scientific research in the area. Glahn, while present at a party and slightly inebriated, deliberately offends the baron by spitting into his ear. He also offends the doctor by whistling to him and coaxing him to jump over his gun, as if it were a stick and the doctor were a dog. Neither the doctor nor the baron is willing to lower himself to Glahn's level, but Mack, who has been accustomed to holding unchallenged power in the area, is not afraid of facing him. Shrewd and manipulative, Mack decides to show Glahn that he is the more intelligent of the two by forcing him to abandon a project. Glahn has been planning to blast some rock out of a cliff as a final salute to the baron, who is leaving, but Mack orders Eva to tar a boat below the cliff, thinking that Glahn will not risk hurting her. Glahn, however, has less regard for Eva's life than for his own pride, and the result is that Eva dies in the explosion.

Glahn behaves erratically on other occasions also. One of the most disturbing instances is found in the book's epilogue, which relates how he goads a hunting companion into shooting and killing him while in India. Not necessarily a happy story, *Pan* clearly sets forth Hamsun's view of the relationship between love, power, and the temperament of the artist.

Summary

The literary career of Knut Hamsun is marked by the contrast between the great artistic quality of his works, which are almost universally admired, and the questionable, even bizarre, behavior of many of his central characters. While social themes became the focus in Hamsun's later novels, resulting in a subordination of character portrayal to the author's ideological concerns, his early works constitute explorations of highly unusual minds. Artists or artists in the making, his protagonists are always memorable although not always to be admired, and their tortured lives are made intelligible to the reader through their occasionally outrageous actions. Through it all, the reader is made acutely aware of the price that has to be paid for creating art.

Bibliography

Ferguson, Robert. *Enigma: The Life of Knut Hamsun.* London: Hutchinson University Library, 1987.

McFarlane, J. W. "The Whisper of the Blood: A Study of Knut Hamsun's Early Novels." *PMLA* 71 (September, 1956): 563-594.

Mazor, Yair. *The Triple Cord: Agon, Hamsun, Strindberg.* Tel Aviv, Israel: Papyrus, 1987.

Næss, Harald. *Knut Hamsun.* Boston: Twayne, 1984.

Turco, Alfred, Jr. "Knut Hamsun's *Pan* and the Riddle of 'Glahn's Death.'" *Scandinavica* 19 (May, 1980): 13-29.

Jan Sjåvik

PETER HANDKE

Born: Griffen, Austria
December 6, 1942

Principal Literary Achievement

Handke is best known for his novels and plays, which are characterized by innovative use of language and radical departure from established literary and theatrical traditions.

Biography

Peter Handke was born on December 6, 1942, in Griffen, Austria, a village in the province of Carinthia near the Yugoslavian border. As a child he lived in the country, except for four years spent in Berlin between 1944 and 1948. He studied law at the University of Graz from 1961 to 1965, which may have influenced his writing style: His attention to detail, precision, and complex sentence structure are all characteristic of legal language.

Handke's first published work appeared in the magazine *Manuskripte* in the mid-1960's; then, in 1966, his first novel, *Die Hornissen* (*The Hornets*), saw print. His book was favorably received by critics, but he did not achieve true recognition until later that year, when he launched a dramatic public attack on German writing and criticism that, he believed, unduly favored traditional descriptive prose and rejected new, experimental techniques. The setting for this attack was a writers' conference in Princeton, New Jersey; the audience (and targets) were the members of Gruppe 47 (Group 47), an influential organization of German writers. Ironically, the writers Handke criticized responded enthusiastically to his remarks, and the incident led to his recognition in the prestigious magazine *Der Spiegel*. The Princeton meeting was a major turning point in Handke's career, bringing international attention to both his work and his controversial and innovative ideas about writing.

Handke's rejection of tradition and interest in artistic experimentation received their first major expression the same year in *Publikumsbeschimpfung* (1966; *Offending the Audience*, 1969), a short play whose title is indicative of its content. Instead of a typical play with scenes, characters, costumes, and sets, *Offending the Audience* consists of four actors in ordinary clothes on a bare stage. Instead of speaking lines of dialogue to one another, the actors directly address the audience, telling them that they are not going to see a play at all, then going on to discuss various ideas about the theater, audiences, illusion, and reality. The title has a double meaning: First, the

expectations of the audience are mocked by the bizarre nature of the play, then the audience is subjected to a barrage of insults from the actors before the play ends. For obvious reasons, some critics called this work an "antiplay" or "antitheater"; Handke prefers the term *Sprechstucke*, or "speaking piece." First performed in Frankfurt as part of a week-long theater festival called Experimenta I, *Offending the Audience* was as startling and intriguing as Handke's Princeton speech; it ensured Handke's status as a major figure in experimental theater in the 1960's.

Other "speaking pieces" followed: *Weissagung* (1966; *Prophecy*, 1976), *Selbstbezichtigung* (1966; *Self-Accusation*, 1969), and *Hilferufe* (1967; *Calling for Help*, 1970). Like *Offending the Audience*, these short dramatic pieces lack the traditional elements of scene, character, and plot and are highly experimental in nature. The year 1968 saw the production of *Kaspar* (English translation, 1969), Handke's first full-length drama, based on the true story of a young man who grew up in isolation and did not learn to talk until late adolescence. Compared by some critics to Samuel Beckett's *En attendant Godot* (1952; *Waiting for Godot*, 1954), *Kaspar* represents Handke's greatest theatrical success. Other notable plays by Handke include *Das Mündel will Vormund sein* (1969; *My Foot My Tutor*, 1970), *Quodlibet* (1970; English translation, 1976), and *Der Ritt über den Bodensee* (1971; *The Ride Across Lake Constance*, 1972).

Handke's literary reputation is based as much on his fiction as on his dramatic works. His first novel to achieve notable success was *Die Angst des Tormanns beim Elfmeter* (1970; *The Goalie's Anxiety at the Penalty Kick*, 1972). The novel deals with the mental breakdown of a working-class man, an ex-soccer player whose psychological deterioration culminates in murder. Murder and mental illness also figure prominently in *Die Stunde der wahren Empfindung* (1975; *A Moment of True Feeling*, 1977). Handke offers a more personal treatment of death in *Wunschloses Unglück* (1972; *A Sorrow Beyond Dreams*, 1974). While classified as fiction in most Handke bibliographies, this work is actually an account of his mother's life and suicide. Other novels include *Die linkshändige Frau* (1976; *The Left-Handed Woman*, 1978) and a collection of short novels published under the English title *Slow Homecoming* (1985).

In addition to novels and plays, Handke published a number of poems and essays, many of which have been collected and translated in several volumes. Two of his better-known collections of poems are *Die Innenwelt der Aussenwelt der Innenwelt* (1969; *The Innerworld of the Outerworld of the Innerworld*, 1974) and *Das Ende des Flanierens* (1976; *Nonsense and Happiness*, 1976). In 1969, Handke, along with ten other writers, established a cooperative publishing company called Verlag der Autoren. He has lectured at universities in the United States and has adapted several of his works to radio and film.

Analysis

Because of their nontraditional form and style and often bizarre subject matter, Handke's works may seem intimidating to readers approaching them for the first time. A play such as *Prophecy*, for example, which consists entirely of statements such as "The chickens will scurry like chickens" and "The weasel will be weasel-faced," resists the kind of straightforward interpretation that more conventional literary works allow. A consideration of some recurring themes in Handke's work, however, can help clarify his often obscure material. Among Handke's most important themes are the uses and significance of language, the analysis of abnormal psychological states, and the nature of the writing process itself.

Handke's writing is filled with strange, innovative, and often playful uses of language. Moreover, language itself is frequently the subject of his writing, as in *Calling for Help*, which consists of a series of sentences and phrases spoken by two or more people on stage, each relating in some way to a need for help: "someone has escaped from death row," "workers at that time were living in inhuman conditions," "in case of emergency." Each sentence or phrase is followed by the response "no," as in a children's guessing game, until the required word, "help," is tried, leading to a "yes!" Handke explains:

> . . . the speakers' objective is to show the way to the sought-after world HELP, a way that leads across many sentences and words. . . . while the speakers are seeking the *word* help they are in need of *help*; once having found the *word* help they no longer need any help. before they find the word they ask *for* help, whereas once they have found the word help they only speak *help* without needing to ask *for* help any longer. once able to shout help, they no longer need to shout *for* help; they are relieved that they can shout help. the word HELP has lost its meaning.

Calling for Help uses irony and wit to examine a fundamental paradox of human relationships: People often find it most difficult to communicate their most urgent needs to others. And, Handke suggests, when communication is finally established, it may lose its original purpose and value. (Note that Handke, like the poet E. E. Cummings, ignores traditional capitalization rules in this work—probably to emphasize its verbal, rather than written, nature.)

If Handke's use of language is sometimes playful, his subject matter is often just the opposite, frequently centering on mental breakdowns or other psychological disturbances. The protagonists of *The Goalie's Anxiety at the Penalty Kick*, *A Moment of True Feeling*, *Kaspar*, and *A Sorrow Beyond Dreams* all exhibit some kind of emotional problem: psychosis, neurosis, childhood trauma, or depression. This emphasis on mental illness might seem morbid at first. Handke is not, however, interested in depicting the sensational or the bizarre for its own sake; his treatment of these subjects is typically low-key and objective. Rather, Handke uses the concepts of mental health and mental illness to examine and comment on the nature of reality, perception, and the place of the individual in society. For example, Joseph Bloch in *The Goalie's Anxiety at the Penalty Kick* walks away from his job, assuming that he is fired because only one of his coworkers looks at him when he arrives at work one day. An obviously neurotic behavior, Bloch's action demonstrates the frightening power of individual perception: His reality has, in a real sense, been altered solely because of the way he views that reality. A similar situation is found in *Der kurze Brief zum langen Abschied* (1972; *Short Letter, Long Farewell,* 1974). The narrator of this novel, an Austrian such as Handke himself, declares, "As far back as I can remember, I seem to have been born for horror and fear." As he travels across America after receiving a letter from his estranged wife ("I am in New York. Please do not look for me, it would not be nice for you to find me"), his troubled perceptions of life are used to shed light on personal interactions, the relationship of Europe to America (the "old world" and the new), and the connections between personal experience and the "real world."

A final element that defines Handke's writing is his treatment of the writing process as a subject in itself (a characteristic of much contemporary, or postmodern, literature). While authors of more conventional literature tend to tell their stories without referring to themselves or to their audience, Handke often interjects into his plays and fiction explicit commentary about himself, his thoughts about what he is writing, and his audience. Obvious examples are seen in *Offending the Audience,* where the relationship of the audience to the presentation on stage is the central concern of the play, and in *Calling for Help,* where audience reaction is crucial to the meaning of the material. Awareness and acknowledgment of the writing process are also found in *A Sorrow Beyond Dreams,* in which Handke repeatedly comments on his motivation for and approach to writing:

> My mother has been dead for almost seven weeks; I had better get to work before the need to write about her, which I felt so strongly at her funeral, dies away and I fall back into the dull speechlessness with which I reacted to the news of her suicide.

Through his direct commentary on the creative process, Handke continually reminds his readers that literature is the end product of a conscious intellectual endeavor, and that writing does not exist in a vacuum but has full meaning only in the context of the relationship between the writer and his audience. While analyzing the psychology of his characters, Handke does not shy away from examining his own as well.

A SORROW BEYOND DREAMS

First published: *Wunschloses Unglück,* 1972 (English translation, 1974)
Type of work: Novella

Handke reacts to his mother's suicide by telling her life story, examining the forces that shaped her life and that ultimately led to her death.

A Sorrow Beyond Dreams is considered by critics to be one of Handke's finest works. Like so much of his writing, it defies pigeonholing in a traditional scheme of literary classification: Is it fiction, is it biography, or is it a personal meditation? Perhaps it is most accurate to say that Handke applies the techniques of fiction— imagination, reconstruction of events, dialogue, thoughts, emotions, and descriptions of characters and scenes—to an account of actual events, much like current historical fiction and television docudramas.

Handke's mother's story begins in a small Austrian village, the site of her eventual death. (Interestingly, the mother is never named—probably to emphasize the conformity and anonymity imposed upon the women in her society.) For most of the villagers, life is full of poverty and desperation—especially for the women. In his mother's day, Handke says, "a girl's future was a joke." This observation is borne out by the mother's subsequent experiences: a loveless marriage, shattered dreams, and life in a society that coerces her into denying her true feelings and personality. While she courageously makes repeated attempts to break free from repression and persecution—leaving home to pursue a career at age fifteen, illegally crossing borders in postwar Europe to escape from Germany and return to Austria, reading literature and involving herself in politics—she eventually succumbs to the negative forces at work in her life, saying, "I'm not human anymore." Following a debilitating illness, probably psychological in origin, she calmly and deliberately ends her own life.

A Sorrow Beyond Dreams is interesting for several reasons. First, it illustrates the cause-and-effect relationship between pressures in society and individual psychological disturbance. The mother's emotional problems—including fear, rigidity, self-blame, and depression—are founded in political and social pressures. Furthermore, by omitting her name and by repeatedly referring to her life's events as "the old story," Handke stresses the universality of her plight: She is not simply an individual but a "type," symbolic of millions of women throughout history.

Second, the book provides a good example of Handke's use of a new, alternative mode of expression, one that places the act of writing at the heart of its narrative. Handke continually interrupts his mother's story to interject comments about his approach to it. Just before describing the suicide, he pauses to inform the reader that "From this point on, I shall have to be careful to keep my story from telling itself." After her death he says, "All at once, in my impotent rage, I felt the need of writing something about my mother." The act of writing does not produce the desired catharsis, however, for he later observes, "It is not true that writing has helped me." By alternating the story of his mother with an account of his telling of her story, giving each equal prominence, Handke allows the reader to gain vivid insight into the creative process. He also demonstrates that the process of writing is just as important and interesting—perhaps more so—as its end product. Appropriately, Handke recognizes that it is an open-ended process as well, ending *A Sorrow Beyond Dreams* with that statement, "Someday I shall write about all this in greater detail."

SLOW HOMECOMING

First published: *Langsame Heimkehr*, 1979 (*The Long Way Around*, 1985);
Die Lehre der Sainte-Victoire, 1980 (*The Lesson of Mont-Sainte-Victoire*, 1985); *Kindergeschichte*, 1981 (*Child Story*, 1985)
Type of work: Novellas

A scientist, an artist, and a child reveal insights about the relationship of people to the world and to each other.

Slow Homecoming is the English title of a collection of three of Handke's short novels, whose individual titles may be translated as *The Long Way Around* (or "Slow Journey Home"), *The Lesson of Mont-Sainte-Victoire*, and *Child Story*. The three works feature separate plots and characters, and different styles. Taken as a group, however, they represent variations on a common theme: the ways in which people view themselves and their place in the world around them.

The Long Way Around tells the story of Sorger, a geologist whose physical journey from Alaska, California, and New York to his home in Europe parallels an inner journey of discovery and self-awareness. At the beginning of the novel, Sorger is a loner who "had done no work expressly useful to anyone" and who "would not have been fit company for anyone"; he tries to comprehend the meaning of existence by obsessively describing the physical world. This approach fails, and Sorger nears a psychological collapse, but eventually he realizes that it is relationships with other people, not his science, that give life its significance. He leaves for home full of confidence and optimism.

The Lesson of Mont-Sainte-Victoire deals with art rather than science, relating the visual art of French painter Paul Cézanne to the literary art of Handke himself. Handke describes his visit to a spot in the Sainte-Victoire mountain range where Cézanne found particular inspiration, and the effects that the experience has had on his own creativity. The "lesson" is that true understanding and insight can be achieved only through the synthesis of form and object, subjective perception and objective reality, the specific and the universal. Handke applies this knowledge in the concluding section, a description of the woods near Salzburg.

Child Story, the final novella in the collection, is Handke's autobiographical account of his relationship with his daughter from her birth through age ten. For Handke, being a parent is both magically fulfilling and horribly trying, and he describes both feelings with equal clarity: His primitive urge to protect and defend his newborn child contrasts starkly with the anger and frustration that, years later, cause him to strike her nearly "hard enough to kill her." Throughout *Child Story*, however, Handke shows the importance of the interaction of parent and child, as she provides him with the same kinds of insights that science and art offered in the two previous novellas.

Slow Homecoming is one of Handke's most complex and difficult works. Often abandoning narrative in favor of meditations on life, knowledge, and nature, the three short novels owe as much to philosophy as to fiction. In their unusual blend of fiction and fact, description and explanation, investigation and revelation, the three sections of *Slow Homecoming* represent some of Peter Handke's most creative, fully developed, and innovative work.

Summary

Peter Handke's works stand on the cutting edge of contemporary literature. Whether playing linguistic games to explore human communication, depicting disturbed characters to reveal the inner workings of the mind, or casting a spotlight on his own creative processes, Handke's literary works are as fascinating as they are unusual. By rejecting the conventional, the typical, and the traditional in both form and subject, Handke's works offer readers unique insights into the mind of an artist as he explores issues and ideas as timeless as literature itself.

Bibliography

Gilman, Richard. *The Making of Modern Drama*. New York: Farrar, Straus & Giroux, 1974.

Hayman, Ronald. *Theater and Anti-Theater: New Movements Since Beckett*. New York: Oxford University Press, 1979.

Hern, Nicholas. *Peter Handke*. New York: Frederick Ungar, 1972.

Klinkowitz, Jerome, and James Knowlton. *Peter Handke and the Postmodern Transformation: The Goalie's Journey Home*. Columbia: University of Missouri Press, 1983.

Schlueter, June. *The Plays and Novels of Peter Handke*. Pittsburgh: University of Pittsburgh Press, 1981.

Charles Avinger

THOMAS HARDY

Born: Higher Bockhampton, England
June 2, 1840
Died: Dorchester, England
January 11, 1928

Principal Literary Achievement
Because of the modernity of vision of both his fiction and his poetry, Hardy is a key transitional figure between the Victorian period and the twentieth century.

Biography

Thomas Hardy was born in the small village of Higher Bockhampton, England, on June 2, 1840. Although his father, a mason, was satisfied with his rural life, his mother encouraged Hardy to get an education and raise his social status. Hardy's first effort to do so was to become the student of Dorchester architect John Hicks. In a fateful accident, the kind of accident that Hardy would later make part of the cornerstone of his fiction, the well-known poet William Barnes had a school next door to Hicks's office. The older poet and the young apprentice became friends, and Barnes became one of the strongest influences on Hardy. Another important influence on Hardy's early life was his friendship with Horace Moule, a classical scholar, essayist, and reviewer. Particularly important was Moule's introduction of Hardy to the works of philosopher John Stuart Mill and the Bible-challenging collection *Essays and Reviews* (1860), both of which served to make Hardy doubt his simple religious faith.

At age twenty-one, Hardy went to London to continue his study of architecture. Once there, however, the publication of Algernon Charles Swinburne's *Poems and Ballads* in 1866 so influenced Hardy that he began writing poems and trying to get them published. After almost two years of being rebuffed by the London publishers, he returned to Bockhampton and decided to try his hand at writing fiction. His first effort, *The Poor Man and the Lady*, was based on a contrast between the rural life of his childhood and the urban life he had experienced in London. Although he did receive some favorable response from publishers, he decided not to publish the work. Instead, based on the advice of the novelist George Meredith, Hardy looked to a popular genre of the time, the detective story, and wrote *Desperate Remedies* (1871). Later, because of the favorable response that editors had made to the rural scenes in his unpublished novel *The Poor Man and the Lady*, Hardy wrote his pastoral idyll *Under the Greenwood Tree* (1872). Although the book did not sell well, critics liked it

and Hardy was encouraged to continue. At the time, the most favorable publishing outlet for authors was serial publication in weekly and monthly periodicals. Hardy began writing such a serial, *A Pair of Blue Eyes* (1872-1873), on the advice of a periodical editor and thus launched his full-time career as an author, having given up architecture forever.

In 1874, Hardy married Emma Lavinia Gifford, who, like his mother, was socially ambitious. After *A Pair of Blue Eyes*, Hardy went back to the rural world for his inspiration and wrote *Far from the Madding Crowd* (1874). The book received many favorable reviews, and Hardy's reputation started growing. Publishers and editors began to solicit work from him. Hardy's next successful work, *The Return of the Native* (1878), was composed while he and his wife were living in a small cottage at Sturminister Newton, although shortly afterward the couple moved to London for the social life that his wife desired. When Hardy became ill, they moved back to Dorset, where he wrote *The Mayor of Casterbridge* (1886) while he was having his home, Max Gate, built. For the next several years, Hardy continued his writing, traveled with his wife, and studied German philosophy.

Although Hardy was well established by the last decade of the nineteenth century, one of the best-known and most widely read authors in England, his last two novels were not well received. First, *Tess of the D'Urbervilles* (1891) was rejected by two publishers (who feared offending the public) before finally being accepted for serial publication. Indeed, many readers did respond with shock and hostility to the book, especially because of the sexuality suggested in the novel. The publication of Hardy's last novel, *Jude the Obscure* (1895), raised an even greater outcry, with a number of thinkers challenging the book on the grounds of its being a threat to public decency and morality. Hardy decided that he had had enough and would write no more novels, a popular literary form that left him open to public criticism.

He thus returned to his first love, poetry, reasoning that because of poetry's subtle indirection and its limitation to a relatively small and select audience, he could say things that would not receive such a hostile response. Indeed, Hardy, who lived to an old age, still had time to create an enviable career as a poet, publishing more than one thousand poems in eight volumes of verse. He also published an epic poem/drama titled *The Dynasts: A Drama of the Napoleonic Wars* (1903, 1906, 1908).

During Hardy's final years of life, he enjoyed the respect of his colleagues and readers, receiving several honors and being hailed as one of the last great authors of Victorian letters. Hardy's wife died in 1912, and four years later he married Florence Dugdale, who had worked for him as a secretary and who cared for him for the rest of his life. Hardy continued to write poetry regularly. His final volume of poems, *Winter Words* (1928), was ready to be published when he died on January 11, 1928, in Dorchester, England. His ashes were placed in Westminster Abbey.

Analysis

Most commentators on the intellectual and artistic life of the nineteenth century are in agreement that the most important event during that period was the so-called death of God, that is, the loss of a unified ground of being, based on Christian faith. These thinkers argue that what is now referred to as the modernist temperament in art and thought actually began with the breakup of a value-ordered universe in the Romantic period. Hardy was one of the most important artists of the period who were powerfully influenced by this loss. Many critics have pointed out that the most significant influence on what has been called Hardy's philosophy was his loss of a notion of a universe governed by a divine power. Indeed, what has often been ana-lyzed as Hardy's philosophy can be summed up in one of his earliest notebook en-tries: "The world does not despise us; it only neglects us." In his autobiographical notes, Hardy presents a picture of himself as a sensitive young man who attended church regularly and believed in a personal God who ruled the universe. When Hardy came to London in his early twenties and discovered such intellectual ferment as caused by Charles Darwin's *On the Origin of Species by Means of Natural Selection* (1859) and the *Essays and Reviews*, he lost his faith and never recovered it.

Many other nineteenth century writers experienced a similar loss, but few felt it so profoundly as Hardy. Furthermore, whereas some nineteenth century writers and thinkers, such as William Wordsworth and Thomas Carlyle, were able to make a leap of faith to an organic concept of nature knowable by the human imagination, Hardy felt the loss of God as a loss with no consequent gain. As one of his most famous poems, "The Darkling Thrush," makes clear, Hardy was unable to ascertain any unity of meaning in the world outside him. He was more like Samuel Taylor Coleridge's Ancient Mariner, who, having experienced the nightmarish chaos of a world without meaning or value, can never really believe in a unified and meaningful world again, but must spend the rest of his life telling and retelling his one story of loss and resultant despair. An understanding of any of Hardy's novels and poems must begin with this basic assumption.

Although Hardy refused to give in to any sense of an external value, he was not content to remain in such an isolated state but was continually trying to find some basis for a ground of being other than that of transcendence. Hardy's ultimate intel-lectual and creative challenge to this loss was what might now be called humanistic existentialism. For Hardy, as it was later for such thinkers as Jean-Paul Sartre and Albert Camus, if any value were to be found in the world for humankind, it lay in not giving in to hope for transcendence but facing the emptiness in the universe—what Hardy called "facing the worst"—and, like the Ancient Mariner, playing this back over and over again in all of his works. Consequently, Hardy's art can be seen as a series of variations in form on this one barren theme of loss.

Hardy's most basic artistic and technical problem in dealing with his loss of God was the incompatibility of the lack of a unified ground of being with the novel form he felt compelled to develop, for the novel as a form depends on some unified social or mythic structure to hold it together. Hardy thus searched about for older forms to imitate to establish a structure for his novels, even though the grafting of his human-istic existential view onto old forms resulted in grotesque distortions. Hardy imitated the detective form and the social comedy form when he was concerned merely with publishing a popular novel, but when he wanted to write a serious work of fiction, he turned to classical Greek and Elizabethan genres such as the pastoral and the tragedy.

This very choice, however, raised a second artistic problem for Hardy in his search for an adequate literary form. Whereas the classical writers saw human life secure within a stable and ordered religious and social context, Hardy saw humanity as isolated and alone, searching fruitlessly for meaning in the world. Because Hardy denied the static and ordered worldview of the past, he was in turn denied the context of myth, symbol, and ritual that derived from that view. Thus, Hardy had to create a modern myth that presupposed the absence of God. Hardy's use of the traditional patterns of tragedy and pastoral, combined with his rejection of the value system that gave meaning to these patterns, resulted in a distortion of the old form that in turn created a grotesque new form.

In a typical Hardy pastoral novel, such as *Far from the Madding Crowd*, nature is not divinely ordered, as it is in the classical pastoral. Although on the surface the story seems to fit the pastoral mode—it is set in a rural community, the main character is a shepherd, and the inhabitants seem content with their lives—the clash of Hardy's atheistic view with the traditional pastoral creates a grotesque inversion of the form. The story is thus a fable of the barrenness and death of the unified pastoral world, the tragic results of wrong choice, and the irrationality of sexual attraction. Although critics have suggested that Hardy's best-known "tragic" novel, *The Mayor of Casterbridge*, is his most explicit use of the Greek tragic pattern, there are many differences that make it difficult to see it as typically Greek. The fall of Michael Henchard, the mayor, at the end is the result of a combination of factors, not the least of which is Henchard's mistaken view that the world around him is unified and dependable. His death symbolizes the disappearance of the old order. What really brings Henchard down is that, given the loss of a transcendent order, he has violated the only order left to humans: the human-created order of humanity itself.

Interest in Hardy's work has followed two basic patterns. The first was philosophical, with many critics uncovering what they saw to be metaphysical structures that supposedly underlay his fiction. Since the early 1970's, however, interest has shifted to that aspect of Hardy's work most ignored before: his technical facility and his generic experimentation. Only since the late 1980's has what once was termed Hardy's fictional clumsiness been reevaluated in terms of poetic technique. Moreover, Hardy's career as a poet, which has always been under the shadow of his fiction, has been reevaluated. During his career, which began in the Victorian era and did not end until after World War I, Hardy was a contemporary both of Matthew Arnold and then of T. S. Eliot. Critics have seen Hardy as an important transition between the Victorian sensibility and the modern era. Like the great moderns that followed him, Hardy realized that the task of the artist was not to try to find an external controlling force but rather to write works that symbolize the modern oriented need to find such a value system.

THE RETURN OF THE NATIVE

First published: 1878
Type of work: Novel

A powerful young woman rebels against her isolation on the desolate heath but is defeated by the crushing indifference of nature to the desires of humankind.

Many readers have noted the formal classical structure of *The Return of the Native* as well as the similarities of the characters to such powerful mythic figures as Oedipus and Prometheus. It is, however, the brooding Egdon Heath itself that becomes the more significant structuring principle. In fact, as many have noted, the heath is one of the principal actors in the drama, for the actions of all the characters are reactions in some way to the indifference that the heath represents. Egdon Heath is the landscape from which God has departed. In its barrenness, it seems like some giant prehistoric monster lying dormant but ready to swallow up anyone who tries to escape its grasp.

As in other Hardy rural idylls, there is a chorus of rustic characters in *The Return of the Native*. They belong on the heath because of their ignorance of the incongruity between the human longing for meaning and the intractable indifference of the external world symbolized by the heath. They still maintain a mythic, superstitious belief in a pagan animism and fatalistically accept the nature of things as they are. The Druidical rites of the fires that open the novel, the insignificance of Christian religion, the voodoo doll of Susan Nonesuch—all these characterize the pagan fatalism of the rustics.

The main characters in the novel are not rustic and make something other than a fatalistic response to the heath. All of them are characterized by their various reactions to the heath's indifference. Mrs. Yeobright is said to have the very solitude of the heath concentrated in her face. Although she knows she no longer has hope of escape, she focuses all of her attention on seeing that her son Clym does. Damon Wildeve is an outsider, the mysterious stranger who seems detached from the heath but who ultimately must answer to its indifference. Tomasin Yeobright aligns herself with the natural world because of her innocence and therefore sees no discrepancy between human wishes and the blindness of the natural world. Diggory Venn, the most puzzling character in the novel, is an outcast, wandering the heath as both a rustic and a demonic figure.

The most towering figures in the novel, however, are Clym Yeobright, the native of the title who returns to the heath, and Eustacia Vye, the powerful, rebellious figure who yearns to escape its bleakness. As is typical of cultural values of the period, Eustacia's only real hope of leaving the crushing suffocation of the heath is by being "loved to madness"; thus her rebellion is often manifested as coquetry. Clym, on the other hand, wishes to remain on the heath, seeing only friendliness written on its face. Having spent some time in the intellectual ferment of the social world, he now wishes to escape the disease of thought and teach the rustics what they intuitively know: that the only life is the life of fatalistic acceptance.

Clym is the disillusioned intellectual trying to return to the mythic simplicity of the natural world; he would prefer not to grapple with the incongruities he has seen. He is indeed blind, as his mother tells him, in thinking that he can teach the peasants the view that life is something "to be put up with" when they have always known and fatalistically accepted that fact. He furthermore reveals his blindness by marrying Eustacia, thinking she will remain with him on the heath, while Eustacia reveals that she is similarly misdirected by idealizing him and thinking that he will take her away. Both characters search for a meaning and a basis for value, but both are trapped by the irrationality of love and vain hopes in a basically irrational world.

After the two marry and Eustacia, in one of Hardy's typical examples of human misunderstandings and the mischance of events, turns Clym's mother away from her door to die on the heath, Clym blames her for his mother's death and drives her away. Eustacia's trip across the heath is one in which the natural world seems inimical to her, for she stumbles over roots and "oozing lumps of fleshy fungi" that impede her path like the organs of some giant prehistoric animal. At the end of the novel, Eustacia's suicidal leap into the pool is less a capitulation to the forces around her than it is a heroic rebellion, for it is an assertion of the absurdity of human hopes by a romantic temperament that refuses to live by such absurdity.

The Return of the Native is probably the most debated of all Hardy's novels, having been called a masterpiece by some critics and a failure by others. Some readers have seen it to be primarily the story of Clym Yeobright's spiritual odyssey, while others have declared as central Eustacia's struggle with the heath. Eustacia herself is one of Hardy's most puzzling creations. While one reader claims that her story is a realistic case history, another calls it a supernatural myth; while one sees her as a tragic heroine, another calls her the parody of a heroine. Even Diggory Venn has been the subject of much debate and argument, being interpreted as both a peasant laborer and a demonic visitant, while Damon Wildeve is seen alternately as a romantic adventurer and Eustacia's demonic familiar. Moreover, the accidents and coincidences that dominate the plot have been the source of much critical disagreement, called both the fault of weaknesses in the characters and the result of Hardy's philosophic determinism, while the framework of magic and superstition that surrounds the action of the work has been termed both grotesque parody and animistic gratuitousness. It is because the novel hovers between realism and romanticism, between the real world and the dynamic world of myth, that both its characters and its actions are so much a subject of critical controversy.

TESS OF THE D'URBERVILLES

First published: 1891
Type of work: Novel

An innocent young rural maiden is cast out of her familiar world after losing her virginity and finally rebels against the injustice of society and the universe.

Tess of the D'Urbervilles centers on Tess's relation to the natural world. As that relationship changes, so does the situation of Tess. At the beginning of the novel, she is a child of nature who is confident that the natural world will protect her and provide her with a value system. When nature fails her, however, she has no value system to which to turn and thus is thrown out of her comfortable world to journey both outwardly and inwardly in search of a way back in to her relationship with the natural world.

Tess first appears "at home" in the world of the small hamlet of Marlott, where, in the May Day dance, she manifests her innocence. Tess, however, is not a typical rustic maid; she is more sensitive than her friends. It is this sensitivity that ultimately undermines her. For example, shame for her father's drunken condition makes her volunteer to take a load of beehives to market, and despair for the laziness of her parents makes her ignore where she is going. As a result, when the family's only horse is killed, her sense of duty makes her overcome her pride to go to her aristocratic relatives for help. It is her first journey outside her secluded and protected world and her first encounter with the corruption of society.

Alec, her cousin, is a stock figure of the antinatural world, and when they meet, the image is a classic one of innocence in the grasp of the corrupt. When Alec takes Tess into the woods, she is not afraid of him, for she feels that she is in her natural element, and she so trusts the natural world to protect her that she falls asleep, only to be seduced by Alec. The antinatural force and her own innocence conspire to make her an outcast among her people. When her illegitimate child is born dead and the church refuses to give it a Christian burial, Tess renounces her religion and leaves the valley of her home in search of some new meaning for her life.

Tess begins her quest in the Valley of the Great Dairies, where the natural world is so lush and fertile as to be a symbolic realm, and Tess hopes for a reintegration with the world she has lost. She puts her moral plight out of her mind until she meets the morally ambiguous Angel Clare. Whereas Tess has challenged formal religion because of her personal experience, Angel has challenged it because of intellectual questioning. Like Clym Yeobright in *The Return of the Native*, Angel has left the intellectual world for the natural world, where he believes innocence and uncontaminated purity and goodness prevail. These qualities are precisely what he sees in the milkmaid Tess.

On the first night of their marriage, however, Tess confesses her previous indiscretion with her cousin Alec, and Angel, unable to accept her as less than pure, leaves her. Tess wanders the countryside once again, until one morning on the road she awakes to find dead pheasants around her. At this point, Tess becomes aware that in a Darwinistic universe, violation, injury, and even death are innate and inescapable realities. Tess realizes that she is not guilty by the laws of such a world. With this new realization, she can go to Chalk-Newton, a land symbolic of the wasteland situation in which she finds herself, and fully accept the blind indifference of the world; she no longer holds out hope of being reintegrated into the natural world of value and meaning.

It is at this point that Alec returns to her life. Taking the path of least resistance, and having given up all hope, she begins living with him. Hope returns, too late, in the form of Angel Clare, who, having come to the same existential realization at which Tess had arrived, returns. Now seeing Alec as the embodiment of all the deception and meaninglessness in the world, Tess kills him, asserting her freedom from social values and her willingness to accept the human penalties of such freedom.

In the final chapter of the novel, Tess and Angel wander until they end up at Stonehenge, where Tess lies down on the pagan altar and willingly gives herself up to the authorities as a kind of archetypal sacrifice. Tess is the embodiment of human rebellion against an empty universe. The basic source of Tess's tragedy throughout the novel springs from her insistent hope that she will find external meaning and value. Only at the end does she achieve true awareness that such meaning does not exist.

JUDE THE OBSCURE

First published: 1895
Type of work: Novel

A young man tries to find meaning in the life of the mind and the spirit, only to be defeated by his own physical desires and the narrow-mindedness of his society.

Jude the Obscure may be thought of as the argument of *Tess of the D'Urbervilles* taken one step farther. Whereas the latter focuses on the loss of a unified order and meaning, the former begins with the premise of that loss and deals with the epic search for meaning. The novel is the archetypal story of everyone who searches for a basis of meaning and value. The problem for Jude is that all of the symbols of meaning for him—education, religion, the beauty of Sue Bridehead—are illusions. Jude is "obscure" because he is in darkness, trying to find an illumination of his relationship to the world but failing at every turn.

The novel begins with Jude as a young man losing his only real friend, the schoolmaster Phillotson, who has been the center of his world. Thus, from the first Jude must find a new center and a new hope to relieve his loneliness. His first projection of hope is toward the celestial city of Christminster, where his teacher has gone. In the first section of the book, his dream is like an indefinable glow in the distance. His ideal value system, represented both by the Christian and the classical framework of Christminster, is put aside, however, when he meets Arabella, described by Hardy as "a substantial female animal." Seduced by the flesh, Jude marries Arabella when she says she is pregnant and gives up his hope of an education. His discovery that Arabella has deceived him is the first disillusionment he suffers in his quest for meaning.

The second phase of Jude's spiritual journey involves his actual journey to Christminster, a city the vision of which is made even more specific by his seeing a picture of Sue Bridehead, who becomes for him a concrete image of his idealizations. Jude's first disillusionment at Christminster comes when he is turned down by all the colleges to which he applies. Thus, he shifts from the life of reason to the life of religion, practicing the rituals of the church.

During the next phase of his search, after having lost Sue to his old schoolmaster Phillotson, Jude becomes aware of the aridity of the religious life and burns all of his theology books. When Sue leaves Phillotson and returns to Jude, he has new hope, in spite of the fact that Sue is unwilling to live with him as a wife. The return of Arabella frightens her into giving in to his sexual desires, and the couple has children together.

When the most morbid of the children kills himself and the others, Sue makes an extreme shift from her former rebellion and accepts a supreme deity whose laws she believes she has transgressed. As penance, she leaves Jude to return to Phillotson. After Sue leaves, Jude goes to "a dreary, strange flat scene, where boughs dripped, and coughs and consumption lurked, and where he had never been before." This is typical Hardy technique for presenting moments of existential realization: The natural world becomes an inimical reflection of the character's awareness of the absurd. Subsequently, Jude's reaction to the world around him is complete indifference. Jude's final journey to see Sue is a journey to death and a final rejection of the indifferent universe of which his experiences have made him aware. *Jude the Obscure* is the most crushing example of Hardy's vision. It may be his final novel because it is difficult to imagine pushing the tragedy of lost hopes beyond this point.

Summary

Thomas Hardy is something of an anomaly in nineteenth century literature. On the one hand, there is something excessively old-fashioned and melodramatic about his fiction; on the other hand, there is also something powerfully symbolic about such characters as Eustacia, Tess, and Jude, who find themselves trapped in a hopeless world not of their own making, a world that seems to offer no meaning and value, and a world against which they quite rightfully rebel even though such rebellion inevitably ends in defeat.

Hardy is one of the two most widely read and discussed novelists of the nineteenth century, second only to Charles Dickens as the writer most representative of the period and most controversial and worthy of study. Every year, new books are published on Hardy that attempt to lay bare the secret of his thought, his art, and, indeed, his continuing power. Hardy was a great existential humanist. His hope for the world was that it would realize that creeds and conventions that presuppose a god-centered origin of value were baseless. His hope was that men and women would loosen themselves from those foolish creeds and become aware of their freedom to create their own human value system. If people would only realize, Hardy reasoned, that all are equally alone and without hope for divine help, then perhaps they would also realize that it is the height of absurdity for such lost and isolated creatures to fight among themselves. At once old-fashioned and modern, Hardy is perhaps the single most important transitional figure between the old world of unity and faith and the new world of fragmentation and doubt.

Bibliography

Brooks, Jean R. *Thomas Hardy: The Poetic Structure.* Ithaca, N.Y.: Cornell University Press, 1971.

Carpenter, Richard. *Thomas Hardy.* Boston: Twayne, 1964.

Cecil, David, Lord. *Hardy, the Novelist.* London: Constable, 1943.

Guerard, Albert, ed. *Hardy: A Collection of Critical Essays.* Englewood Cliffs, N.J.: Prentice-Hall, 1963.

_____. *Thomas Hardy: The Novels and Stories.* London: Oxford University Press, 1949.

Milgate, Michael. *Thomas Hardy: His Career as a Novelist.* London: Bodley Head, 1971.

Miller, J. Hillis. *Thomas Hardy: Distance and Desire.* Cambridge, Mass.: The Belknap Press of Harvard University Press, 1970.

Weber, Carl. *Hardy of Wessex: His Life and Literary Career.* Rev. ed. New York: Columbia University Press, 1965.

Webster, Harvey Curtis. *On a Darkling Plain: The Art and Thought of Thomas Hardy.* Chicago: University of Chicago Press, 1947.

Charles E. May

VÁCLAV HAVEL

Born: Prague, Czechoslovakia
October 5, 1936

Principal Literary Achievement
Havel, who became Czechoslovakia's president in 1989, is one of the best-known contemporary European playwrights and an acclaimed essayist and poet.

Biography
Václav Havel was born in Prague, Czechoslovakia, on October 5, 1936, into a wealthy patrician family. Sharing the fate of their entire class, the Havels lost their property to collectivization when the Communist government came to power in 1948, nationalizing all private enterprises and assets. Because of the bourgeois background of his father, Václav Havel, and mother, Bozena Vavreckova, Václav was barred from institutions of higher learning.

Václav Havel nevertheless attained schooling in night classes while working in a chemical laboratory. After completing his secondary education, he became a stage technician at the ABC Theatre in Prague in 1959. Between 1960 and 1969, he worked in various positions with several playhouses, including the Theater on the Balustrade, beginning as a menial worker and advancing to become a dramaturge and playwright; concurrently, he studied dramaturgy at the Academy of Dramatic Arts in Prague.

During the years that led up to the political liberalization and reforms of the Prague Spring in 1968, the Theater on the Balustrade became the most influential theater company in Prague. Havel coauthored three plays before his first independent effort, *Zahradní slavnost* (1963; *The Garden Party*, 1969), which immediately brought him critical acclaim and wider audiences. Yet all hopes for democratization, evident, for example, in a greater freedom of the press, were crushed in August, 1968, when the invasion of the Warsaw Pact armies headed by the Soviet Union restored a hard-line Communist regime under Gustáv Husák and established rigid control of the political and economic life.

During the brief period of reform, Havel had his previously confiscated passport returned to him and was permitted to travel to New York in mid-1968 to witness the first U.S. production of *Vyrozumění* (1965; *The Memorandum*, 1967) under Joseph Papp, a production that won an Obie Award. Two years later, *Ztížená možnost soustředění* (1968; *The Increased Difficulty of Concentration*, 1969) met with similar success in another New York production. Immediately after the Soviet invasion, Ha-

vel, like other artists and representatives of public life, made radio broadcasts from the underground to appeal to the West for support and to call for continued protest among his compatriots against repression of civil liberties. As a result of his unequivocal championing of human rights, Havel again had his passport confiscated and, along with thousands of others, was forced into various blue-collar jobs, some of which later provided him with subject matter for his plays and infused his vision.

Havel's writings were not published, and his plays were banned from the stage in Czechoslovakia between 1970 and 1989. Yet he categorically refused to emigrate and continued to write regardless of all pressures and hardships. *Žebrácká opera* (*The Beggar's Opera*, 1976; an adaptation of John Gay's *The Beggar's Opera*, 1728) was first performed clandestinely by a Czech amateur troupe in November, 1975. Havel's subsequent plays premiered mostly in foreign productions, with a clear preponderance of one-act plays over full-length plays, such as the seldom-performed *Horský hotel* (1976; the mountain resort).

The play *Spiklenci* (1974; the conspirators) was first performed in the Federal Republic of Germany. The one-act plays *Audience* (English translation, 1976) and *Vernisáž* (*Private View*, 1978) first saw production in 1976 in Austria; the one-act *Protest* (English translation, 1980) was performed in 1978. *Largo desolato* (pb. 1985; English translation, 1987) premiered in Vienna, while the Faustian satire *Pokoušení* (pb. 1986; *Temptation*, 1988) was first performed in 1986 in Vienna and in 1987 in England. Similarly, Havel's essays first appeared abroad, among them "Moc bezmocnych" ("The Power of the Powerless") in London.

For his criticism of the repressive Communist regime, Havel earned its unrelenting hate. During the 1970's, he was arrested and imprisoned several times. Havel became one of the signatories and spokespersons for Charter 77, a human rights declaration of January, 1977. In 1979, Havel, along with other Charter 77 members, was arrested and tried on charges of "subversion of the republic." He was sentenced to four and a half years in prison.

Between his two prison terms, Havel wrote the acclaimed *Protest*, the third part of the trilogy that also includes *Audience* and *Private View*. A selection of letters that Havel wrote to his wife from prison appeared as *Briefe an Olga* (1984; *Letters to Olga*, 1988). For reasons of poor health, which prompted appeals on his behalf from the international intellectual community, Havel was released in February, 1983.

Until the "Velvet Revolution" of November, 1989, which peacefully ousted the hardline Communist regime, Havel was subjected to harassment by secret police and endured a brief imprisonment in early 1989 that again caused an international outcry. In December, 1989, Havel was elected president of the newly democratic Czech and Slovak Federal Republic, an office for which he was reconfirmed in June, 1990, in the first freely held elections since 1948. Two years later, in the wake of the dissolution of the Soviet Union and the political realignments that accompanied that historic event, Havel announced, on July 17, 1992, that he would resign on the following Monday rather than preside over the likely division of his nation into separate Czech and Slovak republics. He planned to continue working for democracy.

Analysis

To view Havel exclusively as a critic of 1960's Communist Czechoslovakia and as a dissident during Husák's so-called normalization period of the 1970's and 1980's would limit his scope as a writer and thinker. Although Havel resisted being called a philosopher, his thinking is firmly grounded in his country's humanistic tradition. The all-pervasive themes of his dramatic fiction and essays are individual responsibility, human dignity and identity, and the burden of human existence. While these themes are central to modern art, Havel's dramatic vision particularly owes a debt to Franz Kafka and the French Theater of the Absurd. Furthermore, Havel was influenced by Martin Heidegger's work, which was conveyed to the Czechs and Slovaks by the philosopher Jan Patočka, who steadfastly applied the principles of individual responsibility to his own life amid persecution.

Paul Wilson, in the introduction to his translation of *Letters to Olga* (1988), rightly notes that phenomenology is congenial to a Central and Eastern European mind that struggles to free itself from ideology and its deterministic worldview. Rather than attributing responsibility for the state of things to external factors, phenomenology seeks the obligation for betterment within the individual. Consequently, human rights, according to Wilson, are not privileges that can be granted or taken away at will but principles that govern responsible human conduct, which in turn revitalizes society.

This philosophical stance in part accounts for Havel's courageous, uncompromising championing of human rights. Havel writes about his own experience—from "below," where he was forced by the political circumstances—in the hope of addressing universal human concerns. Thus, in his work he not only exposes a corrupt, repressive regime in Central Europe but also discloses a universally shared modern condition.

Havel's interest is devoted to questions such as how the individual copes with impersonal power, how people maintain their identities, and how they carry themselves under the burden of existence. Although the author calls for the individual to assume responsibility and to live in the truth (in his essay "The Power of the Powerless"), he is no naïve dreamer who would expect immediate and far-reaching results. Yet Havel seems steadfastly convinced that power is not an external but rather an internal faculty. This responsibility to answer only to one's conscience at all costs is an active and perhaps inescapable endeavor.

Not surprisingly, Havel's plays, particularly the so-called Vaněk trilogy, consisting of the semiautobiographic one-act plays *Audience*, *Protest*, and *Private View*, ironically expose the attempts of individuals to justify their selfish conformity in a repressive political system in which they claim to have no part yet from which they shamelessly benefit. In *Audience*, Vaněk, a dissident, works in a brewery where he is being observed by the secret police with the help of his boss, an informer who, among other unethical proposals, asks Vaněk, the writer, to relieve him from writing reports by composing them himself.

Protest juxtaposes the dissident Vaněk and the successful sellout Staněk; the latter selfishly seeks Vaněk's help against the arrest of his daughter's boyfriend, only to reason artfully against and ultimately dodge the signing of the very petition on the young man's behalf that Vaněk has already prepared. *Private View* attacks the vacuous lives of conformist snobs, depicting a couple who subscribe to materialistic comforts and exhort Vaněk to abandon his obstinate antagonism and its corollary material deprivation. In each of these plays, the mental and linguistic acrobatics and sophistries reveal the absurdity of life in "normalized" Czechoslovakia or, more universally, the schizophrenia of a life lived against one's conscience.

Havel is interested in language, in both its potential benefits and its perniciousness. The essay "Words on Words" restates this theme of the far-reaching "power of words to change history" that is already present in his early plays *The Garden Party* and *The Memorandum*. The two satires are scathing absurdist indictments of the official Communist bureaucratese and its empty clichés that is characteristic of a dehumanized society in which monstrous paradoxes abound. Like these two plays, the vicious comedy *The Increased Difficulty of Concentration* is more than a satire on Communist bureaucracy and an individual's plight to escape its dehumanizing effects; it reiterates Havel's recurrent themes, which range from the schizophrenia of existence to fragmentation, alienation, and the loss of human identity.

THE MEMORANDUM

First produced: *Vyrozumění*, 1965 (first published, 1966; English translation, 1967)
Type of work: Play

This play is a grotesque on the introduction of Ptydepe, an artificial, "logical" language, into a large organization satirizing the dehumanizing officialese of pre-reform Communist Czechoslovakia.

The Memorandum is perhaps Havel's most widely performed play, along with *Private View*. Again, it would not do Havel justice to view the play exclusively as a parody of Communist bureaucracy and its lingo; rather, it is about the dehumanizing effects and the tyranny of language in any system that causes the disintegration of human identity.

The twelve scenes are set in a deliberately "generic" large organization, the purpose of which, like that of any amorphous self-serving bureaucracy, is not plain. Josef Gross, the managing director, and the development of his personality from the introduction to the abolition of the artificial language Ptydepe, are both central to the play. Gross cannot decipher a memorandum directed to him because it is written in Ptydepe, a new office language introduced apparently without his knowledge by deputy director Ballas and his cronies and taught in classes in which every employee seems to have enrolled.

Ptydepe is presumably rational and precise and therefore superior to "dilettantish" natural languages, with their vagueness and ambivalence. Its goal is to eliminate imprecision by limiting all similarity between words and thereby achieve the highest possible redundancy in language. The result is monstrously long words that are formed by the least probable combination of letters. This new doctrine is difficult and complex, so it can be mastered only by discipline and most of all by faith. It is easy to see the parallels between Ptydepe and Communist ideology.

After attempting in vain to stop the spread of Ptydepe, Gross becomes enmeshed in a Kafkaesque catch-22: Even the translation director, Stroll, cannot perform the translation unless Gross's text is "authorized" by a "Ptydepist," a specialist who gives permission for each translation. Prior to an authorization, however, the memo needs to be translated. Gross realizes that since he cannot acquire Ptydepe himself, because of his lack of faith, the only way to learn what his memo contains is to know it already.

Ballas glibly threatens Gross into submission by ridiculous charges, forces him to sign a declaration of compliance to Ptydepe, coerces him into self-indictment for his "wrong-doings," and finally reduces him to the post of "staff watcher," a spy who observes all employees through a crack in the wall. Gross regains his rank with the help of Maria, a sympathetic typist, who translates his memo at a moment when Ballas and his associates already begin to reverse themselves in a total rejection of Ptydepe. The memo itself utterly renounces the artificial language.

Ballas ingeniously justifies his reversal and again pressures the vindicated but naïve Gross into compliance, this time by threatening to expose Gross's forced declaration of advocacy of Ptydepe. A search for culprits ensues. As a result, Maria is dismissed for performing an unauthorized translation. Gross conveniently rationalizes his inaction by claiming that if he maintains his position he will keep Ballas and his cronies in check. Ballas, in the meantime, introduces a new nonsensical bureaucratic language, Chorukor, a very antithesis to Ptydepe. Gross placates Maria by empty, hollow phrases invoking high ethical ideals; he blames the "difficult times" in which humankind, including himself, is fragmented, manipulated, and alienated. This "analysis" is ironic coming from an unwilling conformist who diagnoses in himself the very ills that are Havel's primary philosophical concerns but who fails to assume his individual responsibility.

LETTERS TO OLGA

First published: *Briefe an Olga*, 1984, in German (English translation, 1988)
Type of work: Letters and essays

This publication contains one hundred forty-four selected letters from prison to Havel's wife written between June, 1979, and September, 1982; the last sixteen letters are noted for their philosophical content.

Letters to Olga is a moving document of Havel's imprisonment and, simultaneously, an important philosophical statement, primarily in the final sixteen letters, which were circulated separately and illegally underground.

The letters are particularly interesting in the light of the circumstances under which they were composed. Havel was subjected to hard labor with set quotas that were deliberately high and thus difficult to fulfill. He was permitted to write home only one four-page letter a week to only one person, so it is perhaps not surprising that he chose to address them to Olga Havel, his wife since 1964. Censorship was extremely strict and whimsical. The letters had to adhere to precise specifications: They had to be legible and without corrections, quotation marks, or foreign words. The censors prohibited humor and any thoughts that went beyond what they classified as family matters. The prisoners could not write rough drafts or take notes.

Under such difficult conditions, the weekly letter writing evolved into an anxious guessing game against the arbitrary interpretations of the censors, who ruthlessly confiscated letters that did not fit their specifications. Havel developed a strong dependence on this sole means of intellectual expression permitted to him.

Through her occasional letters, Olga grants him vicarious participation in the cherished life outside the prison. That explains Havel's recurring insistence that Olga write to him more often, in more detail, and answer his questions and requests—an insistence that occasionally culminates in downright petulance and frustration. Havel persistently inquires about such mundane matters as the upkeep of their weekend retreat, Hrádeček, their Prague apartment, or Olga's social life.

Naturally, censorship inhibited intimacy and so the letters may be perceived as devoid of true warmth and feeling. Yet Olga's presence is felt, and Havel's dependence on her, his earnest adviser and first critic of his work, is evident. When Havel became seriously ill in prison in early 1983, it was his wife who alerted the intellectual community abroad, whose interventions on Havel's behalf speeded his release from prison before his sentence was terminated.

The final sixteen letters do not constitute a rigorous philosophical treatise, but even so they show Havel's indebtedness to phenomenological thought and illuminate the tenets of his work. At the center is the image of birth that symbolizes the fundamental condition of humankind, the experience of separation and release, of breaking away: Humanity is cast into an alien world and faces the question of who it is. What essentially characterizes humankind is a boundless primal sense of responsibility for others in a world into which it is cast. All individuals share this isolation in a world from which they cannot escape, and this vulnerability and helplessness cry out for compassion. The misery of others reminds them of their own "thrownness" and isolation in the world. It follows that humankind is not only responsible for others but also obligated to shape the environment, free from scientific or ideological determinism.

Summary

Václav Havel's life and work bear witness to his unwavering humanism, his assertion of individual conscience and responsibility under adverse conditions. His primary interest is devoted to universal dilemmas that transcend the mere historical circumstances of Communist totalitarianism in Central Europe and include questions of human identity, fragmentation and alienation, communicational collapse, and existential schizophrenia.

In his essay "Words on Words," Havel describes the earthshaking potential, both beneficial and detrimental, of language. That words of truth prevail and indeed can change history has been proven by him and the thousands of students, artists, intellectuals, and ordinary citizens who peacefully toppled Czechoslovakia's hard-line Communist regime in 1989.

Bibliography

Havel, Václav. *Disturbing the Peace: A Conversation with Karel Hvížďala.* New York: Alfred A. Knopf, 1990.

_____. *Open Letters: Selected Writings, 1964-1990.* Edited by Paul Wilson. New York: Alfred A. Knopf, 1991.

Keane, John, ed. *The Power of the Powerless: Citizens Against the State in Central-Eastern Europe.* London: Hutchinson University Library, 1985.

Simmons, Michael. *The Reluctant President: A Political Life of Václav Havel.* London: Methuen, 1991.

Vladislav, Jan, ed. *Václav Havel: Or, Living in Truth.* London: Faber & Faber, 1986.

Whipple, Tim D., ed. *After the Velvet Revolution: Václav Havel and the New Leaders of Czechoslovakia Speak Out.* New York: Freedom House, 1991.

Dana Loewy

HEINRICH HEINE

Born: Düsseldorf, Germany
December 13, 1797
Died: Paris, France
February 17, 1856

Principal Literary Achievement

Heine is internationally celebrated as one of the greatest lyric poets of his time, as well as the author of vivid, frequently satiric prose works.

Biography

When Heinrich Heine misstated his birthdate as January 1, 1800, and described himself as "one of the first men of the nineteenth century," he was not only exploiting the dual sense of "first"—earliest and foremost—but also engaging in a characteristic bit of obfuscation. Heinrich Heine was actually born Chaim Harry Heine on December 13, 1797, in Düsseldorf, Germany, the son of Samson Heine, a merchant, and Betty (or Peira) von Geldern Heine. Both his given name, Harry, and his family name derived from Chaim (the latter by way of Heymann or Heinemann). The Jewish antecedents of the poet's parents were impressive, but in his parental home Judaism had been downgraded. The boy received only a spotty Jewish education in a Jewish school, but later he was sent to a lyceum attached to a Franciscan monastery, where the teaching was done largely by French priests. There, Heine received an early taste of the French culture and spirit, coupled with his love of Napoleon I, to which Heine was later to become so attached. Napoleon the conqueror and emancipator had brought hope and freedom to German Jewry, but after his defeat many of the old restrictions were put in force again. Following a brief sojourn in Frankfurt, Heine was set up in business in Hamburg by his wealthy uncle Salomon Heine. A failure in business and in love (his affection for his cousins Amalie and Therese was unrequited), he was nevertheless a published poet at age twenty.

After attending the universities of Bonn and Göttingen, he spent two and a half fruitful years in Berlin, where he studied and frequented literary salons. In 1822, he joined the Verein für Kultur und Wissenschaft der Juden (Society for Jewish Culture and Scholarship), a group that strove to continue Moses Mendelssohn's work of cultural emancipation. That autumn, he visited Prussian Poland and came to appreciate the self-assurance and unity of the eastern Jews, who, unlike German Jewry, were not prey to heterogeneous emotions and resentments. Heine, however, converted to Prot-

estantism on June 28, 1825, shortly before taking a doctorate of laws at Göttingen, and was now called Christian Johann Heinrich Heine. The adoption of Lutheranism, the state religion of Prussia, was to have facilitated the poet's law practice, which he never even attempted, or procured a professorship for him, which did not happen. Referring to his baptism as his "ticket of admission to European culture," Heine often expressed himself in ironic, cynical, and even self-lacerating terms. Paradoxically, his Jewish awareness and education really began with this conversion, and Heine particularly prized the Bible, which he regarded as the "portable fatherland" of the Jews.

Heine spent the last twenty-five years of his life in exile. Attracted by the July Revolution of 1830, but also because he could not find any suitable employment in Germany and was bedeviled by censorship, he went to Paris in 1831, where he was to spend the rest of his life, except for brief and furtive visits to Germany in 1843 and 1844. Associating with such famed French writers as Gérard de Nerval, Théophile Gautier, Victor Hugo, Honoré de Balzac, Alexandre Dumas, and Charles Baudelaire, Heine became an indefatigable cultural mediator, interpreting his native land to the French and vice versa and creating or introducing literary forms new to German literature, such as the travel letter and the *feuilleton* (the latter an elegant, witty, stylistically brilliant essay on many aspects of culture). Until 1848, Heine was supported by a pension from the French government, and he also received an annual subvention from his uncle Salomon, though the latter's death in 1844 marked the beginning of family strife. In Paris, Heine remained what he had always been: a German Jew full of conflicts and contradictions. In 1849, he averred that he was no longer an admirer of the pleasure-loving Hellenes but merely an ailing Jew. After abandoning his flirtation with atheism, polytheism, and hedonistic paganism, he moved closer to a personal and transcendent God, but he remained ambivalent to the end.

After living with a young French shopgirl named Crescentia Eugénie Mirat (whom he called Mathilde) for seven years, he married her in 1841. In his last years, he suffered from a syphilitic infection, a progressive crippling malady that paralyzed his body but not his mind or spirit. During the last eight years of his life, he wasted away in the *Matratzengruft*, his self-styled mattress grave or crypt. Heine died in Paris on February 17, 1856, and was buried in the cemetery of Montmartre, at his own request without the ministrations of clergy.

Analysis

Heine's relatively brief life span encompassed such crucial and formative events as the rise and fall of Napoleon I, the Congress of Vienna, and the failed revolutions of 1830 and 1848. In German literature, the currents during Heine's lifetime were Romanticism, the Junges Deutschland (Young Germany) movement (a journalistic, political, and polemical movement), and poetic realism. Heine described himself as the last of the Romantics and sat in judgment on German Romanticism in *Die Romantische Schule* (*The Romantic School*, 1876), published in 1836 mainly for the benefit of French readers. By virtue of his activism, Heine is widely considered as the leading and possibly only poetic (rather than merely journalistic and ephemeral) member of the group of young revolutionary firebrands, polemicists, and reformers of the Young Germany movement.

Heine grew up when German Jewry was taking its first, faltering steps "from the ghetto into Europe," to use Arthur Eloesser's phrase, a step that these Jews had been enabled to take by the work of two great men—Mendelssohn in the cultural sphere and Napoleon in the political and legal arena. German Jewry's struggle for emancipation is most strikingly symbolized in Heine, and his creative tension derives from the turbulence of his time. In him the *Weltschmerz*, the Romantic pessimism and sadness over the evils of the world and the precariousness of the human condition, mingled with his convoluted Jewishness. When Heine made his famous statement, "Der Riss der Zeit geht durch mein Herz," he meant that the maelstrom of conflicting religious, political, social, and cultural currents near the beginning of the German-Jewish symbiosis and the Industrial Age was producing a rift in his heart.

A remarkable blend of the Jewish and the German past may be found in *Der Rabbi von Bacherach* (1887; *The Rabbi of Bacherach*, 1891), a fragmentary prose work that Heine wrote in an effort to celebrate medieval Jewish life in the manner of Sir Walter Scott's depiction of medieval Scottish life. In the years following his conversion, Heine produced the great works that were to bring him worldwide fame and stature, variously, as the German Aristophanes, the German François Rabelais, the German Lord Byron, the German Voltaire, and the German Jonathan Swift. In 1826-1827, he published a volume of *Reisebilder* (1826-1831; four volumes; *Pictures of Travel*, 1855), and 1827 saw the publication of *Buch der Lieder* (*Book of Songs*, 1856), the most popular poetry collection of the nineteenth century. Like its earlier and later companion volumes, this book contains poems that combine simplicity with sophistication and subtlety, poignance with eloquence, and epigrammatic concision with an expansive folksong quality, in addition to presenting intentional dissonances and vulgarity in the manner of what has been termed romantic irony. In form, Heine's poems range from memorable epigrams of a few lines to brilliant ballads and extensive verse epics. *Book of Songs* contains such major cycles as "Junge Leiden" ("Youthful Sorrows"), "Lyrisches Intermezzo" ("Lyrical Intermezzo"), "Die Heimkehr" ("The Homecoming")—which includes "Lorelei" ("Loreley"), Heine's best-known poem and, in Friedrich Silcher's setting, widely regarded as a folk song—and "Die Nordsee" ("The North Sea"). Heine's poetry inspired musical settings by Franz Schubert, Robert Schumann, Felix Mendelssohn, Franz Liszt, Johannes Brahms, Hugo Wolf, Richard Strauss, and other composers. In general, Heine's works are as much "fragments of a great confession" as Johann Wolfgang von Goethe's are. "Out of my great pains I make little songs," Heine once wrote.

One of Heine's two tragedies is *Almansor* (1823; English translation, 1982) which explores the conflicts between Moors and Christians in medieval Spain and may be regarded as a parable of the situation of German Jewry in Heine's day. In it, the Moor Hassan's reply to Almansor's horrified remark about the burning of the Koran in the marketplace of Granada contains these words of chilling prescience: "That was only a prelude; where one burns books, one is going to wind up burning people, too."

Louis Untermeyer, an outstanding biographer and translator of Heine, has pointed out that the poet's ethnic inheritance is expressed in the flavor of his writings, which is not bittersweet, as it has often been characterized, but sweet and sour, the result of generations of cultural, as well as culinary, pungency. Heine's wry wit and comic stance have led another noted critic, S. S. Prawer, to discern a "reasonably straight" line from Heine to Philip Roth, Woody Allen, or Mel Brooks.

GERMANY: A WINTER'S TALE

First published: *Deutschland: Ein Wintermärchen*, 1844 (English translation, 1892)
Type of work: Poetry

Based on his furtive trip to his native Germany from his Parisian exile, this work takes an irreverent look at many aspects of Germany's history, culture, and present conditions.

The title of *Germany: A Winter's Tale* is reminiscent of William Shakespeare's play *The Winter's Tale* (c. 1610-1611), and the work shows Heine at the poetic peak of his radical phase. This frequently lighthearted but rarely lightweight verse epic is an impishly witty chronicle of the exiled writer's first visit to Germany in October of 1843. Heine's work was published as a supplement to his collection *Neue Gedichte* (1844; *New Poems*, 1858) in September, 1844, was reprinted separately the following month, and then appeared uncut in installments in the Paris revolutionary journal *Vorwärts* (forward) in October and November, the first two printings having been proscribed and confiscated by the German authorities. Representing Heine's answer to the bombastic political poetry of his time, *Germany: A Winter's Tale* takes a refreshingly irreverent look at many German conditions and attitudes, particularly symbols of German nationalism and conservatism. The poet attempts to bring some fresh air into the musty corners of the German past and sweep away the Romanticists' fascination with an idealized medievalism. It helps to remember that Heine's native country was still decades away from being united; in his time, Germany was an agglomeration of thirty-six petty principalities, each headed by a king, a duke, a bishop, or another kind of potentate. Heine excoriates the backward political and social structure, as well as the hidebound mentality, of a land that was still under the spell of absolutism, feudalism, and nationalism.

Heine's poetic sequence consists of twenty-seven sections, each called a *caput* (head, heading, or chapter). In his four-line stanzas, the poet employs colloquial language and a meter based on iambic stresses. The second and fourth lines are rhymed, frequently in the comic punning fashion familiar to American readers from the poems of Ogden Nash or Dorothy Parker. The vibrant, dynamic effect achieved by Heine is reminiscent of facile folk poetry or folk songs and has inspired a number of imitations and updated adaptations.

In the opening caput, the traveling poet describes his emotions as he, Antaeus-like, touches the soil of his native country again for the first time in a dozen years. A sort of pie-in-the-sky song sung by a harp-playing girl makes him think of replacing the lullabies of institutionalized religion with rousing secular songs about liberty and a good life for everyone here on earth. In the next section, Heine reflects on the connection between snooping Prussian customs agents and censors looking for intellectual contraband. Caput 3, set in Aachen, is a satiric sally against the stiffness of Prussian soldiers and the outworn relics of medievalism. In Cologne, the poet remembers the clerical narrow-mindedness of that city and the legend that the bones of the Three Wise Men from the East are interred in its famous cathedral. Caput 5 presents a hilarious conversation with Father Rhine, the river having long been a bone of contention between the Germans and the French. The poet then symbolically communes, in the nocturnal city, with the ax-bearing executor of his ideas, who then smashes, in the poet's dream, the skeletons of the Wise Men, representing false beliefs. After remembering Napoleon the libertarian, Heine reaches Westphalia and enjoys succulent German food again. Traveling through the Teutoburg Forest, where the Cheruscan chieftain Arminius (or Hermann) vanquished the Roman legions of Varus in A.D. 9, Heine wonders what Roman greatness his mediocre contemporaries would have achieved if the outcome of that battle had been different. A nocturnal breakdown of his carriage gives Heine a chance to make a pompous speech to some wolves and assure them that he is one of them. A roadside crucifix stirs thoughts of Christ and the dangers faced by idealists.

In caputs 14, 15, 16, and 17, Heine concerns himself with the so-called Kyffhäuser Legend, according to which Emperor Frederick Barbarossa (Friedrich I) and his retinue are asleep in a Thuringian mountain cave and will come to the aid of their country in its hour of need. The poet fantasizes that the emperor shows him around and asks to be updated on political and cultural figures; but the two quarrel, though an apologetic Heine admits, somewhat ironically, that some aspects of the past are preferable to the present. Following a nightmarish encounter with the Prussian eagle, a symbol of confinement and oppression, and after slogging through the mud of Bückeburg, Heine finally reaches Hamburg (caput 20) and is reunited with his beloved (and quintessentially Jewish) mother, who serves her son a sumptuous meal. The poet comments on the people and places of Hamburg, a large part of which was destroyed in a conflagration of May, 1842. On a street, he encounters a majestic woman who, far from being a lady of the evening, turns out to be Hammonia, the "guardian goddess" of Hamburg, and claims to be the daughter of Charlemagne. The rest of Heine's work contains his conversations with her. Assessing his situation and stature, she warmly invites him to return to Hamburg and even vouchsafes him a glimpse of Germany's future in a sort of enchanted chamber pot, but the poet is almost overcome by the stench. (It is interesting to note that a German recording of this work, complete with music and sound effects, briefly presents the voice of Adolf Hitler at this point). In a rather weak conclusion, Heine describes himself as an heir of

Aristophanes and, referring to the *Inferno*, the first canticle of Dante Alighieri's *La divina commedia* (c. 1320; *The Divine Comedy*, 1802), entreats the king of Prussia to treat poets well, while warning him that they would be able to condemn him to eternal damnation.

HEBREW MELODIES

First published: "Herbräische Melodien," 1851 (English translation, 1859)
Type of work: Poetry

The poet celebrates the Sabbath observance, remembers one of the great figures of medieval Hebrew poetry, and passes a sardonic judgment on representatives of both Judaism and Christianity.

Heine's sequence of three poems on Jewish themes forms part of his collection *Romanzero* (1851; English translation, 1859). The title was undoubtedly suggested by the *Hebrew Melodies* (1815) of Lord Byron.

The poems reflect both continuity and change as far as the poet's attitude toward Judaism and his Jewish heritage is concerned. "Prinzessin Sabbat" ("Princess Sabbath") presents, in thirty-eight unrhymed stanzas, a warmly evocative account of the Sabbath observance in a synagogue. On the eve of the Jewish day of rest, Israel (that is, a Jew) is temporarily freed from the witch's curse that has transformed him into a dog and enters the house of prayer like a prince ready to meet his princess, the personification of the Sabbath, who is as humble and quiet as she is beautiful. Heine describes the richly symbolic festive bustle in the synagogue as the princess promises her beloved culinary delights. Such treats stir visions of biblical scenes, but the waning of the Sabbath threatens to transform the observant Jew into a workaday beast again. The poem ends with a description of the traditional *Havdalah* ceremony. The smell of a spice box sustains the worshipers, who are saddened and weakened by the need to bid the Sabbath farewell, and a few drops of wine serve to extinguish the candle and thus the day of rest.

"Jehuda ben Halevy," the longest poem in this sequence, has twenty-four stanzas and almost nine hundred lines, and yet it is a fragment with an elegiac beginning and undertone, for in his age-old mourning for devastated Jerusalem the poet invokes the exemplary figure of Judah Halevi, a scholar, physician, and poet. Heine gives a flowery description of the making of the poet and his study of the Torah and the Talmud, but he also integrates him into the mainstream of Christian medieval Europe and calls him the equal of the great Provençal poets, though his muse was Jerusalem rather than some lady love. In a long digression, Heine concerns himself with jewels found by Alexander the Great after his victory over the Persian king Darius III in 331 B.C., specifically the wondrous wanderings of a pearl necklace. He also pays tribute to the other great poets of that age, Salomon ben Judah ibn Gabirol of Malaga and Moses ibn Ezra of Granada.

"Disputation" consists of 110 unrhymed stanzas. The witty narrator gives a mordant account of a fourteenth century public debate between a Franciscan friar and a rabbi at the Toledo court of King Pedro I of Castile. The question to be settled in this grotesque variant on a medieval tournament is which is the true God, the threefold Christian God of love or the Hebrews' stern deity. Since the loser will have to adopt the religion of the winner, each dueling debater has assistants ready with baptismal basins and circumcision knives. The friar gives a crude, absurd account of Christian beliefs, and the more rationalistic rabbi emphasizes that Jehovah is a strong living presence. In this twelve-hour mental marathon, the arguments become increasingly heated and vituperative, and when the king asks his queen for her judgment, she comes to the unsettling conclusion that "both of them stink."

Summary

Heinrich Heine's fame rests primarily in his body of lyric poetry. It led to some of the most well-known German folk songs ever produced and has appeared in numerous foreign translations. While calling himself the last of the Romantics, he often criticized the Romantic movement for its lack of social and political commitment. In the turbulent period before the revolution of 1848, he advocated a new German literature addressing such important issues of the day as human rights, women's emancipation, and equal representation of the masses in national government. He continues to be regarded as one of Germany's most outspoken champions of the liberal cause.

One of Heine's early translators, the American poet Emma Lazarus, has pointed out that Heine was a German Jew with the mind and eyes of a Greek, a beauty-loving, myth-creating Pagan soul housed in a somber Hebrew frame. Certainly Heine's poetic persona encompassed the German literary heritage and the Western tradition, as well as classical antiquity and timeless popular legend.

Bibliography

Butler, E. M. *Heinrich Heine: A Biography.* London: Hogarth Press, 1956.

Fairley, Barker. *Heinrich Heine: An Interpretation.* Oxford, England: Clarendon Press, 1954.

Liptzin, Sol. *The English Legend of Heinrich Heine.* New York: Bloch, 1954.

Prawer, Siegbert S. *Heine's Jewish Comedy.* Oxford, England: Clarendon Press, 1983.

Robinson, Ritchie. *Heine.* New York: Grove Press, 1988.

Sammons, Jeffrey L. *Heinrich Heine: A Modern Biography.* Princeton, N.J.: Princeton University Press, 1979.

Spencer, Hanna. *Heinrich Heine.* Boston: Twayne, 1982.

Tabak, Israel. *Judaic Lore in Heine: The Heritage of a Poet.* Baltimore: The Johns Hopkins University Press, 1948.

Untermeyer, Louis. *Heinrich Heine: Paradox and Poet.* New York: Harcourt, Brace, 1937.

Wormley, Stanton L. *Heine in England.* Chapel Hill: University of North Carolina Press, 1943.

Harry Zohn

HERMANN HESSE

Born: Calw, Württemberg, Germany
July 2, 1877
Died: Montagnola, Ticino, Switzerland
August 9, 1962

Principal Literary Achievement

Hesse combined elements of German Romanticism, Eastern religion, and Jungian psychoanalysis to explore the themes of the isolation of the artist and the fundamental duality of existence.

Biography

Hermann Hesse was born in Calw, Württemberg, Germany, on July 2, 1877, to Johannes and Marie Hesse. The family moved to Basel in 1881, where Hesse acquired Swiss citizenship. He returned to Calw in 1889 and in 1890-1891 attended Latin school in Göppingen in order to prepare himself for the Württemberg regional examinations. To qualify he had to renounce his Swiss citizenship. In 1891-1892, he was a student at the seminary in Maulbronn, which he left after seven months because he wanted to be a writer. In 1892, he underwent exorcism treatments in Bad Boll, attempted suicide, spent three months in a clinic for nervous diseases at Stetten, and was admitted to the Gymnasium in Cannstatt. Over the next ten years he worked in a clockworks factory in Calw and in bookshops in Tübingen and Basel. During this time he began writing a novel, "Schweinigel" (the hedgehog), the manuscript of which has disappeared. In 1899, he published his first prose work, *Eine Stunde hinter Mitternacht* (an hour beyond midnight).

In 1901, Hesse made his first trip to Italy, returning in 1903 to finish *Peter Camenzind*, his first successful novel, which appeared in 1904 (English translation, 1961). That same year he married Maria Bernoulli and moved to Gaienhofen on Lake Constance, where he began a career as a free-lance writer. In 1905, his first son, Bruno, was born. In 1906, he published *Unterm Rad* (*The Prodigy*, 1957; also published as *Beneath the Wheel*, 1968) and founded *März*, a liberal weekly directed against the personal authority of Kaiser Wilhelm II. His second son, Heiner, was born in 1909, and his third son, Martin, in 1911. Meanwhile, he published *Gertrud* (1910; *Gertrude and I*, 1915; also published as *Gertrude*, 1955) and *Unterwegs: Gedichte* (1911; on the road). That same year he traveled to India, a journey that resulted in *Aus Indien* (1913; sketches from an Indian journey) and a lifelong interest in Eastern philosophy.

Hesse published *Rosshalde* in 1914 (English translation, 1970), the year that World

867

War I began. He volunteered for active duty but was found unfit for military service and was assigned to the embassy in Bern, where he edited newspapers and established a publishing company for prisoners of war. In 1915, when his father died and his wife and youngest son fell seriously ill, Hesse suffered a nervous breakdown that led to psychotherapy with J. B. Lang, a student of C. G. Jung.

In 1919, Hesse moved to Montagnola, Switzerland, where he lived until 1931. The year 1919 also saw the publication of *Demian* (English translation, 1923), a book that gathered a cult following throughout Europe. *Blick ins Chaos* (in sight of chaos) was published in 1920. *Ausgewählte Gedichte* (selected poems) appeared in 1921, the same year Hesse suffered an emotional crisis that lasted eighteen months, during which time he underwent psychoanalysis with Jung himself. *Siddhartha*, Hesse's most popular novel, appeared in 1922 (English translation, 1951). In 1924, Hesse became a Swiss citizen again; in 1926, he was elected a member of the Prussian Academy of Writers, from which he resigned in 1931 after expressing fears that the academy was deceiving people about contemporary German politics.

In 1927, Hesse turned fifty; his second wife, Ruth, divorced him; Hugo Ball published a biography of him; and *Der Steppenwolf* (*Steppenwolf*, 1929), his most bizarre work, appeared. In 1930, Hesse published *Narziss und Goldmund* (*Death and the Lover*, 1932; also published as *Narcissus and Goldmund*, 1968) and in 1931, the year of such works as *Weg nach Innen* (the inward way) and "Klein and Wagner," married Ninon Dolbin and moved into a house in Montagnola built especially for him by H. C. Bodmer with a lifetime right of occupancy. In 1932, Hesse published the third work inspired by his travels in the Far East, *Die Morgenlandfahrt* (1932; *The Journey to the East*, 1956).

Between 1932 and 1943, Hesse wrote and published many stories and poems but spent most of this time composing his masterpiece, *Das Glasperlenspiel* (1943; *Magister Ludi*, 1949; also published as *The Glass Bead Game*, 1969), the novel that not only capped a lifetime of supreme literary achievement but also led directly to his being awarded the Nobel Prize in Literature 1946. Between 1939 and 1945, many of Hesse's works, including *Steppenwolf* and *Narcissus and Goldmund*, were banned in Germany. *The Glass Bead Game* was published in Switzerland in 1943, but by 1946 publication of his works was resumed in Germany, and that same year Hesse was awarded the Goethe Prize in Frankfurt.

Gesammelte Dichtungen (collected works), in six volumes, appeared in 1952 in honor of Hesse's seventy-fifth birthday, and succeeding years saw publication of facsimile editions, correspondence, incidental pieces, and new and old poetry. In 1956, the Hermann Hesse Prize was established by the Society for the Advancement of German Art in Baden-Württemberg. In 1962, the 1937 edition of *In Gedenkblätter* (in memoriam) was published and included fifteen additional texts. On August 9 of that year, Hesse died in Montagnola.

Analysis

Hesse's first published work, *Eine Stunde hinter Mitternacht*, is a romantic novel overflowing with sentimental posturing and romantic clichés, a style Hesse soon came to call sick and incomprehensible, but which he simply refined rather than repudiated. In his next work *Hinterlassene Schriften und Gedichte von Hermann Lauscher* (1901), the hero with a split personality became the model for a long line of alter egos (*Doppelgänger*), including Narcissus and Goldmund, Emil Sinclair and Max Demian, and Hans Giebenrath and Hermann Heilner.

The early works contain many of the themes that appear in Hesse's later writings. One of these is the author as confessor-observer who looks at life objectively and perceives a higher resolution above its superficial contradictions. A similar theme is that of the child who views the world in the eternal present and lives as in a paradise, unaware of the passage of time. Other familiar themes are those of the mirrored image, the outsider, and the Earth Mother. There is also a pervasive love of nature throughout Hesse's works. The hero of *Peter Camenzind*, Hesse's next major novel, strives to obey his own inner law the way seeds obey theirs. His experiences as a student in the city expose him to the artificiality of humankind, and he comes to feel that his mission is to lead the world back to God through Nature. *Peter Camenzind* also contains another of Hesse's central themes: a moment of awakening when intuition and intelligence ignite in a burst of inspiration. *Beneath the Wheel* is a school novel much like James Joyce's *A Portrait of the Artist as a Young Man* (1916), John Knowles's *A Separate Peace* (1959), and J. D. Salinger's *The Catcher in the Rye* (1951). Like Joyce's novel of initiation, this novel chronicles the rebellion of its main characters, Hans Giebenrath and Hermann Heilner, against a dehumanizing educational system. Heilner has the courage to escape, but Giebenrath retreats into a world of madness and ultimately commits suicide. The theme of the inaccessible woman dominates Hesse's next novel, *Gertrude*. Similar goddess figures can be found in *Peter Camenzind* and particularly in *Demian*, where Frau Eva, Demian's mother, is portrayed as a shadowy Earth Mother and an object of veneration to those few who bear the mark of Cain.

Discouraged by the events of World War I, branded a traitor by his country, and devastated by a series of domestic disasters, Hesse underwent psychoanalysis to emerge spiritually reborn. The artistic reflection of this rebirth is *Demian*, in which Hesse makes conscious use of dreams, memories, and associations. Hesse published it under the name of its narrator, Emil Sinclair, because he wished to express the change of personality he (Hesse) had experienced with psychoanalysis and because he wished to appeal to a more intellectual kind of reader. There is only one principle that *Demian* teaches: that people have a duty to be themselves. Those who abide by this principle will be the ones qualified to lead humanity into the future. In *Demian*, these people bear the mark of Cain as a badge of honor, not shame, a sign that they have the courage to break old rules and create new ones. From *Demian* on, Hesse's theme is the fundamental oneness of all being. This vision of the unity of all life is central to *Klingsor* (1920; *Klingsor's Last Summer*, 1970) and *Knulp: Drei Geschichten aus dem Leben Knulps* (1915; *Knulp: Three Tales from the Life of Knulp*, 1971), Hesse's personal favorites among his own works, as well as to *Klein and Wag-*

ner and to his most popular work, *Siddhartha*. Although Siddhartha's life closely parallels that of the Buddha, the novel, with its synthesis of all major religions, is really the profession of faith of a seeker who cannot accept any doctrine but who, when he finds his "way," is able to approve each doctrine and share in the universal brotherhood of all of those who have glimpsed something of the divine and the eternal.

Steppenwolf is, like all Hesse's work, the biography of a soul. In this novel, Harry Haller purges his soul of time and personality in a vain attempt to attain the realm of the Immortals. Although he fails because he has not learned to see the eternal behind the temporary and to laugh at the game of life, the novel ends on a note of hope for Haller. In *Narcissus and Goldmund*, the conflict between Spirit and Nature is embodied in the relationship between Narcissus, the analytical thinker and theologian who represents the Spirit, and Goldmund, the dreamy artist who represents Nature. Narcissus inhabits a monastery, the World of the Father, while Goldmund lives in the outside world, the World of the Mother. Ultimately, a mystical union of these opposites is realized.

After *Narcissus and Goldmund*, Hesse's perspective again changes, and in his last two prose works the individual quest is no longer the center of the novel. In *The Journey to the East*, the message is that the willful, personal self must die and the suprapersonal self must increase. This means the liberation of the true self and the ability to view life as a game. The journey Hesse describes in this work is not geographical but spiritual. All wayfarers are drawn irresistibly eastward in search of the home and youth of the soul, the everywhere and nowhere, the unification of all times. The east becomes a metaphor for the Kingdom of the Spirit, and the whole book is an appeal to a way of life that runs against the currents of the time. When Hesse speaks of the order of the wayfarers, he perceives them as a wave in the eternal stream of the human spirit toward the East, toward Home. This novel also celebrates artists as artist-saints, for among the travelers are famous painters, writers, and musicians. *Demian* expresses the belief that it is through those who bear the mark that humanity progresses. Now, years later, this belief is reaffirmed. *The Journey to the East* announces that it is good for those who bear the mark to know that they have comrades and to know that they are part of the journey.

The Glass Bead Game is Hesse's masterpiece. Like *The Journey to the East*, *The Glass Bead Game* expresses faith in the indestructibility of humanity's spiritual culture. Regardless of differing interpretations, *The Glass Bead Game* repeats the major motifs of Hesse's other works, particularly the essential duality of human nature, which is represented by contrasting characters who form bonds that ultimately transcend their differences and result in an all-encompassing oneness. The artist-saint and the millennium are the principal themes of *The Glass Bead Game*. The artist-saint—the self-fulfilled individual—is embodied in such characters as Goldmund, Demian, Siddhartha, and the Wayfarer to the East. In *The Glass Bead Game*, the artist-saint Josef Knecht is formally installed in the eternal and invisible Kingdom of the Spirit, the end of the Inward Way.

SIDDHARTHA

First published: 1922 (English translation, 1951)
Type of work: Novel

A young Brahman searches for ultimate reality through profligacy and asceticism and learns that wisdom cannot be taught but must come from one's inner struggle.

Siddhartha combines two universal myths, that of Everyman searching for enlightenment and that of the hero on the way to sainthood. Siddhartha takes the journey common to all of Hesse's later heroes, passing from the irresponsible paradise of childhood through the purifying conflicts of youth to the liberation of adult wisdom, the "higher irresponsibility" of absolute faith. Throughout Hesse's works is the reminder that one can learn how to live only from life itself, not from books or teachers. Thus, Siddhartha, the eternal seeker, goes his own way, bowing to no one. He must disregard the wishes of his father, the advice of his friend Govinda, and finally even the counsel of the great Buddha. Only thus can he find his way to his true self.

The story of *Siddhartha* is also built on the myth of the quest. For Siddhartha, the quest begins when he feels that the teachings of Brahmanism do not lead to salvation and decides to try other paths. He leaves home with his friend Govinda to join the ascetic Samanas, with whom he spends three years. When he realizes that asceticism and yoga are only leading him further away from himself, he goes with Govinda to hear the teachings of Guatama the Buddha. Govinda remains with the great teacher, but Siddhartha decides that he must seek his own path through immersion in the world of the senses.

He travels to a large city, where he falls in love with Kamala, a famous courtesan. With her help Siddhartha becomes wealthy, able to afford anything he wants—including Kamala herself. Eventually he realizes that this life of indulgence is just as pointless as a life of denial, that both luxury and asceticism can be extremes that obstruct the path to spiritual illumination. He decides, therefore, to turn his back on the world of Sansara and illusion. Unaware that Kamala is now pregnant with his child, Siddhartha flees the city and returns to the river, where, in despair, he almost commits suicide.

Realizing that suicide is an evasion, not an answer, he decides to stay by the river and to try to understand himself. He looks upon the contrary experiences of asceticism and indulgence as necessary opposites that define and neutralize each other, leaving him once again in his original state of innocence but with a knowledge of good and evil. Living with the wise ferryman Vasudeva, Siddhartha learns many secrets from the river, the most important ones being that time is an illusion, that all being is one, and that for knowledge to be significant, it must be conditioned by love.

Twelve years later, Kamala comes to the river with her son in search of Buddha. When she dies from a snake bite, Siddhartha begins to care for the boy. He loves his son desperately, but the boy longs to escape the two old boatmen and return to life in the city. Eventually he escapes, and Siddhartha, realizing how deeply he loves his son, also realizes that loving him means letting him go. Vasudeva soon dies, and Siddhartha takes his place. Govinda appears one day and is struck by the change that has overtaken Siddhartha, for it is clear to Govinda that Siddhartha, like Buddha, has at last achieved absolute peace and harmony.

When Hesse talks of peace and harmony, he means the perfect balance of opposites. Every truth is made up of equally true opposites. In order for Buddha to teach about the world, he had to divide it into Sansara and Nirvana, illusion and truth, suffering and salvation. The world itself, however, is never one-sided. A deed is never wholly Sansara or wholly Nirvana, just as a person is never wholly a saint or a sinner. These absolutes persist because people are under the illusion that time is real. Time is not real; and if time is not real, then the dividing line between this world and eternity, between suffering and bliss, between good and evil, is also an illusion.

The lesson Siddhartha learns is that the world is perfect at every moment, that every sin carries the hope of grace within it. During deep meditation it is possible to dispel time, to see simultaneously all of the past, present, and future, and then to see everything as good, everything as perfect, everything as Brahman. Thus, everything that exists is good—death as well as life, sin as well as holiness, wisdom as well as folly. Everything is necessary; it needs only the concurrence of true believers. Then all will be well with them and nothing can harm them.

STEPPENWOLF

First published: *Der Steppenwolf*, 1927 (English translation, 1929)
Type of work: Novel

An idealistic artist, struggling to accept the crassness of the real world, learns how to relate to humanity without compromising his integrity.

Steppenwolf is Hesse's most surrealistic novel. With its cast of dreamlike characters, its Magic Theater, and its nightmarish imagery, it comes closer than any of his other works to re-creating the fevered intensity of the lost soul adrift in time and space, ensnared in its own smothering web. The only way back is the mystical process of depersonalization. Harry Haller, the main character, is a man in deep despair because he doubts his ideals and his vocation. Life has become senseless; he longs for new values. Haller first has to learn to accept himself wholly, then to perceive life as a game, and finally to expand his soul to include the whole world in its totality.

On the surface, a bourgeois world is a world of sanity. Haller looks about him at the comfortable routine of domestic existence, and although he feels nostalgia for it, he can no longer accept it. Thus when he sees a sign that says "Magic Theater; Entrance Not for Everybody; For Madmen Only," he tries to enter, because only madmen can make any sense out of a bourgeois world. Until Haller reads the pamphlet entitled "Treatise on the Steppenwolf," he has always thought of himself as a double personality: man and wolf, the civilized human being and the freedom-loving outlaw. So great is this inner tension that Haller has often been on the point of taking his life and indeed is able to keep living only because he plans to commit suicide on his fiftieth birthday.

After reading the treatise, however, Haller realizes that he is wrong in supposing that he is a twofold person. All people, he learns, have manifold personalities, and the common notion that each person is a single ego is false. The road to enlightenment is to surrender the idea of a central ego and to expand the soul until it includes nothing less than everything. To achieve this enlightenment, one must experience certain symbolic rites of passage that will remove one from the clutches of the bourgeois.

Haller has such an experience when he encounters a professor of comparative folklore with whom he once studied and accepts an invitation to dine with him and his wife. During the meal, Haller is forced to behave courteously and exchange social lies with his host and hostess. When the professor, a right-wing nationalist, ridicules a newspaper article denouncing the kaiser, however, Haller declares angrily that he is the author of the article and cares nothing for the professor, his scholarship, or his politics. Calling himself a schizophrenic who is no longer fit for human society, Haller storms out, relieved; the lone wolf in him has triumphed over the bourgeois.

Haller then meets Maria, who becomes his mistress, and Pablo, a handsome young musician with extensive experience in sex and drugs. One evening Pablo invites Haller to his quarters for a little entertainment—"for madmen only," he explains—the ticket of admission being one of Pablo's drugs. When Haller has succumbed to the influence of the drugs, Pablo holds up a small mirror in which Haller sees himself in a double vision, as a man whose features blend with those of a shy, beautiful, dazed wolf with smoldering, frightened eyes. Next Pablo leads him into a theater corridor where there is a full-length mirror. Standing before it, Haller sees himself in a hundred forms: as child, adolescent, mature man, both happy and sad, dressed and naked. One form, an elegant young man, embraces Pablo.

Turning from the mirror, Haller walks down the corridor, off of which are dozens of doors, each offering the fulfillment of a thwarted or unrecognized aspect of Haller's personality. Haller goes through a sequence of bizarre experiences climaxing in the symbolic murder of Hermine and culminating in his appearance before a dozen robed judges who, instead of sentencing him to death as he expects, condemn him to "eternal life." Then all but Haller laugh. He is left feeling that he still has much to learn about how to live but promises himself that he will work at it and one day even learn to laugh.

NARCISSUS AND GOLDMUND

First published: *Narziss und Goldmund*, 1930 (*Death and the Lover*, 1932;
Narcissus and Goldmund, 1968)
Type of work: Novel

Two close friends lead contrasting lives, one spiritual, one sensual, ultimately
realizing that they are but opposite sides of the same nature.

In *Narcissus and Goldmund*, Hesse reaches into the past to explore the theme of
the reconciliation of opposites. The conflict between artistic and scholarly existence
had always been a problem for him, and in this novel Hesse embodies those opposites in the personalities of two close friends whose interdependent lives take meaning from each other. Both young men meet as novitiates in a monastery, but it is
clear from the beginning that they are destined for very different vocations. Narcissus is a scholar who searches for meaning in abstractions, whereas Goldmund is a
sensualist who seeks meaning in the concrete world of the senses.

At the end of his novitiate, Narcissus takes final vows and starts his prescribed
ascetic exercises, dedicating himself to a life of service to the spirit even though he is
aware of its one-sidedness. Goldmund, on the other hand, runs away from the monastery and meets a young gypsy who surrenders herself to him and then leaves him to
return to her husband. Thus Goldmund's first experience in the world of the senses
teaches him how unstable and fleeting it is. Yet he continues his search for worldly
satisfaction. He has an adventure with a peasant woman, then joins the household of
a knight, from whom he flees after getting involved in a triangle with the knight's two
daughters. Shortly thereafter Goldmund experiences the violence of the world when
he kills a thief, hides the corpse, and escapes.

Goldmund next becomes a disciple of Master Nicholas, a sculptor whose statue of
St. Mary he admires. When Goldmund fashions a statue of the Disciple John, the
features are clearly those of Narcissus. Master Nicholas realizes Goldmund's possibilities and decides to admit him to the guild and give the young man his daughter in
marriage. Goldmund, however, does not want to live a bourgeois life and deserts his
master. It is the period of the Black Death, and Goldmund meets two refugees, a
vagabond cleric and a girl the cleric thinks he has rescued from the plague. For a
time the three live together in a country cottage, but once the girl falls ill with the
disease, the cleric flees, leaving Goldmund to nurse her until her death. Goldmund
then returns to Master Nicholas, who, he learns, has died from the disease.

Soon thereafter Goldmund is caught in bed with the governor's mistress and condemned to death. When a priest comes to give him extreme unction, Goldmund considers killing the priest and escaping in the priest's habit, but the priest turns out to
be Narcissus, who has become Abbot John. As Narcissus had promised, he has come

to his friend in the hour of his direst need, when the world of the senses and the world of violence and disease have led him to contemplate the sin of premeditated murder. Through Narcissus' influence, Goldmund is released, and the two friends return to the monastery, where Goldmund is given a shop in which he can create sculptures. Once again Goldmund cannot submit to the discipline of monastic life and flees. Years later he returns to the monastery as a tired old man. The world has become too much for him; he longs for peace but harbors no grudge against fate. He has no faith in a life after death but still looks forward to dying, seeing it as a happiness in which his mother will take him by the hand and lead him back into the innocence of nonexistence.

Although Narcissus is portrayed from the beginning as being well on the way to perfection, in the end he has not yet achieved it. His life seems complete only when it is seen as a frame of reference within which Goldmund's experiences acquire meaning. The life of Goldmund is developed in stages as he moves upward from innocence through experience to attain, through sensuality, the higher innocence that Narcissus has sought through spirituality. Neither, however, can make it alone. As halves of the same entity, they need each other. This reality is the interdependence that is the theme of all of Hesse's works.

THE GLASS BEAD GAME

First published: *Das Glasperlenspiel*, 1943 (*Magister Ludi*, 1949; *The Glass Bead Game*, 1969)
Type of work: Novel

A young man in a futuristic utopian society renounces the emphasis on pure intellect and the world of the spirit, leaves the Order, and dies.

The Glass Bead Game is Hesse's masterpiece. He wrote it over a period of eleven years (1932 to 1943), during a time when the world seemed bent on self-destruction. Because *The Glass Bead Game* is, among other things, an urgent plea for an all-embracing humanitarianism, it has a more didactic tone and a more explicit linkage with spiritual ideas from the past. The result is a book subject to many interpretations. On one level it restates Hesse's belief in the individual's ability to attain perfection and to help others by serving as an example, creating an eternal circle of master and disciple. By affirming faith in the individual's perfectibility and will to serve, Hesse implies his belief in the coming of a better humanity that will conquer chaos and barbarity.

For many readers, the significance of *The Glass Bead Game* lies in the synthesis that it represents in Hesse's art and life. It is the work in which he reaffirms most strongly his belief in the Kingdom of the Spirit, seeing in the Game an eternal approach to this Kingdom. The central figure's name, (Josef) Knecht, means "servant" in German, suggesting that his purpose is to serve the hierarchy. His ultimate service is as supreme Magister Ludi, an office he holds for eight years, but he is plagued by doubts from the beginning. Slowly he realizes that he is aware of the polarities of the light World of the Father (Castalia) and the dark World of the Mother (the outside world). Knecht harbors two opposing feelings within his breast—one toward service to the Order, the other toward "awakening."

The irrational strain grows. As with Goldmund, it is the artist in him that desires liberation. When he does decide to leave the Order, the reason he gives is that he fears that devotion to the spiritual life in seclusion from the world leads to degeneration, that the glass bead game is nothing but an esoteric play as pastime. He prefers to become a Castalian teacher in the outside world. Not long after Knecht leaves Castalia in his quest for self-fulfillment, he drowns in an icy lake one morning right at sunrise. Hesse himself saw Knecht's death as a sacrifice made to free Tito, his pupil, to take up Knecht's cause. This affirmative conclusion is symbolized by the way Tito takes up the robe Knecht has left behind and puts it on after Knecht's death.

By writing *The Glass Bead Game*, Hesse tried to achieve mainly two goals: to build a spiritual realm in which he himself could live and breathe in spite of the poisoning of the world around him and to strengthen the resistance of his German friends against the barbaric powers under which they had to suffer. In order to create this spiritual realm, however, it was not enough to return to the past or to dwell on the present. Instead it became necessary for Hesse to project his ideas into the future, when the unbearable present would have become history. The utopian character of the novel, therefore, is not a gimmick but a need to view the present from a clearer perspective.

Summary

Hermann Hesse's works are all fragments of a long confession, reflecting a single human being and his relation to the world and to his own self. Although they are primarily concerned with self-recognition and self-realization, these spiritual autobiographies deal with the human condition in general. They have a mystical quality in the way Hesse traces the quest for identity in a universe that is either hostile or indifferent. Yet the quest is not undertaken within the dogma of an established religion, for then obedience to an established law would suffice. To Hesse, one finds the way according to one's own inner law.

Bibliography

Freedman, Ralph. *Hermann Hesse: Pilgrim of Crisis, a Biography.* New York: Pantheon Books, 1978.

Marrer-Tising, Carlee. *The Reception of Hermann Hesse by the Youth in the United States: A Thematic Analysis.* New York: Lang, 1982.

Michels, Volker. *Hermann Hesse: A Pictorial Biography.* New York: Farrar, Straus & Giroux, 1975.

Mileck, Joseph. *Hermann Hesse: Life, Work, and Criticism.* Fredericton, Canada: York Press, 1984.

Norton, Roger C. *Hermann Hesse's Futuristic Idealism: "The Glass Bead Game" and Its Predecessors.* New York: Lang, 1973.

Stelzig, Eugene L. *Hermann Hesse's Fictions of the Self: Autobiography and the Confessional Imagination.* Princeton, N.J.: Princeton University Press, 1988.

Ziolkowski, Theodore. *The Novels of Hermann Hesse.* Princeton, N.J.: Princeton University Press, 1965.

Thomas Whissen

E. T. A. HOFFMANN

Born: Königsberg, East Prussia
January 24, 1776
Died: Berlin, Prussia
June 25, 1822

Principal Literary Achievement

The author of four novels and the composer of the opera *Undine*, Hoffmann wrote bizarre Romantic tales. A few provide the text of Jacques Offenbach's *Les Contes d'Hoffmann* (*The Tales of Hoffmann*) and of Peter Ilich Tchaikovsky's the *Shchelkunchik* (*The Nutcracker Suite*) ballet.

Biography

Ernst Theodor Wilhelm Hoffmann is known as E. T. A. Hoffmann, because he changed the name "Wilhelm" to "Amadeus" as a tribute to Wolfgang Amadeus Mozart, the German composer. Hoffmann was born on January 24, 1776, in Königsberg, then known as East Prussia, but later called Kaliningrad and located in the Soviet Union. He came from a family of lawyers with a long tradition of service to the state, a calling that he also felt obliged to follow. His parents were separated when he was three years old, and he was cared for by a bachelor uncle, who was eccentric and demanding but a great lover of music. Hoffmann's thorough education in instrumental music and theory may have been the only positive aspect of his lonely childhood.

Hoffmann displayed virtuoso talents. He wrote music throughout his career and was middle-aged before he abandoned the notion that he would be remembered by posterity as a composer. Hoffmann was also a gifted artist and an inspired caricaturist, an ability that had a negative effect on his career. Yet his irrepressible humor and dualistic personality contributed to his genius. Hoffmann displayed a lifelong tendency toward excess in his life-style and in the consumption of alcohol, factors that help to explain his early death at the age of forty-six.

From 1792 to 1795, Hoffmann attended the university in Königsberg as a law student. He passed difficult examinations, making him eligible for service as a high-ranking legal official in the Prussian government. His life, like that of the writer Franz Kafka a century later, was compartmentalized into pursuit of the traditional legal career during business hours and devotion to his artistic talents during his off-hours. Hoffmann also gave private music lessons and fell in love with one of his pupils, Cora Hatt, who was married.

Nach der eigenen Zeichnung Hoffmann's.

E. T. W. Hoffmann

geb. den 24ten Januar 1776.

gest. den 25ten Junius 1822.

From 1797 to 1807, Hoffmann held positions in Prussian courts of law in Posen, Plozk, and Warsaw. He was sent to the remote hamlet of Plozk because of an indiscretion involving the caricature portrait of one of the leading military personalities in Posen, who was not amused by the likeness. In 1802, Hoffmann married Michalina (Rohrer) Trzynska. During the years from 1797 to 1807, he continued to study both painting and composition, completing an opera and a symphony. He also began to write fiction at this time.

Because he refused to swear an oath of fealty to Napoleon I's occupation government, Hoffmann was dismissed from public service in 1807. After a time of personal hardship and near starvation in Berlin, he succeeded in obtaining the position of musical director and in-house composer at the Bamberg theater, where he stayed from 1808 to 1813. After the failure of his first production as music director, Hoffmann resigned but retained the job of composer of stage music and ballets. He gave private music lessons again, and he fell in love with another pupil, Julia Marc. This unfortunate passion drove him to thoughts of suicide, a theme often adumbrated in his fiction. Divorce was not an option in Hoffmann's time and situation. In these difficult years, Hoffmann continued to write instrumental or choral music, published his first short story, "Ritter Gluck: Eine Erinnerung aus dem Jahr 1809" ("Ritter Gluck"), and functioned as a theatrical designer.

In 1813, Hoffmann was appointed music director for the opera company of Joseph Seconda in Dresden and Leipzig. He wrote such stories as "Der goldene Topf: Ein Märchen aus der neuen Zeit" ("The Golden Flower Pot"), an essay titled "Beethoven's Instrumental Music," and his own opera, *Undine*, with libretto supplied by the writer Friedrich de la Motte Fouqué. This charming story of a water sprite in love with a mortal knight was produced in Berlin in 1816 for fourteen popular performances. The opera house burned to the ground, however, while Hoffmann watched, horrified, from his room across the street. *Undine* was soon forgotten. Contemporary music historians view it as one of the most unjustly neglected operas of Romanticism.

Hoffmann's months at Seconda's opera were brief. He returned to Berlin in 1814 to take the position of deputy judge in the court of appeal, a prestigious appointment that he held until his death in 1822. He continued to write stories, reviews of musical performances, novels, and sketches. He was well known in artistic circles, befriending the famous actor Ludwig Devrient and counting many Romantic writers among his close friends. He was also a habitué of the renowned wineshop Lütter and Wegner. Late in his life, he was appointed commissioner of inquiry for a set of important trials, where he acquitted himself with honesty and efficiency. He also returned to the fatal error of caricature, this time of people at the trial, whom he pilloried in a short story titled *Meister Floh: Ein Märchen in sieben Abenteuern zweier Freunde* (1822; *Master Flea: A Fairy Tale in Seven Adventures of Two Friends*, 1826). A man with, in his own words, "too much reality" to devote himself entirely to writing, Hoffmann continued to function in two spheres, even up until paralysis claimed his life. He dictated his last story, "Der Feind" ("The Enemy"), until a few days before his death on June 25, 1822, in Berlin, Prussia. Hoffmann is among the most famous of all Romantic tellers of tales, particularly in England, France, and America.

Analysis

Hoffmann's fiction is noted for its astonishing depiction of pathological psychological states, for the use of description emulating the detail of dreams, for the introduction of grotesque, supernatural, and bizarre elements into his narratives, for its sometimes macabre humor, and for the portrayal of characters torn between two conflicting desires. His work, like his life, is dualistic, full of two-sided heroes leading frenetic, eccentric lives.

Hoffmann came to fame as a writer after having considered the calling of an artist or a composer-musician. He accompanied his efforts as a lawyer and author with the writing of operas, symphonies, and a wealth of smaller compositions. He often gave private music lessons to augment his precarious income and published critical articles about the music of his time.

Musicians and other kinds of artists play a significant role in Hoffmann's fiction as ambivalent heroes. The most famous (partly autobiographical) character that he created was Kapellmeister (Conductor) Johannes Kreisler, the hero of a cycle of stories, which served as the inspiration for the occasional music titled *Kreisleriana* by the nineteenth century composer Robert Schumann. Kreisler was also the hero of Hoffmann's avant-garde novel *Lebensansichten des Katers Murr, nebst fragmentarischer Biographie des Kapellmeisters Johannes Kreisler in zufalligen Makulaturblättern* (1819, 1821; *The Life and Opinions of Kater Murr, with the Fragmentary Biography of Kapellmeister Johannes Kreisler on Random Sheets of Scrap Paper*, 1969). In this novel, Hoffmann's dualism is graphically displayed, since the book purports to be the autobiography of a tomcat, who uses the reverse sides of the musician Kreisler's autobiography for his own story. Thus, each page of the cat's life alternates with pages of the musician's confessions. Murr (Purr) is the very embodiment of a limited and judgmental member of the middle class, and the composer's struggles are caused precisely because of such attitudes.

The eighteenth century composer Christoph Willibald Gluck is a main character in Hoffmann's earliest story, "Ritter Gluck." In this tale, as in most, the supernatural plays a role because the composer is a ghost. Other magical, often humorous, elements figure prominently in the stories, including fire spirits and salamanders, in "The Golden Flower Pot"; twisted demonic characters who appear in various guises and may be in league with the Devil, such as Coppelius in "Der Sandmann" ("The Sandman"); or eccentric violin collectors, who build houses symmetrical only on the inside, like Councillor Krespel in "Rat Krespel" ("Councillor Krespel"). Titles such as "Das öde Haus" ("The Deserted House") from *Nachtstücke* (1817; night pieces) *Die Elixiere des Teufels: Nachgelassene Papiere des Bruders Medardus, eines Kapuziners* (1815-1816; *The Devil's Elixirs: From the Posthumous Papers of Brother Medardus, a Capuchin Friar*, 1824), "Der Elementargeist" ("The Nature Spirit") attest to the range of fantasic themes that crowd Hoffmann's tales.

Hoffmann often wrote about people who were obsessed by one peculiar idea. For example, he depicted the slightly mad obsession of Counselor Krespel for taking violins apart in order to see where their beautiful tone resided. That is analogous to the futility of doing an autopsy on a human body to search for the soul or the cause of a beautiful singing voice. Indeed, Krespel, a lawyer like Hoffmann, has been unhappily married to an operatic soprano from Italy (where the best violins were also made) and has a daughter who will die if she sings. Of course, she has a divinely beautiful voice, and, inevitably, she succumbs to the fatal temptation to sing. This theme is taken up by such later authors as Thomas Mann in his short story, *Tristan* (1903; English translation, 1925). It is also typical of Hoffmann's fiction that more than one related theme is treated in the same story, for example, building an inwardly symmetrical house, dismantling violins, and enforcing silence on a gifted, but physically frail, singer.

Hoffmann was the first author to write mystery fiction, when he published, "Das Fräulein von Scuderi" ("Mademoiselle de Scudéry") in volume three of *Die Serapionsbrüder* (1819-1821; *The Serapion Brethren*, 1886-1892), twenty-two years before Edgar Allan Poe. It contains a fanciful description of an artist-criminal, obsessed with a beautiful work of art, a theme that has enjoyed wide currency since Hoffmann's time.

The author arranged his stories into collections, with names such as *The Serapion Brethren*, perhaps a reference to his own friends and fellow Romantics, or *Fantasiestücke in Callots Manier* (1814-1815; *fantasy pieces in the style of Callot*). In all, he wrote nearly fifty tales. Although an entire collection may not be remembered, individual stories have entered the canon of world literature and, aided by their use in musical compositions, have become part of the Western heritage, particularly through the use of "Nussknacker und Mausekönig" ("Nutcracker and the King of Mice") in *The Nutcracker Suite* ballet of Russian composer Peter Ilich Tchaikovsky.

Fascinated by mesmerism, an early fad related to hypnosis, and by the ways in which the human spirit is drawn to conflicting realities, one of which may be fatal, Hoffmann captured the imagination of a Romantic generation. He is still read in numerous translations throughout the world.

THE SANDMAN

First published: "Der Sandmann," 1816 (English translation, 1844)
Type of work: Short story

A promising young author becomes the victim of an obsession with the identity of the two women whom he loves, and plunges to his death.

"The Sandman," justly regarded as one of Hoffmann's greatest stories, is the basis for a scene from the opera *Les Contes d'Hoffmann (The Tales of Hoffmann)* by

Jacques Offenbach and for the Léo Delibes ballet *Coppélia*. It is a typical example of Hoffmann's use of doubles.

While studying at the university, Nathaniel, a sensitive aspiring writer, believes that a barometer maker and binocular salesman named Coppola is a terrifying figure from his childhood. Dabbling in alchemistic experiments with a lawyer named Coppelius, Nathaniel's father died in a laboratory explosion. So that she could hurry the children into bed whenever Coppelius visited Nathaniel's father, Nathaniel's nurse had used the figure of Coppelius to scare the children with stories of the Sandman, who steals the eyes of children for his nefarious purposes. Although rationally, the two men cannot be identical, despite the similarity of their names (Coppelius/Coppola), an encounter with Coppola reminds Nathaniel of his father's death.

Nathaniel's agitation at encountering Coppola is soothed by a trip to his home. His fiancée, Clara, a name suggesting the clarity and reason recommended by the Enlightenment, exercises a healing influence on him, although she does not comprehend his confessional and deeply felt poetic art. In Clara's opinion, Nathaniel's preoccupation with emotionally stimulating poetry is not good for him.

Upon his return to the university, Nathaniel discovers his rooming house destroyed by fire. His new lodgings face the apartment of the mysterious scientist Spalanzani and his daughter Olympia. Using the binoculars purchased from Coppola before Nathaniel's restorative trip home, he observes and falls hopelessly in love with Olympia.

After meeting her at a gathering at the professor's home, Nathaniel is confirmed in his opinion that she is a woman who truly understands his artistic soul. She listens to his compositions by the hour, sometimes punctuating Nathaniel's reading with the single cry, "Oh!" Olympia, however, is an automaton, built by the scientist and fantastically endowed with "life" from the essence of Nathaniel's eyes, stolen by the "Sandman" Coppola when Nathaniel bought the binoculars. Thus, when Nathaniel looks into Olympia's eyes he sees and loves himself.

Nathaniel goes mad one day because he chances to see Spalanzani and Coppola struggling over ownership of Olympia and tearing her limb from limb in the process. Again nursed back to health by Clara, Nathaniel accidentally turns his binoculars on her. He suddenly understands that it is Clara who is really a lifeless doll. He attempts to murder her, but instead he falls from a great height onto the city square, just as the barometer maker is walking by.

In this tale, the themes of identity, the supernatural, demonism, alchemy, and automata, reflecting a fear of scientific innovation and the dilemma of the artist in society, combine to create the typical Hoffmannesque thrill of fear and alienation, combined with horror and tragic disappointment. One can see why such tales influenced writers such as Poe and may be the forerunners of modern science fiction.

MADEMOISELLE DE SCUDÉRY

First published: "Das Fräulein von Scuderi," 1820 (English translation, 1826)
Type of work: Short story

The obsessive desire of a master jeweler to possess his creations leads him to murder and death in seventeenth century Paris.

"Mademoiselle de Scudéry," considered to be Hoffmann's supreme achievement, may be the earliest mystery story. It served also as the inspiration for the opera *Cardillac* by twentieth century composer Paul Hindemith. Like many of Hoffmann's tales, it provides a psychologically accurate portrait of a pathological personality, in this case a split personality, or a Jekyll-and-Hyde figure, the master jeweler Cardillac. Written with attention to historical accuracy, and the creation of the mood in Paris during the reign of Louis XIV, the story is also a masterpiece of narrative technique, using a minor poet and spinster of advanced age, Mademoiselle de Scudéry, as the agency by which the fiendish criminal-artist is brought to justice.

A lengthy tale, "Mademoiselle de Scudéry" includes a narrative about a rash of notorious poisonings and the consequent creation of a special tribunal in Paris to hunt down malefactors. This reference serves to explain the mood of Parisians, who are almost hysterical even before the murders are perpetrated by Cardillac. It also calls into question the kind of justice available in society when a citizenry is roused, a query pertinent to events not only in Hoffmann's time but also in the present age.

In the main story, a young couple, portrayed as shining examples of virtue, Cardillac's apprentice Olivier, who has Mademoiselle's special "pet" as a baby, and Madelon, the jeweler's daughter, are wrongfully accused of the theft of Cardillac's jewels and his murder. Scudéry must clear up the confusion to save the innocent couple.

In what proves to be a tortuous process, Cardillac's criminal behavior is revealed, but, to protect Madelon from knowledge of her father's crimes, Mademoiselle de Scudéry must secretly narrate the true events to the king himself, whose heart is softened by Madelon's resemblance to a woman whom the King once loved but lost to the convent. Formal procedures are circumvented in the interest of subjective and arbitrary considerations. Only the honesty of individuals assures that the streets of Paris are safe and that justice has been served.

Cardillac is revealed to be the victim of a prenatal influence—his mother's pathological appetite for jewelry during her pregnancy. He is driven to create masterpieces of jewelry in his daytime identity as the irreproachable jeweler for Paris nobility (Dr. Jekyll). At night, however, he is obsessively compelled to steal the lovely baubles back, killing their rightful owners (Mr. Hyde). After many baffling murders, one of Cardillac's victims parries the knife thrust intended to kill him and stabs Cardillac instead. Olivier, who has discovered his master's secret, drags the jeweler back to his apartment, only to be taken for the thief-murderer himself. After Mademoiselle has explained the unique situation to the king, the young couple is permitted to emigrate to another country, thus keeping the truth from Madelon and the public while providing a rather questionable and subjective kind of justice.

Summary

E. T. A. Hoffmann's tales call into question the nature of the artist and of art itself, or they provide puzzling views of a reality only imperfectly comprehended. They are grotesque parodies of the ideal of harmonious beauty in art and narrative fiction. Typical Hoffmann heroes are talented but obsessive. They cannot conform to society, and thus they are compelled to seek understanding in unnatural ways. They are crushed by society or find themselves utterly unable to discern where reality lies. They are swept along by forces that they cannot control and forced to participate in bizarre, irrational events. Yet, the reader is captivated by Hoffmann's masterful storytelling. Ever the ironic humorist, he softens the harshness of his tragic vision with fantasy, wit, and humor.

Bibliography

Cobb, Palmer. *The Influence of E. T. A. Hoffmann on the Tales of Edgar Allan Poe.* Chapel Hill: University of North Carolina Press, 1908.

Daemmrich, Horst. *The Shattered Self: E. T. A. Hoffmann's Tragic Vision.* Detroit: Wayne State University Press, 1973.

Hewett-Thayer, Harvey W. *Hoffmann: Author of the Tales.* Princeton, N.J.: Princeton University Press, 1948.

McGlathery, James M. *Mysticism and Sexuality: E. T. A. Hoffmann.* Part 1, *Hoffmann and His Sources.* Las Vegas: Lang, 1981; part 2, *Interpretations of the Tales.* New York: Lang, 1985.

Negus, Kenneth. *E. T. A. Hoffmann's Other World: The Romantic Author and His "New Mythology."* Philadelphia: University of Pennsylvania Press, 1965.

Schafer, R. Murray. *Hoffmann and Music.* Toronto: University of Toronto Press, 1974.

Taylor, Ronald. *Hoffmann.* New York: Hillary House, 1963.

Watts, Pauline. *Music: The Medium of the Metaphysical in E. T. A. Hoffmann.* Amsterdam: Rodopi, 1972.

Erlis Glass

HOMER

Born: Ionia(?), Greece
c. early eighth century B.C.
Died: Greece
late eighth century B.C.

Principal Literary Achievement

The Homeric *Iliad* and *Odyssey* provide both the finest examples of Greek epic and valuable testimony on the nature of the Mycenaean world.

Biography

The ancient Greeks recognized the advantage of keeping vague the identity of the poet whom they universally called *Omeros*. The *Iliad* and *Odyssey* became, in effect, national epics half a millennium before anything like pan-Hellenism actually existed. In them, ancient Greece saw its tradition and its history, and they alone marked the transition from a nonliterate culture to a literary one. It is hardly surprising, then, that seven cities claimed the poet as their own or that a mass of manifestly false genealogical material appeared in ancient times, concocted to demonstrate that the poet of the *Iliad* (eighth century B.C.; first codified early second century B.C.; English translation, 1616) and *Odyssey* (eighth century B.C.; first codified early second century B.C.; English translation, 1616) was their native son.

Ionia becomes, essentially because of the predominance of Ionian dialect, the region most often cited by modern scholars as Homer's place of birth. Still, this general agreement contributes little toward settling the infinitely more important question of how a presumably blind poet from a rural and relatively unsophisticated region of the Greek world could have written two poems as cosmopolitan as the *Iliad* and *Odyssey*. An explanation unacceptable to modern sensibilities is that there was no single poet called Homer, or even if there had been, that his poems were passed by oral tradition throughout the Greek world and received successive refinements through the rhapsodes, professional reciters who presented them. The episodic nature of the poems themselves lends credence to the argument that they originally had been separate shorter works reconciled into epics. There again, nineteenth century etymologists deduced that the name "Homer" meant "the united." In plural form, the *Omeroi* would thus be guild members entrusted with maintaining the legends of the Trojan War at an appropriate standard. This original group, so the argument runs, became identified with the succeeding generation of Homeric imitators, called *Homeridae*

(sons of Homer) even in ancient times. Reconciling this patronymic with the plural form yielded the name *Omeros*.

Because no definitive biography of Homer existed, even in ancient times, wildly contradictory dates appear to frame his life span. Modern scholars reject the ancient assumption that Homer lived within chronological proximity to the historical Trojan War, now generally set from 1194-1184 B.C. The majority of ancient opinion, following the historian Herodotus (484-c. 430 B.C.), accepted a mid-ninth century B.C. period for Homer's mature years, as Herodotus claims (2.53) that Homer could not have lived more than four centuries before his own. Early Christianity found it expedient to place Homer's birthdate as close as possible to the period assigned to biblical codification, primarily to reconcile the Greek and Hebrew traditions.

Until the mid-twentieth century, a ninth century dating for Homer remained the most popular; even so, an eighth century Homer is more logical and has become widely accepted based on several arguments. Post-Homeric literature, including the epic imitations of the *Homeridae*, Hesiod and the Hesiodic continuations, and the earliest lyric and elegiac poems of Greek literature, are firmly placed in the seventh century B.C. All depend on Homeric influence as their most important internal feature. It is clear that Homer precedes Hesiod, and also as clear that relative chronological proximity exists between the two poets. That would place Homer's birth in the eighth century, not the ninth. It is also probable that Herodotus calculated the number of generations that existed between himself and Homer, for it is clear from another place in his work (2.142) that Herodotus calculates three generations as one hundred years.

None of these speculations settles the essential question of the poet's identity. Indeed, many people have become lost in various aspects of the question. An Ionian identity makes sense, and perhaps one might localize it even further to Smyrna on the coast of Asia Minor or to the offshore island of Chios, a stronghold of the *Homeridae*. The *Iliad* contains two specific references to the area: a description of the birds that gather beside the Cayster, the Ionian river, and a description of the northwest winds that blow from Thrace. Even so, that is hardly conclusive. Who Homer was, and whether one poet by that name actually existed, must essentially remain unanswered questions.

Analysis

Accepting an eighth century dating for composition of the *Iliad* and *Odyssey*, as most modern scholars do, logically raises questions regarding the appropriateness of the Homeric poems as historical testimony. Such questions do not grow substantially fewer by moving Homer's century back to the ninth. Archaeological methods developed since Heinrich Schliemann's excavations at the site of Troy in the 1870's have set the dates for the historical Trojan War between 1194 and 1184 B.C. That would mean that Homer's *Iliad* and *Odyssey* describe a historical period four or three hundred years anterior to his own. Since the Greek world was still at its preliterate stage (the ability to write existed, but the written language was not used for literary purposes),

Homer had no written records upon which to rely. Even so, memory remains strong in preliterate societies. Mythic storytelling becomes a privileged art, one that does not tolerate deviation from elements considered essential. Descriptions of personalities, places, and events and outcomes must remain consistent. Numbers involved and chronological frames for these events assume considerably less importance. Given that classical Greek identifies all numbers above ten thousand as *myría* (myriad), no ancient reader would have expected a precise inventory of numbers in the "Catalogue of Ships and Heroes" that fills *Iliad* 2. In fact, Greek notions of history before Thucydides differed as much as their understanding of biography before Plutarch (c. A.D. 50-120).

Nevertheless, archaeology supports much of what Homer provides regarding the Trojan War. Read emblematically, the *Iliad* implies a major clash of Greek and non-Greek cultures. Even ancient historical sources document the friction between the Peloponnesic Greeks and the inhabitants of Ionia, Caria, and Anatolia, and it is likely that the theft of Helen (whose value is material, not human, by Mycenaean standards) represents the mercantile friction that existed between the Peloponnesus and Asia Minor.

Moreover, the internal consistency of the Homeric poems constitutes a strong argument in favor of their reliability. Both *Iliad* and *Odyssey* rely extensively on verbatim repeated passages, epithets regularly assigned to people, places, and things, and massive lists known as epic catalogs. Formulaic endings often fill out the hexameter verse, implicitly supporting the authenticity of the line in question. All of these techniques effectively become mnemonic devices that facilitated oral transmission of the poems by rhapsodes, who originally circulated the Homeric poems throughout the Greek world. It is clear that the *Iliad* and *Odyssey* had assumed privileged status at a period that approximates their composition. With this understood, it is unlikely that the rhapsodes would have altered the essentials of the poems in any substantive way. Late second century B.C. codification by Aristarchus and Xenodotus appears limited to division into books and a choice of likely readings between or among variant readings not significantly affecting the poems themselves. Obviously, stability of text cannot guarantee reliability of content, but, given the pre-Thucydidean conception of history, it is clear that the Homeric epics can provide valuable insights into the Mycenaean world.

Of course, Homer was not Mycenaean. Archaeological evidence shows that pre-Greek culture died following, and perhaps partly in consequence of, the power vacuum created by the absence of traditional power structures on the Peloponnesus during the years of preparation and fighting at Troy. It is another question whether the Mycenaean kingdoms fell by a Dorian invasion or simply by neglect. Still, the *Odyssey* would support the latter contention, one sustained as well by modern archaeology. The instability of Odysseus' Ithaca is clear, and the poem clearly contrasts the Mycenaean outlook of Odysseus, Nestor, and Eumaeus with that which the suitors of Penelope have imposed. Likewise, it is easy to detect the unease that Menelaus shows upon his return to Sparta with the reclaimed Helen. Even young Telemachus, the son of Odysseus, senses how much the war has cost and the unhappiness that prevails in its aftermath.

One typical characteristic of Homeric epic is thus its ability to restrict a massive theme such as the Trojan War both chronologically and to its human dimension. The *Iliad*, though its theme is indeed the fighting at Troy, treats its subject only in terms of the conflict of Achilles and Agamemnon. Chronologically, it covers no more than ninety days, perhaps as few as sixty. It also initiates what would become the accepted practice of beginning *in medias res* (in the middle of events) and ending before the final conclusion of the events that it describes. There is nothing of the nine years that preceded the quarrel of Achilles and Agamemnon, nor is there anything of the strategy that would result in Greek victory: the wooden horse. Homer's narrative ends with the return of Hector's body to his father, Priam. The effect is to underscore the importance of *moira* (fate) as a controlling factor in Achilles' life. Readers know that once Achilles has made the decision to remain at Troy he will kill Hector and will himself die soon after. That Achilles' acceptance of *moira* would become a moral imperative as a result of Hector's killing of Patroclus thus emerges as the climax of Homer's narrative.

Narrative pattern in the *Odyssey* resembles that of the *Iliad* insofar as it begins *in medias res*. Odysseus has spent approximately seven years on Calypso's island as the epic begins. His adventures with his crew are behind him, and he recalls them subsequently to his Phaeacian hosts only by way of flashback. Most of the ongoing narrative of the *Odyssey* concerns itself with recognition scenes, and these culminate with Odysseus' recognition by the suitors and his gory slaughter of them and the unfaithful handmaidens. Another slaughter, that of the fathers of the suitors, appears about to start when the goddess Athena suddenly appears and ends the entire narrative by *dea ex machina* (goddess from the machine, describing any unnatural termination of narrative). Readers learn nothing through the *Odyssey* regarding how well (or badly) Odysseus resumes his position as king, husband, or father.

ILIAD

First compiled: Eighth century B.C.; first codified, early second century B.C. (English translation, 1616)
Type of work: Epic poem

Homer's *Iliad* presents the Trojan War in terms of the conflict between Achilles and Agamemnon; fate, willingness to accept death, courage, and pettiness are its timeless themes.

Though the myths describe the Trojan War as a thirty-year cycle of preparations, conflict, and homecomings, the chronological period that the *Iliad* covers is actually quite restricted, not more than ninety days in the final year of fighting. Despite its focus on the quarrel of only two of its warriors, both of them Greek, Homer nevertheless conveys the full range of human emotions that prevails in war, even as he provides a vivid portrait of Mycenaean culture. The result is that his *Iliad*, bold and all-encompassing though it is, remains essentially quite limited; that is undoubtedly one of the most distinctive features of Homer's epic. Homer makes the limits of his intentions clear from the outset. His invocation to Caliope, the Muse of epic, specifies that he will sing of Achilles' anger.

Obviously, the anger of Achilles operates on several levels and has far-reaching consequences. On the personal level, it refers to the quarrel between Achilles and Agamemnon for possession of Briseis, a young woman originally given to Achilles by the Achaeans as his prize of honor. Agamemnon, too, had a captive mistress, Chryseis; yet, she was the daughter of a priest of Apollo named Chryses. When Agamemnon haughtily refuses to return Chryseis to her father, Chryses invokes Apollo himself, who sends a plague upon the Achaeans. Once he realizes that the army will be decimated by disease if he takes no action, Agamemnon returns Chryseis to her father, though he simultaneously demands that Achilles surrender Briseis to him as her replacement. Agamemnon fears that the Achaeans will consider him weak if he does not enforce his will upon Achilles in this way, yet the reader perceives only Agamemnon's pettiness and insecurity.

Achilles reviles Agamemnon in the *agora* (assembly) of leaders, yet he surrenders Briseis to him without active resistance. More significantly, Achilles announces his intentions to withdraw his Myrmidons from battle and return with them to Phthia, their home in southern Thessaly. These dramatic announcements made, Achilles throws down the *skeptron* (staff), which gives him the uncontested right to speak, and dashes from the *agora*. This extraordinary behavior at the least implies weakness and apparently cowardice. It seems to complement the pettiness of Agamemnon, but there are clearly other reasons for Achilles' actions.

Thetis, the goddess-mother of Achilles, subsequently appears to comfort her son, who is all too aware of how the Achaeans could interpret his sudden withdrawal and threat to return home. She reviews the alternatives that *moira* (fate) has assigned to him: either to slay Hector, the first of the Trojan warriors, and to be killed at Troy soon thereafter or to live a long and undistinguished life in Phthia, dying there of old age. Achilles well knows these alternatives. His withdrawal, which extends from *Iliad* 1 to *Iliad* 22, represents an essential pause to consider these alternatives at a crucial juncture of his life. Worth noting is the fact that Achilles undertakes no preparations to return home; also, although the war initially goes badly for the Achaeans, to the extent that Agamemnon offers Achilles an impressive series of gifts (including restoration of Briseis) for his return, Achilles' prolonged absence makes relatively little difference overall.

Agamemnon's embassy to secure Achilles' return contains elements of magnanimity and self-interest. Significantly, Agamemnon does not personally entreat Achilles. Instead, he enlists the cunning Odysseus and Diomedes (who would together devise the strategem of the wooden horse), as well as Achilles' old tutor Phoenix. The appeal thus emerges through a combination of clever argument and sage advice, and the collection of gifts (listed in catalog form) is calculated both to impress the Achaeans with Agamemnon's *megalapsyché* (great-heartedness, generosity), as much as it is to force Achilles to make his decision. That is one of several places in which the humanity of the poem emerges. Achilles' concern for his old tutor, seen in his insistence that Phoenix remain overnight rather than attempt to return immediately, shows that he values privileged relationships such as master and student. It has its counterpart in Achilles' relationship to Patroclus, his young protégé in the art of war. This relationship, severed by Patroclus' death, will ultimately provide the impetus that Achilles needs to accept the short but glorious life that *moira* has offered him.

In one sense, all the characters of the *Iliad* recognize the inevitability of *moira* yet remain essentially powerless to change it. The tears of Achilles that precede his mother's appearance are an indication of this human frailty, but so is Hector's meeting with his wife, Andromache, and their infant son, Astyanax. In *Iliad* 6, long before Achilles returns to battle, the Achaeans have advanced to the very walls of Troy. Hector, the bravest of the Trojan warriors, searches for Alexandrus (Paris), whose theft of Helen had been the immediate cause of the war, and finds him in Helen's rooms. His reproaches make Alexandrus recognize his obligations, and Alexandrus takes up his arms to defend the city, but the primary contrast is clear. Andromache recognizes and regretfully accepts the likelihood of her husband's death in battle, but Helen belittles Alexandrus as a sensualist willing to allow others to fight for him. Andromache's fears for Hector correspond to those of the child, Astyanax, who does not recognize his father because of the helmet that he wears. When Hector removes the helmet, the child accepts his father's embrace, and the couple laughs. There, then, is a contrast between pure love and simple sensual attraction as well as between responsibility and weakness.

Even the deities of Olympus display the flaws of their human counterparts. They, too, remain tied to *moira* and are essentially powerless to change it. They, too, govern by *agorai*, and these assemblies inevitably end as inconclusively as those of the human warriors below. The gods and goddesses have taken sides in the war, but these reflect their previous personal antagonisms rather than their concern with humanity. Thetis, for example, does intercede with Zeus for her son Achilles but is aware that doing so will necessarily provoke the jealousy of Hera, Zeus's wife. She must also know that any favor that Zeus grants to Achilles would necessarily be in the context of glory on the battlefield. Ironically, any such benefaction would necessarily hasten her son's death. Just as Agamemnon prevails in the human order, so does Zeus in the divine; yet neither appears able to take meaningful and decisive actions that affect outcomes. The power of both is limited to immediate actions and short-term results.

The peculiar powerlessness of Zeus emerges clearly in the Sarpedon episode, *Iliad* 16. At this point, Patroclus has received Achilles' permission to reenter battle wearing his master's armor. Patroclus experiences his *aristeia* (moment of glory), a series of combats in which he defeats one opponent after another. Sarpedon, a beautiful boy loved by Zeus, is one of those whom *moira* has determined that Patroclus will defeat. Zeus raises the scales of *moira*, watches Sarpedon's weight descend, and realizes that he must accept the young man's death. His resignation to *moira* parallels that of Andromache, even as it underscores the similarity of mortals and immortals.

Though Achilles allows his protégé, Patroclus, to enter battle, he himself remains apart. Patroclus is effectively Achilles' surrogate, however, and his appearance in his master's armor emphasizes this relationship. So devastating is the effect of his presence that the Trojans at first believe Achilles has returned. In one sense that is true, for Patroclus looks very much like Achilles, and the *aristeia* that he enjoys is equivalent to any that his master could have enjoyed. It is also true that once Patroclus has entered battle, the *moira* of Achilles is sealed, for the lives of master and student are tied by the bonds of friendship and obligation. Patroclus dies at the hands of Hector, and while Hector succeeds in claiming the armor of Achilles, the body of Patroclus remains with the Greeks. The announcement of Patroclus' death sends Achilles into a threnody and leads to his construction of an extravagant pyre for the corpse. This development provides the opportunity for another catalog listing the offerings that formed the pyre. Averse as human sacrifice was to Greek sensibilities, the pyre includes young Trojans captured in battle.

Achilles now recognizes that his obligations to Patroclus have forced his return, but he has no armor worthy of the event. Thetis intervenes again, this time to secure armor crafted by the artisan deity Hephaestus, and once again Thetis' intervention hastens her son's *moira*. In effect, the alternatives that had existed in *Iliad* 1 are no longer available. The period of introspection has ended, and Achilles reenters battle knowing that he will kill Hector but equally aware that his own death will follow soon after. When Achilles meets Hector in battle, he is, in effect, encountering an aspect of himself. Hector wears the armor of Achilles, and Achilles has donned the glorious new armor that his mother, Thetis, had secured for him. In killing Hector, especially because Homer has already portrayed that warrior's character so sympathetically, Achilles eliminates his ties to the past and fully accepts the alternative of a short but glorious life. It is his true destiny and, like the armor provided by Thetis, the only *moira* that is appropriate for him.

The humanity that lies behind so much of the bravado in the *Iliad* emerges in the final scene of the poem. Old Priam, King of Troy, comes to Achilles to beg for the return of his son's body. Even though Achilles realizes that Hector had been the immediate cause of his beloved Patroclus' death and that Hector had forced Achilles to accept his own *moira*, he grants Priam's request and declares a truce for ritual mourning and appropriate burial of the dead on both sides. The *Iliad* thus ends in a suspension, rather than a resolution, of events.

ODYSSEY

First compiled: Eighth century B.C.; first codified, early second century B.C.
(English translation, 1616)
Type of work: Epic poem

The return of Odysseus to Ithaca nearly twenty years after his departure for
Troy represents his personal struggle, often against larger forces, to restore the
stability that war had cast aside.

Read at its most basic level, the *Odyssey* recounts Odysseus' struggles to return to
his native island of Ithaca after ten years of fighting at Troy. It appears to be a highly
particularized account of one warrior's struggles and sufferings. No doubt exists that
Odysseus remains the focus; though names of his crew appear at intervals, they collectively constitute a vehicle that gets their master part of the way home, and all of
them die long before their master reaches home. Even the mythic Phaeacians, who
literally place the sleeping hero on his remote western island, remain peculiarly nameless, except for the family that rules them, but Alcinous, Areté, and Nausicaä merely
approve this final phase of the journey. The seafaring Phaeacians themselves suffer
permanent hardship for their good deed: Poseidon landlocks their harbors in retri-
bution for Odysseus' having blinded Polyphemus the Cyclops, the sea-god's monster son.

Once Odysseus finally realizes that the Phaeacians have actually returned him to Ithaca, and not merely abandoned him on a forsaken island, in order to steal the treasure that their king had given to him, the hero proceeds to test everyone he meets,
starting with Eumaeus, his swineherd, and Telemachus, the son whom he had had to
abandon in infancy in order to honor his commitment to fight at Troy. He tests his old
nurse, Eurycleia, who, when she recognizes his scar received in youth during a boar
hunt, appropriately venerates him. He tests his wife, Penelope, who has waited for
Odysseus more than nineteen years, resisting more than a score of much younger
suitors. Her stratagem of weaving and unweaving a funeral shroud for the aging Laërtes, Odysseus' father, allows her to delay choosing a new husband, but it also allows this assortment of brash young men with decidedly uncourtly manners to move
into Odysseus' great hall and deplete the wealth of his household through their cease-
less banquets and irresponsible behavior. This irresponsibility extends to the moral
sphere as well, for the suitors, in short order, corrupt the handmaidens of the household.

True to form, Odysseus arrives disguised as a beggar, tests the suitors, finds that
they have abused the laws of hospitality, and kills them all. He ratifies this action by
pronouncing moral judgment on the handmaidens, as well. Once they have cleaned
the great hall of the suitors' blood, he orders the handmaidens to be collectively

hanged in the courtyard. While this mass slaughter is in progress, Phemius, the court rhapsode, is ordered by Odysseus to sing as loudly as possible to the loudest of musical accompaniments in order to cover the screams of those being killed. Furthermore, Odysseus enlists both Telemachus and Eumaeus as accomplices. The first thing that Odysseus and his nineteen-year-old son do together is, in effect, commit mass murder, then retreat to the suburban vineyard at which old Laërtes is awaiting the arrival of the fathers of the suitors, who are avid for vengeance. Another slaughter is about to begin when the goddess Athene, the mentor of Odysseus from the outset, calls a halt, and the *Odyssey* ends.

Seen in this way, Odysseus does not appear to be a very nice man, and certainly not very heroic. Even so, his epithet *polutropos* (many-wiled) implies that there is more to his character, and correspondingly to Homer's poem, than this rather negative reading implies. Indeed, virtually every action of Odysseus admits of positive and negative interpretations. In this respect, Homer's Odysseus mirrors humanity at large. To assess Odysseus positively, it is necessary to consider external particulars more carefully than has been done above. It is also important to bear in mind details that Homer assumes his audience knows and therefore does not, given the limited parameters of epic poetry, feel particularly obligated to supply.

First of all, Odysseus had never wanted to fight at Troy. He had been perfectly happy as king of his rural island with his young wife, Penelope, and infant son, Telemachus. He had even feigned madness by sowing his fields with salt instead of seed in order to escape his obligation to restore Helen to Menelaus. Canny Agamemnon, brother of Menelaus, recognized immediately, however, that this was a typical Odyssean ruse. To test Odysseus' sanity, Agamemnon placed Telemachus in the path of the plowshare, and of course Odysseus had to turn the plow aside to spare the "seed" that he prized most of all: his son and heir. Homer knows that his audience will recognize immediately the disparate values of Odysseus and Agamemnon, for the latter would be willing to sacrifice his own daughter Iphigeneia in order to ensure a favorable wind for the departing armada. Agamemnon would, of course, pay the price for his moral lapse. Having escaped ten years of war with barely a scratch, his wife Clytemnestra, ironically Helen's half sister, would murder him on the day of his return as he emerged from his bath.

Placing these sets of events beside each other shows the essential difference between Odysseus and Agamemnon. Odysseus privileges the values of home and family; Agamemnon quickly recognizes affronts to the honor of his clan but is willing to avenge these at the cost of his immediate family. Yet it is clear that the Trojan War has no positive effect on Odysseus. It forces him to place domestic considerations to one side and use his wiles in order to survive. Odysseus is, above all, a survivor, and his stratagems of the theft of the Palladium (the great statue of Athene in the citadel of Troy) and of the wooden horse ultimately bring victory to the Greek forces. Without them, the war would have continued even beyond the ten years specified in the myths.

That is the knowledge that Homer assumes, and the first item that he includes among Odysseus' postwar exploits is that, after leaving Troy, Odysseus and his crew sack a town, that of the Cicones, who had been Trojan allies. Like many warriors, Odysseus has trouble laying aside the ways of war. What would have been acceptable behavior in the context of war becomes unacceptable afterward, yet Odysseus cannot recognize this fact. When he and his men arrive on the island of the Cyclopes, the first thing that he and his men do is raid the stores of the Cyclops Polyphemus. Polyphemus is hardly a sympathetic creature. He is a giant, nonphiloprogenitive son of the sea-god Poseidon; like all Cyclopes, he has in the middle of his forehead an eye the size of a wheel. This heterotopic eye effectively makes Polyphemus a symbol of irrationality, corresponding to the displaced moral environment in which Odysseus has functioned in the years since leaving Ithaca.

As Odysseus had eaten the food of Polyphemus without leave to do so, it is justifiable by the irrational standards of Polyphemus for the Cyclops to eat some of Odysseus' crew, and he does so. When Polyphemus asks to know the name of their leader, Odysseus appropriately calls himself *Outis* (nobody), for he has, in effect, lost the dignity of a name derived from the infinitive *odyssasthai* (to be angry, wrathful). Wrath implies righteousness and reasonable cause, but the immediate history of Odysseus has allowed little chance for righteous anger. Once he blinds the Cyclops, however, Odysseus has neutralized one symbol of unreason in his world. When he follows this act by devising his crew's escape from the Cyclops' cave, strapping them to the undersides of Polyphemus' sheep, he declares not only his name but also his patronymic and epithet to the monster: He is Odysseus, son of Laërtes, the sacker of cities.

Ironically, Odysseus' bold insistence on his proper identity allows the anger of Poseidon to find its mark. Still, Odysseus has to identify himself fully in this way, even as he and his crew have to accept the consequences: long and hard struggles for the master and death by attrition for the crew. The crew, like the mass of humanity, satisfies itself with apparently easy courses of action and thereby defines life as existence that precedes death. As Homer kills them, singly and in groups, his audience wastes no mourning upon them; nor does Odysseus.

Though the crew appears largely as a collective entity, Homer makes clear that its individuals freely choose their doom. For example, the Lotos Eaters offer Odysseus' crew lotos-fruit, which, when eaten, causes them to forget home and enjoy the earthly paradise of the present in which they find themselves. Forgetting one's past is tantamount to abandoning the cause that produced the present and the impetus that impels the future. It is apparently easier to live in the eternal present, but doing so robs life's journey of reason. The crew members who eat the lotos-fruit accept a form of the irrational with the excuse of world-weariness, but the drug culture of the Lotos Eaters is merely death in life.

When Odysseus' crew taste the potion of the witch Circe, she transforms them into swine. Their almost unanimous collective identity had at least been human. After their transformation, they lose rationality, the highest human faculty; that happens because they had made insufficient use of the faculty. Hermes, Zeus's messenger but also, fittingly, the guide to the Underworld, warns Odysseus' to prepare himself for

Circe's magic by applying the *molü* (wild garlic), which he finds at his feet, before encountering the witch. Hermes also admonishes Odysseus to extract a promise from Circe not to emasculate him. In both respects, Hermes' advice focuses on the weed to preserve a sense of personal identity and power. The herbal drug is as secondary in importance to the state of mind that it produces as the lotos-fruit had been in the Lotos Eaters episode. What is important is its obvious availability and the self-assurance that follows its use. It is worth noting that Odysseus temporarily loses sight of his personal mission to continue life's journey, for he remains on Circe's island until pressured to resume his adventures. In doing so, he comes dangerously close to accepting the paradisiacal present, essentially what the Lotos Eaters had offered. This lapse from obligation characterizes even the most heroic, however, and it underscores the fact that life's journey is nonlinear; it rather assumes varying degrees of circularity that resemble the past, which spring from it but always differ. Life returns to its origins at its end, though the origins themselves appear other than what they had been.

Perhaps the Aeolus episode emphasizes the difference between Odysseus and his crew most profoundly of all. The king of the winds entrusts Odysseus with a sack filled with all winds, which could conceivably oppose Odysseus' homeward journey. Aeolus appears to offer Odysseus an easy passage to his destination, but Odysseus must stay at the tiller nine days and nine nights, since he needs all his faculties to maintain his course. Within sight of Ithaca, Odysseus falls asleep, and this temporary loss of reason is enough to allow the jealousy and curiosity of his crew to surface. The crew resents the universal recognition that Odysseus receives and opens the sack thinking that it contains some special treasure that Odysseus does not wish to share. Immediately, the hostile winds blow Odysseus and his crew away from his homeland, and when the Ithacans reappear before Aeolus to request a second sack, the king refuses. This refusal is only right: Any benefaction requires personal responsibility for its proper use. Absent this responsibility, it becomes an imposed control that predetermines an outcome. Reaching the goal of the journey ultimately requires the skill of the traveler, not counting on the good fortune of meeting one's personal equivalent of a sympathetic Aeolus to smooth the passage.

Even as the Phaeacians are returning Odysseus to Ithaca, Telemachus, at the instructions of Athene disguised as the traveler Mentes, is about to set sail in search of Odysseus' whereabouts. The first four books of Homer's poem thus belong firmly to Telemachus and represent the young man's personal odyssey. Telemachus has never known his father, has seen only the aberrant, extended family that the arrival of the suitors has caused. His adventures in *Odyssey* 1 to 4 show him one family that respects moral values (that of Nestor of Pylos) and one that is entirely secular (that of Menelaus and Helen). Menelaus and Helen appear content, though the unease of their relationship is plain. It is only through an anodyne, which Helen adds to their wine, that they maintain this fragile equilibrium. They, like the crew members who had succumbed to the lotos-fruit or Circe's potion, have chosen existence rather than life. Telemachus also refines his understanding of the laws of hospitality through gifts mutually offered and tactfully refused, as well as through his sagacity, the polytropic quality that characterizes his father. He manages to elude the suitors, who plan his assassination upon his return, and returns to the other side of his island and to the hut of Eumaeus, to be reunited with Odysseus and plot the extermination of the suitors.

Summary

One could question whether even Odysseus and Penelope could recapture the same degree of happiness that they had enjoyed before the Trojan War and before the arrival of the suitors. Alfred, Lord Tennyson, in his poem "Ulysses," strongly implies his hero's disgust both with the Ithacans and with an "aged wife." Nikos Kazantzakis, in his *Odysseia* (1938; *The Odyssey: A Modern Sequel*, 1958), even more definitely describes Odysseus' need to face death in the midst of an active life. Happiness takes the form of completing the heroic mission, and Homer's Odysseus and Achilles do this. For Achilles, completing the mission consists in the willingness to accept the destiny of a brief but glorious life, the only kind appropriate to his heroic nature. The life of Odysseus is longer, perhaps even more demanding because of its challenges, but no less worthy.

Bibliography

Bowra, C. M. *Homer.* Oxford, England: Oxford University Press, 1972.

Edwards, Mark W. *Homer: Poet of the "Iliad."* Baltimore: The Johns Hopkins University Press, 1962.

Kirk, G. S. *Songs of Homer.* Oxford, England: Oxford University Press, 1962.

Page, Denys. *History and the Homeric "Iliad."* Berkeley: University of California Press, 1972.

Parry, Milman. *The Making of Homeric Verse: The Collected Papers of Milman Parry.* Oxford, England: Oxford University Press, 1971.

Pucci, Pietro. *Odysseus Polutropos: Intertextual Readings in the "Odyssey" and the "Iliad."* Ithaca, N.Y.: Cornell University Press, 1987.

Seymour, Thomas Day. *Life in the Homeric Age.* New Haven, Conn.: Yale University Press, 1907. Reprint. New York: Biblo & Tannen, 1963.

Silk, Michael. *Homer: The "Iliad."* New York: Cambridge University Press, 1987.

Whitman, Cedric. *Homer and the Heroic Tradition.* Cambridge, Mass.: Harvard University Press, 1958.

Robert J. Forman

GERARD MANLEY HOPKINS

Born: Stratford, Essex, England
July 28, 1844
Died: Dublin, Ireland
June 8, 1889

Principal Literary Achievement

Hopkins' vigorous poetry was first published after his death, when he became a major influence on modern poetry.

Biography

Gerard Manley Hopkins was born on July 28, 1844, in Stratford, a suburb of London, England. His father, Manley, was a devout Anglican, a well-educated and successful author of marine handbooks and some poetry. At Oxford, Hopkins studied Greek and Latin and wrote poetry on nature and religious subjects. Among his teachers was Walter Pater, whose aesthetic and social theories influenced Hopkins; Hopkins' friends included Robert Bridges, the poet who encouraged him throughout his career and eventually published his poems.

At Oxford, Hopkins came under the influence of the Oxford Movement to revitalize Anglicanism by returning to its Roman Catholic roots, and this influence led him to John Henry Newman. Hopkins read Newman's autobiographical *Apologia pro Vita Sua* (1864), which described his conversion to Catholicism. Conversations with Newman led Hopkins to convert in 1866. Hopkins' conversion radically changed his life, alienating him from his family and leading him into a religious vocation. After completing his B.A. at Oxford with honors, Hopkins decided to take holy orders as a Jesuit. To mark this change in his life, he burned copies of his poems, though he had asked Bridges to save the best of his work. For seven years, he wrote no poems, and for the rest of his life he remained unwilling to publish except when this was approved by his superiors in the Church.

Though Hopkins eventually resumed writing poetry, most of his energies from 1868 until his death were devoted to teaching, study, and, for a time, the duties of a parish priest. Having decided to seek ordination, he studied theology as he taught at various Catholic institutions. One of these was St. Beuno's in Wales, where he learned Welsh, which influenced his uses of alliteration and word arrangement in his poems. During

900

this period, he produced his great ode "The Wreck of the *Deutschland*," a beautiful but forbiddingly difficult consideration of the drowning of five exiled Franciscan nuns. Ordained in 1877, he served as teacher and as priest in England and Scotland and served several terms in slum parishes in towns such as Liverpool and Glasgow.

During the last five years of his life, he was professor of Greek and Latin at University College, Dublin. Though the position was an honor, the work was very demanding, and he was unhappy away from England.

He died from typhoid fever on June 8, 1889, in Dublin, Ireland.

In 1918, when Bridges published the poems that he had lovingly saved as his friend sent them to him, contemporary writers immediately recognized that Hopkins was a major new voice in poetry. Even though he had been dead for twenty-nine years, his innovations in form and style impressed the early moderns such as William Butler Yeats, W. H. Auden, and T. S. Eliot as refreshingly new.

Analysis

Hopkins is, above all, a Christian poet. He is also a difficult poet, who in his best work produced a density of diction and experimented with syntax, rhythm, and sounds in ways that can daunt an inexperienced reader. In fact, however, the difficulties of language and structure in his poems are not so great as they may seem at first. With a dictionary, patience, and a little imagination, any reasonably mature reader can make sense of Hopkins' unusual word choices and arrangements.

The more serious difficulty of Hopkins is his Christian point of view. While some forms of Christianity continue to hold great popular appeal, the number of readers who understand and appreciate traditional Christian doctrines has continued to decline since Hopkins' death. Most modern readers, even those who are practicing Christians, probably will need to use a commentary or reader's guide in order to make sense of Hopkins' uses of Christian scripture and doctrine.

An overview of Christian belief is helpful in order to understand the central concept of his poetic theory, "inscape." Traditional Christians believe that a single perfect and loving God, usually envisioned as a father, created the universe and all life. He made humankind with free will, which humankind then asserted against God, opening a division between humanity and God, called sin, that humanity could not heal by itself. This rebellion is called "the fall of man." God desires a communion, or intimate spiritual relation, with humanity that remains impossible as long as humans feel separated from God.

To make this communion possible and heal the division, God descended to earth in human form. He was born as Jesus Christ of Nazareth to Hebrew parents, Mary and Joseph, in the first year of the modern calendar. Jesus lived a short life as a holy man, performing miracles and preaching an ethic of brotherhood and love on the grounds that God required it and that each individual possessed an immortal soul that connected that person with God. Then Jesus was accused of a variety of crimes and was executed on a cross near Jerusalem. Three days after his death, he was resurrected and appeared to a number of people in his physical body. Forty days later, he ascended into the realm of God the Father and is expected by Christians to return at an undefined future date. At that time, he is expected to make judgments about all human souls that have ever lived to determine the ultimate quality of their afterlives.

Ten days after the ascension of Jesus, now celebrated at Pentecost, a new aspect of God entered into the world, a spiritual being called the Holy Spirit, that is said to flow through those who accept as true the story of Jesus and who work at conforming their wills to his teachings. The original division from God that humanity initiated is healed by God, who through Jesus Christ and the Holy Spirit reaches out to humanity with offers of communion. Though traditional Christian doctrine contains many more ideas and images and though many of these are disputed in various sects, most Christians agree on this central narrative.

Hopkins' literary models and mentors were Romantics such as John Keats and Walter Pater. This background disposed Hopkins to view nature sacramentally, as a kind of book upon which the messages of divinity were addressed to mankind. Romantic pantheism was not, however, consistent with Christian theology. In the theology of the medieval philosopher John Duns Scotus, Hopkins found ideas that helped him to resolve his vivid experiences of divinity in nature with Christian theology. From this thinking, the idea of "inscape" emerges.

Literary critics have differed considerably about the nature of inscape. Hopkins seems to have concluded that every object in the universe had a central organizing principle that could be called its identity. This spirit of the object was not a simple thing but a dynamic principle, the actuating core of its identity or being, and Hopkins called it the inscape of the object. Human beings are capable of recognizing the inscapes of other people and of objects. When they do so, they experience "instress," which can be described as a feeling of communion with the "soul" of the object. When one experiences instress, one finds Christ in the object, the imprint of God the creator upon His creation. Many of Hopkins' poems are about the experience of instress, the discovering of inscape, and the momentary union with God through Christ in the contemplation of natural objects. This set of ideas justifies critics in labeling Hopkins a Christian Romantic poet.

GOD'S GRANDEUR

First published: 1918
Type of work: Poem

> The poet reflects on the persistent human failure to see God's presence in nature.

Hopkins' ideas of inscape and instress seem to imply that every object in creation has something like a soul, that is, a power that points toward its divine creator. He begins "God's Grandeur," composed in 1877, with the assertion that the world as a whole has this inscape: "The world is charged with the grandeur of God." Though several senses of the word "charge" may be relevant in this statement, the primary sense seems to be of electric force. God is like an electric charge present in the world. This image is continued in the statement that this divine force "will flame out." While conveying the idea of a lightning strike implicit in the image of an electrical charge, this new image also suggests the Pentecostal tongue of flame, which introduces one of the aspects of God's presence in the world as the Holy Spirit, the idea with which the poet ends. Hopkins extends this idea into that of blinding light, another familiar biblical image associated with God, when he says that the flaming out of the grandeur of God is "like the shining of shook foil." In a letter, Hopkins said that he was thinking of gold foil, which "gives off broad glares like sheet lightning and . . . owing to its zigzag dints and creasings and network of small many cornered facets, a sort of fork lightning too." Other senses of foil may also enrich this image—for example, the idea of a sword, with its suggestions of challenge and judgment. The next image compares the gathering of the force of God in nature to the way oil gathers in a container as seeds or olives are crushed.

Having asserted the presence, greatness, and force of divine power in nature, the poet poses the main question: "Why do men then now not reck his rod?" He asks why, given the visible power of God in nature, people fail to see it and to show regard for God. The phrase "reck his rod," which may seem archaic and needlessly difficult, like the entire grammatical arrangement of the question, nevertheless is carefully chosen. "Rod" seems mainly to refer to the scepter, symbolic of power to judge, that points to and rhymes with God; but rods are also often thought of as instruments of punishment. "Reck" is a little used and archaic term, meaning to regard or care for, and both meanings are relevant here. It is also however, related to words such as "recognize" and "reckoning," with their various connotations. Such meanings amplify the question in several ways. For example, these ideas remind readers that recognizing the power of God in the world leads to knowledge (reckoning in the sense of navigation) about the purpose of one's life.

As this look at the first quatrain of the sonnet demonstrates, one characteristic of Hopkins' poetry is a density of diction that allows the reader to pursue individual word choices into areas of meaning that nearly always enrich the depth and suggestiveness of the poem. Hopkins chooses words and images that reverberate deeply. Even though the above analysis may seem to some readers to have "overread" the first four lines, professional readers typically find much more of interest to say about them simply on the basis of word choice and images, and even more when they consider aspects of rhythm, sound, and grammar.

The second quatrain of the octave (or first eight lines) answers the question of the first quatrain. The reason people do not honor God as they should is that they are unaware of God's grandeur. The poet says that generations have walked the earth, searing or burning it for business purposes, blearing or making it difficult to see and smearing it or making it less visible with work of all kinds. It is a complex idea that has at least two meanings. First, the world itself is altered by human labor so that it reveals God's grandeur less clearly and directly. Second, however, the processes of trade and labor alter human perception, so that people are less attuned to seeing the inscapes of nature. The poet repeats this idea in the last two lines of the octave, where he says that nature is smudged by man and smells like man and that, because people wear clothing, they are less likely to perceive nature directly.

Having asserted that God's power in nature is brilliantly if sporadically visible but that human labor obscures its visibility and weakens the human ability to perceive it, the poet turns to the miracle of Spirit's continuing presence in the sestet, the last six lines of the sonnet. The poet says that even though labor blinds people to it, God's grandeur persists. At the center of every natural thing is a freshness that the poet can see. This realization is just as true as that the darkness of sunset does not presage eternal darkness but rather a new dawning. These observations mean that the Holy Ghost is present, that it continually renews the "bent" or misshapen world, just as a bird—a typical image of the Holy Spirit—broods over its nest, pouring energy into its egg (the world) so that it will hatch to reveal a new bird, the double of itself within.

The richness and depth of "God's Grandeur" is apparent in Hopkins' use of diction, imagery, and metaphor, but these techniques do not exhaust the art of the poem. One can learn a lot more about it by studying how Hopkins arranges alliteration, meter, and rhyme. For example, one of the astonishing features of this poem is that while it is especially rich in language, it is very confined in form. Not only did Hopkins use one of the most restrictive forms in English poetry, the sonnet, but he chose one of the most difficult forms of the sonnet, the Italian, which uses only four rhyming sounds at the ends of its lines. Such a choice seems quite appropriate for a poem about how the infinite eneregy of God is constrained in the physical form of the world.

THE WINDHOVER

First published: 1918
Type of work: Poem

The poet sees Christ represented in a falcon's flight and dive in pursuit of its prey.

Dedicated "To Christ Our Lord," this sonnet in the Italian form was composed in 1877. While diction, image, and metaphor are central technical elements in the poem's success and meaning, "The Windhover" nicely illustrates Hopkins' more radical experiments with meter and sound.

In the octave, the poet says that while walking in the morning he saw and admired a falcon in its flight. In the first three lines of the sestet, he recounts a visionary experience, his narration shifting into present tense. The vision comes upon him as he watches the bird dive in pursuit of its prey, and several levels of meaning "burst" forth from this motion. The vision begins with the word "buckle." When the bird buckles, it collapses, pulling back its wings for a swift, controlled descent. Yet this verb also means to put on armor, to prepare for action as in a battle, and it also means to fasten together, as in buckling the ends of a belt. Furthermore, collapse can mean at least two things, the drawing in of the bird as it dives or the folding up of one who experiences pain or momentary weakness. These are only a few of the many interesting meanings critics have found in nineteenth century uses of this word.

Fire bursts forth from the bird when it dives, and this fire makes the bird "a billion/ Times told lovelier, more dangerous." This vision leads the poet to address the bird: "Oh my chevalier!" A chevalier is a knight, one who serves a king in battle and who is often represented as rescuing the weak and oppressed from evils both natural and supernatural. One key suggestion of the knight image is the idea of putting on armor to enter into a battle. This image connects with the divinity to whom the poem is addressed, Christ. The knight putting on his armor is parallel to Christ's incarnation, the son of God entering a physical body to become Jesus, thereby entering the world to do battle with human sin.

This suggestion of incarnation is one way in which God descends to human beings and in which God is like the falcon that descends to grasp its prey, except that God's intention is benevolent. For this reason, among others, the falcon's dive may be seen as a billion times lovelier, but why a billion times more dangerous? Perhaps the poet there reflects upon the human experience of grace. Trapped in sin as humans are, in the smudged world of "God's Grandeur," they are unlikely to welcome the radical changes that God's "dive" requires of them. This negative aspect of grace is reflected in another descent suggested by the bird's dive, the descent into the grave, by which Christ's incarnation is completed as he shares death with humankind and by means of which Christ's "prey" is figuratively snatched up from the earth, as Christ makes possible the human ascent into heaven that completes the act of divine grace. Just as the bird will rise after its dive, so Christ arose after his death, and humans who accept this graciousness may rise after their deaths.

In the last three lines of the poem, the poet asserts almost humorously that his vision really is not a wonder. After all, a mere plough shines as a result of its plowing the earth, and almost burnt coals, when they fall and break, flash forth red-gold fire. While he may appear to retreat from the intensity of the vision of the diving bird, he cannot really reduce his own or the reader's impression of the profundity of that vision. Though he chooses an ordinary plough as his next image of comparison, that image evokes the idea of a descent into the earth in order to prepare a new resurrection, and its shining evokes the fire that broke from the windhover. When he turns to the burnt coals, he cannot avoid an exclamation of affection—"ah, my dear"—addressed to the bird and to Christ as they reveal themselves in the coals. In breaking to reveal flames within, they remind him of the breaking of Jesus' body on the cross, the fall that sent forth the gleams of resurrection and Pentecost.

When Hopkins composed "The Windhover," he had been thinking about altering the rhythmic patterns of contemporary poetry. In Old English poetry he noticed metrical arrangements that he came to call "sprung rhythm." Much of the poetry written before Hopkins in modern English made use of fairly strict syllable counts to determine basic poetic forms. For example, a sonnet would contain as close as possible to 140 syllables, fourteen lines of ten syllables each, and the rhythm of each line would be made of five iambic feet (iambic pentameter), as can be illustrated in the first line of this poem: "I caught this morning morning's minion, king-" (the accented syllables are marked). Though it does not make grammatical sense presented this way, this line shows the pattern of iambic pentameter, five pairs of syllables, the first in each pair unaccented, the second in each pair accented. In "The Windhover," there are no more lines that follow strict iambic pentameter so closely. Yet a carefully studied and prepared oral reading will reveal that each line has five heavily accented syllables. For the main rhythmic pattern of Hopkins' poem, unaccented syllables are not counted, though how they are accented is important to preparing a performance of the poem. Sometimes, as in line 12, Hopkins marked some syllables he intended to have accented; otherwise, the reader must make judgments about which five syllables should receive the major accents in reading. The result of careful thought and analysis, however, is usually an exciting and provocative performance of the poem.

That Hopkins gave so much attention to his rhythm and that he modified, without abandoning, the basic sonnet form underscores the degree to which he thought of his poems as intended for oral performance. When one studies the poem, it becomes clear that one of the many functions of Hopkins' frequent alliteration, especially the repetition of consonant sounds, is to control or at least suggest where accents should fall within the lines.

It is sometimes difficult to believe that a poet would give so much attention to what might seem the minor aspects of a poem, such as its rhythm and sounds. Yet even if one did not have the evidence of his correspondence, the sheer quantity of alliteration and the stress marks in this poem would indicate that Hopkins must have thought about these things. Hopkins not only thought deeply about how he would organize the sound and rhythm in his poems but also worked to integrate those aspects with the overall meaning and experience he hoped to convey. This effort can be seen, for example, in the opening of the poem, where no line has an endstop—a final punctuation mark—until the exclamation point after "ecstasy." To perform this opening is to realize that it is designed to make speaker and listener feel breathless and, thereby, to convey the wonder of seeing and of almost feeling the flight of the windhover. That this breathless line ends in ecstasy suggests even deeper thought in Hopkins, whether intuitive or conscious, which may have whispered to him that, in a poem about a visionary experience, a good first place to pause is on the word "ecstasy."

HURRAHING IN HARVEST

First published: 1918
Type of work: Poem

In this Italian sonnet of 1877, the speaker is so moved by his spiritual vision of the harvest season that he leaps into the air.

Though "Hurrahing in Harvest" is just as rich in diction and ideas as "God's Grandeur" and "The Windhover," it may seem more accessible to beginning readers of Hopkins because the poet's vision and actions are simpler. In the first quatrain, he observes with wonder the beauties of the harvest season, the piling of the grain for threshing, and the wind and clouds of the sky. On both levels, he sees harvest, for he finds in the clouds images of winnowing grain. In the second quatrain, he recounts his experience of walking through such a landscape. As he walks, his heart and his eyes glean, or gather, the remains of the harvest, and what they glean is Christ, "our saviour." Gathering up visions of Christ in the landscape, he sees Christ as a lover speaking to him through the landscape: "What lips yet gave you a/ Rapturous love's greeting of realer, of rounder replies?" Rapturous love, however, points beyond a comparison of Christ with a lover, for "rapture" shares the root meaning of "raptor," a bird of prey like the windhover, that seizes its prey and carries it into the sky. For a Christian, the Rapture is that moment when the soul is caught up into Heaven for the final judgment. Christ as rapturous lover is, therefore, an apt image of Christ the savior and the judge, who in the variety of ways observed in "The Windhover" offers to bring the faithful soul out of sin and into the bosom of God.

In the sestet, the poet sees the autumn hills beneath the rich blue sky as Christ's shoulders, capable of lifting the world like a strong but sweet-smelling stallion. He reflects that this world is always present, waiting to speak in this way to a beholder. When the beholder, in this case the poet, appears, then his heart grows bold wings with tremendous strength to hurl the earth away from his feet. In this way, the heart becomes the raptor, drawing the body with it heavenward, toward God.

Though this poem is clearly typical of Hopkins in its themes and technique, it also can remind readers vividly of seventeenth century Metaphysical poetry, where the figure of Christ as a lover is not uncommon, as in John Donne's "Batter My Heart, Three-Person'd God." Like his American contemporary, Emily Dickinson, Hopkins was drawn to Metaphysical conceits, those sometimes shocking comparisons, so delightful in Donne's poetry, that are capable of moving and astonishing effects. Such an effect occurs when the wings of the poet's heart carry his body into the air, wittily and somewhat humorously suggesting his imminent ascension into Heaven.

I WAKE AND FEEL THE FELL OF DARK, NOT DAY

First published: 1918
Type of work: Poem

The poet meditates upon his alienation from God and his self-imprisonment.

In 1885, during the difficult years of exile in Dublin and demanding labor as a professor, Hopkins wrote a series of poems that Robert Bridges called "the terrible sonnets." In most of these poems, Hopkins explores the theme of exile from God, the alienation and doubt that all believers feel at times. These feelings tend to lead to self-loathing, because it is the human self that stands as a barrier to permanent union with God.

In "I Wake and Feel the Fell of Dark, Not Day," the poet awakens in the dark, implicitly awaiting the light of day. The word "fell," however, indicates that this is more than a literal awakening in the night. A fell is the hide, or pelt, of a dead animal. His feeling the fell of dark suggests imprisonment in an animal body and the desire to escape into a "body of light."

In the rest of the first quatrain of this modified Italian sonnet, the poet addresses his heart, lamenting the "black hours" they have spent, the terrors they have experienced together in this seemingly endless night. In the second quatrain, he says that he has been speaking metaphorically, that where he has said hours he means years. In fact, his whole life has been lived in the dark of separation from God, yearning for the light of final union. All of his prayers to God have been like dead letters, sent to one who is distant. Dead letters are not delivered and may be returned to the sender. This comparison emphasizes the speaker's despairing sense of entrapment. Unable to communicate with God, he is caught forever in painful communion with his suffering heart.

In the sestet, he says that he understands that God has deliberately given him this experience of exile, though here he says little about why this is the case. In another dark sonnet, "Carrion Comfort," he suggests that God's purpose may be to strengthen or purify him in some way, but in this poem he concentrates on the experience of being made to experience the bitterness of his own flesh.

Though his imagery repeatedly suggests loathing of his physical body, it is not clear that it is the body itself that he hates. Rather, what hurts him is that being in a body prevents his union with God. He says "Selfyeast of spirit a dull dough sours." This line seems to say that his body is like dough and his spirit like yeast. That yeast should raise and "ennoble" the dough, but instead it sours it. The problem seems, therefore, not to be in the body or the dough but in the isolation of the spirit, the "selfyeast." What is needed is a renewing influx of the Holy Spirit as it is presented in "God's Grandeur." Perhaps a brilliant visionary experience as in "The Windhover" or "Hurrahing in Harvest" would seem a consoling reply to one of his dead letters, a glimpse of light that would promise a greater light to come. Nothing of that kind, however, comes to the speaker in this poem. His final reflection is that this experience is like that of the damned, except that for them it is worse. He does not explain why at the end of the poem, but the beginning has made this clear: because the damned have no expectation of the day; they have no faith and, therefore, no hope.

Summary

Gerard Manley Hopkins was a brilliant Christian poet. He produced a small number of finely crafted and moving poems in his lifetime but, for religious reasons, made little effort to publish them. When they were published twenty-nine years after his death by Robert Bridges, Hopkins quickly took a place of honor among modern poets. His radical and difficult experimentation with diction, sound, syntax, and rhythm made him especially attractive to early twentieth century poets. Though his poems seem difficult, they are accessible to patient readers who are willing to inform themselves about Hopkins' traditional Christian beliefs. Indeed, his poems repay repeated study with new discoveries that make them seem increasingly rich and moving as one comes to know them better.

Bibliography

Bender, Todd K. *Gerard Manley Hopkins: The Classical Background and Critical Reception of His Work.* Baltimore: The Johns Hopkins University Press, 1966.

Bump, Jerome. *Gerard Manley Hopkins.* Boston: Twayne, 1982.

Hartman, Geoffrey H., ed. *Hopkins: A Collection of Critical Essays.* Englewood Cliffs, N.J.: Prentice-Hall, 1966.

Hopkins, Gerard Manley. *The Correspondence of Gerard Manley Hopkins and Richard Watson Dixon.* Edited by C. C. Abbott. New York: Oxford University Press, 1955.

_____. *Further Letters of Gerard Manley Hopkins.* Enlarged 2d ed. Edited by C. C. Abbott. New York: Oxford University Press, 1956.

_____. *The Letters of Gerard Manley Hopkins to Robert Bridges.* Edited by C. C. Abbott. New York: Oxford University Press, 1970.

MacKenzie, Norman. *A Reader's Guide to Gerard Manley Hopkins.* Ithaca, N.Y.: Cornell University Press, 1981.

Mariani, Paul. *A Commentary on the Complete Poems of Gerard Manley Hopkins.* Ithaca, N.Y.: Cornell University Press, 1970.

Sulloway, Alison, G., ed. *Critical Essays on Gerard Manley Hopkins.* Boston: G. K. Hall, 1990.

Terry Heller

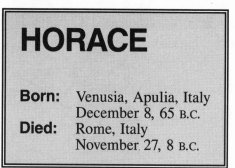

HORACE

Born: Venusia, Apulia, Italy
December 8, 65 B.C.
Died: Rome, Italy
November 27, 8 B.C.

Principal Literary Achievement

One of the most important authors of Rome's Golden Age, Horace excelled at both satire and lyric poetry, while adapting the form and rhythms of Greek verse to the Latin language.

Biography

Horace was born Quintus Horatius Flaccus on December 8, 65 B.C., in the small Apulian town of Venusia in southeastern Italy. The date is recorded in the brief profile of Horace attributed to Suetonius, which appears as an appendix to some of Horace's early manuscripts. The place is recorded in Horace's own *Satires* (35 B.C., 30 B.C.; English translation, 1567), where the author frequently provides information about his own life. These two sources, Suetonius and Horace himself, permit the biography of Horace to be reconstructed in greater detail than is possible for most other ancient figures.

Horace's father was a freedman (*libertinus*, a slave who had bought his freedom), who made his living by collecting money at auctions. Horace was born, therefore, into nearly the lowest ranks of Roman society. Yet Horace's father was thrifty and managed to save enough money to buy a small farm in Venusia. Moreover, he wanted his son to have greater opportunities than his own. That meant that the young Horace needed to receive a better education than could be obtained in the local schools of Apulia. For this reason, Horace's father moved the family to Rome and enrolled his son in a school attended by the children of equestrians and senators. There Horace's education consisted largely of memorizing passages of early Latin poetry under the stern tutelage of Lucius Orbilius Pupillus. Later in his life, Horace would question the lavish praise that many of his contemporaries heaped upon the early Roman poets. Horace came to believe that much of the language used by authors such as Livius Andronicus and Gaius Lucilius was awkward and uninspired.

Horace's mother is never mentioned in his works. It seems likely, therefore, that she died early in Horace's life, perhaps even before the family left Venusia. On the other hand, the relationship between Horace and his father seems to have been quite

911

close. Lacking money for a servant, Horace's father escorted the boy to school himself. Moreover, in one of his *Satires*, Horace describes the practical lessons in morality that his father gave him during these years: Horace's father would point out examples of Roman citizens whose way of life was noble and whom Horace was to imitate. He would also mention those whose character was base and whose habits the boy was to avoid. This sort of "education by example," important to both Roman satirists and historians, was to be a major stylistic technique in Horace's own *Satires* and *Epistles* (c. 20 B.C., 13 B.C.).

When Horace was about twenty years old, he went to Athens to pursue an advanced course of study. While in Greece, Horace became absorbed with the political intrigues that were occurring throughout the Roman world at the end of the Republican period. He abandoned his studies during the autumn of 44 B.C. and joined the forces of Marcus Junius Brutus, one of the principal assassins of Julius Caesar. After Brutus was defeated by Octavian (later the Emperor Augustus) and Marc Antony at the Battle of Philippi in 42 B.C., Horace returned to Rome. There he found that his father had died and that his family's small farm in Apulia had been confiscated to provide land for Octavian's veterans.

As a result, Horace became a legal secretary or treasury clerk in order to support himself. In his spare time, he began to write verse. It was during this period of his life that some of the *Epodes* (c. 30 B.C.) and *Satires* were written. Horace's poetry began to be circulated among other members of the Roman intelligentsia, and, in this way, Horace met the poet Vergil. Vergil's literary patron was the wealthy Etruscan aristocrat Gaius Maecenas, and, through Vergil, Horace secured his own introduction to Maecenas. In 38 B.C., Maecenas became Horace's patron as well, freeing the poet from financial concerns for the rest of his life. Moving in such elevated literary and political circles, Horace met a number of the most influential persons of his day. He became reconciled with Octavian and appears to have been present at the conference that led to the Treaty of Tarentum in 37 B.C.

After Vergil died in 19 B.C., Horace virtually became the poet laureate of Rome. In 17 B.C., ten years after Octavian had assumed the title of Augustus, Horace composed a great choral hymn in honor of the emperor. This poem, the *Carmen saeculare* (17 B.C.; *The Secular Hymn*, 1726), was sung by a choir of twenty-seven boys and twenty-seven girls. Its theme was that Rome, under Augustus' leadership, had entered a new era of peace and reform. Augustus also encouraged Horace to write a fourth book of the *Odes* (23 B.C., 13 B.C.; English translation, 1621) long after the first three books had been published. He asked Horace to compose an epistle on the art of poetry and commissioned him to write the official hymn celebrating the military victory of his stepsons Drusus and Tiberius.

Horace died on November 27, 8 B.C., in Rome, only a few months after his patron, Maecenas. Their tombs were built beside each other on the Esquiline Hill in Rome. In his own works, Horace describes himself as short, fat, delicate in health, and prematurely gray. His contemporaries added that the poet was congenial though independent in spirit, promiscuous, tactful, kindly, and sensitive to the feelings of others.

Analysis

The body of work published by Horace is rather small, reflecting the author's belief that a poem that is tightly crafted and highly polished is superior to a work that is longer and less refined. For this reason, Horace's models were not the ponderous Saturnian lines of Andronicus or the lengthy satires of Lucilius. Rather, Horace turned for inspiration to the Greek poetry of Archilochus, Sappho, and Alcaeus, imitating both their meters and their style in Latin verse.

Horace claims to have been the first Latin poet to have adopted Archilochus' iambic meter and to have introduced the style of Alcaeus to a Roman audience. The influence of these Greek predecessors are already apparent in Horace's earliest published works, the seventeen iambic (or iambic-dactylic) poems known as the *Epodes*. A number of the *Epodes* reflect a satirical approach intentionally reminiscent of Archilochus; this humorous style was to be repeated in the *Satires* and the *Epistles*, as well. Not even Horace's patron, Maecenas, is spared, bearing the (admittedly rather gentle) brunt of Horace's satire in Epode 3.

Even in these early and derivative works, however, something of Horace's originality may be seen. For example, apart from his closest friends, Horace rarely mentions specific individuals in these poems. In fact, the object of Horace's satire is frequently not an individual at all, but a general type of character or a particular human flaw. Satire 1.1 thus criticizes the human inability to be contented with one's lot in life, Satire 1.3 ridicules intolerance, and Satire 1.9 presents Horace's encounter with a persistent, but unnamed, bore.

In this way, Horatian satire lacks the topicality of the Athenian playwright Aristophanes or the bitter invective of the Roman satirist Juvenal. Horace's satirical tone tends to be one of bemused ridicule of common human faults, tempered always with tolerance and the poet's awareness of his own imperfections. To some extent, Horace's unwillingness to criticize individuals is a reflection of the political turmoil that occurred during his youth—it would not have been prudent for a former partisan of Brutus to ridicule political figures who had sided with the victorious Octavian—but it may be attributed to Horace's own personality. Throughout his works, Horace appears to be a genuinely amiable human being who disliked conflict and who was willing to adapt to a changing political climate.

Horace's preference for dealing with general literary types rather than specific individuals may be seen even in his greatest literary works, the *Odes*. For example, the women to whom Horace addresses his odes of love tend to be imaginary female "types" rather than identifiable women of his own day. Their names are usually drawn from Greek lyric or elegiac poetry and are indicative of their appearance or character. Thus, *Odes* 1.5 is addressed to Pyrrha (Greek for "blonde"), *Odes* 1.22 speaks of Lalage ("chatterbox"), and *Odes* 1.23 mentions Chloe ("fresh young thing"). The presence of these type characters makes Horace's love poetry quite different from that of his contemporary Catullus, whose passionate love affair with Lesbia (an actual Roman woman, whose real name was probably Clodia) may be charted in his poetry from first infatuation to final, bitter rejection.

Horace's love poetry thus lacks, at times, the passion and intensity of Catullus' lyrics. Horace's poems tend to be highly polished and charming, even studied, rather than realistic depictions of a young man in love. Yet what Horatian love poetry may miss in spirit, it more than compensates for in the perfection of its language. Not a word is out of place in one of Horace's *Odes*, and these works have no parallel in Roman poetry for the beauty of their imagery or allusions.

Horace composed 103 *Odes* in all, arranged in four books published at various periods of his life. Their meters were borrowed from Greek lyric poetry and are amazingly diverse. Indeed, each of the first nine poems in Horace's first book of *Odes* is composed in a different meter. Each of the odes usually has an addressee (such as Augustus, Maecenas, Pyrrha, or some other person, real or imaginary) and an occasion that, at least as a literary device, prompts the composition of the ode. Within this general framework, Horace mixes traditional Greek themes such as the pleasures of love and drink with more familiar Roman concerns such as the greatness of the state, the nature of the ideal citizen, and the need to preserve one's integrity in a chaotic society. Satirical themes, such as the notion that one's heirs will only waste tomorrow the wealth that one hoards today, familiar from the *Satires* and *Epistles*, also sometimes appear.

One of the innovative features of the *Odes* is Horace's ability to combine these traditional themes in new and unexpected ways. A drinking song, for example, may unexpectedly include patriotic themes, or a poem on the passing of the seasons may suddenly draw a parallel to the ages of a person's life. The freshness of the *Odes* is attributable, in large part, to the novel way in which these poems recombine traditional literary themes.

Certain phrases introduced by Horace in the *Odes* have become so famous that they are commonplaces in the Western literary tradition. These phrases include *nil desperandum* ("never despair"), *carpe diem* (usually translated as "seize the day," but a more accurate rendering would be "pluck the day like a flower"), *integer vitae* ("the man whose life is pure"), *auream mediocritatem* ("golden moderation") and *"Eheu fugaces"* ("Alas the fleeing" years slip away).

SATIRE 1.9

First published: 35 B.C. (English translation, 1567)
Type of work: Poem

While strolling along the Sacred Way, Horace encounters a bore, who persists in accompanying him despite his hints that he would prefer to be alone.

Horace's description in Satire 1.9 of his encounter with a bore is an excellent example of his satirical style. The bore is never named, and though several critics have attempted to identify him with the poet Sextus Propertius, Horace provides no clues as to his identity. The reason is that Horace does not wish to create a poem filled with invective against a particular individual. Rather, Horace's intention is to satirize dullness in general. Humor in the poem is derived from the reader's identification with Horace's predicament. Everyone can recall an incident in which an annoying individual would not leave despite numerous hints. In this way, Horace criticizes the behavior of the bore and of others like him rather than attacking the person by name.

During their (rather one-sided) conversation, the bore reveals that he is a poet and is hoping that Horace will introduce him to Gaius Maecenas (Horace's wealthy patron). In so doing, the bore alienates Horace still further by completely misunderstanding the relationship that poets such as Horace have with their patron, by stressing his ability to write quickly (elsewhere in the *Satires*, Horace makes it clear that he prefers polished writing to swift writing), and by assuming that Horace wants to compete with the other poets in Maecenas' circle. The bore, therefore, appears shallow and insensitive, as well as annoying.

It is unlikely that Horace, in this satire as elsewhere, really sought to correct the fault that he is ridiculing. Few readers will leave this work with a renewed desire to be more interesting and less annoying to others. Rather, by gently mocking this common human flaw, Horace leaves his readers smiling at a situation that they will recognize and a type of folly with which they are well familiar.

ODES 1.9, THE SORACTE ODE

First published: 23 B.C. (English translation, 1621)
Type of work: Poem

On a winter day, Horace looks out from the warmth of a friend's house and sees the snows covering Mount Soracte.

The charm of *Odes* 1.9, the Soracte ode is derived from Horace's ability to combine the traditional themes of lyric poetry in new ways. The poem begins with an image of winter: Mount Soracte, twelve miles north of Rome, is covered with snow, and the trees are laden with ice and frost. This image, then, is set into strong contrast with the poet's description of the warmth inside the house of Thaliarchus (Greek for "master of the festivities"), where wine flows abundantly and logs are heaped upon the fire. This contrast reminds Horace, rather abruptly, of how all things, such as the winter cold, are determined by the gods and must be entrusted to them. As a result, humankind, the poet says, should enjoy its youth while it can, taking delight in such simple pleasures as the warmth of the fire and the distractions of love.

In this way, Horace moves from a description of a natural scene to a commentary on the human condition. The Soracte ode may be read on a number of levels. It captures, as does much of Greek lyric poetry, the particular feeling that its author had at a given moment. Yet it is also a symbolic commentary on the contrast between youth (the fire inside) and old age (the white snow outside).

ODES 1.37, THE CLEOPATRA ODE

First published: 23 B.C. (English translation, 1621)
Type of work: Poem

The Romans may rejoice again, now that Cleopatra has been defeated.

A combination of drinking song, victory ode, and political manifesto, *Odes* 1.37, the Cleopatra ode, is a celebration of Cleopatra VII's defeat by the forces of Octavian and Marcus Vipsanius Agrippa in 31 B.C. It is also another example of Horace's ability to combine diverse themes and poetic genres in an interesting way. While the poem begins with a simple invitation to drink in celebration of the Roman victory, the tone of the work gradually becomes more serious as the work progresses. Cleopatra is first presented as a queen plotting mad destruction for the Capitoline Hill (line 37), then as an accursed monster (*fatale monstrum*, line 21), then as "no submissive woman" (*non humilis mulier*, line 32) but a queen who preferred death to humiliation. There is, in the end, a grudging admiration by Horace for Cleopatra's heroism, even though she had been an enemy to the Roman people.

Marc Antony, who had been defeated along with Cleopatra, is not mentioned. (He had been similarly ignored in Octavian's declaration of war against Cleopatra.) Horace does not think it suitable to revel in the defeat of Antony, a fellow Roman citizen. Nevertheless, Antony's presence is felt throughout the poem in the frequent references to wine and drunkenness. Before the battle, Octavian, Cicero, and others had attempted to depict Antony as a drunk. The poem's structure as a drinking song, its references to Caecuban and Maeotic wine, and its (historically inaccurate) image of Cleopatra as inebriated at the battle are all attempts to remind the reader indirectly of Antony.

The meter of the work is borrowed from the Greek lyric poet Alcaeus, who also wrote drinking songs and victory odes. The repetition of the word "now" (*nunc*) three times in the opening line established an immediacy as though a great threat, long impending, has only now been removed. In addition to the imagery of drunkenness and wine, symbolism of the hunter (Octavian) and hunted (Cleopatra) appears throughout the work. Cleopatra fled, Horace suggests, from the pursuit of Octavian; but when death proved inescapable, she met it nobly as befits a queen.

THE SECULAR HYMN

First published: *Carmen saeculare*, 17 B.C. (English translation, 1726)
Type of work: Poem

At a festival proclaiming the dawn of a new age, the chorus invokes the gods' blessings upon the Roman people.

Originally sung by a double choir of twenty-seven boys and twenty-seven girls on June 3, 17 B.C., *The Secular Hymn* is an important statement about the Romans' view of their empire in the time of Augustus. Stemming from an Etruscan belief that a new age of humanity was inaugurated each eleven (or, in some cases, ten) decades, the Centennial Festival reflected Augustus' view that, with his reign, a new period had begun. For this reason, the poem is filled with images of the rising and setting sun, the passing of the seasons, and, most of all, symbols of birth.

The goddess of childbirth, Eileithyia (or Ilithyia), is mentioned both because a new age is being born and because of Augustus' belief that Rome needed to return to its traditional values. The emperor rewarded Romans who produced large families and imposed a higher level of taxation upon those who remained single. In this way, Horace is able to use the figure of Eileithyia to shift from the birth imagery at the beginning of the poem to advocacy of Augustus' social policies in the second group of verses.

Moreover, Eileithyia is only one of the deities invoked in this hymn. Horace also addresses Apollo and Diana, the Sun, the Fates, Ceres, and a host of other gods and goddesses. The resulting image is that Rome's destiny is guided by all the deities in the Roman pantheon. It was the will of the gods that Rome should become great, and it was through their efforts that Augustus rose to rule the state.

The fertility of the Italian countryside and the founding of the Roman people by the Trojan warrior Aeneas, alluded to in this poem, appear also as major themes in the works of Vergil and on the Altar of Peace (*Ara Pacis*), erected in Rome between 13 and 9 B.C. These images represent, therefore, a consistent view of how Augustus wished his rule to be portrayed. As the one who brought about the end of the Roman Civil Wars, Augustus is depicted as making it possible for battlefields to become wheat fields once again. As the new Aeneas, Augustus is depicted as fulfilling the gods' plan begun at the very beginning of human history.

The poem ends with an invocation of Apollo and Diana, as it had similarly begun. This "ring composition" allows Horace to tie the poem directly to the human cycles that the Centennial Festival honors. Even as the hymn itself begins, rises, and ends, so (Horace suggests) do the ages of human life. The poet expresses Augustus' belief, however, that the current age would be one of unparalleled peace and prosperity.

THE ART OF POETRY

First published: *Ars poetica*, c. 17 B.C. (English translation, 1640)
Type of work: Poem

In a letter addressed to Gnaeus Calpurnius Piso, Horace offers a wide-ranging critique of literature and practical advice on how to write various types of poetry.

Horace's *Epistles* (c. 20 B.C., 13 B.C.) are written in the same meter, and with much the same style, as his *Satires*. In form, they are poetic letters intended for a recipient who is named in the first few lines; in actuality, they are general commentaries about human weaknesses or other issues of concern to the author himself.

The Art of Poetry is a reiteration of many of the same arguments found in *Epistles* 2.1, written at the request of Augustus. In that work, Horace discussed his views about the proper role of literature and the place of Roman poetry within the ancient literary tradition. In *The Art of Poetry* itself, Horace expands upon these and couples them with specific suggestions for the authors of his day.

Horace begins by praising consistency as the highest virtue of poetry. A work that attempts to be now one thing, now another, is eventually, according to Horace, being nothing at all. For this reason, authors must maintain the same tone throughout a work, not attempt to improve an inferior effort with a "purple patch" (*purpureus . . . pannus*, lines 15-16) of fine words every now and then. Moreover, authors should not attempt subjects that are beyond their powers. If they do, the result will make them look ridiculous.

Each incident and word in a poem should be chosen with care. Precise selection of what is needed, rather than a torrent of words, creates the most polished result. The meter, too, should be chosen with care: Dactylic hexameter, the meter of Homer (and, coincidentally, of *The Art of Poetry*), is appropriate for epic; elegiac couplets are appropriate for sad subjects and songs of thanksgiving; iambic verse lends itself to satire; lyric meters are suitable for victory odes and drinking songs. These meters had all become traditional by Horace's day, and the poet warns his readers that audiences expect them: A serious thought may unintentionally be made to seem comic if presented in an improper poetic form.

In dramatic poetry, language assigned to a character must both suit the traditional depiction of that character and be consistent within the work itself. In epic poetry, it is best not to prolong the story by starting at the very beginning but to thrust the reader right "into the middle of things" (*in medias res*, line 148). Brevity, as well as an ability to convey both wisdom and pleasure, are essential to the skilled poet.

The reader should not, however, find fault with a poet who occasionally fails to fulfill these high standards since, in the phrase of Horace, "even great Homer sometimes nods" (line 359). Still, the public will not long endure a second-rate poet, and it is the author's goal to see that such passages are rare. This lapse tends to occur, Horace suggests, when poets distribute their work without sufficient editing. Thus, instead of publishing a work immediately, the poet should set it aside for a time—at line 388, Horace recommends, with satirical exaggeration, that it be set aside for nine years—to see if it still seems as inspired later.

The advice that Horace provides in *The Art of Poetry* is thus a combination of common sense, practical observations drawn from a lifetime of writing, and views inherited from earlier literary critics such as Aristotle, Neoptolemus of Parion, and Philodemus. Probably the last work that Horace wrote, *The Art of Poetry* has played an important role in defining both the classical style and the canons of good writing developed in later periods.

Summary

Horace's own works adhere to the principles that the author set forth in *The Art of Poetry*. His poems are consistent, well crafted, brief, and highly polished. Their language is chosen both for its appropriateness to the topic and for the emotional force of its imagery. This achievement is all the more impressive in light of the incredible variety of Horace's poetry. He perfected both satire and lyric poetry. He was at home with the simple charm of the *Epistles* as well as the lofty grandeur of *The Secular Hymn*. Through his works, the reader comes to understand Horace both as an individual and as a representative of the values of Augustan Rome.

In each of his poems, Horace emphasizes the general human condition instead of particular situations. His satire is not filled with invective against individuals, but with parody of common folly. His love poetry does not reflect his own experiences but, rather, is written to imaginary characters. Even in those lyric poems where he begins by capturing the experience of a specific moment, Horace will usually generalize, using the incident as a way of commenting upon a larger truth.

Bibliography

Commager, Steele. *The Odes of Horace: A Critical Study*. New Haven, Conn.: Yale University Press, 1964.

Frank, Tenney. *Catullus and Horace*. New York: Russell & Russell, 1928.

Fränkel, Edouard. *Horace*. Oxford, England: Oxford University Press, 1957.

Perret, Jacques. *Horace*. Translated by Bertha Humez. New York: New York University Press, 1964.

Richardson, Leon J. *Quintus Horatius Flaccus*. Berkeley: University of California Press, 1935.

Rudd, Niall. *The Satires of Horace*. Berkeley: University of California Press, 1966.

Sedgwick, Henry Dwight. *Horace: A Biography*. New York: Russell & Russell, 1947.

Showerman, Grant. *Horace and His Influence.* New York: Cooper Square, 1963.
Wilkinson, L. P. *Horace and His Lyric Poetry.* 2d ed. Cambridge, England: Cambridge University Press, 1951.

Jeffrey L. Buller

A. E. HOUSMAN

Born: Fockbury, Worcestershire,
England
March 26, 1859
Died: Cambridge, England
April 30, 1936

Principal Literary Achievement
Although he operated under self-imposed limitations of theme and form, Housman is known as one of the most gifted lyric poets in the English language.

Biography

Alfred Edward Housman was born on March 26, 1859, the eldest of seven children born to Sarah and Edward Housman. Although Housman was born in Fockbury, Worcestershire, England, he grew up in Bromsgrove, near Birmingham, to where the Housman family moved when he was still in infancy. Bromsgrove is in close proximity to the Shropshire hills that would become the central setting in Alfred's most famous collection of poems, *A Shropshire Lad*, published in 1896.

A. E. Housman's childhood was mostly unhappy. He was frail, often sickly, very devoted to his mother, and alienated from his father. His mother's death in 1871 on young Housman's twelfth birthday further served to alienate his father, a masculine, sporting, practicing attorney who fancied himself as a country squire and who displayed some disappointment that his eldest son did not share these same characteristics or inclinations. The elder Housman soon remarried a cousin, however, and young Housman found in his stepmother, Lucy Housman, a devoted and supportive person who helped make the remainder of his early life bearable, if not altogether happy.

Housman's education began at the Bromsgrove School, where he distinguished himself in his studies from the outset. In fact, at Bromsgrove, Housman was at the top of his class and upon graduation won a scholarship to Oxford in 1877. At Bromsgrove, he developed a taste for classical languages and excelled in both Latin and Greek. He continued these studies at Oxford, becoming especially interested in the Roman poet Sextus Propertius. In addition, Housman read the works of English writers Matthew Arnold and Thomas Hardy, both contemporaries, whose ideas and forms influenced much of Housman's poetry.

While Housman was matriculating at Oxford, he met Moses Jackson, a classmate

who would have a profound effect on the rest of Housman's life. Although Jackson and Housman were from similar backgrounds, Jackson was everything that Housman was not—tall, handsome, well built, athletically inclined, and confident in his own abilities. Jackson and Housman became not only fast friends but also roommates for most of their college careers, along with A. W. Pollard, another Oxford undergraduate. Housman, however, desired more than simply Jackson's companionship; in short, Housman found himself deeply in love with Jackson, a situation from which he apparently never recovered. The exact nature of Jackson's rejection of Housman's affections is not clear, for while they remained lifelong friends, Jackson's rejection left Housman emotionally impaired.

During Housman's first years at Oxford, he continued to succeed brilliantly in his studies, often earning top honors in his examinations, so it was quite unexpected on everyone's part when, in 1881, he miserably failed his final examination in the classics. Housman left Oxford in 1881 without a degree, although he did manage to qualify for a lower degree the following fall. Having received this degree, Housman returned to Bromsgrove, where he taught lower grades while preparing to take the civil service examination, which he took and passed successfully in the fall of 1882. He took a job as a clerk in Her Majesty's Patent Office in London and moved there in December, 1882, to share an apartment with Jackson and Jackson's younger brother, Adalbert. Housman remained in this job for ten years, until 1892. During this period, Housman continued to study Latin and Greek, working especially on emendations to the texts of various classical authors and preparing scholarly articles for publication in the *Journal of Philology* and *The Classical Review*, while earning a respectable reputation as a classical scholar.

In 1886, Housman moved to his own apartment and lived in near seclusion, devoting most of the time away from work to his studies. In 1887, Moses Jackson took a teaching job in India, and the grief over his departure pushed Housman even further into seclusion. His grief became even more pronounced two years later when, in 1889, Jackson married Rosa Chambers. Housman recorded his feelings in a commemorative poem, "Epithalamium," that he began writing in 1890 but did not publish until 1922 in his last collection, *Last Poems*.

In 1892, Housman won an appointment to the Chair of Latin and Greek at University College in London. Although his record was marred by the previous failure of the examination in the classics at Oxford, his reputation as a careful and brilliant scholar was confirmed by a number of leading scholars in the field. Thus, Housman delivered his opening lecture to the University College faculty in October, 1892, and began a long career as a teacher and scholar of considerable renown.

In November, 1892, the painful death from typhoid of Adalbert Jackson caused a tremendous shock to the customarily sensitive Housman. Not only was the grief over his friend's death intense, but it also triggered a flurry of poetic creativity through which Housman poured out all of the emotion, the sadness, and the pain with which he had lived for so long. Over the next several years, Housman wrote numerous poems, sixty-three of which were assembled into *A Shropshire Lad*. Although the book sold slowly at first, when the Boer War began in 1899, sales had increased considerably, and by World War I, *A Shropshire Lad* had become one of the most popular poetry collections ever.

In 1911, Housman was named Kennedy Professor of Latin at Cambridge and a Fellow of Trinity College. He taught there for the remainder of his career, during which time he continued to devote his time to classical scholarship but wrote only a few new poems. Housman's composition of poems seems to have ceased with the death of Moses Jackson in 1923. Thereafter, Housman devoted his remaining years to his teaching duties and his scholarly interests until his death on April 30, 1936, in Cambridge, England, from complications of heart disease.

Analysis

Housman's poems all seem to be motivated by one of several emotions: grief and sadness over loss, unrequited love, and a strong sense of fate or destiny. Within this narrow focus, however, Housman created many memorable poems, several of near classic standing, and all imbued with a sense that life, after all, is something to be endured rather than enjoyed.

Housman is frequently termed a minor poet. This classification results in large part from Housman's refusal, or inability, perhaps, to move beyond a handful of themes and to his limiting himself to the lyrical ballad for much of his poetry. Furthermore, the entire corpus of Housman's published poems consists of 178 short works, far fewer in number than most career poets. It must be noted, however, that the bulk of Housman's poetry was produced within the ten-year period from 1892 to 1903, and that Housman perhaps preferred praise for his scholarly studies of the Roman poet Manilius.

Despite Housman's status as a minor poet, however, *A Shropshire Lad* is among the most popular books of poems in the English language. In this short collection of sixty-three poems is found the essential Housman: the superb lyric form, the precise, unornamented language, the extraordinary simplicity in style and tone, and the hauntingly poignant mood that characterizes nearly every poem.

A Shropshire Lad is certainly no haphazardly arranged collection of poems; indeed, it is a consciously arranged selection, both chosen and numbered to reflect and emphasize several recurrent themes, among them, praise and celebration of rural life, the constancy of death, especially the death of the young, love lost or unreturned, the special qualities of the soldier, and suicide. These themes are also addressed in *Last Poems*, as well as those poems collected and published posthumously by Housman's younger brother, Laurence Housman.

A typical Housman poem, then, may have a fixation on death, on lost love, or on the unbearableness of human life. Furthermore, Housman's persona of Terence Hearsay figures importantly in many of the poems as one who understands the pulse of Shropshire society and who feels compelled to articulate its feelings, concerns, and general way of life. Terence Hearsay, name symbolism included, gives the poems authority, authenticity, and objectivity.

From a technical standpoint, Housman's poems are quite often miniatures wrought to perfection. The lines are short, even, and to the point; furthermore, the language is clear and direct. Yet for all the simplicity of form, language, and theme, there is a formal elegance to Housman's poetry, from the regularity of the meter to the precision of the rhyme. Note, for example, in the opening poem of *A Shropshire Lad*, the following stanza:

> From Clee to heaven the beacon burns,
>   The shires have seen it plain,
> From north and south the sign returns
>   And beacons burn again.

The iambic pattern alternates between tetrameter and trimeter lines; alternate lines rhyme as well, giving the poem a lyrical impression; and the combination of these features, then, gives the very high degree of formality to the poems. This first poem repeats the stanzaic form above in seven additional stanzas, and many of the poems throughout the collection repeat the pattern, or a similar one, as well.

Housman did not venture or experiment beyond the miniature poems in his first collection. In subsequent collections, rather than showing any broad growth as a poet, Housman only varied the themes and forms that had established his reputation as a poet many years earlier. These later poems perhaps provided more depth to the examination of these themes. Further, Housman's body of work seems intent on advancing the idea that limitation and concentration make for excellent poetry. In the final analysis, these characteristics are what readers remember and appreciate about Housman.

1887

First published: 1896
Type of work: Poem

On the eve of the fiftieth anniversary of the reign of Queen Victoria, the poet muses about the condition of England.

In "1887," the first poem in *A Shropshire Lad* (1896), Housman establishes the main themes, the main technique, the chief setting, and the main mood that would characterize the remainder of the sixty-three short poems that constitute the collection. For this reason, "1887" is often referred to as a "frame poem," along with poems LXII and LXIII, for a very deliberately arranged collection.

During the otherwise festive occasion of the eve of Queen Victoria's Golden Anniversary, when others are poised for, or already engaged in, celebration, the persona in Housman's poem adds a strong sense of melancholy as he recalls the past and ponders the future. In short, there is considerable lament over the fact that many friends have made the transition from life to death, many by the horrors of war. The speaker fully understands that the soldiers have performed their duty as "saviours" of the queen and England proper, but he interjects a tone of bitterness that on this happiest of occasions they could not join in the celebration because "themselves they could not save."

Despite the gloominess of the poem, however, the speaker pledges continued love and allegiance to England, the queen, and God, seemingly fully realizing that death is a natural part of life and that life, despite its many travails, must be endured. Thus, the poem ends with a grave admonition that

> Oh, God will save her, fear you not
> Be you the men you've been,
> Get you the sons your fathers got,
> And God will save the Queen.

Indeed, England's continued success and the Queen's protection are dependent upon the strength of the Shropshire lads and their many counterparts.

LOVELIEST OF TREES

First published: 1896
Type of work: Poem

In springtime, a young man muses over the brevity of life.

"Loveliest of Trees" is one of the finest examples of Housman's lyrical poems. The rural setting of the Shropshire woodlands in springtime is a beautiful sight to behold, with the cherry tree—the loveliest of trees—in full white bloom to celebrate the time of rebirth and rejuvenation associated with Easter. Yet the beauty strikes a chord of melancholy in the speaker, who realizes that life is indeed short; and even if he lives to his full life expectancy, that, too, will be too short a time to behold such splendor as these trees in bloom.

While there is present the popular *carpe diem* theme in "Loveliest of Trees," Housman adds to it a somber sense of impending doom as the speaker resolves to view the beauty of the world while he is yet alive. The attitude and the mood that it creates is typically Housman, in that even in the face of immense beauty, there is always the discomfort of knowing that life has no real permanence, that death and doom are, without question, imminent.

TO AN ATHLETE DYING YOUNG

First published: 1896
Type of work: Poem

Upon the death of a young runner, the poet celebrates his life and premature death.

"To an Athlete Dying Young" is one of Housman's most often anthologized poems. Its quiet, melancholy tone, its theme of the comfort of death, and its simplicity of form and style combine to make the poem a classic celebration of release from the difficulties of life.

In this short elegy, written upon the death of a young, celebrated athlete, Housman advances the idea that it is far better to die in one's prime, while one can be remembered for his or her youthful accomplishments, than to become infirm, forgotten, ignored, or replaced in the memories and hearts of one's townspeople. With the typical detached, observant tone often employed by Housman, the speaker hails the dead youth as a

> Smart lad, to slip betimes away
> From fields where glory does not stay

who will not suffer the fate of many other

> Runners whom renown outran
> And the name died before the man.

Technically speaking, "To an Athlete Dying Young" is indicative of Housman's gift of poetic craft. The even meter and the taut rhyme add to the deliberate, somber, reflective mood established from the first stanza onward. In addition, contrasting symbols and images—the victory parade and the funeral cortege, the laurel and the rose—add complexity to a deceptively simple poem.

The poem concludes with the projection of what the speaker perceives as victory for the dead young athlete, now a "Townsman of a stiller town":

> And round that early laureled head
> Will flock to gaze the strengthless dead
> And find unwithered on its curls
> The garland briefer than a girl's.

Thus, Housman insists that death, especially for youth, is a victory over the impending difficulties, tragedies, and heartbreak that accompany life.

TERENCE, THIS IS STUPID STUFF

First published: 1896
Type of work: Poem

A friend chides Terence, the poet figure, about his melancholy poetry, and Terence responds.

"Terence, This Is Stupid Stuff," poem LXII of *A Shropshire Lad*, is commonly considered Housman's apologia. As this next-to-last poem in *A Shropshire Lad*, Housman moves toward the conclusion of his presentation of his many themes and offers justification for the melancholy tone of his poetry.

The poem is structured as a dialogue between Terence, the poet figure, and one of Terence's friends, who initially chides Terence for writing poetry that is somber and thought provoking rather than uplifting and celebratory. The friend warns Terence, jestingly, that he is driving his friends "Moping melancholy mad" with his serious poetry, and that they would prefer something happier, "a tune to dance to."

Terence responds that the purpose of his poetry is not to entertain but to strengthen and instruct. In fact, Terence suggests that if all that his friends want to do is to have a good time, then there is dancing and drinking for them in which to participate, but that these are hardly answers for life's many problems. Terence claims to know that from personal experience. Therefore, Terence explains, because life is full of uncertainties, heartbreak, and pain, people should prepare themselves accordingly. His poetry, then, is written to prepare each person for "the dark and cloudy day" that each one will surely face.

Terence concludes his response to his friend's complaint by relating the ancient tale of King Mithridates, who, anticipating that rivals would attempt to poison him, took small amounts of arsenic and strychnine and developed an immunity to them. Thus, when the attempted assassination occurred, Mithridates was prepared to ward off the ill effects of the poison. Likewise, Terence insists that the poetry will help immunize his readers against "the embittered hour" when they come face to face with adversity.

In "Terence, This Is Stupid Stuff," Housman reemphasizes his theme of stoicism and suggests, once again, that life is made bearable by concentrating on its tragedies, and by doing so, one learns to live in the face of adversity.

EPITAPH ON AN ARMY OF MERCENARIES

First published: 1922
Type of work: Poem

The poet celebrates heroism.

"Epitaph on an Army of Mercenaries" is a short, occasional poem of eight lines, one of the many poems that Housman wrote to celebrate the extraordinary bravery of soldiers in the face of great odds. In this poem, the poet honors the British mercenaries, professional soldiers who performed with great valor and heroism at the battles of Ypres during the early stages of England's entry into World War I.

In short, Housman says that these soldiers, although paid for their work, saved a world that was fast crumbling; further, had it not been for these hired soldiers, much, if not all, would have been lost. Unfortunately, despite being paid for their services, many of the soldiers were killed in battle; those who were not were often victims of the harshest criticism. Housman both laments their predicament and celebrates their most important contributions.

Housman's antireligious sentiments are also revealed in this poem. These sentiments were no secret and had been expressed in many of the poems in *A Shropshire Lad*. In "Epitaph on an Army of Mercenaries," however, the poet, in the process of applauding the soldiers' defense, is bitterly critical of a God who would abandon the world, let the heavens fall, and allow the foundations of the world to crumble.

Summary

A. E. Housman's poetry has many enduring qualities, among them the intensity of feeling, the fastidious care with which the setting is etched, the careful maintenance of tone and mood, and the poignancy of the moments of experiences captured and preserved in time. Housman has frequently been accused of being "bitterly critical" and even sardonic in his poetry. The careful reader, however, will recognize Housman's sincere presentation of actual experiences, experiences that he or she perhaps would rather not confront but that are almost certain to occur. That is perhaps Housman's chief contribution to poetry—the strong medicine that the world needs to immunize it against the ills of life.

Bibliography

Allison, A. F. "The Poetry of A. E. Housman." *Review of English Studies* 19 (1943): 276-284.

Bishop, John Peale. "The Poetry of A. E. Housman." *Poetry* 56 (June, 1940): 144-153.
Braithwaite, William Stanley. Introduction to *A Shropshire Lad*. Boston: International Pocket Library, 1919.
Brooks, Cleanth. "The Whole of Housman." *Kenyon Review* 3 (1941): 105-109.
Haber, Tom Burns. *A. E. Housman*. Boston: Twayne, 1967.
Page, Norman. *A. E. Housman: A Critical Biography*. New York: Schocken Books, 1983.
Spender, Stephen. "The Essential Housman." *Horizon* 1 (1940): 245-301.

Warren J. Carson

TED HUGHES

Born: Mytholmroyd, Yorkshire, England
August 17, 1930

Principal Literary Achievement
Hughes is recognized as one of England's leading poets writing after World War II; his work is especially noted for its compressed syntax and rhythms, as well as its often violent portrayal of nature.

Biography

Edward James Hughes was born on August 17, 1930, in Mytholmroyd, on the Calder River, one of England's first industrialized rivers yet also near the wildness of the moors. Hughes was the youngest of three children of Edith Farrar (who traced her ancestry back to the martyr Bishop Farrar) and William Hughes (a carpenter, who was one of only seventeen of an entire regiment to have survived at Gallipoli in World War I). When Hughes was seven, the family moved to Mexborough; there, Hughes led a double life of living in town but often roaming about on nearby farms and estates. The landscape and the language of West Riding and South Yorkshire were undoubtedly significant in shaping Hughes's sensibility: his fascination with animals, natural processes, and archaic myths; the conflict between wilderness, farm, and industrialization; the rhythms of collapse and renewal; and the spare, physical language of the people are present throughout his poetic career.

In 1948, Hughes won an Open Exhibition to Cambridge. Hughes postponed his studies at Cambridge until 1951, choosing to serve for two years in the National Service, in the RAF (Royal Air Force) as a mechanic at an isolated radio transmission station in Yorkshire. Though he planned to study English literature at Pembroke College, Cambridge, he changed in his third year to archaeology and anthropology. He was graduated in June, 1954, the same month that his first poem, "The Little Boys and the Seasons," appeared in the Cambridge journal *Granta*. For the following two years, he worked as a rose gardener, a night watchman in a steel works, a zoo attendant, and a schoolteacher.

In late February, 1956, Hughes met Sylvia Plath, who had arrived from the United States on a Fulbright scholarship to study. Her own literary career had begun in 1950 with the publication of her poetry. Four months after their first meeting, Plath and Hughes were married. In Plath's *Letters Home* (1975), she states that she learned through Hughes "the vocabulary of woods and animals and earth" and felt herself

like "adam's woman [*sic*]." Hughes brought to Plath's attention the mythologic underpinnings of poetry as conceptualized by the British poet, novelist, and essayist
Robert Graves in his *The White Goddess: A Historical Grammar of Poetic Myth*
(1948). In turn, Plath brought Hughes into contact with the poetry being published in
the United States. On his behalf, Plath typed and sent the manuscript of *The Hawk in
the Rain* (1957), which was selected by the poets W. H. Auden, Stephen Spender, and
Marianne Moore in a competition for the publication of a first book of poems in
English. Published simultaneously in England and the United States, *The Hawk in
the Rain* gained immediate critical recognition.

In 1957, Hughes and Plath went to the United States to teach, Plath at Smith College and Hughes at the University of Massachusetts. After a year, they abandoned
their teaching so as to spend more time writing. In the spring of 1959, Hughes received a Guggenheim Fellowship, and in December they returned to London. In 1960,
Hughes's second collection of poems, *Lupercal*, appeared, and Plath published her
collection of poems *The Colossus*. In 1960, their first child, Frieda Rebecca, was
born. Growing weary of the city, the family moved to a thatched rectory in Devon,
and in 1962 their second child, Nicholas Farrar, was born. During this period, Hughes
was at work not only on some of the poems and stories in *Wodwo* (1967) but also on
plays and articles; Plath was completing her novel *The Bell Jar* (1963) and was at
work on her *Ariel* (1965) poems. By the middle of the year, their marriage was col-
lapsing, with Hughes leaving her for another woman; they returned to London separately, where in February, 1963, Plath committed suicide.

By holding imaginary dialogues with his children, Hughes created three children's
books, *How the Whale Became* (1963), *The Earth-Owl and Other Moon-People* (1963),
and *Nessie the Mannerless Monster* (1964), also published as *Nessie the Monster,*
(1974), and thereby avoided falling into silence. In 1967, *Wodwo* was published, as
was his text, *Poetry in the Making,* which describes to students the practice of writing. In 1970, Hughes married Carol Orchard, the daughter of a Devon farmer. In 1970,
Crow: From the Life and Songs of the Crow was published; this cycle of poems is
perhaps Hughes's most important contribution to Anglo-American poetry because of
its spare language, the trickster figure of Crow, and the desperate vitality of the voice.

In 1971, Hughes collaborated with the director of the National Theatre, Peter Brook,
to create and produce *Orghast* for the Fifth Shiraz Festival in Iran. *Orghast,* both the
name of the play and the play's invented language, is based on various myths and
folktales, especially that of Prometheus. Hughes continued his interest in dramatic
and cyclical poems with *Prometheus on His Crag* (1973) and *Gaudete* (1977). Simultaneously, Hughes's vision of the natural world became increasingly acute in *Remains
of Elmet* (1979), *Moortown* (1979), *River* (1983), and *Wolfwatching* (1989). In December, 1984, Hughes was named England's poet laureate, succeeding Sir John Betjeman.

Analysis

Much of the sensibility of Hughes's poetry can be defined by several consistent
elements. The influence of *The White Goddess,* the landscape of Hughes's child-

hood, and the connection between literary influences and the vernacular speech of his Yorkshire environs are essential elements of Hughes's poetics. Familial concerns are less self-evident; Hughes seldom seems overtly autobiographical or confessional. Nonetheless, it should be noted that Hughes has written of his family, such as his mother's ancestry ("The Martyrdom of Bishop Farrar" in *The Hawk in the Rain*) or his father's ordeals in World War I ("Dust as We Are" and "For the Duration" in *Wolfwatching*).

Perhaps the earliest and most intellectually formative influence was that of *The White Goddess*. Given as a prize to Hughes from his grammar school, Graves's work initiated an interest that continued at Cambridge in Hughes's anthropological studies and has continued to develop. Hughes remained an assiduous reader of myths, folklore, ethnology, and poetry. Graves proposes that myth, particularly of fertility and renewal, is the authentic language of poetry. Hughes considers poetry or myth as the means for reintroducing the community to its origins or sources of the energy of renewal. In many ways, Hughes's long dramatic poem *Gaudete* (1977) is the culmination of his vision of division, struggle, and atonement through transformation as described in *The White Goddess*. In this work, nature and the human world are divided; there is a human desolation and the impending apocalyptic aftermath of a psychomachy. At each turn, the poem's mock-epic hero, Lumb, faces a distorted vision of the White Goddess as an expression of death.

Directly linked to the idea of mythopoeia is Hughes's attention to the natural landscape. The physicality of Hughes's diction corresponds to his focus on natural objects. As a child, Hughes would accompany his older brother in the hills and moors, retrieving what his brother shot. In his *Poetry in the Making,* Hughes describes that "at about fifteen my life grew more complicated and my attitude toward animals changed. I accused myself of disturbing their lives. I began to look at them, you see, from their own point of view. And about the same time I began to write poems." To be a mythmaker, Hughes implicitly knew that he must be a naturalist. Examples of Hughes's engagement with his natural landscape are to be found throughout the collections of his poetry. Perhaps most noteworthy, however, is the sequence of thirty-four poems in the collection *Moortown*. In these poems, Hughes details the human toil of farming, the rhythms of farm life, and the profound intersection of the human world and the natural world beyond. It is the toil of the farm, the continual birthing and death, and the seasons' demands that reinitiate an understanding of nature and the intimate connection between the human body, the psyche, and the world of nature.

Hughes's influences are often cited as the poets Geoffrey Chaucer, William Shakespeare, Gerard Manley Hopkins, Dylan Thomas, and D. H. Lawrence. In an interview with the critic Ekbert Faas, Hughes argues that whatever "speech you grow into, presumably your dialect stays alive in a sort of inner freedom, a separate little self . . . [I]n the case of the West Yorkshire dialect, of course, it connects you directly and in your most intimate self to middle English poetry." The title poem of the collection *Wodwo* illustrates this point. The word "wodwo" appears in the anonymous middle-

English poem *Sir Gawain and the Green Knight* (c. 1375-1400) and means a wild man of the woods, and in Hughes's poem represents the centrality of the unconscious and the mythic demand to be named: "But what shall I be called am I the first/ have I an owner what shape am I." The childhood core of experience—language and landscape—remain in the poet and provide the energies for the writing of poetry.

In the collection *Crow,* Hughes offers several directions in understanding these various influences: The figure of Crow is the consummate poet-bard, the primordial storyteller and memory for an entire culture; an Everyman, hero, and clown—the prototypic figure of the Trickster found throughout the world's mythologies. The language of the poems is direct and vernacular; it rejects Latinate words for words rooted in the archaic and Anglo-Saxon. *Crow* investigates the centrality of the Anglo-Saxon-Norse-Celtic roots in the English language and psyche that are, Hughes argues, constantly repressed.

Hughes's work is also often described, or disparaged, as violent. Such violence is, in fact, the violence of transformation, part of Graves's interpretation of myth as a movement through birth, life, death, and renewal. The violence ascribed to Hughes's work is also an attribute of the language and rhythms that he uses: The language is compact, highly stressed, and direct. Hughes responded to the question of violence in his interview with Faas by stating that "Any form of violence—any form of vehement activity—invokes the bigger energy, the elemental power circuit of the Universe." Throughout his work, Hughes argues that the epoch's destructive activities—particularly World Wars I and II and the environmental crisis—have destroyed both humanity's contact with the natural world and the rituals that maintained the health of the world's communities. Hughes's poetry attempts to renew contact with nature, not through accommodation but on nature's own elemental terms. "Hawk Roosting," from *Lupercal,* is often cited as an example of Hughes's celebration of violence. Through its utterly direct language and its inhabitation of the perching hawk, the poem, however, provides a needed contact with the natural world and its powers. The hawk comes to represent nature thinking. The poem contains echoes of the biblical book of Job; indeed Job's inability to understand his unmerciful God parallels the fruitless efforts to understand nature. The poem warns against confusing human identities with those of the hawk, for to do so will distort nature, as well as humankind. In Hughes's vision, nature offers no compromises.

THE THOUGHT-FOX

First published: 1957
Type of work: Poem

The poet imagines a fox's approach through the night, which is a metaphoric reverie of the writing of poetry.

"The Thought-Fox" appeared in Hughes's first collection of poems, *The Hawk in the Rain* (1957), and is one of his most celebrated and anthologized poems. This poem contains many of the stylistic and thematic elements that have come to define Hughes's poetry. In terms of Hughes's poetic development, this poem was unmistakably his breakthrough, signaling his departure from the rhetorical and metaphysical poetry and his movement toward mythmaking.

The poem comprises a reverie by immediately invoking the imagination in the first line: "I imagine this midnight moment's forest." The alliteration in this line suggests a casting of a spell. The first stanza of this twenty-four-line poem arranged in quatrains evokes solitude; plainly, the writer is working late at night alone, the only sound being "the clock's loneliness." Beyond the writer's domain of time and the blank page exists the primordial force of the imagination.

The poet becomes actively aware of the approach of the nearness of the other or the imagination in the second stanza. The poet stands at literal and figurative thresholds: He stares at a blank page, which becomes the dark window, the starless sky, and then into the forest's darkness. In the third stanza, the poet has crossed these various thresholds to make contact with this totem-figure of the unconscious or the imagination. Both the poet and the metaphorical fox are tentative in their approaches. The rhythm enacts the moment-by-moment movement of the reverie. The selection of simple words underscores the directness of the experience and the rhythm of the poem's trancelike chant: "Two eyes serve a movement, that now/ And again now, and now, and now/ Sets neat prints into the snow."

The fourth stanza traces the movement of the fox through the trees. Gradually the blank, snowy page fills with print, the tracks of the thought-fox. The poem is simultaneously depicting the transcription of a poem from the imagination onto the page and describing the moment of inspiration. The fifth stanza is the most abstract while also seeking to convey the fullness and primordial magic of reverie as the poet is swept into the "deepening greenness," or vitality, of the imagination. The force of the reverie overwhelms the poet, until the sudden physical presence and departure of the fox in the sixth stanza occurs: "Till, with a sudden sharp hot stink of fox/ It enters the dark hole of the head." The imagination at this moment shows its immediacy and power; the fox is no longer a shadow but dangerously close before vanishing and leaving the page printed, scented with its presence, its territory marked. The imagination, for Hughes, is a primordial force; its presence is both creative and predatory. The poem implies that it is necessary, however, to engage these archaic powers if one is to write an authentic poetry.

SALMON EGGS

First published: 1983
Type of work: Poem

The poem is a meditation on the sanctity and continuity of the river, the salmon, and life.

"Salmon Eggs" is the closing poem of Hughes's collection *River* (1983). The collection itself is a sequence of forty-three poems offering both description of river life and meditations on the spiritual and physical ecology. "Salmon Eggs," as the final poem, offers an affirmation: "Only birth matters/ Say the river's whorls."

There are two movements in the poem. One is the horizontal flow of the river, its journey downstream, oceanward, toward conclusion and, implicitly, extinction. The other movement is vertical, from the sky, penetrating the water's surface, probing the sediments. The poet occupies the intersection of these two movements and travels their axes. The poem opens in the past tense, suggesting had the reader arrived sooner he or she, too, would have seen the salmon. The second stanza, cast in the present moment, gives witness to the salmon's fatal exhaustion after spawning. Throughout the poem, there are images of fertility and birth, as well as exhaustion and extinction. These two conditions are never isolated; one always informs the other. For Hughes, the essential role for the poet is to be at the intersection of these movements, to witness and record them. "Salmon Eggs" continues with the poet or speaker describing his reverie: "I lean and watch the water/ listening to water/ Till my eyes forget me/ And the piled flow supplants me." Rather than the incantatory archaic and totemic being invoked, as in "The Thought-Fox," this poem's reverie carries the poet into the geologic and biological world of catkins, spiders, "mud-blooms," and "Mastodon ephemera."

The speaker notes that "Something else is going on in the river/ More vital than death." Death is merely part of nature's overarching processes. Hughes sees everywhere the continuity of life—"The river goes on/ Sliding through its place, undergoing itself/ In its wheel." The conventional symbol of the river as a coursing of life is certainly evoked here, as well as the vision of life as cyclical. The river is also understood in poetry and myth as the process of time, encompassing both time's passage and eternity—rivers, such as the Styx of Greek mythology, lead to death, as well as to immortality. Hughes's image of the wheel becomes identified as the water mill, a common image in the English landscape, and one that has come to represent both time and fate. The poet communes with the river and invokes a blessing upon the river and upon the salmon, "Sanctus Sanctus/ Swathes the blessed issue." The river becomes a holy "font . . . swaddling the egg." In the course of the river *"Only birth matters."* The poem closes with the river's movement spreading to encompass the sun and earth. The final line—"mind condenses on old haws"—suggests the crystallization of consciousness or awareness in the same way that dew condenses on the leaves of a hawthorn hedge.

Summary

Ted Hughes offers a powerful vision of the world and of poetry. While the underpinnings of much of his thought may seem esoteric, his poetry is direct and sensory; the poems' immediacy brings the reader into contact with the archaic, mythic, or primordial forces explored by Hughes. Hughes certainly belongs to the tradition of English landscape poets, such as Andrew Marvell, William Wordsworth, or D. H. Lawrence; however, his vision of the natural world suggests that any attempt to control nature results not only in damaging the natural world but also in the distortion and destruction of the human spirit.

Bibliography

Bedient, Calvin. "Ted Hughes's Fearful Greening." *Parnassus: Poetry in Review* 14, no. 1 (1987): 150-163.

Faas, Ekbert. *Ted Hughes: The Unaccommodated Universe.* Santa Barbara, Calif.: Black Sparrow Press, 1980.

Sagar, Keith. *The Art of Ted Hughes.* 2d ed. Cambridge, England: Cambridge University Press, 1978.

Seigaj, Leonard M. *The Poetry of Ted Hughes: Form and Imagination.* Iowa City: University of Iowa Press, 1986.

Uroff, Margaret. *Sylvia Plath and Ted Hughes.* Champaign: University of Illinois Press, 1979.

West, Thomas. *Ted Hughes.* London: Methuen, 1985.

James McCorkle

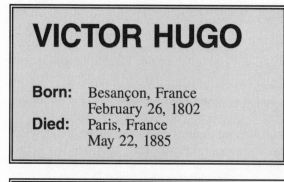

VICTOR HUGO

Born: Besançon, France
February 26, 1802
Died: Paris, France
May 22, 1885

Principal Literary Achievement

Recognized as a guiding force of the Romantic movement in Europe and the leader of the Romantic rebellion in his own country, Hugo provided nineteenth century France with its greatest novels, verse drama, and lyric poetry.

Biography

Victor-Marie Hugo was the third son of Major Joseph Léopold Sigisbert Hugo and Sophie Trébuchet Hugo. He was born in Besançon, in eastern France, on February 26, 1802, in the third year of Napoleon Bonaparte's (Napoleon I's) First Republic. He was a slight, somewhat misshapen child, who at birth seemed to the doctor to have little chance for survival. No omen could have been more false, as Victor Hugo became a titan of strength and energy, living during one period of his life with the equivalent of three marriage partners and, as an octogenarian, outliving all five of his children.

Hugo's parents quarreled much and separated frequently, gaining legal separation in 1818. His father distinguished himself in a military career, serving Napoleon's brother, Prince Joseph, under whom he obtained a colonelcy and the governorship of Avellino in Italy; he later became count of Siguenza in Spain when Joseph Bonaparte, having become king of Naples, went on to the kingship of Spain and the Indies. It was in Spain that the young Victor Hugo developed a penchant for Spanish history, legend, and grandiloquence that would materialize in works such as *Hernani* (1830; English translation, 1830) and *Ruy Blas* (1838; English translation, 1890). Victor's father attained the rank of general but, after the defeat of Joseph Bonaparte, returned to France, where he commanded a garrison in Thionville. The three Hugo brothers, after their parents' separation, went to Paris to live with their mother.

Victor Hugo married Adèle Foucher in 1822, three years after he and his brothers had founded *Le Conservateur littéraire*, a magazine for which Hugo wrote over 120 articles and more than twenty poems in its first two years of existence. In 1821, the magazine had merged with *Les Annales de la littérature et des arts*. That was the year in which his mother died and during which he was at work on his first novel,

Han d'Islande (1823; *Hans of Iceland*, 1845), a romantic extension of the love shared by Adèle and himself. In the year of his marriage, his first book was published, *Odes et poésies diverses* (1822, 1823); it was dedicated to Adèle.

Adèle and Victor Hugo had three sons and two daughters—Léopold II, Léopoldine, Charles, François-Victor, and Adèle. The marriage was filled with uncertainty and marred by infidelity, especially on Victor's part, but was never dissolved. After the publication of *Odes et ballades* in 1826, Victor Hugo befriended Charles Augustin Sainte-Beuve, who had reviewed *Odes et ballades* very favorably and who came, after a time, to carry on an extended amorous liaison with Adèle. The true love of Victor's life was Juliette Drouet, who devoted herself to him from 1832 until she died in his arms in 1883.

Hugo's long and imposing verse drama, *Cromwell* (English translation, 1896), appeared in 1827; it was not successful, but the prose preface written for it later was a great success as a Romantic manifesto. It champions Romantic against French classical literature, upholds the grotesque as an essential artistic development, calls for new rules and models of composition, and associates nature with truth.

French Romanticism may be said to have begun officially at the first performance of Hugo's play *Hernani* on February 25, 1830. One of the cardinal rules of French classical dramaturgy (no carryover, or enjambment, of a phrasal unit from the end of a verse-line to the beginning of the next) was broken in the first two lines of the drama. The vociferous protest against Hugo's audacity was outshouted by the Romantics in the audience, and *Hernani* went on to an acclaimed run.

The fame that *Hernani* brought to Hugo was sustained by his second novel, *Notre-Dame de Paris* (1831; *The Hunchback of Notre Dame*, 1833), published when he was only twenty-nine. It was at this period in his life that Hugo had to contend with his losing much of Adèle's love for him as she responded favorably to Sainte-Beuve's amatory overtures. Hugo translated his heartache into his fifth volume of poetry, *Les Feuilles d'automne* (1831).

His personal problems were in fellowship with his deepening social consciousness. He deplored the gross disadvantages suffered by the poor at the hands of the wealthy, and he despised the powerlessness of the lower echelons of society against injustices. Two of his works—*Le Dernier jour d'un condamné* (1829; *The Last Day of a Condemned*, 1840) and *Claude Gueux* (1834)—established an outcry that would culminate in *Les Misérables* (1862; English translation, 1862). Of his personal problems there appeared both the intensification and the solution in the young actress Juliette Drouet, whom Hugo met when she was cast in one of his plays, *Lucrèce Borgia* (1833; *Lucretia Borgia*, 1842). Adèle was as tolerant of Victor's love for Juliette as he had been of his wife's consorting with Sainte-Beuve. When Victor Hugo and Sainte-Beuve parted company permanently in 1834, the break resulted from professional differences and not personal conflict.

Juliette Drouet abandoned her own career and committed her entire life to Hugo, copying his manuscripts and serving him with a selfless devotion that became a mainstay of his emotional life. In October, 1837, he returned alone to Metz, where he and Juliette had first consummated their love. Troubled in spirit and shaken by his initial failure to be elected to the Académie Française, Hugo composed his poem "Tristesse d'Olympio" ("Olympio's Sadness"). "Olympio" is the name by which Hugo identified himself as a literary Romanticist. Hugo was elected, in his fifth candidacy and in the lingering triumph of his play *Ruy Blas*, to the Académie in 1841, by which time Juliette had become the equivalent of his second wife.

His triumphs and publications continued, and his fame grew. His personal joys alternated with personal tragedies. In 1843, his daughter Didine and her husband drowned in a boating accident. In 1844, he began his love affair with Léonie d'Aunet, wife of the painter Auguste Briard. In 1845, elevated to the peerage, he became Vicomte Hugo; shortly afterward, he and Madame Briard were surprised in their love nest by the police. In 1848, Hugo founded a newspaper, which within a short time placed itself in opposition to Louis Napoleon (Napoleon III). The editors, including his two brothers, were arrested in 1850, and Hugo himself went into an exile that was to last for twenty years. He was joined in exile by Juliette. His literary productivity flourished during these two decades. He published *Les Châtiments* in 1853; an enormously successful (and perhaps his very best) volume of poetry, entitled *Les Contemplations*, in 1856; *La Légende des siècles* (*The Legend of the Centuries*, 1894) in 1859-1883; the monumental *Les Misérables* in 1862; *William Shakespeare* (English translation, 1864) in 1864; and *Les Travailleurs de la mer* (*The Toilers of the Sea*, 1866) in 1866, among many other works.

During the last years of his exile, his son Charles presented Hugo with the author's first grandchild, Georges, born in 1867. Hugo's wife Adéle died the following year. Then, as the Second Empire, under Napoleon III, came to an end, Hugo returned to Paris, was received triumphantly, and embraced the Republican cause. His continued political activities, along with his literary and polemical work, did not abate, despite his advancing age. His last novel, *Quatre-vingt-treize* (*Ninety-three*, 1874), was published in 1874 and is, according to André Maurois, one of his finest. Three years later, Hugo was elected to the senate.

In 1878, Hugo and Juliette moved into a house at 130 Avenue d'Eylau. Hugo's eightieth birthday was celebrated as a national holiday, and the Avenue d'Eylau was renamed the Avenue Victor Hugo. Juliette died on May 11, 1883; Victor Hugo followed her in death on May 22, 1885, in Paris. At the news of his death, the senate and the chamber of deputies adjourned abruptly in initiation of a national mourning. Hugo's body lay in state beneath the Arc de Triomphe and was carried in triumphal procession to the Pantheon, where the remains of one of France's greatest literary giants was given a burial befitting a conquering hero.

Analysis

Hugo's literary artistry has as its base a definitive Romanticism, a religious sensibility, and a constant regard for the oppressed; its superstructure—a huge corpus of lyric poetry, an important group of verse dramas, and a soaring succession of novels—rises like a Gothic cathedral above the less excessive and more orderly monuments of nineteenth century French literature. For Hugo, excess confirmed and did not suppress greatness: "Heaven," he wrote, "is excess." His religious sensibility was nurtured by his sense of the divine, both in all things, in accordance with pagan depths of imagination, and above all things, in keeping with the Judeo-Christian concept of a deity of creation and succor. His regard for the oppressed is evident in his novels, with their pageantry of victimized innocence, and in his political tracts in favor of revolutionary changes to better the lot of workers and the poor.

To select from his works those most patently representative of the respective constituents of his literary artistry's base, one would perhaps choose the play *Hernani*, which ensured the victory of Romanticism for an entire generation, the novel *The Hunchback of Notre Dame*, with its personification of God as human expression and female force, and the novel *Les Misérables*, with a christological pilgrim of immortality as its hero.

For the inner Hugo, the subjective Olympio, one may turn to the Romanticism of his deeply subjective lyric poems. While the lyrics are replete with Romantic excess and concern for the downtrodden, they offer the reader the religious insight and the sense of personal triumph that Hugo experienced in the complex dimensions of human sadness. His Romantic melancholy is born of a joy in life and nature that reacts poignantly to its own curtailment by its own realization of the brevity and imperfection of human life before the lasting grandeur and magnificent beauty of nature.

In his 1856 collection of poems, *Les Contemplations*, his attitude toward poetic composition is most explicit. The collection is divided into six books, inclusive of 156 poems written during the period from 1830 to 1856, along with preface, prefatory poem, and long eight-part valedictory poem addressed "To Her Who Has Remained in France," that is, his daughter Léopoldine, who had died in 1843 and whose spirit pervades the second half of the collection. In the first book, "Aurore," the seventh poem, "Réponse à un acte d'accusation" ("Answer to an Accusation"), written in 1834, constitutes his *ars poetica*. He pleads guilty to trampling upon good taste and traditional French verse, to saying "Let there be darkness" in the manner of God saying "Let there be light," and to ravaging the "old A B C D." He asserts his disregard of Aristotelian limitations and his declaration of the equality, independence, and maturity of words. He sees himself as a revolutionary force taking art by the neck and standing as the instigator of a revolution of words.

In his declaration of the independence of words, he is like Jacques Derrida and the twentieth century deconstructionists who see words as Protean in their resistance to inflexible denotation and lexical boundaries. Just as the deconstructionists came to see words as objects, and objects as words, Hugo, in "À Propos d'Horace" ("Apropos of Horace"), had seen nature as "alphabet des grandes lettres d'ombre" (the alphabet of the great literature of darkness). Darkness or shadow, in Hugo's perspective, is where the truth lies: Light is the mask of Apollo, the disguise of darkness.

"Suite" ("Continuation"), a poem written in 1855 on the island of Jersey, is placed directly after "Answer to an Accusation" in "Aurore." It personifies the word (*le mot*) as a creative entity. The word says "My name is FIAT LUX"—Let there be light. The word, antedating its speaker, is like writing, which for Derrida antedates and creates language (and speech, which is the use of language). For both writers, what is posited is the Logos. "Continuation" concludes with "le mot, c'est le Verbe, et le Verbe, c'est Dieu" (the word is the Logos, and the Logos is God).

Hugo lyrically identifies himself with artistic expression by Romantically revolutionizing artistic expression, which in turn is Divinity itself. Prior to the publication of *Les Contemplations*, Hugo had begun work on two theological poems, the unfinished *La Fin de Satan* (1886; the end of Satan) and the never completed *Dieu* (1891; God); both long fragments were published posthumously. Oriented from Christianity, Hugo's religious sensibility found its tentative expression in a post-Christian spiritualism, not unrelated to the occultism of séances, which stabilized his belief in his personal immortality.

His unorthodox Christianity is discernible in *The Hunchback of Notre Dame*, in which architecture is seen as a form of writing (one might say, with the deconstructionists, a statement of Writing, or Logos), and in which Notre Dame (Our Lady) is not only the actual cathedral in Paris but also the spirit of the Virgin Mary, for whom the cathedral is named, as well as the virgin Esmeralda, who takes sanctuary within it. Hugo has in this novel already objectified his trinity of God, Soul, and Responsibility: God is the Logos expressed in the architecture, Soul is the female force of Our Lady, and Responsibility is the sanctuary given to "our lady" Esmeralda.

The magisterial *Les Misérables* is a prose parallel to *La Fin de Satan* and very much of a piece with the spiritualism of his 1850's poetry. The theological directions of the novel are apparent in the valley of the shadow—the life of danger, flight, concealment, injustice, and violence—through which the Christlike figure of Jean Valjean passes and in which he is witness to truth. The name "Valjean" itself means "John of the Valley."

Images of the valley of the shadow, of the world of truth in darkness or of dark truths, are dominant in Hugo's work. True light is the spiritual radiance experienced in the darkness, which is the shadow of God; it is the understanding provided by the shadow of the Logos, by "Ce que dit la bouche d'ombre" (what the mouth of shadow says). Conjunctive with his theological apprehension of true light in the darkness of shadow is his aesthetic notion of beauty in the grotesque. In his *La Préface de Cromwell* (1827; English translation, 1896), he speaks of the grotesque as one of the supreme beauties of drama. His own mastery of the grotesque can be seen in his Quasimodo, the hunchback of Notre Dame. Grotesquerie appears in tandem with theological shadow in *Ninety-three*, his last novel, in which the sun rises over a stone monster, the Tourgue (a prison), and a wooden monster, the guillotine. Characteristically, he calls the building a "dogma" and the machine an "idea"; and he adds, "The Tourgue was the monarchy, the guillotine the revolution."

In general, Hugo probes deeply the paradoxes of religion and lyric Romanticism and expresses these as a divine happiness situated in human sadness.

THE HUNCHBACK OF NOTRE DAME

First published: *Notre-Dame de Paris*, 1831 (English translation, 1833)
Type of work: Novel

A beautiful young woman, reared by gypsies, becomes the beloved of an ineffectual poet, a lecherous priest, and a grotesquely deformed bell ringer.

The Hunchback of Notre Dame, Hugo's second novel, emphasizes the theme of *anankē*, the Greek word for fate or necessity. *Anankē* appears in the novel chiefly as inevitable transition; stylistically, the transition is from classicism to Romanticism and, ultimately, from the human to the divine. The cathedral of Notre-Dame is the embodiment of what must be recognized as the permanence of transition. In origin a Gallo-Roman temple to the classical deity Jupiter, it became a Christian basilica and, later, in the twelfth century, a Romanesque cathedral; as its construction continued into the thirteenth century, the Gothic style overtook and succeeded the Romanesque configuration; and the cathedral, completed in 1345, stood as the architectural scripture of its own history. The novel is about this cathedral as a statement of *anankē* more than it is about any particular one of its many characters. In that sense, to translate the title, *Notre-Dame de Paris*, into *The Hunchback of Notre Dame* is seriously to delimit the magnitude of the novel.

The action of the novel begins on January 6, 1482, and ends in July of the same year, with an epilogistic chapter disclosing the fate of Quasimodo, the hunchback, dated to mid-1484. Esmeralda, a sixteen-year-old woman, identified as a gypsy and dancing in the company of her trained goat, catches the eye of Archdeacon Frollo, who orders his misshapen ward, Quasimodo, to kidnap her. Gringoire, a poet, fails in his efforts to intervene, but Esmeralda is rescued by Captain Phoebus and falls in love with him. She becomes the "bride" of Gringoire in a mock ceremony produced by a "court" of beggars. She later becomes the "bride" of Captain Phoebus, who promises marital commitment in his seduction of her but is murdered by Frollo before he can consummate his desire. Frollo frames her for the murder of Phoebus and offers to save her life if she will yield to his desire. She refuses and is then temporarily saved from execution by Quasimodo, who engineers sanctuary for her in the cathedral of Notre-Dame. Quasimodo also loves her and ultimately, after her actual execution, embraces her in death as his "bride" and achieves burial with her. Esmeralda, loving the one man who does not really love her and being loved by three men whom she does not love, remains a virgin through three "marriages," as Hugo reconstructs the Christian Trinity through Our Lady: Mother, Daughter, and Holy Spirit. Esmeralda is the point at which virginity, motherhood, and divinity intersect. Esmeralda, issuing from the womb of Our Lady (the cathedral that had been her sanctuary) is executed in an analogue to crucifixion. By the same spiritual geometry, Notre-Dame, the cathedral of the Mother Church, with its eponymous Virgin Mary as divine Mother, is the temporal-spatial point at which ancient, mediaeval, and modern architectural *logoi* (words) intersect in permanent transition. The transition is marked by the fifteenth century invention that will supersede the Logos of architecture: the printing press, which will prevail as the new Writing of humankind. The printed book is identified, in a chapter titled "Ceci tuera cela" (this will kill that), as the killer of architectural scripture and as the new representation of the human mind.

The narrative integrates some of the standard devices of ancient romance—such as the switching of infants, with the gypsy-infant Quasimodo substituted for Agnes, the daughter of Paquette la Chantefleurie, and the infant's shoe by which the mother sixteen years later recognizes Esmeralda as her daughter—and Hugo's Romanticism, in which truth reposes in darkness and grotesquerie. The true depth of the human spirit is sounded in the emotions of the shadow-concealed, deformed, one-eyed Quasimodo. The falsity of exterior light is explicit in the shallow, shining-knightlike Captain Phoebus, whose name is a metonym of the sun.

LES MISÉRABLES

First published: 1862 (English translation, 1862)
Type of work: Novel

A saintly fugitive from justice improves the lives of those whom he befriends and loves, achieves ascendance over his relentless pursuers, and redeems himself.

The title, *Les Misérables*, is Hugo's revision of his original title, "Les Misères." The choice is affinitive with Hugo's Romanticism, as it indicates a preference of the concrete (*the wretched ones*) to the abstract (*miseries*), of persons to situations. The full connotative strength of neither title can be retained in literal English translation, and it is good that English translations of the novel appear under the French title. The word *misérables* supports the double sense of "those who are wretched" and "those who are to be pitied." The second sense implies the possibility or presence of pitiers. The readers of the novel, then, may participate in the narrative as those who pity the pitiable. Pity is, etymologically, an act of *pietas* (piety). It is in this subjective inclusion of the reader in the art work that Romanticism differs from classicism. With regard to *Les Misérables*, the reader's pity is an experience of piety; and piety, in the full Latin sense of *pietas* (devotion, dedication, commiseration), is as much the theme of the novel as it is a manifestation of Hugo's deep religious sensibility.

The story begins with an account of the exemplary piety of a Christian bishop, Monseigneur Myriel Bienvenu, who selects as the most beautiful name of God, not Creator, Liberty, Light, Providence, not even God or Father, but the name given by Solomon, Miséricorde (compassion or pity). He is contrasted with men who dig for gold: He is one who digs for pity. To this seventy-five-year-old bishop, in the year 1815, comes Jean Valjean, a paroled convict who has spent nineteen years in prison. He is seeking lodging for the night, and no room has been found for him at the inns of the town. The priest offers him food, lodging, and trust. Valjean had been sentenced to prison, first for the theft of bread to feed his widowed sister and her seven children, and subsequently for four unsuccessful attempts to escape. Hardened by imprisonment and the reception given him by those who had either despised or exploited the ex-convict, he is capable now of crime for its own sake, as well as for survival. Checking his movement to murder the bishop as he sleeps, Valjean settles for stealing the household silverware. Apprehended and returned to the bishop, he is released, as the bishop, insisting the silverware was not stolen, adds a pair of candlesticks to the "gift." Valjean's receipt of mercy restores him to piety, the showing of mercy to others, although the first stage on his new journey involves his reflex theft of a coin from a boy, in his tearful remorse for which he undergoes repentance: He awakens to see a semblance of "Satan in the light of Paradise," returns to the door of Monseigneur Bienvenu, and prays in the predawn darkness.

Valjean's life of altruism takes the forms of various *personas* after his moment of truth in the shadow. The first of these is that of the good mayor of a town; his appropriate pseudonym is Père Madeleine (translatable as Father Magdalene, that is, a priestlike layman converted from wrongdoing). He intercedes with a police inspector, Javert, to save a woman, Fantine, from a six-month prison sentence. Then, learning from Javert that another man had been arrested as Valjean, in connection with the goods stolen from the bishop, Valjean turns himself in. Later, he escapes from prison and becomes the protector of Fantine's daughter, Cosette. Living under cover in Paris, he rears Cosette as his daughter and becomes devoted to her. Eventually, Cosette falls in love with Marius, a political activist, toward whom Valjean will bear a paternal resentment; he is once again a "father," and Cosette addresses him as such. Marius is wounded in the republican uprising of 1832; Valjean rescues him and carries him to safety through the labyrinthine Parisian sewers. The strictly honorable Javert, who finally discovers his unceasing pursuit of Valjean to have been unjust, commits suicide. Cosette and Marius are wed. Valjean, vindicated and at last content, dies in peace in the light of candles held by the "gift" candlesticks.

The novel incorporates a number of subplots and a great variety of characters. All of its narrative elements contribute in the manner of an epic, which it is, to a broad perspective of the Napoleonic era. The Emperor Napoleon I himself appears in the long episode devoted to the Battle of Waterloo. Marius' father is an officer in Napoleon's army whose life is saved by Thénardier, to whom accordingly Marius is in debt and by whom Valjean comes also to be pursued. The history of postrevolutionary France, its changing social institutions, the persistence of its religious customs, and its political turmoil, along with realistic depictions of Parisian life and converse, much of which is embodied in the character of a street-smart boy named Gavroche, are interstitial to the vast fabric of Hugo's tale. To his Romantic tale Hugo adapts much of the machinery of classical epic.

Hugo includes two parenthetical disquisitions: one on the Convent as an abstract idea and as historical fact (part 2, book 7) and one on argot, or slang (part 4, book 7). These slow down the narrative but greatly intensify its substance. The Convent, according to Hugo, is abstractly right in its nurture of religious sensibility but concretely wrong in its preservation of outmoded ritual and dogma. Argot is *la langue des ténébreux* (the language of the shadows). It is the language mainly of wrongdoers (those abominated by society), like "cant" in Henry Fielding's *The History of the Life of the Late Mr. Jonathan Wild the Great* (1743, 1754) and "nadsat" in Anthony Burgess' *A Clockwork Orange* (1962), but it is also the language of poverty and is, in its rebelliousness and poetic turn, a language of true life.

Rebelliousness, religious sensibility, and poetic concretion make *Les Misérables* an epical testament to Romanticism. In its five parts, comprising forty-eight books, themselves comprising 361 chapters, the novel discloses the failure of rationalism and of rigidly organized religion. The first two chapters of the first book in part 1 are significantly titled "Un Juste" (a just man) and "La Chute" (the fall). The just man is Monseigneur Bienvenu; the fall is that of Jean Valjean, but it is a fall, not from, but into, grace as he becomes the bishop's successor in justness. His passage through crime and, climactically, through the Dantesque hell of the sewers of Paris is a pilgrimage of redemption, a movement not toward a paradisiacal light but into the true light at the core of darkness. The last chapter of the concluding book is titled "Suprème Ombre, Suprème Aurore" (supreme darkness, supreme dawn). The supreme darkness is the life that Valjean has fully lived; the supreme dawn is his death.

ECSTASY

First published: "Extase," 1831 (English translation, 1883)
Type of work: Poem

The poet expresses an affinity with nature.

The "Ecstasy" that Hugo describes in this twelve-line poem is his experience of himself in nature as nature identifies itself with God. The poem reads, in prose translation, as follows:

> I was standing alone by the waves on a starry night, under a cloudless sky and by a sea unbothered by sails. My eyes saw more than the material world; and the woods and mountains and all of nature seemed to question, in mingled murmur, the waves of the sea and the fires of heaven. And the countless legions of golden stars were answering, in voices raised and lowered in a host of harmonies; and the blue waves, which nothing controls or hinders, were saying, as their crest foamed back in an arc, "It is the Lord, the Lord God!"

The solitary stance of the individual in an almost but not quite pantheistic communion with nature is a characteristic posture of nineteenth century Romantic poets, in

Germany and England, as well as in France. During the eighteenth century, "nature" was "human nature," which could be improved by rationalism and enlightenment, and ecstasy was as suspect an irrational quality as it had been to Plato. With Johann Wolfgang von Goethe, William Wordsworth, and Hugo, however, "nature" was the terrestrial and physical universe with which an individual could establish a subjective relationship that was predispositional to spiritual gratification and religious satisfaction. Hugo intones that relationship in this short lyric, in which ecstasy and the night transcend reason and daylight.

OLYMPIO'S SADNESS

First published: "Tristesse d'Olympio," 1840 (English translation, 1883)
Type of work: Poem

The poet makes a solitary retreat to the valley in which he and his mistress began their love affair.

"Olympio's Sadness" is Hugo's realization that nature, endlessly beautiful, can be seen as cruel to human beings, whose beauty, in love and as part of nature, is fleeting and cannot, or will not, be sustained by nature: "How little time it takes for you, Nature, with your unwrinkled brow, to change everything, disregardingly, and, in your acts of transformation, to snap the mysterious threads that bind our hearts." Hugo saw himself as an Olympian, both in his unorthodox religiousness, which was closer to Greek paganism than to Christianity, and in his sense of personal greatness. For him, sadness was not the opposite of happiness but the comprehension of happiness, even as he considered the true light of the religious soul to be implicit in the darkness and not external to it.

The poem was composed in October, 1937, and is rich in autumnal resonance; but the day is bright with light, and the sky is unvaryingly clear. The external light brings the poet no joy. Joy is to be remembered only in the natural things—birds, streams, the sky, lakes, and such—that have no remembrance but are themselves remembered and, in being remembered, are for lovers "the shadow of love itself." The thirty-eighth, and last, stanza locates the soul in a pitch-black night, where the holiness of memory, the essence of human happiness, sleeps in the shadow.

In making this sentimental journey to the scene of his early days of love with his mistress Juliette Drouet, Hugo is following the examples of his fellow Romantic poets Alphonse de Lamartine and Alfred de Musset, each of whom had written superb poems about such retreats.

The first eight stanzas of the poem, each consisting of a pair of two and a half Alexandrine verses, is a third-person narrative of the poet's return to the scene of his love: the pond, the garden, the orchard, the chestnut tree where the poet and his mistress held trysts and which they used as a repository for love letters. These stanzas are followed by thirty Alexandrine quatrains in which the poet recounts in direct statement his reactions to the loss of subjective syntony over a three-year passage of time.

The poem opens with "The fields were no longer dark," and, in the smiling autumn light, the poet finds the sadness of his soul. The poem closes with "this night which no light spangles," in which darkness his soul senses the pulsation of memory. The progression of the day from light to darkness defines the progression of the soul from melancholy to the bliss enclosed in what Wordsworth calls "the still sad music of humanity."

Summary

Viewing philosophy as, in the words of his character Jean Valjean, "the microscope of thought," Victor Hugo chose lyric poetry, the verse drama, and the novel to produce his macroscopic depiction of human feeling. He is the consummate Romanticist, for whom the dark reaches of the emotions hold more truth than do the logic and science of the Enlightenment. "Science," he wrote, "has the first word on everything, the last word on nothing"; and he urged artists always to oppose "shadow to light" and "invisible truth to visible fact."

The three *r*'s evident in Hugo's life and work are revolution, Romanticism, and religion; and, in his writing, each is implicit with his apprehension of the female force: The fictional women in his novels and the actual women who inspired most of his poetry all attest to his belief that "the poem that is Woman pervades the history of Man."

Bibliography

Brombert, Victor. *The Romantic Prison: The French Tradition.* Princeton, N.J.: Princeton University Press, 1979.

———. *Victor Hugo and the Visionary Novel.* Cambridge, Mass.: Harvard University Press, 1984.

Grant, Richard B. *The Perilous Quest: Image, Myth and Prophecy in the Narratives of Victor Hugo.* Durham, N.C.: Duke University Press, 1968.

Houston, John Porter. *Victor Hugo.* Rev. ed. Boston: Twayne, 1988.

Hugo, Victor. *Victor Hugo's Intellectual Autobiography,* (*Being the Last of the Unpublished Works and Embodying the Author's Ideas on Literature, Philosophy, and Religion*). Translated by Lorenzo O'Rourke. New York: Haskell House, 1971.

Maurois, Andre. *Olympio: The Life of Victor Hugo.* Translated by Gerard Hopkins. New York: Harper and Brothers, 1956.

———. *Victor Hugo and His World.* Translated by Oliver Bernard. New York: Viking, 1966.

Richardson, Joanna. *Victor Hugo.* London: Weidenfeld & Nicolson, 1976.

Roy Arthur Swanson

ALDOUS HUXLEY

Born: Godalming, Surrey, England
July 26, 1894
Died: Los Angeles, California
November 22, 1963

Principal Literary Achievement
Widely renowned as a satiric novelist, Huxley contributed significantly to literary modernism's skeptical reassessment of the scientific and technological tendencies of twentieth century society.

Biography
Aldous Leonard Huxley was born on July 26, 1894, in Godalming, Surrey, England, the third son of Dr. Leonard Huxley, a teacher, editor, and writer, and Julia Arnold, niece of Matthew Arnold and sister of novelist Mrs. Humphrey Ward. Aldous was also the grandson of Thomas Henry Huxley, a well-known scientist, and the brother of scientist Sir Julian Huxley.

Huxley had planned on a career as a physician, but an affliction with nearly total blindness while studying at Eton altered his plans, and, upon partial recovery three years later, he entered Balliol College, Oxford, and earned a degree in English literature. While Huxley was at Oxford, World War I began, and he was refused enlistment because of his poor eyesight; eventually, he became totally disillusioned about the war and about the direction of twentieth century society, particularly after a visit to America in the Roaring Twenties, during which he was appalled by the material excesses and what he saw as a pervasive spiritual emptiness. The death of his mother when he was fourteen and of his brother Trevenen when Aldous was eighteen may have contributed to the skeptical bent of Aldous' mind. The Oxford years, however, did establish important literary connections for Huxley, since during his years there he met Bertrand Russell, the Sitwells, D. H. Lawrence, and Lytton Strachey, among others, as well as his future wife, Maria Nys.

After graduation, Huxley worked briefly for the Air Board as a patriotic duty until his poor vision forced his resignation. He then taught at Eton, the preparatory school from which he had been graduated, but did not enjoy teaching, perhaps because of his somewhat introverted nature. He switched to a position as second assistant editor of *The Athenaeum,* a literary review; the increased salary allowed him to marry Maria Nys in 1919. Then, in 1920-1921, he worked as drama critic for *The Westmin-*

ster Gazette, at the same time writing *Chrome Yellow* (1921), his first novel, which began the development of his reputation as a skillful satiric novelist. (Although he had been publishing poetry and short stories since his college days, including *The Burning Wheel,* 1916, his first poetry volume, none had been very successful.)

The even more successful novels *Antic Hay* (1923) and *Those Barren Leaves* (1925) followed, allowing Huxley the financial security to leave journalistic work and travel widely in Europe and even once around the world, with stops in India, the Dutch East Indies, and the United States. In fact, from 1923 until his death in 1963, Huxley lived elsewhere than in England, returning there only for visits. From 1923 until 1930, he lived in Italy, studying and admiring Italian architecture and landscapes (painting being a hobby) but expressing contempt for Fascism. While there, he wrote *Point Counter Point* (1928), which was second only to *Brave New World* (1932) in popularity. The latter was written during Huxley's years in southern France, at Sanery-sur-Mer; he had moved there in 1930 because of the pleasant climate and reasonable cost of living. During these years of residence in France, he also took a trip to Central America that was the basis for his successful travel book *Beyond the Mexique Bay* (1934). Given his diverse knowledge and interests, Huxley also wrote book reviews, newspaper articles, plays, short stories, and forewords, introductions, and prefaces for others' works—a total of some eighty-five works being written or edited by Huxley by the time of his death in 1963.

That death came in the United States, to which Huxley had immigrated from France in 1937 for several reasons, including not only his belief in impending disaster in Europe (on the eve of World War II) but also his love of the Mojave desert and its climate. The latter, particularly, in combination with the Bates method of visual re-education, improved his eyesight.

Huxley remained politically engaged in the 1930's and early 1940's, attending to his humanistic concerns, working to avoid World War II, even writing a book, *Ends and Means,* in 1937 on war's motives and futility. Yet both during and after World War II, he turned to less practical considerations and embraced a kind of psychological and philosophical/religious mysticism as a solution to the lack of wholeness, to the fragmentation, of the modern world. That mystical focus is evident even in the 1941 study of Father Joseph, *Grey Eminence,* and in his important later novels *After Many a Summer Dies the Swan* (1939), *Ape and Essence* (1948), and *The Island* (1962). Paradoxically, however, given the Huxley family's scientific tradition, that mysticism was also pragmatic and empirical, involving an attempt to synthesize all of life's diverse elements. Thus, during his years in America, Huxley wrote scripts for Hollywood movies and articles for *Playboy* and *Esquire* while at the same time writing essays on parapsychology and mystical novels (novels that also include the very earthy, such as the sexual elements in *The Island*). Nor did the mystical concern preclude some political and social activity, such as Huxley's work for the United Nations Food and Agriculture Organization based on his concern with overpopulation, or his help in the Campaign Against Hunger in 1963.

Socially, too, he was active, talking with Igor Stravinsky, taking walks with Thomas

Mann, having picnics with Anita Loos and Charlie Chaplin, and even going for drives with a juvenile delinquent (Huxley enjoyed and studied automobiles throughout his life).

The mystical concern did help Huxley deal with his wife's death from cancer in 1955 and with his own long struggle with cancer that ended on November 22, 1963, in Los Angeles, California. His life and work indeed reflect a highly varied but impressively unified mind that continually developed in a consistent way from early satiric skepticism to the confident mysticism of the later years, and which throughout shows the constant human conflict between the intellectual and emotional polarities of the human personality. Huxley did in fact achieve the synthesis and unity that were the object of his lifetime search.

Analysis

Huxley's primary thematic concern in his fiction is with the ramifications of humanness: what the authentic human values are, what life-styles humans should adopt, and what type of society or world humans should create. He is particularly concerned, in that context, with the issue of modernist alienation and isolation in a complex scientific and technological society that, particularly in 1928 and 1932 (the respective dates of publication of his two most important novels, *Point Counter Point* and *Brave New World*), was in great upheaval because of the economic problems of capitalism that were all too evident. As a humanist in the classical and Renaissance sense of a broadly educated and talented person with a devotion to improving life on earth, Huxley particularly focuses upon the psychological effects of twentieth century life, of a life on nonstop action as it shapes human attitudes toward love, material possessions, and political structures, but especially as it affects the personal balance and happiness of individual human beings. If humans were not happier in the twentieth century than in the past (and Huxley firmly believed that they were not), then why not? Where did they err and lose the normal human balance of intellect and emotion, body and soul, love and hate, self-concern and concern for others—all the balances involved in being naturally adjusted and contented?

Implicit in such an assumption of balanced "naturalness" is the Romantic conception of humans living in harmony with nature, with all of the created, living world, and thus with themselves. Such a Goetheian Romantic stance inevitably led Huxley to be critical of science and technology and of any positive human future based upon such products of the rational side of human beings. Hence, Huxley continuously presents the scientist as a threat and his creations, his machines, as a similar danger because they control those who use them. The use of machines is implicitly connected to corrupted values in *Point Counter Point* and *Brave New World*, for example. In the former, this theme is depicted in Lucy Tantamount's fascination with airplanes and fast travel as a way to avoid real emotion in relationships, as a way to speed to a new and superficial love relationship. Hence, Lucy deserts Walter Bidlake because he is too caring: too deep in his attachments, too unlike the mechanistic superficiality and temporariness and rapid pace of Lucy's modern life. Similarly, machines in *Brave New World* adversely affect the normal freedom and balance and harmony in life; for example, mechanical birth processes that allow the creation of perfectly planned, robotic humans who are further controlled by science-created soma, a drug for pleasure and distraction that deprives humans of the pain and suffering that motivate thought and questioning, and thus intellectual development. The result is an acceptance of controlled, thoughtless, superficial lives that lack both emotional depth and intellectual attainment.

It was this kind of presentation of science and technology that led H. G. Wells, the positivist science-fiction writer, to write a letter to Huxley damning him for treason to science after *Brave New World* was published. Such presentation also led to Huxley's being criticized for cynicism, with many critics not wanting to, or at any rate failing to, note the real human potential for success implicit in both *Point Counter Point* and *Brave New World*. Those successes include the balanced-living Mark and Mary Rampion in the former (who do their own housework, read and discuss ideas, and live emotionally and fully, as well) and Bernard and Helmholtz in the latter.

There are also unbalanced and tragic characters in Huxley's novels, characters who embody Huxley's ideas about flaws in human development, flaws that lead to unnaturalness and psychological aberration. The purpose of these characters in Huxley's novels of ideas is to illustrate the causative forces of psychological aberration, such as Spandrell's unnatural closeness to his mother, which causes him to hate her, himself, and everyone else when she remarries. He is led to murder as a product of his hate-filled imbalance. Yet such scenes merely illustrate one type of human perversion and do not indicate the cynical views of the author.

More justified criticisms of Huxley's novels are that the concern with ideas is so pervasive that characterization is often limited to speeches and dialogue as a way to present ideas, and that plot unity is often lacking because too many characters are used to represent the mélange of ideas involved. Yet both *Point Counter Point* and *Brave New World* present positive, hopeful ideas as well as negative ones, as Huxley conveys his messages about the need for more human psychological balance and for more skeptical analysis of the "advancements" in science and technology.

POINT COUNTER POINT

First published: 1928
Type of work: Novel

In early twentieth century England, a range of interrelated characters illustrate the modern world's complexity and the difficulty of harmonious, sane existence within it.

Point Counter Point, Huxley's greatest novelistic success except for *Brave New World,* is a complex work involving a multitude of characters who represent various extremes of imbalance in earthly life, imbalances that detract from naturalness and harmony. As such, these characters are the most inclusive presentation of Huxley's ideas about erroneous human values and actions, and about the complex social, political, economic, and psychological causes of such actions and values.

The novel unfolds in a very diffuse way. The introductory section is structured around a party given by Lord Edward Tantamount and his wife, which is attended by a multitude of the "rich and famous," including nearly all of the characters whose lives are alternately focused upon in the rest of the novel. At the party, the central conflict is also foreshadowed, that between the socialist Illidge, Lord Tantamount's scientific assistant, and the ultraconservative, capitalistically privileged leader of a reactionary political group, Everard Webley. That plot line then develops with Spandrell's very Freudian and psychologically violent perverseness contributing to the radical violence implicit within Illidge's perspective. (Spandrell has been too psychologically attached to his mother, and her remarriage devastates him, turning him into a pathological being, the villain of the novel.) At Spandrell's urging, he and Illidge eventually perform the central action of the novel, the murder of Everard Webley. That murder leads to the novel's climactic moment, the somewhat tragically heroic decision by Spandrell to destroy himself by forcing the police to kill him, illustrating the destructiveness of the social, political, and psychological counterpoints in twentieth century society.

The other plot line counterpoints develop in similarly tragic ways. The painter John Bidlake's psychosexual excessiveness is paralleled by that of the editor Burlap and the Tantamounts' spoiled daughter Lucy, all three characters pursuing sexual pleasure at the expense of other characters, such as John Bidlake's wives and models, Burlap's rejected secretary Ethel Cobbett (who commits suicide), and Walter Bidlake, from whom Lucy drifts away out of boredom in her pursuit of sexual adventures. These psychosexually excessive characters are themselves also seen as tragic, John Bidlake unable to cope with death, Lucy pursuing sexuality in a desperate attempt to escape thought and deep feeling, and Burlap regressing to an almost infantile sexual relationship with Beatrice Gilray.

The tragic lives of the psychosexually excessive are counterpointed by the equally tragic lives of the religiously and intellectually excessive. Fanatically Christian Rachel Quarles almost totally retreats from her husband and children into religious isolation, in the process bringing Walter Bidlake's mistress, Marjorie, into the same kind of mystical isolation, which leaves Marjorie totally incapable of helping Walter cope with his rejection by Lucy Tantamount. Similarly, Walter's intellectual excessiveness makes him incapable of contentment with either Marjorie or Lucy, since, like Don Quixote, he has read so much idealistic literature that he is continually searching for more than reality affords. Thus, his life is continual tragic dissatisfaction. Also, the philosophically excessive Philip Quarles continually withdraws into thought and avoids feeling, and thus cannot relate to his son, little Phil, or even feel very affected by Phil's death. He is also so withdrawn that he nearly drives his wife into an affair with Everard Webley, a circumstance prevented only by Phil's sudden illness and

Webley's murder. Philip Quarles's future is as bleak as that of most of the other characters, since he remains trapped within his personal imbalance. The intellectually scientific are also presented as a counterpoint to the psychosexually excessive, with Lord Edward Tantamount embodying the withdrawn, socially dysfunctional scientist who cannot sexually relate to his wife and who is only happy doing experiments in his laboratory. Thus, at the novel's end, only the Rampions, Mark and Mary, remain as embodiments of the possibility of synthesis and balance in an imbalanced, fragmented modern world that is resoundingly rejected by Huxley in this profoundly satiric novel.

BRAVE NEW WORLD

First published: 1932
Type of work: Novel

In the future world imagined in this novel, there is no provision for complete and emotional human existence.

Brave New World continues the presentation of human psychological and other imbalances of *Point Counter Point,* but in a more creative and unified way. It is set in a future society in which control over individuals is nearly absolute and in which there is virtually no possibility of maintaining a sane, balanced, and fully human existence. Through the future setting of a scientifically created and controlled technological society, operating in artificial harmony by virtue of nearly deadened human emotional and intellectual attributes, Huxley focuses on the danger of what twentieth century society could become if the values of order, profit, and power continue to prevail over spontaneous creativity, mutual respect and pleasure, and cooperative idealism.

The citizens in this "brave new world" are controlled and conditioned from birth, in fact before birth, by means of genetic engineering, or mechanical childbirth processes. Humans are then subjected to a variety of operant conditioning techniques, including hypnopaedia, or sleep-teaching, which fit them for their carefully planned roles in the society. This role preparation is involved even in the genetic engineering, too, as the embryonic rocket engineers' birth tubes are kept in constant motion to prepare the engineers to work in weightless environments in which right-side-up and upside-down positions alternate constantly. In the words of the director of the genetics institute, "They learn to associate topsy-turvydom with well-being; in fact, they're only truly happy when they're standing on their heads." The conditioning continues throughout life, the sleep teaching reinforced by the entertainment drug soma, which encourages narcissistic self-indulgence and thus lack of concern for larger decisions of societal direction made by the few in power.

The system of scientific and technological control, directed by Mustapha Mond, is not yet perfect. Some humans continue to be dissatisfied and want more than what is prescribed for them. Mond, who fears real human experience and thus uses control and artificial creation to avoid such balance, has trouble particularly with the emotional and intellectual longings of several characters, with their often subconscious desire to be whole. Specifically, Bernard keeps longing for real love, not just entertainment sex, and the same is true to some extent of Lenina (thus the important Freudian psychology element again in Huxley's work). Also, Helmholtz keeps feeling unfulfilled because of some deeply suppressed need that has not been totally eliminated.

The Savage, though, is particularly problematic for Mond. The Savage realizes the total imbalance, the total inhumanness, of the society in its elimination of both deep feeling and intellectual attainment. He believes in feeling, in living, and in experiencing real human pain and thus real human joy—even the pain of death, which defines and creates human joy. When Mond questions him, the Savage admits that he is "claiming the right to be unhappy." Mond responds with the following:

> Not to mention the right to grow old and ugly and impotent; the right to have syphilis and cancer; the right to have too little to eat; the right to be lousy; the right to live in constant apprehension of what may happen tomorrow; the right to catch typhoid; the right to be tortured by unspeakable pains of every kind.

The Savage's response is simply, "I claim them all." They are all part of being human, of being in the real world, and Huxley sees the drug-induced life of scientific and technological society as destructive of that real world. Thus, the Savage dies tragically by hanging himself, in primitive reaction against a world that has eliminated the side of human beings that he represents.

Summary

In *Brave New World,* which describes a future society that seems perfectly orderly, harmonious, and controlled but which is actually depraved, unhappy, and hellish, Aldous Huxley embodies his principal ideas. He also embodies them in *Point Counter Point,* in a diffuse portrait of imbalanced characters in early twentieth century England.

One of those principal ideas is that humanness and authentic human values involve recognition of and participation in all the dichotomies of human existence: emotion and intellect, mind and body, body and soul, love and hate, self-concern and concern for others. Without that balance and total development, humans are doomed to incomplete, and often tragic, lives. The other principal belief is that modern society is itself unbalanced in its overly scientific and technological orientation, leading to intellect dominating emotion and thus to final tragedy unless drastic adjustments are made. It is that idea that continues to make Huxley's two great novels tremendously important in solving the problems of today's world.

Bibliography

Baker, Robert S. *The Dark Historic Page: Social Satire and Historicism in the Novels of Aldous Huxley, 1921-1939.* Madison: University of Wisconsin Press, 1982.

Bass, Eben E. *Aldous Huxley: An Annotated Bibliography of Criticism.* New York: Garland, 1981.

Bedford, Sybille. *Aldous Huxley: A Biography.* New York: Knopf, 1974.

Birnbaum, Milton. *Aldous Huxley's Quest for Values.* Knoxville: University of Tennessee Press, 1971.

Huxley, Laura Archera. *This Timeless Moment: A Personal View of Aldous Huxley.* New York: Farrar, 1968.

Kuehn, Robert E., ed. *Aldous Huxley: A Collection of Critical Essays.* Englewood Cliffs, N.J.: Prentice-Hall, 1974.

Rolo, Charles J., ed. *The World of Aldous Huxley.* New York: Grosset, 1947.

Watt, Donald, ed. *Aldous Huxley: The Critical Heritage.* Boston: Routledge, 1975.

Woodcock, George. *Dawn and the Darkest Hour: A Study of Aldous Huxley.* New York: Viking Press, 1972.

John L. Grigsby

HENRIK IBSEN

Born: Skien, Norway
March 20, 1828
Died: Christiania (now Oslo), Norway
May 23, 1906

Principal Literary Achievement

Ibsen is widely regarded as the most important dramatist since William Shakespeare, not only for the depth and complexity of the major characters in his plays but also for his technical innovations and his subtle use of symbolism.

Biography

Henrik Johan Ibsen was born in Skien, a small town on the east coast of Norway, on March 20, 1828, to Knud and Marchinen Altenburg Ibsen. By all accounts, he was a withdrawn and introspective child, much given to reading, painting, and creating puppets for the tiny theater that he had constructed in a storehouse attached to his childhood home. The financial decline of the Ibsen family severely curtailed his formal education. Though he had hoped to go to the university and study medicine, in 1843 he left school and became an apprentice to an apothecary in the small coastal town of Grimstad, where he was to spend nearly seven years. The revolution of 1848 in France, coupled with his study of Cicero's oration against the Roman senator Lucius Sergius Catalina (Cataline), inspired the young Ibsen to write his first play, an unsuccessful verse tragedy entitled *Catalina* (1850; *Cataline*, 1921), which treats Cataline not as a traitor to Rome but as an idealistic reformer.

In 1850, Ibsen left Grimstad for Christiania, where he tried his hand at journalism while studying for the examinations that would qualify him to enter the university. Although his second play, *Kjalempehøien* (1850; *The Burial Mound*, 1912), was accepted by the Christiania Theater and performed three times that autumn, his other projects met with little success. While he was struggling to make his mark in literary circles in Christiania, a Norwegian National Theater was established in Bergen to encourage Norwegian playwrights to develop an independent dramatic tradition. In the autumn of 1851, Ibsen was offered a position as "dramatic author" in this new theater. The next spring, the directors of the theater sent him abroad to study theatrical methods. He spent six weeks at the Royal Theater in Copenhagen and about a month in Dresden, seeing plays and studying stage machinery. After his return to Bergen, he signed a five-year contract as "scene instructor," a position that placed

961

him in charge of blocking, decor, and costumes. He was also expected to write a new play each year for performance on the anniversary of the opening of the theater. In this capacity, he wrote *Sancthans nat ten* (1853; *St. John's Night*, 1921), *Fru Inger til Østraat* (1855; *Lady Inger of Østraat*, 1906), *Gildet paa Solhaug* (pb. 1856; *The Feast at Solhaugh*, 1906)—his first theatrical triumph—and *Olaf Liljekrans* (1857; English translation, 1911).

In 1856, nineteen-year-old Suzannah Thoreson, a young woman of strong character and progressive views, accepted Ibsen's proposal of marriage; they were married on June 18, 1858, nearly a year after Ibsen had left Bergen to become the artistic director of the Christiania Norwegian Theater. Though it was a great success at the Norwegian Theater, his next play, *Hærmænde paa Helgeland* (1858; *The Vikings at Helgeland*, 1890), could not offset the growing financial difficulties of the theater, which finally had to close down in the summer of 1862. Ibsen's negative views of marriage in *Kjærlighedens komedie* (1862; *Love's Comedy*, 1900) stirred up a storm of protest, and not even the success of *Kongsemnerne* (pb. 1863; *The Pretenders*, 1890), a historical drama of Shakespearean proportions, could rescue him from the desperate financial situation into which he had fallen. Disillusioned by failure in his chosen career, he felt like an outcast. Supported by a state grant for foreign travel, he and his wife and young son left Norway in 1864 for what was to be twenty-seven years of self-imposed exile—with only two short visits to his homeland before his return to Christiania in 1891.

The Ibsens settled first in Italy, where they remained for the next four years. The verse drama *Brand* (pb. 1866; English translation, 1891) proved so successful in book form that it made Ibsen financially independent for the first time in his life. Though less successful with critics than *Brand*, its companion piece, *Peer Gynt* (1867; English translation, 1892), quickly went into a second edition. It was first produced at the Christiania Theater in 1876 with a musical suite by Norwegian composer Edvard Grieg and has been staged frequently ever since. In 1868, the Ibsen family settled in Dresden, Germany, where they remained for nearly seven years, during which time Ibsen wrote *De unges forbund* (1869; *The League of Youth*, 1890), a five-act political comedy satirizing liberal politicians. Immensely popular in its day, this play has not earned a permanent place in the modern repertory, nor has *Kejeser og Galilæer* (1873; *Emperor and Galileau*, 1876), a two-part drama in ten acts about the Roman Emperor Julian, called Julian the Apostate.

In 1875, Ibsen moved his family to Munich, Germany, where he wrote *Samfundets støtter* (1877; *The Pillars of Society*, 1880), a play that signaled a new direction in his work. This play and the eleven that followed it all deal with problems in contemporary life. Between 1878 and 1891, the Ibsens divided their time between Munich and Rome with vacations in Berchtesgaden and Gossensass in Tyrol and (in 1885) a summer in Norway. During this period, Ibsen achieved international fame with a series of fascinating, often controversial plays: *Et dukkehjem* (1879; *A Doll's House*, 1880), *Gengangere* (1881; *Ghosts*, 1885), *En folkefiende* (pb. 1882; *An Enemy of the People*, 1890), all of which have a social emphasis. In the next four plays, *Vildanden* (pb. 1884;

The Wild Duck, 1891), *Rosmersholm* (pb. 1886; English translation, 1889), *Fruen fra havet* (pb. 1888; *The Lady from the Sea*, 1890), and *Hedda Gabler* (pb. 1890; English translation, 1891), Ibsen becomes increasingly interested in exploring the psychological depths of his dramatic figures.

In 1891, Ibsen left Munich to spend the rest of his life in Christiania. His last four plays, *Bygmester Solness* (pb. 1892; *The Master Builder*, 1893), *Lille Eyolf* (pb. 1894; *Little Eyolf*, 1894), *John Gabriel Borkman* (pb. 1896; English translation, 1897), and *Naar vi døde vaagner* (pb. 1899; *When We Dead Awaken*, 1900), are deep philosophical meditations on the conflict between life and art. In the spring of 1900, Ibsen became gravely ill; the next year, he suffered his first stroke. In 1903, another stroke broke his health completely. He died on May 23, 1906, in Christiania and was buried with great honor by the Norwegian state.

Analysis

Ibsen's protagonists generally have great difficulty in coming to terms with the ideas, institutions, and laws that exist to direct their lives. For that reason, they battle for freedom and truth, though their efforts are frequently undermined by the fact that their own past misdeeds threaten to destroy them. This pattern is already evident in *Cataline*, the protagonist of Ibsen's first play. An ardent idealist, Cataline is powerless to reform a corrupt society because he is haunted by the ghosts of his own past. The two women in his life, his gentle wife Aurelia and the avenging Furia, represent the opposing forces at war within him. The alternative to active engagement with the forces that limit our freedom is aesthetic withdrawal. The conflict between Ibsen's own desire to retreat into aesthetic contemplation and his need to act is clearly expressed in "On the Fells," a poem about a hunter who contemplates life from the heights. Ascent to the mountain top, a common Romantic symbol of artistic detachment, is nearly always connected with the aesthetic view of life in Ibsen's plays.

Many of the concerns of Ibsen's early plays come into sharp focus in the two verse dramas *Brand* and *Peer Gynt*, both of which raise the question of how one can be true to one's self. Loosely based on some of the ideas of Danish philosopher Søren Kierkegaard, *Brand*, with its insistence on total commitment ("all or nothing"), is an existentialist tragedy. Brand is a fiery young pastor who carries Romantic individualism to the extreme. After an unrelenting struggle against "the spirit of compromise," a struggle that costs the lives of his infant son and his wife, he is swallowed up by an avalanche, which reproves him with the words, "He is the God of love." If Brand represents commitment to duty and to a high-minded way of life that kills joy and denies love, Peer Gynt, the hero of Ibsen's next play, learns—almost too late—that only by rejecting the self-sufficiency of the romantic individualist and committing oneself to love can one transcend the limits of the self.

The opposition between Brand's self-denial and Peer's self-indulgence is restated in *Emperor and Galilean* as the conflicting claims of Christian aceticism (the Tree of the Cross) and pagan hedonism (the Tree of Knowledge). In this play, the Emperor Julian dreams of effecting a synthesis between these two views of life by establishing a mysterious "third empire." The hope that some such synthesis will open a new path for happiness and self-fulfillment recurs in many of Ibsen's subsequent dramas. *Emperor and Galilean* was Ibsen's last historical play; *Peer Gynt* was his last verse drama. After *The Pillars of Society*, all Ibsen's plays deal with contemporary life. *The Pillars of Society* is a thesis play designed to show that society is built on rotten foundations. Following the pattern of the popular French "well-made play," Ibsen makes the gradual unveiling of past misdeeds the source of dramatic tension in this play, but instead of trivializing and resolving all conflicts in the last act, he adds psychological depth and social significance to this technique by pressing forward to an unmasking and a confession. A similar pattern underlies all of his subsequent dramas: The protagonist is forced to confront a problem from the past.

In most of these plays, personal conflict is rooted in ideological differences. Ultraconservative characters, usually businessmen or lawyers, oppose any sort of social change that will jeopardize their wealth or their authority. Their outmoded ideas are challenged by rebellious, idealistic individualists who may be political reformers, artists, or women. The truth-seeking idealists in *The Pillars of Society*, *A Doll's House*, and *An Enemy of the People* believe that it is their duty to identify and label "lifelies," that is, the evasions and distortions of the truth in the light of which most people lead their lives. Serving as foils to Ibsen's female rebels are a number of female figures for whom ideas or moral issues are less important than security and the opportunity to be devoted wives and mothers. Many of Ibsen's important characters have lost their chance for happiness by marrying for money rather than for love. Others have an unfortunate tendency to misjudge or overestimate the people whom they are trying to reform or to dominate.

Ibsen first began to question the power of the truth to make humanity free in *The Wild Duck*, where he seems to conclude that most people have a very limited capacity for facing the truth and that harmless illusions are much less dangerous than fullblown ideals. In each of the next three plays, *Rosmersholm*, *The Lady from the Sea*, and *Hedda Gabler*, he gives searching psychological portraits of women whose inner struggles threaten to destroy them. Isolated male figures tend to dominate the plays that he wrote after his return to Norway—*The Master Builder*, *Little Eyolf*, *John Gabriel Borkman*, and *When We Dead Awaken*—all of which deal with impotence, old age, and the lack of love. In one way or another, all four of these plays raise once again the question of aesthetic withdrawal, only to show that love, not art, is the only means of self-fulfillment.

More a gadfly than a preacher, Ibsen frequently poses problems without attempting to solve them. The master of the strong curtain, he favors contrapuntal endings: Two opposing views of life collide, leaving motivations and outcomes in doubt. Ibsen believed that the playwright's task was to raise questions, not answer them.

PEER GYNT

First produced: 1876 (first published, 1867; English translation, 1892)
Type of work: Play

A romantic dreamer tries to find an empire within himself but finally discovers that his empire really lies in the love of Solveig, the woman who loves him.

Peer Gynt, the title character of *Peer Gynt*, is man in search of himself. His problem is that he misunderstands "self-realization" and seeks fulfillment in his poetic dreams because he fears life and love. In order to show the full range of his negative development, Ibsen shows Peer first as a feckless young man of twenty, then as a middle-aged tycoon, and finally as a broken old man returning to his native Norway.

As a youth, Peer lives fictional adventures so vividly in his imagination that they almost become his own life experiences. He dreams of being an emperor but is never ready when opportunity knocks. While he has been playing hooky in the uplands, Ingrid of Hegstad, an heiress whom he might have married, has been betrothed to another young man. Looking for trouble, Peer sets off for Hegstad to engage in belated courtship. Among the wedding guests is Solveig, a pure young woman whom Peer instantly loves. When Solveig refuses to dance with him, he gets drunk and steals the bride. Abducting Ingrid makes Peer an outlaw. Though Ingrid is quite willing to marry Peer, he sends her back to her father because he loves Solveig. In what may be a dream sequence, he encounters a woman in green, the daughter of the Troll King, who takes him to her father's kingdom, where everything is reversed: Black seems white and foul looks pure. Peer is a candidate for the hand of this troll princess, a negative counterpart of Solveig, but in order to win her father's full approval he must wear a tail and accept selfishness as a way of life. Peer is quite willing to accept these conditions, until he learns that in doing so he can never return to humanity.

After his narrow escape from the trolls, Peer's path is blocked by a languid monster called the Boyg, who tells him to "go roundabout." The Boyg seems to be a portmanteau symbol for everything that prevents Peer from being himself. By having church bells rung, his mother, Åse, and Solveig—the women who love Peer—manage to save him both from the trolls and from the Boyg. Yet they cannot save him from himself. What little remains of Åse's property is seized to compensate Ingrid's father; yet she gladly suffers for her son. Solveig makes an even bigger sacrifice for Peer: She leaves her beloved family and searches for Peer in his mountain hut. When the troll princess arrives accompanied by their troll son, however, Peer realizes how unworthy he is of Solveig's love and "goes roundabout," abandoning her there.

Many years later in North Africa, Peer is a middle-aged millionaire who owes his fortune to all sorts of unprincipled enterprises. Though still apparently human, he has espoused the troll way of life, which he now defines as "the Gyntian self." Most of the fourth act takes place in a symbolic desert that represents the aridity of this "Gyntian self." Riding a stolen horse, he encounters a group of Bedouins who take him for a prophet. He falls in love with the exotic dancer, Anitra, and believes he is emperor of her thoughts, but she strips him of his rings and clothes and rides off on his horse, abandoning him as he once abandoned Ingrid. While contemplating the Great Sphinx, Peer meets Begriffenfeldt, the mad director of an insane asylum in Cairo. At the asylum, the only place where illusion truly triumphs over reality, the inmates hail Peer as one of them, and Begriffenfeldt crowns him the Emperor of Self.

One brief scene in act 4 shows the faithful Solveig still waiting for Peer's return. In act 5, the aged and embittered Peer does return to Norway, where everything that he encounters reminds him of his wasted life and points to his impending death. Near his old mountain hut, he hears Solveig singing and realizes that this was where his true empire lay. Yet he is still afraid to face her. Haunted by the emptiness of his stillborn visions, he next encounters the eerie Button Moulder, a mysterious figure who has been sent to dissolve him, since he has never become the self that he was intended to be. During the final scenes in the play, Ibsen illustrates what "being oneself" really means. Only in the loving arms of Solveig does the dying Peer discover that he has always been himself in her faith, her hope, and her love.

A DOLL'S HOUSE

First produced: *Et dukkehjem*, 1879 (first published, 1879; English
translation, 1880)
Type of work: Play

After eight years of marriage, a woman discovers that her husband has never understood her and that marriage has prevented her from becoming herself.

In *A Doll's House*, Nora Helmer returns home on Christmas Eve with a Christmas tree that must be hidden from the children until it is trimmed. Indeed, hiding is a major theme in this play. Later in the first act, Nora plays hide-and-seek with her children, and she hides the macaroons that her husband, Torvald, has forbidden her to eat. A more dangerous secret is the fact that, years earlier, she had borrowed a large amount of money to pay for the sojourn in Italy that enabled Torvald to recover from a serious illness. She had borrowed the money illegally from a usurer named Krogstad, and she has secretly been repaying the loan out of the small sums that she is able to earn by copying documents or save from her household budget. To spare her dying father, who was to have been her cosigner, she even forged his signature on the contract.

That something is wrong with the Helmers' marriage quickly becomes evident in the first scene: Torvald treats Nora more like a favorite child than a wife, and to please him she seems perfectly willing to pretend to be his little "skylark" or his "squirrel." In other words, she is content to live in a dollhouse. Nora's old school friend, Mrs. Linde, is one of those Ibsen characters who has married for money, not for love. The man she did love—and jilted—was Krogstad. Now a penniless and childless widow, she would be very happy to settle down in a dollhouse, but necessity forces her to beg Nora to help her get a job in Torvald's bank.

The plot hinges upon Nora's ignorance of three important facts: Krogstad holds a minor position in the bank of which Torvald is shortly to become manager; Torvald is so embarrassed by Krogstad's presumptuous familiarity that he plans to fire him; and forgery, no matter what the motivation, is a serious crime. Ironically, Torvald fires Krogstad and promises his position to Mrs. Linde. This act prompts Krogstad, who is trying to regain his respectability, to use his knowledge of Nora's forgery to blackmail her: If he loses his job, he will expose her and ruin Torvald. Nora's attempt to persuade Torvald to retain Krogstad precipitates the crisis: Torvald angrily dispatches the letter of dismissal. Her situation worsens when Krogstad delivers an ultimatum and leaves a letter exposing her crime. In desperation, Nora tells Mrs. Linde about the incriminating letter now locked in the mailbox and urges her to use whatever power that she may still have over Krogstad to persuade him to ask for it back unread. By the end of the second act, Nora sees only two possible ways out of her dilemma: Either she will save her beloved husband's reputation by committing suicide, or what she calls "the miracle" will happen, and he will magnanimously assume full responsibility for her crime. In an interview with Krogstad, Mrs. Linde succeeds in reviving his love for her, but she precipitates the final crisis by forbidding him to retract his letter.

Torvald's explosive reaction to Krogstad's letter shows Nora that the man for whom she was willing to sacrifice her life, the man capable of "the miracle," is a fiction. Discovering that he is self-centered, petty, and unfeeling, she can no longer love him. To challenge his outmoded ideas about marriage, she becomes a female rebel and informs him that she is leaving him and the children. When he admonishes her that she is duty bound to remain, she says that she has discovered a higher duty: her duty to herself. She exits, slamming the door on a bewildered Torvald.

Part of the play's effectiveness on stage depends on Ibsen's suggestive use of props, costumes, and activities (for example, the Christmas tree, the macaroons, the game of hide-and-seek) to illustrate psychological states or to underscore symbolic meanings. In its day, *A Doll's House* was extremely controversial. While many applauded Nora's determination to "be herself," many more condemned her as "unnatural" for deserting her children. More than a century later, the play still raises questions that stimulate readers and spectators.

AN ENEMY OF THE PEOPLE

First produced: *En folkefiende*, 1883 (first published, 1882; English
                    translation, 1890)
Type of work: Play

When a doctor tries to reveal that the water supply for a planned health resort
is infected, he is discredited and ostracized because the truth threatens the economic stability of the community.

In *An Enemy of the People*, Dr. Thomas Stockmann is chief medical officer at The
Baths, a health resort that is soon to open. Though he first conceived the idea of
developing this resort, his older brother, Peter, the mayor of the town, had the business sense and political connections to put it into effect. Ibsen uses the contrast between the two brothers to establish the ideological framework of the play: Thomas is
a liberal but impractical idealist; the ultraconservative Peter is motivated chiefly by
self-interest and what he calls "the good of the community." Dr. Stockmann's home
is a haven for people with liberal ideas: Billing and Hovstad, who edit the town's
liberal newspaper; Horster, an open-minded sea captain; and Stockmann's free-thinking
daughter, Petra, a schoolteacher. Petra is the first character to raise what is to become
the major theme in the play, the "life-lie." When she complains that, at school, she is
forced to teach children to believe in lies, Captain Horster encourages her to found a
school where children will learn the truth.

The crucial issue in the play emerges when Dr. Stockmann receives a laboratory
report confirming his suspicions that the water supply for The Baths is polluted. Jubi-
lant that he has detected the contamination in time to prevent a disastrous epidemic,
all the liberals offer their support and declare him a public hero. Peter Stockmann,
however, intends to discredit his brother, because the enormous costs of reconstructing the water system spells financial ruin for the investors and, ultimately, for the
whole town. Because he has the liberal press and the compact majority on his side,
and, above all, because he is right, Dr. Stockmann is confident of victory. The battle
lines are quickly drawn, but the motives on both sides are mixed. His wife, Katherine, sees the impending fight as a threat to the security of her family. The mayor
fears financial ruin and the erosion of his political power. Hovstad is a spineless
political opportunist who will espouse any cause that promises to increase his power.
Katherine's surrogate father, Morten Kiil, wants revenge for having been voted off
the town council. Because Stockmann and Petra are the only combatants free of self-
interest, it proves easy for the mayor to swing the entire community to his side.

Unable to get his message across through the press, Stockmann calls a public meeting in Captain Horster's house, where he intends to expose the fact that the whole
town's prosperity is rooted in a lie. His opponents take charge of the meeting, how-

ever, and rule all discussion of The Baths out of order. Goaded to fury, Dr. Stockmann abandons his intended subject and develops the symbolic significance of the situation: The town's spiritual sources are polluted, and the whole civic community is built over a cesspool of lies. The authorities may be stupid and inflexible, but the worst enemy of truth and freedom is the compact majority. He launches into a diatribe against the whole notion of a democratic society. The majority is always wrong, he claims, because most people are fools, too lazy to think for themselves and therefore easily led by demagogues. Truth is relative and always changing; by the time that truths filter down to the majority, they are so outdated that they can hardly be distinguished from lies. One such lie is that the common herd has the same right to criticize, govern, and counsel as the few intellectuals. The elitism and incipient racism of his remarks about the relation between class and intelligence so incense the crowd that he is voted "an enemy of the people."

The hostility of the mob does not stop with a vote of censure; the Stockmann family is assaulted on every front. The mayor and his supporters visit Stockmann and appeal to his self-interest in the hopes of getting him to retract his report on the pollution at The Baths. The final test comes when old Morten Kiil informs him that all the money that he would have left to Katherine's children is invested in The Baths and will be lost unless Stockmann says he was mistaken about the contamination. All of these threats to his integrity convince Stockmann to abandon his plan to take his family to the United States. He realizes that he must stay in Norway and fight. He and Petra vow to open a school in Horster's house, where they will try to train the "mongrels" to become decent and independent-minded people.

One problem that arises in interpreting this play stems from the disparity between Stockmann's facts, which are correct, and his opinions, some of which are indeed questionable. He is frequently ridiculous, and his elitism (his talk of "mongrel" people) clashes sharply with the progressive views that he claims to cherish. Ibsen apparently undermines his protagonist in this manner because there is no reasonable spokesman for the other points of view. In adapting this play for the American stage, American playwright Arthur Miller eliminated Stockmann's disagreeable or ridiculous traits, as well as his "fascistic" opinions.

HEDDA GABLER

First produced: 1891 (first published, 1890; English translation, 1891)
Type of work: Play

An unsuccessful attempt to shape the destiny of the man whom she once loved deprives a bored aristocratic lady of her last remaining sense of freedom.

While the familiar Ibsenian patterns remain intact in *Hedda Gabler*, the conflict is no longer rooted in ideology. Though she loved the glamorous and dissolute Eilert

Løvborg, fear of scandal and of her own repressed sexuality prevented Hedda Gabler from giving her love free rein. As a last resort, she has married George Tesman, a humdrum, middle-class historian, whom she does not love. While George is astonished that he has had the good fortune to marry the daughter of the late General Gabler, Hedda is despondent to find herself trapped in the hopelessly bourgeois Tesman family. George and Hedda have both returned from their long wedding trip with expectations: George fully expects to be appointed to a professorship, and Hedda, much to her dismay, is expecting Tesman's child. George has assumed that the appointment will automatically be his, because Eilert Løvborg, his only serious rival, has long suffered from acute alcoholism. He soon learns, however, that Eilert has stopped drinking and has published a very successful book. He is not aware, however, that Eilert is still deeply in love with Hedda.

Eilert has recently completed another book, which promises to be his masterpiece. When Thea Elvsted, the wife of Eilert's former employer, beseeches Tesman to keep an eye on Eilert because she fears that he may start drinking again, Hedda is intrigued. Without difficulty, she gets Thea to admit that, though she has managed to reform Eilert, she has never been able to win his love, because he is still haunted by the shadow of another woman. Thea is unaware that Hedda is that woman, and Hedda is extremely gratified to learn that she may still exercise great power over Eilert. She puts this power to the test when she successfully tempts him to take a drink and then to accompany George to a party. Hedda wants to shape Eilert's destiny by freeing him from fear of alcoholism. Though she assures Thea that he will return "with vine leaves in his hair," by which she means that his debauchery will have been translated into Dionysian creativity, she is also aware that he may instead succumb to his weakness. Either way, she will have gained control over him.

Unable to control himself, Eilert becomes so drunk at the party that he loses the manuscript of his new book. Tesman, who finds it, entrusts it to Hedda for safekeeping. When the distraught Eilert enters near the end of act 3, he tells Hedda and Thea that he has destroyed the manuscript. Thea, who regards this book as her and Eilert's "spiritual child," is crushed. After Thea's departure, Eilert confesses to Hedda that he dared not tell her that he had simply lost "their child," and he intimates that he intends to "end it all" as soon as possible. Firmly believing that his sense of honor will not allow him to live with his failure to master his weakness, Hedda gives him one of her father's duelling pistols and tells him to "do it beautifully." After he leaves, she gleefully burns Eilert's and Thea's "child."

Though the first account of Eilert's death suggests that he has fulfilled Hedda's expectations, the audience subsequently learns that he has not committed suicide at all. In fact, he has been fatally shot by accident in a brothel, where he was raving about "a lost child." Hedda's failure to shape his destiny brings her face-to-face with her own failure to achieve selfhood. The final degradation occurs when Judge Brack, who recognized the gun that killed Eilert as one of General Gabler's pistols, intimates that the price of his silence is Hedda's agreement to become his mistress. This final loss of freedom seems to motivate her to shape her own destiny. While Thea and George are patiently working at the task of reconstructing Eilert's lost book from notes that Thea has kept, Hedda goes into the adjacent room and shoots herself in the temple.

Summary

Henrik Ibsen's impeccable craftsmanship and his deep understanding of human psychology place him in the first rank of dramatists. His plays complement and correct one another in a dialectical manner. Though some of the ideas in the plays are now dated, he continues to hold the stage because of the vitality of his characters. By linking the dramatic device of gradual revelation of the past with the "ghosts" in the past lives of his characters, he finds a way to make psychological development his main subject. In skillfully exploiting the relations between his characters and their environment, he uses sets and props to suggest a psychological complexity usually considered beyond the scope of the theater. By means of these and other reforms of tired dramatic conventions, Ibsen remade the drama.

Bibliography

Beyer, Edvard. *Ibsen: The Man and His Work*. Translated by Marie Wells. New York: Taplinger, 1980.

Bradbrook, Muriel. *Ibsen the Norwegian: A Revaluation*. London: Chatto & Windus, 1966.

Downs, Brian W. *A Study of Six Plays by Ibsen*. Cambridge, England: Cambridge University Press, 1950.

Durbach, Errol. *Ibsen the Romantic: Analogues of Paradise in the Later Plays*. Athens: University of Georgia Press, 1982.

McFarlane, James W. *Ibsen and Meaning: Studies, Essays, and Prefaces, 1953-1987*. Norwich, England: Norvik Press, 1989.

Meyer, Michael L. *Ibsen: A Biography*. Garden City, N.Y.: Doubleday, 1971.

Northam, John. *Ibsen's Dramatic Method: A Study of the Prose Dramas*. London: Faber & Faber, 1953.

Wiegand, Herman J. *The Modern Ibsen: A Reconsideration*. New York: E. P. Dutton, 1960.

Barry Jacobs

EUGÈNE IONESCO

Born: Slatina, Romania
November 26, 1912

Principal Literary Achievement

Hailed as one of the most important playwrights of the Theater of the Absurd and one of its leading defenders, Ionesco wrote plays that use Surrealist techniques, based on the language and activities of daily life, to show more fully the human condition.

Biography

Eugène Ionesco was born in Slatina, Romania, on November 26, 1912, the son of Eugène and Marie-Thérèse (Icard) Ionesco. His father was Romanian, and his mother was French. In 1913, his family moved to Paris, and it was there that he was reared until 1925, at which time his family moved back to Romania. In 1929, he began to study at the University of Bucharest, where he specialized in French. By 1930, he was writing articles for a literary review, and in 1931 he published a collection of verse. Ionesco married Rodica Burileano on July 12, 1936, and was a teacher of French in Bucharest in the years 1937-1938. In 1938, he obtained a government-sponsored scholarship to travel to France in order to write a thesis on the themes of sin and death in French poetry since the time of Charles Baudelaire. In 1939, he and his wife went to France, settling first in Marseille and later in Paris. He never finished his thesis, and during World War II he worked for a publishing firm in Paris.

In 1948, Ionesco wrote his first play, a one-act "antiplay" called *La Cantatrice chauve* (1950; *The Bald Soprano*, 1956), which had, as a starting point, a manual on the study of English, and which made use of clichés and conversational patterns. It was produced in Paris, at the Théâtre des Noctambules on May 11, 1950. The following year, his second play, *La Leçon* (1951; *The Lesson*, 1955), billed as a "comic drama," was produced. This play did indeed involve a real lesson, between a dominant professor and a young pupil. Even though his first plays were not immediately very successful and in fact received some adverse criticism, little by little there began to be a more favorable reception by the public and the critics alike. This receptivity increased when his third play, *Les Chaises* (1952; *The Chairs*, 1957), a "tragic farce," was produced in 1952. In this play, Ionesco expressed the importance of the total self; the chairs for the imaginary guests represented that part of a person's identity that is made up of more than a mere surface reality. Another early one-act play is *Jacques:*

Ou, La Soumission (pb. 1954; *Jack: Or, The Submission*, 1958). This play, billed as a "naturalistic comedy," deals with the influence of the family on the individual. A sequel to *Jack* is *L'Avenir est dans les œufs: Ou, Il Faut de tout pour faire un monde* (1953; *The Future Is in Eggs: Or, It Takes All Sorts to Make a World*, 1960), which shows a young couple at the mercy of their families as they are ordered to produce offspring.

Ionesco stated that these early plays were largely exercises. He was trying to set in motion the mechanism of the theater, to free the theatrical language from its literary aspects. His plays were also exorcisms of his own anxieties; he presented, through himself, the anxieties and hopes of other people.

In his second period, Ionesco tried for a kind of amplification of his early style, in which objects themselves become a language. He wanted to find a visual language of the stage that would be more direct, more shocking, and stronger than that of words. Two important plays of this second period are *Victimes du devoir* (1953; *Victims of Duty*, 1958) and *Amédée: Ou, Comment s'en débarrasser* (1954; *Amédée: Or, How to Get Rid of It*, 1955). The hero of *Victims of Duty*, a "pseudo drama," returns, in his mind's eye, to the world of his childhood and looks for the person that others insist that he find, but he can find only fragments of the many selves that he has been. Ionesco's first three-act play, *Amédée*, dealt with the creative instinct and with the inner life, which in this hero has been almost killed by the humdrum activities of his life.

Beginning with *Tueur sans gages* (1958; *The Killer*, 1960), Ionesco began to write a more traditional kind of play, but one that still incorporated surrealistic overtones. *Rhinocéros* (1959; English translation, 1959) and *Le Piéton de l'air* (1962; *A Stroll in the Air*, 1964) belong to this later period. *Rhinoceros*, perhaps more than any other of his plays, established Ionesco as a world-famous dramatic author. It was first performed in Düsseldorf in 1959, in Paris and in London in 1960, and in New York in 1961. Of note in these plays is that they revolve around one protagonist, Bérenger, a kind of Everyman, who is also, as Ionesco admitted in an interview, an aspect of himself. Bérenger reappears in *Le Roi se meurt* (1962; *Exit the King*, 1963), which deals with Ionesco's obsession with death. His later plays, *Jeux de massacre* (1970; *The Killing Game*, 1974; also known as *What a Bloody Circus* and *Wipe-out Games*), *L'Homme aux valises* (1975; *Man with Bags*, 1977), and *Voyages chez les morts: Ou, Thèmes et variations* (pb. 1981; *Journeys Among the Dead: Themes and Variations*, 1985), have not achieved the success of his earlier ones.

Ionesco also wrote a novel, *Le Solitaire* (1973; *The Hermit*, 1974), and a collection of short stories under the title *La Photo du colonel* (1962; *The Colonel's Photograph*, 1967). The title story was, in fact, the basis for his play *The Killer*. His *Journal en miettes* (1967; *Fragments of a Journal*, 1968) and *Présent passé passé présent* (1968; *Present Past Past Present*, 1972), both contain autobiographical writings.

In many ways, Ionesco is considered a spokesperson for the avant-garde theater, and he has published a considerable amount of explanatory writing on it. Many of these articles have been collected in *Notes et contre-notes* (1962; *Notes and Counter-*

Notes, 1964). In these articles, Ionesco states his position against theater with a message or with any kind of political ideology.

Ionesco has received great critical acclaim, and his plays are now considered among the most important in the Theater of the Absurd. In 1966, Ionesco was awarded the Grand Prix du Théâtre de la Société des Auteurs, and in 1971 he was admitted to the prestigious Académie Française.

Analysis

The theme running throughout the work of Ionesco is that one's inner life is not as fully developed as the exterior one, thus causing a certain malaise and a feeling of alienation from one's environment. His protagonists go on quests for their identity or try to recall bits of their dreams or express their hopes, aspirations, and desires. Perhaps the special quality of Ionesco's theater comes from the fact that he is dealing with both the exterior reality of his characters and their inner life. Ionesco's characters feel trapped in the prison of their daily lives and want to escape. Their social identities do not fully represent them.

In presenting the life from which his protagonists desire to escape, Ionesco draws attention to the sheer mechanical aspect of living, as his characters perform routine actions without really knowing why they are doing them or what purpose they serve. This characteristic is especially noticeable in *Victims of Duty* and *Amédée*. The characters in these plays appear to be going through a ceremony, but one that has lost all meaning for them. They perform fantastic actions, but actions that are based on everyday habits and customs. Ionesco uses such mechanical movements to show how absurd and inhuman the social aspect of life can be.

Even though many of these plays have as their setting a typical middle-class living room, there are fantastic elements amid these banal settings: a clock in *The Bald Soprano* that tells the opposite of the correct time, a girl who has three noses in *Jack*, a body that grows in the bedroom in *Amédée*, and a young married couple who give birth to hundreds of eggs in *The Future Is in Eggs*. One notices the influence of Surrealism in these plays, as Ionesco made use of objects, as well as decor, lighting, action, and dialogue—all of which are well integrated. He also uses language in striking ways in many of his plays, employing, for example, repetition of dialogue, or words that may be in perfect grammatical order but do not make much sense when taken literally, or proverbs rewritten by him and spoken in such a way that they seem authentic. His characters utter clichés and set formulas of speech, which they substitute for meaningful conversation. Also important is what is *not* seen: the imaginary guests, for example, in *The Chairs*, or the search for the self in *Victims of Duty*, or the feeling of alienation that many of his characters try to express. Ionesco also made effective use of movement: The characters in *Victims of Duty* and *The Chairs* rush around the stage like automatons as they rapidly bring onto the stage dozens of cups of coffee or chairs, the professor does a sort of Indian scalp dance in *The Lesson*, and the families of the young couple do a sort of initiation ritual at the end of *Jack*.

Ionesco's theater has several elements that have probably been influenced by the work of the Surrealists: language used in striking ways, an exaggerated use of gesture and movement, unusual lighting and other special effects in the decor, and the integration of objects into the action. Other similarities include a search for the lost paradise of childhood, an attempt to express the internal world of the characters, and the idea that the theater not be a mere copy of surface reality, but that it should go beyond this to reveal an inner reality. The extraordinary thing about Ionesco's theater is that, while dealing with serious themes and being in some ways pessimistic, it accomplishes its end through comedy. Yet this laughter comes from the tension between comic and tragic. The comic springs from the absurd when language and actions are pushed beyond credibility, yet it is tragic in its human implications.

Ionesco's theater is concerned with conditioned human beings, whose habits, both physical and mental, are formed for them. In *Jack*, for example, he is especially concerned with the role of the family in the formation of the individual's identity, showing how one's behavior is controlled, how one's decisions are forced, how one's freedom of expression is taken away, and even how one's emotional responses are modified by the family. Ionesco draws the audience's attention to the sheer mechanical ritual of living, which further separates people from their true selves. One becomes identified, as did the Smiths and the Martins in *The Bald Soprano*, with one's social milieu, function, and possessions. Furthermore, one's mental habits are formed by society, as one comes to accept clichés and slogans that take the place of real thought and genuine communication. Ionesco sees, especially in *Rhinoceros*, the danger of the direction of the mind by schools of thought and political ideologies.

In his writings, Ionesco calls for total liberty of thought, the use of artistic creation, and the exercise of the imagination as ways to regain part of one's basic self, which has been lost to the demands of social life. He refuses to limit himself, in his writings, to any form of commitment or ideology, instead insisting on freedom of artistic expression. He has expressed, in *Notes and Counter-Notes*, that few authors dare to take advantage of the immense possibilities of the theater. In his own plays, however, Ionesco has dared to use not only realism but also Surrealism in order to present a more complete reality.

THE BALD SOPRANO

First produced: *La Cantatrice chauve*, 1950 (first published, 1954; English translation, 1956)
Type of work: Play

The activities and thought patterns of social living can cause people to become little more than their social identity.

In *The Bald Soprano*, Ionesco has created characters who are guided in everything by formality and routine. They act according to their social role, not from any individual motivation. They are essentially nothing more than their exterior qualities. Their language and gestures are automatic; they have nothing personal to say because they have no inner life. In writing about his first play, Ionesco stated that such people are part of the mechanical aspect of daily life to such an extent that they are indistinguishable from it. The Smiths and the Martins of this play do not think for themselves, no longer are moved by anything, no longer have any passions. Thus, they can become, and are in fact, interchangeable with anyone else.

This play shows people who live the perfect serenity of a life preserved by solid institutions. They are satisfied with their way of life, and they do not question it. The opening scene reflects this peace of mind, as Mr. and Mrs. Smith, a typical middle-class couple, are sitting in their living room engaging in a typical middle-class after-dinner conversation. Mr. Smith mentions an old friend of the family named Bobby Watson. This recollection causes some confusion in pinning down the exact identity of this person, as there are many people they know who are named Bobby Watson. In fact, however, it does not really matter what their names are, since all of their middle-class friends have similar lives. Minor distinguishing characteristics such as physical appearance and names are not important; there is no real difference in their pattern of living.

Mary, the maid, enters and recounts her daily routine. When Mrs. Smith asks her what she has done that day, the question incorporates what Mary has just said, almost word for word. Her question is only a formality, since she knows what Mary always does on her day off. Another couple enters: the Martins. There follows a delightfully comic scene, in which Mr. and Mrs. Martin, by careful reasoning, conclude that they are married to each other. They sit opposite each other, and each one, in turn, says that it seems as if he or she has seen the other one somewhere before. From their questions and answers it comes to light that they both live at the same address and both have a little daughter named Alice. All this seems to them to be a strange coincidence. They conclude that they must be man and wife. They embrace, but without emotion, then sit down and go to sleep.

It would seem that there is no spark of vital life left in either the Smiths or the Martins. This absence is made especially evident at the entrance of the fire chief, who comes looking for a fire. He is told, however, that there is not even a little spark. This fire is perhaps symbolic of vital life, which has been smothered by bourgeois routine. The high point of the scene comes when the fire chief tells an anecdote in which, after about two hundred words of introduction, he comes to the point: A certain person sometimes catches a cold in the winter. After the fire chief leaves, the characters' behavior deteriorates to the point of absurdity. The people become like robots out of control and finally speak syllables that are nothing but sounds. At this point, the lights go down and then come up again, and the play begins exactly where it started, this time with the Martins taking the places of the Smiths. This "rebeginning" serves to point up the lack of a meaningful life of these characters. The lack of a plot corresponds to their lives without purpose. It does not matter who takes which role in the social structure; one person can be replaced by another.

RHINOCEROS

First produced: *Rhinocéros*, 1959 (in German, 1959; in French, 1960; English translation, 1959)

Type of work: Play

The power of public opinion and conformity is far-reaching and can break down the resistance of even a well-meaning individual.

Rhinoceros is a play of great simplicity and deals with the mindless following of others in order to be like the herd. Ionesco preserves the symbol of the rhinoceros throughout the play, as he shows how people lose their freedom of will and their individuality in order to be cast into the common mold, all happy to have the same appearance, the same desires, and the same thoughts as the next person.

In the first scene, Bérenger, a kind of Everyman, is being reproached by his friend, John, for not being like other people. In the midst of their discussion, a rhinoceros comes charging down the street. Everyone makes a few remarks about where such a beast could have come from, but their initial surprise soon wears off. A few minutes later, another rhinoceros comes from the opposite direction. People say that something must be done, but still, after a few minutes, their surprise again wears off.

Act 2 takes place in Bérenger's office, as his colleagues discuss the newspaper account of the incident. Then an unusual thing happens: M. Boeuf, who had been absent that day, turns into a rhinoceros. Now they realize that a person has changed into one of these creatures. Bérenger pays a visit to John, who tries to defend the rhinoceroses. As he talks, he turns into a rhinoceros himself and attempts to run Bérenger underfoot. On his way out, Bérenger discovers that the other tenants have also changed into rhinoceroses.

In act 3, Bérenger's colleague Dudard comes to visit him. Dudard tries to find a rationale to explain the motives of the rhinoceroses, and he makes it seem that Bérenger is the abnormal one. Bérenger's girlfriend, Daisy, comes to visit and informs Bérenger that even his friend Botard, who had been so opposed to the rhinoceroses, has now become one. Daisy also reports that even some of the intellectuals of the day have now converted. Bérenger tries to summon the others to rally but receives only excuses and protests. Even though others suffer from this situation, they refuse to do anything about it. Now, even Dudard turns into a rhinoceros, and there are only two people left: Bérenger and Daisy. The attraction of the herd is too much for Daisy, however, and she goes out to metamorphose. Bérenger is left entirely alone and says that he will never follow the others. Yet he is disturbed over being completely alone. He tries to become a rhinoceros but cannot, so he decides to make the best of things and stand his ground. He is the last person, and he will resist to the end. It seems as if, in reality, he is trying to make the best of a bad situation. He regrets his individuality and comes to feel that it is the majority, after all, that is right.

What Ionesco tried to accomplish in *Rhinoceros* was to show the danger of ideology. The personages of this play make use of slogans, clichés, and ideology in order to rationalize their desires of wanting to be part of the herd. They make broad statements and generalities that they do not bother to prove. Bérenger does his best to defend the values of civilization against the onslaught of this evil.

Ionesco did not wish to show Bérenger as a superman, only as a simple man who has the courage to speak against the general opinions of his time. Bérenger cannot escape what he calls the reality of the facts, and he refuses to cover them over with theory. By trying to defend the values of civilization, he is forced into solitude. Thus, Ionesco shows that the liberty to be an individual carries with it grave consequences.

Summary

Eugène Ionesco's special field of endeavor is that of conditioned human beings. He calls into question the conventional social virtues and many other qualities that are thought to be important in the social person. By carrying to the extreme certain aspects of daily life, he presents a picture of humanity in the full absurdity of its condition.

There is within Ionesco's writings his belief that social life restricts the individual's mind and life into narrow channels and that society's obligations cause part of one's basic nature to be killed. People are imprisoned in a workaday world, and their inner life is often at odds with their exterior life. To Ionesco, dreaming, imagination, and artistic creation can be the means to give the inner life freer rein and allow greater expression of the insufficiently exercised basic self.

Bibliography

Bonnefoy, Claude. *Conversations with Eugene Ionesco.* New York: Holt, Rinehart and Winston, 1971.

Coe, Richard W. *Eugene Ionesco: A Study of His Plays.* 1961. Rev. ed. London: Methuen, 1971.

Esslin, Martin. *The Theatre of the Absurd.* 3d ed. New York: Penguin Books, 1983.

Fowlie, Wallace. *Dionysus in Paris: A Guide to Contemporary French Theater.* New York: Meridian Books, 1960.

Hayman, Ronald. *Eugene Ionesco.* New York: Frederick Ungar, 1976.

Lamont, Rosette C., ed. *Ionesco: A Collection of Critical Essays.* Englewood Cliffs, N.J.: Prentice-Hall, 1973.

Pronko, Leonard. *Eugene Ionesco.* New York: Columbia University Press, 1965.

George Craddock

CHRISTOPHER ISHERWOOD

Born: High Lane, Cheshire, England
August 26, 1904
Died: Santa Monica, California
January 4, 1986

Principal Literary Achievement
Considered one of the finest English novelists of his talented generation, Isherwood wrote his best work on life in Berlin during the last days of the Weimar Republic.

Biography
Christopher William Bradshaw-Isherwood was born in High Lane, Cheshire, England, on August 26, 1904. His family, owners of a large Elizabethan mansion, was well established in the upper-middle class of England, and his father, Francis Bradshaw-Isherwood, rose to the rank of lieutenant colonel in the military before his death in action during World War I. His mother's name was Kathleen Machell-Smith. Isherwood's early education, first at St. Edmund's School and then at Repton School, was significant largely for the friendships that he formed with W. H. Auden and Edward Upward—both of whom would become, like Isherwood, important literary figures in the 1930's. They remained friends for life, most intensely during their Cambridge years. Isherwood wrote poetry and an unpublished novel while at Cambridge; eventually deciding on literature as a career, he purposely failed examinations and subsequently left the university without a degree. While writing *All the Conspirators* (1928), he tutored students and served as secretary to the Mangeot family. After a brief stint as a medical student, he left England to join Auden in Berlin.

The move to Berlin was the most significant of Isherwood's early life. From 1929 to 1933, Isherwood taught English and lived a marginal existence in a city that was bordering on moral and political chaos. In Berlin, he met many people, English and German, who were to serve as models for the characters in his major works. *The Memorial: Portrait of a Family* (1932), his second novel, was published while he was a resident in Berlin. His "Berlin stories" were published several years after he had left the German capital because of the Nazi takeover: *The Last of Mr. Norris* appeared in 1935; *Goodbye to Berlin*, in 1939. In between the two Berlin novels, Isher-

wood collaborated with Auden on two plays, *The Dog Beneath the Skin: Or, Where Is Francis?* (pb. 1935) and *The Ascent of F6* (pb. 1936), both influenced by German expressionist theater. In 1938, soon after the publication of Isherwood's first autobiography, *Lions and Shadows: An Education in the Twenties* (1938), he and Auden traveled to China to report on the outbreak of war there. The result of this journey was another collaboration with Auden, the excellent travel book *Journey to a War* (1939).

At the beginning of 1939, Isherwood left Europe for good and settled in California, which was to be his permanent residence until his death. The move to the United States coincides with a transition in both his life and his work and thus serves as a convenient dividing line in Isherwood's biography. One of the important results of this move was Isherwood's introduction to another British writer, Aldous Huxley, who prompted a profound change in Isherwood's religious life by introducing him to the Indian guru Swami Prabhavananda. Isherwood subsequently became a pacifist and a Vedantist.

A growing interest in Hindu philosophy occupied much of his time in the 1940's. He was the editor of the magazine *Vedanta and the West*, and along with Prabhavananda translated the Hindu religious text *Bhagavad Gītā* (1944). Isherwood was sometimes criticized for his apparent withdrawal from the conflicts confronting his native country. His move to the United States and preoccupation with Hinduism were considered the acts of an escapist. Yet Isherwood remained faithful to the pacifist cause, even spending two years working for the American Friends Service Committee hostel for refugees in Pennsylvania.

The year 1945 saw the publication of Isherwood's much-admired novel *Prater Violet*. He also worked for several Hollywood studios during these years, including Metro-Goldwyn-Mayer and Warner Bros. Finally, in 1946 he became a citizen of the United States.

In the late 1940's, Isherwood traveled through South America; the result of the journey was his second travel book, *The Condor and the Cows* (1949). Although he was a well-established writer by this time—his South America book had been commissioned, for example—he remained relatively unknown outside a small group of interested critics and devoted readers. In 1951, however, John Van Druten's play *I Am a Camera* (1951), based on *Goodbye to Berlin*, was performed in New York. The success of the play, and later of the 1968 Broadway musical version and 1972 film *Cabaret*, insured renown for the novelist.

In the 1950's, Isherwood continued to work on translations of Hindu writings, including *How to Know God: The Yoga Aphorisms of Patanjali* (1953). Additionally, he published his own work, the novel *The World in the Evening*, in 1954. In 1959, he began teaching as a guest professor at Los Angeles State College. Throughout the 1960's, Isherwood received appointments at California universities, including the University of California at Los Angeles, at Riverside, and at Santa Barbara. Three works appeared in these years: *Down There on a Visit* (1962), *A Single Man* (1964), and *A Meeting by the River* (1967).

In the final years of his life, Isherwood devoted himself to autobiography and to arguing for the acceptance by society of homosexuality. The two efforts are combined in his last great work, *Christopher and His Kind, 1929-1939* (1976), a frank account of his own homosexual awakening. Christopher Isherwood died on January 4, 1986, in Santa Monica, California.

Analysis

The aspect of Isherwood's writing that is most immediately apparent is the extent to which his fiction is all but inseparable from his autobiography. For Isherwood, the process of creation began with his own experience and observation. While he certainly invented material, even those inventions tend to be but slight variations of his actual experiences. In some of his best work, most notably *The Last of Mr. Norris* and *Goodbye to Berlin*, Isherwood uses his own name or his middle names for the protagonist.

That noted, it must also be recognized that the "Isherwood" or "Bradshaw" of the novels is never a perfectly autobiographical presentation of the author. There are significant differences, and Isherwood does not hesitate to assume a mask, even if the voice remains his. There is, for example, an aloofness and ingenuousness to the narrator that is not characteristic of Isherwood himself. The boundaries are so imprecise in Isherwood's work, however, that many readers have confused the writer and the protagonist. Isherwood has even been criticized for some of the faults that he purposely assigned to his fictional self. Likewise, his best work has sometimes been mistaken for mere journal or diary extracts strung together in a loose framework.

The more general opinion, however, is that Isherwood is one of the best writers of his generation. Isherwood stands out in part because of the lucidity and ease of his style. Along with novelist and essayist George Orwell, he is representative of the power that a colloquial or vernacular style can achieve. It was a style that he developed after early experimentation with a prose derived from modernist novelists such as Virginia Woolf and James Joyce. E. M. Forster was particularly influential in the career of the young Isherwood. Consequently, his early novels, such as *All the Conspirators* and *The Memorial*, rely on a tone of ironic understatement by which significant events are treated only slightly while trivial events are presented in full detail. Isherwood referred to this characteristic as the "tea-table technique"; that is, subjects worthy only of the tea table receive undue attention. The intention is entirely ironic. For example, Isherwood might juxtapose memories of a dead husband with anxieties over cooking and shopping, thus highlighting for the reader the way in which a fragmented postwar society has imposed triviality and isolation on its members.

Though Forster remained the most important influence in his literary career, Isherwood abandoned the techniques of modernism in favor of a more restrained and pared-down realism. Starting with *The Last of Mr. Norris*, he avoided the complexities of a fragmented story line and a jumbled chronology, along with the interior monologue of his earlier novels. Bradshaw's account of his encounters with the strange Mr. Norris is straightforward and colloquial. Yet the simple diction conceals a sense of incongruity that can only be called ironic. There is always the slightest sense of mockery and denigration in Isherwood's subtle prose. Indeed, the prose is so subtle that the reader must avoid assuming, mistakenly, that the narrator is merely a neutral or transparent observer—the camera to which the narrator compares himself in *Goodbye to Berlin*. He is not merely a camera; he comments on the subjects of his vision, and the commentary is persistently, if not overtly, ironic.

The source of the irony is the sensibility of Isherwood's detached narrator. He calls little attention to himself, and he does not dramatize himself. He is an unobtrusive guide leading the reader through "the freak museum of our neurotic generation." The narrator's strong urge to be that guide provides the incentive for the documentary style of the Berlin novels. The nature of the political circumstances demands of him a lucid and objective presentation, insofar as objectivity is possible. Isherwood's changing technique exemplified some of the concerns of his generation, particularly the belief that communication was more important than aesthetics.

His work after 1939, the year that he moved to the United States, is generally thought to be inferior to his early work, at least in terms of style. Instead of his quintessential "thirties prose," considered by many to be the best of the decade, Isherwood's later style is more melodramatic and sentimental. According to many critics, the excursions into Oriental philosophy that inform his later work, *A Meeting by the River*, for example, weaken the universal appeal that was so marked in his early novels. Not all, however, are in agreement on this particular point. Brian Finney, Isherwood's biographer, finds that his later novels compare favorably with the early ones.

The most important aspect of Isherwood's later career remains his public defense of homosexuality. *A Single Man*, for example, is a sympathetic portrait of an aging homosexual. This defense was an inevitable result of his intensely autobiographical approach to fiction. While he suppressed it in his early career, by the 1960's he no longer hedged on the issue. Isherwood had to be courageous in his frankness, since homosexuality had long been a taboo subject in literature. Eventually, he came to see it as a cause and claimed that, in defending this one minority, he was speaking out for all minorities. This sympathy for those who have been marginalized by a brutal society is the most persistent theme in Isherwood's work.

THE LAST OF MR. NORRIS

First published: 1935
Type of work: Novel

A young Englishman is captivated by a quirky con artist in the Berlin of the Weimar Republic.

The Last of Mr. Norris (the British title is *Mr. Norris Changes Trains*), Isherwood's third novel, takes place in the year 1930. Two strangers, sharing a compartment on the train to Berlin, begin speaking to each other as the train crosses the border from Holland into Germany. The younger one is William Bradshaw, a young man looking to escape from the restraints of England to the sophisticated and dissolute German capital. The older one is Arthur Norris, a well-dressed man with expensive accoutrements. By the time they reach Berlin, the two are on friendly terms. Eventually, Bradshaw's experiences in Berlin revolve around his somewhat puzzling compatriot.

At first, Bradshaw is blind to Norris' corruption. He consistently underestimates Norris' depravity. Only very slowly does he learn that Norris is practicing blackmail and fraud in order to maintain his accustomed gentlemanly life-style. Through Norris, Bradshaw is introduced to the world of sexual deviation and political machination. Without a doubt, Norris is a charming character, and Bradshaw's ingenuousness is understandable. Ultimately, however, the charm is superficial, and the reader understands before the narrator does that this Norris is a crook who hides behind a mask of snobbery and wealthy appearances. Bradshaw seems incapable of reading these signs and resists detaching himself from a man who has become something of a father figure for him.

Mr. Norris's self-centered depravity is suggestive of the city in which the story takes place. The final years of the Weimar Republic are presented as years of political confrontation marked by the debasement of meaning through distorted language and deliberate lies. Near the end of the novel, the political situation comes center stage, as Bradshaw describes the showdown between Nazis and Communists. Hitler's shadow looms over the final pages. The German populace is taken in by the Nazi leader in much the same way that Bradshaw has been deceived by Norris. Norris, however, is a comic bungler whose designs are exposed and foiled. By contrast, Hitler seems even more brutal and dynamic. Isherwood's novel is a fascinating account of a personal relationship set against a society in disintegration.

SALLY BOWLES

First published: 1937
Type of work: Novella

A young Englishwoman meets and overcomes various setbacks in Weimar Berlin.

Sally Bowles is the most renowned of Isherwood's famous "Berlin stories," a "loosely-connected sequence of diaries and sketches," as he called them, that together form the novel *Goodbye to Berlin*. Both the story and the character Sally Bowles brought Isherwood his first fame. That fame was attributable in large part to the role of Sally as played by Julie Harris in the play *I Am a Camera*.

Sally Bowles is a young Englishwoman living in Berlin, who is befriended by the narrator (whose name is Christopher Isherwood, though he is not to be identified completely with the author). Sally is a cabaret artist of little talent but much charm. Indeed, she lives primarily by her charm, wit, and peculiar beauty. Christopher soon learns that her Bohemian life-style involves entertaining gentlemen, but he does not pass judgment on her.

In fact, Christopher finds Sally to be the most attractive of his Berlin friends, because watching her is like watching "a performance at the theater." Sally's performances are certainly eccentric and, to a degree, pretentious. Yet these pretensions do not bother the narrator. He rather likes her masquerades and disguises. In this sense, Sally has much the same effect on Isherwood that Norris had on Bradshaw. Nevertheless, she is more ingenuous than Norris, and this ingenuousness makes her more transparent. Her charm thus mitigates her obvious dishonesty and artificiality. Sally uses people without compunction, but she is also innocent and childlike. This childishness is the source of her appeal.

In a way, Sally is a peripheral character. Her upper-class connections allow her to escape from Berlin when life there becomes tiresome or boring. While she is unquestionably one of the "lost" characters in Berlin ("The Lost" was Isherwood's working title for *Goodbye to Berlin*), she somehow manages to escape from the impending devastation that the other Berliners must confront. Great disasters leave her unchanged. Despite rejection from lovers, robberies, and an abortion, Sally remains strangely untouched, and indeed she recovers nicely from these setbacks. She is a misfit; she is a sexual outcast; but she is also a survivor, untouched by the disease and death attacking the Berliners. Isherwood's novella presents a successful character study and raises questions about those human qualities that can prevail in desperate and degenerate circumstances.

GOODBYE TO BERLIN

First published: 1939
Type of work: Novel

In the last days of the Weimar Republic, a young Englishman befriends several Germans and foreigners whose doom is inevitable.

The world of *Goodbye to Berlin*, possibly Isherwood's finest novel, is a grim world where the decaying past is about to be transformed into a horrible future. Isherwood writes of the period of transition, the period when change is ineluctable and yet few people seem to see it coming, or at least to recognize the significance of this change.

The reader is introduced to this world in the first section, "A Berlin Diary (Autumn 1930)." This first of two diaries in the novel introduces objects and people that the narrator can observe from the window of his room. The famous phrase from this diary—"I am a camera"—establishes the technique of the "diary" and something of the narrator's character: He is passive in his perceptions (though not neutral), an observer more than an actor. A certain ironic vision of life is established as well, with an emphasis on the fragmented and discontinuous nature of the world in which the narrator finds himself.

Christopher, called "Herr Issyvoo" by the Germans, turns his attention to four characters of the Berlin scene. The four—Sally Bowles, Peter Wilkinson, Otto Nowak, and Bernhard Landauer—are representatives of "the lost" (as Isherwood's first, unfinished version of the novel was called). These are people whom "society shuns in horror," according to Isherwood. Christopher tells their stories in a series of episodes that are unified by this theme of the lost.

The novel concludes with another "Berlin Diary," this time dated "Winter, 1932-3." By this time, Nazi brutality is everywhere in evidence, and at novel's end the reader realizes that the coming turmoil will destroy the lost characters of whom Christopher has grown so fond.

Summary

Another novelist and Christopher Isherwood's coeval, Angus Wilson, placed Isherwood at the moral center of their generation. Both terms, morality and generation, are useful in fixing Isherwood's status: His voice, so clear and precise, is the voice of morality in a world gone chaotic; perhaps more than any other novelist of his time, he speaks for the generation of writers who first achieved prominence in the 1930's. Isherwood's documentary style, combined with a reserved yet persistent moral tone, makes the Berlin stories some of the best in the English language.

Bibliography

Finney, Brian. *Christopher Isherwood: A Critical Biography*. New York: Oxford University Press, 1979.

Fryer, Jonathan. *Isherwood*. Garden City, N.Y.: Doubleday, 1977.

Heilbrun, Carolyn G. *Christopher Isherwood*. New York: Columbia University Press, 1970.

Hynes, Samuel. *The Auden Generation: Literature and Politics in England in the 1930's*. Princeton, N.J.: Princeton University Press, 1972.

King, Francis. *Christopher Isherwood*. Harlow, Essex; England: Longman House, 1976.

Piazza, Paul. *Christopher Isherwood: Myth and Anti-Myth*. New York: Columbia University Press, 1978.

Westby, Selmer, and Clayton M. Brown. *Christopher Isherwood: A Bibliography, 1923-1967*. Los Angeles: California State College at Los Angeles Press, 1968.

Wilde, Alan. *Christopher Isherwood*. New York: Twayne, 1971.

Stephen Benz

KAZUO ISHIGURO

Born: Nagasaki, Japan
November 8, 1954

Principal Literary Achievement
Read by an international audience, Ishiguro's texts center around themes of human dignity and loyalty pledged to dubious or ambiguous causes; his novels have won major literary prizes.

Biography

Kazuo Ishiguro was born on November 8, 1954, in the Japanese city of Nagasaki, the son of Shizuo and Shizuko (née Michida) Ishiguro. In 1960, Shizuo Ishiguro, an oceanographer, moved with his family to Guildford, near London, because the British government offered the scientist a job in connection with the exploration of the North Sea oil fields. Even though the family assumed that they would return soon to their native land, they found many practical reasons to stay. Helped by the fact that the father loved the comparative lack of social obligations in his new country, the family's temporary stay became a permanent one, and Kazuo Ishiguro, together with his two sisters, found himself immersed in British culture.

Sent to what he described as a typical British school, Ishiguro felt fully integrated there. Reading with pleasure the novels of classic nineteenth century British writers such as Charles Dickens and Charlotte Brontë, and growing up with the works of other influential European writers such as Russian dramatist Anton Chekhov, as a boy and young man Ishiguro nevertheless retained certain crucial ties to his native culture. His vision of Japan was formed by means of strong childhood memories, Japanese films of the 1950's, and the Japanese books that arrived every month at home, where the family conversed in Japanese. His interest in the films portraying a past Japan that he himself remembered has remained very strong, and he acknowledges them as a major artistic influence.

In the 1970's, after completing his high school education, Ishiguro traveled and sustained himself with a variety of odd jobs. Taking his cues from his young British peers, he set out for countries, such as America and Canada, that fascinated them all; he did not feel a need or desire physically to explore a Japan with which he felt connected through his imagination. After a short stint as a grouse beater for the British Queen Mother at Balmoral Castle in 1973, and employment as social worker both before and after his B.A. (with honors) in English and philosophy from the University

of Kent in 1978, Ishiguro decided to try his hand at writing. He was twenty-five. He had already aborted a brief and unsuccessful career as a singer and songwriter when, in 1979, he enrolled in the creative writing program at the University of East Anglia, where British novelist Malcolm Bradbury taught courses, and where Ishiguro earned an M.A. in 1980.

Having started to write short fiction in the summer before his first term at East Anglia, Ishiguro garnered immediate acclaim with his work. Three of his short stories were published in *Introduction 7: Stories by New Writers* (1981), and his first novel, *A Pale View of Hills* (1982), received the Winifred Holtby Award from the Royal Society of Literature. Although the novel was translated into thirteen different languages, it failed to make a visible impact in America, where his next work, *An Artist of the Floating World* (1986), remained similarly undiscovered despite having earned the Whitbread Fiction Prize as Whitbread Book of the Year 1986, another important British literary distinction.

The financial rewards for his second novel, however, enabled Ishiguro to end his part-time work in a hostel for London's homeless and allowed him to focus exclusively on his fiction and his film scripts for television; in the latter field, his *A Profile of Arthur J. Mason* (1984) and *The Gourmet* (1986) were well received. While working with characteristic intensity on his third novel in 1986, Ishiguro married Lorna Anne MacDougall, a fellow social worker; when *The Remains of the Day* (1989) was published, the couple was still living in an unpretentious corner of London, a fine piano their most valuable possession.

It was *The Remains of the Day* that cemented Ishiguro's international success with its triumphant reception. It became the 1989 winner of the Booker Prize, Great Britain's most prestigious literary award. Finally, the novel also marked Ishiguro's breakthrough in America, where it earned for him a sudden recognition as a major voice in the chorus of contemporary fiction.

Analysis

As a writer, Ishiguro has remained very modest about his fame. In particular, he has rejected claims that his first two novels, despite their setting and Japanese characters, offer a realistic picture of his home country, which he did not see between 1960 and 1989. Instead, he has insisted that it is a character's memory of a conflict in life that held his artistic interest in the writing.

Ishiguro's choice of protagonists evidences his basic reluctance to look for obvious links between his characters and himself, an authorial strategy that he rejects. Thus, even his Japanese characters rely for their existence primarily on the author's imagination and his artistic skills, rather than on his self-observation. Neither Etsuko Sheringham, the widowed Japanese mother who moved to England with her second husband, a Briton, and who tells the story of Ishiguro's first novel, *A Pale View of Hills*, nor the old painter Masuji Ono, whose diary constitutes the text of *An Artist of the Floating World*, can be seen to represent an authorial alter ego. By making the quintessential English figure of a butler his third protagonist, in *The Remains of the Day*,

Ishiguro attempted a quantum leap of the imagination. In return, the brilliant success of his butler, Stevens, entangled in the question of whether he has wasted his life serving a corrupt lord, triumphantly demonstrates his author's mastery of his artistic goal of focusing on the human condition as it is revealed through the crises of diverse characters anywhere in the world.

Apart from their determination to avoid simple realism and rely instead on sheer artistic imagination to make their points and create their worlds, Ishiguro's novels are linked by the prominence of their first-person narrators, through whose meandering thoughts the stories unfold. The reader soon discovers, moreover, that these central voices are rather unreliable in their accounts of past reactions to crises. For all of them, there lurks in the past an experience that may invalidate their projected sense of self and destroy their human dignity. Yet what exactly it is that hovers in the dark as each novel opens is a mystery that unravels only slowly, and the process keeps the reader on edge until a final climactic revelation. Even then, though, pieces of the central mystery are still left to the reader to put together.

In a move that would become typical for his fiction, Ishiguro opens *A Pale View of Hills* with the narrator seemingly in control, living through a brief, critical moment in the present. As small events trigger a stream of personal memories, answers emerge to questions that the narrator—like all Ishiguro's central characters—refuses to discuss openly. Accordingly, the novel moves along two temporal planes after Etsuko Sheringham is visited at her home in England by Niki, her younger daughter by her late second husband; that visit comes soon after the suicide of Niki's older, Japan-born half sister, Keiko. In a similar vein, Ono's worries in *An Artist of the Floating World* that his artistic support for the imperialists during World War II may endanger the marriage chances for his second daughter, Noriko, and the even less dramatic occasion of Stevens' first holiday after a lifetime of service, in *The Remains of the Day*, function as catalysts for the protagonists' surveys of their lives.

In a pattern that again foreshadows how later characters will interact with one another, in the first novel, mother and daughter communicate on a very formal, restrained level that allows neither to say what is really on her mind and that, at the most, admits a bitter irony that may hint at the truth; instead of discussing their problems openly, Ishiguro's pair hovers together on the abyss opened by Keiko's death. It is only through Etsuko's memories, and her haunting recurring dream about a young girl, that the extent of her pain becomes visible: Indelibly impressed in her mind is the question of whether her divorce, her subsequent marriage to a Westerner, and her departure from her native land somehow caused the desperate act of her eldest daughter. Ono and Stevens, too, have a characteristic, roundabout way of dealing with their problems, the very existence of which is unearthed only slowly.

While *A Pale View of Hills*, which receives its title from the view of Nagasaki's hills visible from Etsuko's apartment in Japan, centers mostly around a question of personal guilt, it also contains the story of Etsuko's first father-in-law, Seiji Ogata, a former teacher now publicly denounced by one of his former students for his imperialist leanings during World War II. This conflict of a man trying to come to terms with his past actions in a broad historical setting is made the artistic center of Ishiguro's second novel, *An Artist of the Floating World*, and is also a powerful theme for *The Remains of the Day*, where Stevens' dead master is revealed to have been a Nazi sympathizer.

While Etsuko's thoughts are related to the reader with common directness, Ishiguro's next novels more ambitiously try to call attention to the fact of their narrators' subjective coloring of events. A first step to distance them is to have them write, rather than think, their narratives; the next action involves the creation of an unmistakably personal voice for each character. While Stevens' English approximates the language used by a servant to the upper classes in mid-twentieth century Great Britain, Ono's voice is even more complexly constructed. The proposition, advanced by the text, is that his narrative is really a translation from the painter's original Japanese and thus reflects the limitations of his vision. Ono himself confesses to this idea as he tries to explain why he created patriotic paintings that the war party used as propaganda before and during World War II:

> But then I for one never saw things too clearly. A narrow artist's perspective. . . . Why, even now, I find it hard to think of the world extending much beyond this city.

After putting his characters through a mental wringer that forces and squeezes them into confronting what they have made of their lives, however, Ishiguro does offer a glimpse of hope for them. Etsuko, purified by her memories, is able to wave good-bye to Niki with a smile; the old Japanese men of the war generation, Ono and Ogata, win a tranquillity of spirit that allows them to retire from active life with grace and leave the field to their children, even though the punishment represented through their loss of prestige and social esteem should not be underestimated. Stevens, after he has realized what his "great" service to his lord has really cost him— he has denied his affection for his father and never allowed himself to see the love in the eyes of a female colleague—finally understands what he has lost and, with typical understatement, decides on some crucial changes in his no-longer-cheerless life.

AN ARTIST OF THE FLOATING WORLD

First published: 1986
Type of work: Novel

> After World War II, a Japanese painter, whose work had glorified the war, learns that the next generation does not blame him only because it considers him irrelevant.

Addressing the reader like an old friend in what reads like portions of a diary, the old Japanese painter Masuji Ono, the narrator of Ishiguro's second novel, *An Artist of the Floating World*, uses the imminent marriage negotiations for his younger daughter Noriko, in 1948, to reflect on his life and his career as an artist. Characteristically for Ishiguro, everything that the reader learns comes directly from the first-person narrator, whose account freely wanders from the present to various instances in the past, deliberately refusing to tell a chronological story. The narrator's voice also is highly subjective and cannot be trusted blindly.

Thus, through Ono's musings, the reader becomes gradually acquainted with the narrator's troubled career, which is related in a total of four diary entries spanning the years 1948 to 1950. Starting as a fashionable artist who took his themes and motifs from the underworld—the Japanese term is "Floating World"—of the bohemians, artists, and geishas of his unnamed city, Ono eventually denounced his "decadence" during the rise of imperialism in Japan in the 1930's. As a rebel against his old master Matsuda, the young Ono now painted pieces that, like his masterpiece "Complacency," attacked what he felt was the corruption of an aimless, modern world—here represented by three drinking men—and juxtaposed it with "heroic" images such as the band of angry young men confronting the well-dressed drinkers in his picture.

Success came almost immediately, and Ono did not have to illustrate comic books, as his master scornfully predicted. Yet Ono's masterful pictures became powerful tools of imperial propaganda, as well. To reinforce the issue of Ono's personal guilt, Ishiguro creates a close parallel between Ono's earlier rejection by his bohemian teacher, Matsuda, who cruelly confiscates Ono's pictures when he changes artistic directions and joins the "patriotic" cause, and Ono's own denunciation of his favorite pupil to the secret police in the 1930's.

Like the ex-teacher, Seiji Ogata, in Ishiguro's first novel, *A Pale View of Hills* (1982), Ono supports the imperialist Committee on Unpatriotic Activities—an institution that is Ishiguro's symbol for the wrongs of a system that betrayed the idealism of those who, with exuberant naïveté, put their talents in its service. Confronted with the consequences of his patriotism, Ono now must ask himself whether he wasted or abused his talents by serving the Devil.

Ishiguro's resolution to Ono's crisis, however, is marked by a disarming, gently ironic humanism. Finally ready to admit to his daughter's potential in-laws that he has, in fact, erred and been guilty, Ono's grand confession is brushed aside by the groom's family, who tell the old man that they regard his former political leanings as irrelevant to their son's marriage; the painter was never that important. Guilty but ignored by a young generation too busy to worry about old men, Ono can watch mirthfully as the young prepare to embark on their own lives.

THE REMAINS OF THE DAY

First published: 1989
Type of work: Novel

Given his first holiday by his new American master, an old British butler reflects on a lifetime of service as he travels to meet an old friend.

Ishiguro's great third novel, *The Remains of the Day*, which won Great Britain's
prestigious Booker Prize for 1989, undertakes to demonstrate with beautiful clarity
how high the human price can be for a person who has dedicated his or her life to a
goal that becomes tainted. Set in southern England in the summer of 1956, the novel
consists of the diary-like notes composed by Stevens, a British butler whose lifelong
goal was to serve Lord Darlington. Now, after the death of the lord, the mansion,
complete with its prime servant, has been taken over by an American. Offered his
first vacation, Stevens sets out for Cornwall to meet Mrs. Alice Benn, who, as Miss
Kenton, had worked with him in the heyday of Darlington Hall.

In the course of Stevens' travels to his final destination, his personal recollections
evoke an imaginary England that is made perfect by reason of an understated greatness that simply exists, refusing pompously to announce itself. The source of Stevens' pride, contentment, and self-worth has always been that he has served at the
"hub" of his great island's society; his greatest goal was always to be a perfect butler
to a perfect lord.

Steven's ideal is tested in a variety of ways as he remembers amusing anecdotes,
and darker experiences. When the reader is first told how William Stevens, the butler's father, had to serve a general whose incompetence had killed his oldest son, and
how he did so with "great" composure, the full price for Stevens' ideal becomes
visible. Following his father's steps, Stevens later flawlessly serves Lord Darlington at
a crucial function while his own father, whom old age saw descending in rank to that
of a glorified busboy, dies in the attic, and Miss Kenton—and not Stevens—closes
his eyes.

Another ambiguity is examined as the reader gradually learns that Lord Darlington—
required by Stevens' definition to be a great man, in order to bestow greatness on his
butler—has fallen far short of that distinction. Moved by private pity for the defeated
Germans after World War I, the lord gradually becomes an avid sympathizer with the
Nazis, and his reputation is destroyed by a related scandal. By 1956, the late Lord
Darlington's name has become a badge of shame.

If Stevens is made to suffer like the millions of citizens of the Axis nations—
among them Japan—who decided to trust and follow leaders who pursued aggression and atrocities until defeated in a bitter collapse, Ishiguro's novel constitutes a
highly critical examination of the price of self-neglecting, uncritical, and total ser-

vice. Though Darlington's betrayal is bitter, *The Remains of the Day* points out that, even if Stevens had served a better lord, he would still have suffered.

The key is the character of Miss Kenton. Stevens' utter failure to decipher her signals of affection bestows an exquisite sense of melancholy upon the book. The saddest moment arrives when the two meet again in Cornwall, and she finally spells out her now-impossible love for Stevens, whose heart breaks for a moment before he accepts his fate and politely helps her onto the bus for her return to her husband. Now Stevens achieves full tragic status and realizes that his talents may well have been wasted on Lord Darlington. Yet, in a decision that echoes existential philosophy, Stevens decides to try to be a better butler to the American by improving his skill in "bantering," light irony that he hopes may bring some human warmth to Darlington Hall. Thus, Ishiguro gives his most tragic character a ray of hope that may guide him beyond the sadness of a life falsely sacrificed.

Summary

Kazuo Ishiguro's desire to craft complex protagonists whose experience is radically removed from the life of their author has led to the creation of a remarkably diverse array of powerful literary characters who have fascinated an international audience. All of his first-person narrators tell of the primal conflict in their lives in their very own, intensely unique ways; they must all come to terms with past actions that have tainted their lives.

Despite their various shortcomings, which most often result from half-blind disregard for the consequences of their actions or the happiness of others (and themselves), Ishiguro's characters are nevertheless offered a final vision of grace that redeems rather than condemns them. This ultimate expression of a guarded optimism is a trademark of Ishiguro's fiction.

Bibliography

Gurewich, David. "Upstairs, Downstairs." *The New Criterion* 8 (December, 1989): 77-80.

Ishiguro, Kazuo. Interview by Gregory Mason. *Contemporary Literature* 30 (Fall, 1989): 335-347.

Mason, Gregory. "Inspiring Images: The Influence of the Japanese Cinema on the Writings of Kazuo Ishiguro." *East-West Film Journal* 3 (June, 1989): 39-52.

Parrinder, Patrick. "Manly Scowls." *London Review of Books* 9 (February 6, 1986): 16.

Yoshioka, Fumio. "Beyond the Division of East and West: Kazuo Ishiguro's *A Pale View of Hills*." *Studies in English Literature* (1988): 71-86.

R. C. Lutz

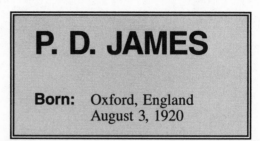

P. D. JAMES

Born: Oxford, England
August 3, 1920

Principal Literary Achievement
P. D. James's detective novels are realistic, psychoanalytical studies of character and motive, with intricate plots and a strong visual sense of place.

Biography

Phyllis Dorothy James was born in Oxford, England, on August 3, 1920. She attended Cambridge Girls School from 1931 to 1937, then clerked in a tax office for a few years until she found more interesting work as assistant stage manager of the Festival Theatre, Cambridge. During World War II, while a Red Cross nurse and an assistant at the Ministry of Food, she married Ernest White; they had two daughters, Clare and Jane. When White returned from the front a severe schizophrenic and was permanently institutionalized, providing for the family fell to James.

Thus, in 1946, James began her long civil service career, first as a National Health Service clerk and then, after earning diplomas in hospital administration and medical research, as a principal administrative assistant with the North West Regional Hospital Board, London. The latter position provided her with a detailed knowledge of illness, aging, and institutions that makes her novels authentic and credible. At forty-two, James published *Cover Her Face* (1962) and was immediately recognized as a major crime novelist. Her husband died in 1964. In 1968, she took the highly competitive Home Office exams and became a senior civil servant in the criminal department, specializing in juvenile delinquency and criminal law policy. This position, which she held until she retired in 1979, provided her with a working familiarity of forensic science laboratory routines, police procedures, and law. It also helped her understand better the juvenile mind, depicted so effectively in *Innocent Blood* (1980) and *Devices and Desires* (1989). In 1979, she began writing full-time but continued to serve as a Fellow of the Institute of Hospital Administrators and as a London magistrate. She was made an Officer of the Order of the British Empire in 1983 and taught a detective fiction course at Boston University's Metropolitan College in 1984.

Analysis

One of England's most prominent mystery writers, P. D. James became a skilled novelist. Her works are restrained, their internal tensions resulting from close associ-

997

ates facing painful and unforgiving inquiries into secret fears and obsessions. Keen and inquiring, James faces unpleasant truths about the human frailty, the complex and sometimes self-destructive relationships among people, and humankind's potential for psychic and physical violence. Kindly characters murder to protect family, hearth, or reputation; suspects prove culpable. Despite credible plots, meticulously provided clues, and convincing motives, "Whodunit?" is secondary to ambience and character, a realistic world of professionals whose jealousies and rivalries in the close confines of narrow communities produce Byzantine relationships.

James's novels build on a strong sense of place, with her initial inspiration coming from "a desolate stretch of coast, an old and sinister house, an atmospheric part of London, a closed community such as a Nurses Home, a village, a forensic science laboratory." In *A Mind to Murder* (1963), an elegant, stately Georgian home turned psychiatric outpatient clinic provides an ironic counterpoint to sinister events. Toynton Grange of *The Black Tower* (1975), a nursing home, commune, hotel, monastery, and "dotty lunatic asylum," reflects the bleak desolation of the Dorset coast. In *Devices and Desires*, a nuclear power plant dominates a coastal town and its inhabitants. *Shroud for a Nightingale* (1971) most effectively draws analogies between a nurse's training center and a Nazi prison camp to demonstrate the ambiguous nature of rules and of humans.

James's murder investigations turn on relationships and routines that are dependent on place. The initial murder in *Shroud for a Nightingale*, for example, results from student nurses who, while practicing intragastric feeding, witness a ghastly, nightmare death beyond their capacities to cope: carbolic acid added to warm milk in the inserted tube. In *Death of an Expert Witness* (1977), a despised physiologist is murdered in his lab while examining physical evidence from another murder. A suspect in *Devices and Desires* plunges to his death in the reactor room, the heart of a nuclear power plant whose dangerous power feeds the latent heart of darkness in those associated with it. James's writing captures the "minutiae of ordinary life": the internal rivalries, the jockeying for advancement up the bureaucratic ladder, the unhappy home lives, the daily pressures, the jealousies, the strife.

All of James's highly visual novels communicate a sense of an intricate mind at work, meticulously and precisely calculating every twist of plot. James keeps an hour-by-hour chart of her characters so that each detail fits logically and each piece of physical evidence is psychologically right. Her style is leisurely, with intricately woven sentences reflecting the complex musings of intelligent, but not always reliable, characters. Her narrator is third person—the omniscient author, a particular character, even the murderer. Her easy movement from one perspective to another adds a rich, varied texture to detailed descriptions of place and character. Her metaphors are of bleak wastelands; her characters casually allude to William Shakespeare, Jane Austen, and Thomas Hardy and talk of murder while taking tea or admiring a rose garden. Overall, character study outweighs action, but in the final analysis the realities of human behavior prove to some degree too complex to be fully known; even as they act, her characters often fail to understand their own motives.

James explores complex interpersonal relationships, particularly in closed communities. For instance, she describes hierarchical medical communities whose personnel share a language and a professional mystery that leave patients vulnerable outsiders. She studies stress and psychological consistency. Her respectable middle-class characters, literate and cultured, prove to be consumed by hidden emotions and desperate to preserve their façade of respectability or the reputations of those dearest to them. James's victims are often disagreeable—selfish, narcissistic, lascivious, greedy, hot-tempered, catty; her killers appear normal on the surface but are really emotionally maimed, beset by secret torments that ultimately evoke sympathy and pity— an abused childhood, a sexual compulsion, a tragic loss. Her plots frequently include apparent suicides that prove to be murders and interlocking or copycat crimes. Her main detective, Adam Dalgliesh, brings critical intelligence, sensitivity, and professionalism to his job. He is a "lonely man in a lonely profession," observing the bleakness of the human condition and seeing himself as an instrument of justice. Tall, dark, morose, and sometimes testy, he is the son of a London clergyman, versed in articles of faith, but a born skeptic whose distrust of simple creeds the tragic death of his wife in childbirth has deepened. Well-read and introspective, he internalizes his horror at unnatural death and comes to terms with it through poetry (titling one volume "Invisible Scars") and through enforcing a civilizing legal code. A private man with personal compulsions, he avoids deep emotional attachments. He is brutally honest, patient, "ruthless, unorthodox"—a master interrogator with an instinct for asking the right questions to uncover evil. His determined quest for the truth of his cases speeds his rise from detective chief-inspector to commander. Cordelia Gray, in *An Unsuitable Job for a Woman* (1972), is a cordial rival who shares Dalgliesh's love of Jane Austen and Thomas Hardy, old churches, and fine art. Though sensitive to human responses, calm, and detached amid mayhem, she is Dalgliesh's opposite in optimism and hope, remaining spunky, self-reliant, upbeat, good-natured, and capable despite a series of foster homes and her father's suicide. Overall, a James novel, with its dense prose, shrewdly realized characterization, and sound plotting, examines human interaction, rationalization, and despair with a unique combination of compassionate understanding and uncompromising analysis.

INNOCENT BLOOD

First published: 1980
Type of work: Novel

An adoptee seeking self-identity discovers the painful truth of her parentage and unknowingly becomes part of a revenge plot.

The title, *Innocent Blood*, refers to a twelve-year-old girl who is lured into the home of a pedophile, raped, and then strangled by the molester's wife. It also suggests a second victim, eighteen-year-old Philippa Rose Palfrey, an adoptee burdened by her natural parents' crime. Adopted before the murder occurred, the intelligent but difficult Philippa is adoptive father/sociologist Maurice Palfrey's living proof of nurture countering genetics. Her blood is not shed, but she must confront her parents' guilt. Ironically, she proves far more cold-blooded and ruthlessly egocentric than either parent, and her rejection of her long-suffering, docile mother results in the final bloodshed. James's narrative skill and deft psychological analysis suggest that the final "innocent" blood shed is that of the murderess/mother, who commits suicide when rejected by the daughter she has come to love and on whom she has come to depend.

Innocent Blood grew out of James's musings, on a real murder case, about a child's knowledge of parental culpability and about the potentially disastrous effects of the Children Act of 1975, which permitted adoptees to learn the identity of their natural parents. A regular novel, it shares the detective story's interest in guilt and innocence, crime and punishment, love and revenge. Despite her fine education and comfortable home, Philippa fantasizes about her real parents when irritated by her adoptive ones. In a sociological/psychological experiment of the sort of which she accuses Maurice, she finds, and, for the summer months before entering Cambridge, takes in, her real mother, Mary Ducton, a murderess just released from prison. Her act purposefully thwarts Maurice, whose approval and love she seeks, and rejects her adoptive mother, Hilda, whose timidity and lack of self-worth she scorns.

As mother and daughter share a small London flat, work together in a restaurant, spend time on "educational" tours of museums and galleries, and seek intimate moments of self-revelation (a program Philippa establishes and her mother passively accepts), the father of the murdered child, Norman Scase, dogs their steps, bent on revenge in fulfillment of a deathbed promise to his wife. James skillfully interweaves the two plot lines—the golden youth searching for identity, the ugly, bumbling, and sweet-tempered but driven older man seeking release from a haunting obligation—drawing them closer and closer as the man becomes as obsessed with Philippa as he is with killing her mother. Ironically, at the moment of final vengeance, Scase finds his act thwarted, the murderess already dead, a victim of her own guilt and rejection by her only child. When his knife plunges into her throat, she has already stolen away the life he seeks. Philippa, recognizing her personal responsibility for her mother's death, protects Scase from the police.

James's basic argument is that identity comes from within, that parents provide few clues about their progeny, and that relinquishing necessary fantasies can bring "a kind of death." Philippa is more the daughter of Maurice than of her real parents, sharing his intellectual distancing, cold disdain for weakness, and narcissistic self-absorption. Maurice's marital and sexual conflicts are but psychological responses to Philippa. A final brief, incestuous affair frees them from their mutual obsession and allows a more normal life thereafter. One set of fantasies, purged by reality, is replaced by another; even Mary Ducton's long, careful confession reworks reality to win back her daughter. According to James, a person's account of his or her life is an interesting psychological study, but it is not reality.

Questions of guilt and innocence shade into blurred grays, with the "criminals" providing sad, pitiable victims of physical compulsions or of traumatic childhoods, and with the "innocents" proving disturbingly culpable. Environment outweighs heredity in molding individuals, but some sort of unique, individual personality proves to be the true final determiner.

A TASTE FOR DEATH

First published: 1986
Type of work: Novel

The violent deaths of an important political figure and a lowly tramp endanger a young witness and a fledgling investigator.

The title *A Taste for Death* suggests a murderer whose appetite for power increases with each murderous act. It refers more particularly to Sir Paul Berowne, the murdered Tory minister who, weighed down with guilt at the automobile death of his first wife, had lost his taste for public life, undergone a religious conversion, abandoned a flourishing political career, and accepted death. It encompasses Detective Dalgliesh's questions about his and his profession's obsession with violent death, as well as Lady Barbara Berowne's taste for death (she enjoys the "power," "mystery," and "ruthlessness" of her gynecologist/surgeon/lover, Stephen Lampart, whose hands determine a patient's life or death). Even the local vicar at whose picturesque church the murders occur finds himself and his congregation infected by a taste for death.

In this dense and detailed police procedural novel of manners, Dalgliesh heads a homicide squad to investigate politically sensitive crimes, assisted by the conservative, opinionated, and able but jealous John Massingham and a bright new recruit, Kate Miskin, whose resourcefulness and ambition irritate Massingham but impress Dalgliesh. James explores the sacrifices and compromises that Miskin, as a career policewoman, must make to maintain a personal life, fulfill family obligations to her aged and contrary mother, and escape the poverty and illegitimacy that have fueled her ambition. This case involves Dalgliesh personally, for he not only liked the murdered Berowne, having consulted him about blackmail, but also finds that he and the victim had much in common. Both were cultured, private men, dedicated to preserving civilization and art, schooled in language and literature, and aware of ambiguous human relationships and of the need for commitment to enduring values. Interested in church architecture, nineteenth century novelists and poets, philosophical questions of life and death, both had a cerebral, detached way of coping.

This close study of the frustrations and precision of police procedures and of the intelligence and instincts that transform the minutiae into details of great moment depends on a single bloodstain under a corpse, a struck match, a moved diary, and a missing button. James's argument throughout her depiction of the investigation—the gathering of physical evidence, the taking of testimonies, the checking and recheck-ing of alibis—is that murder changes everyone it touches; investigators, suspects, witnesses—none can ever be the same. Mother, wife, mistress, friends, brother-in-law, and business associates cannot escape the questions that lay bare their secret hearts. Dalgliesh knows murder destroys privacy through "the intimate detritus" of a victim's life and "through the mouths, truthful, treacherous, faltering, reluctant" of family, friends, and enemies; he also knows that "exploitation" of a suspect's fear, vanity, insecure need to confide, and lonely grief is "at the heart of successful detec-tion." Disturbed by the activities of his trade, he nonetheless recognizes their neces-sity. Actions bring consequences and the burdens of guilt and responsibility must be accepted.

Here again James explores the effects of environment on adolescents. Kate Miskin escapes her origins through hard work and sheer grit; Barbara Berowne escapes simi-lar limitations through cold-blooded sexuality (producing a legitimate heir). Barbara's brother, Dominic Swayne, warped by a loveless childhood and a succession of step-fathers, seduces an unattractive household servant to confirm an alibi, feigns friend-ship to win trust, and hides murder behind a façade of frankness to assure a con-tinued life of luxury. Tough, competent, ten-year-old Darren Wilkes, in turn, controls his environment, despite an alcoholic, prostitute mother, by attaching himself to the kindly sixty-five-year-old spinster, Miss Emily Wharton, whose safety he guards as they provide each other with companionship. Sarah Berowne, in contrast, wealthy and aristocratic, opts for an affair with a committed communist to embarrass her aloof, reticent father.

Ironically, the murderer helps each of these characters: killing Miskin's contrary mother but freeing Miskin from a limiting psychological and economic burden that prevented her commitment to love and career; frightening young Darren but thereby calling attention to an unnoted illness, leukemia; forcing Sarah to realize the obliga-tions of birth and education, reevaluate her relationship to her lover, and understand that she has been a pawn of the radical left; and seemingly confirming Barbara as heir of the Berowne fortune, an inheritance that her suspicious mother-in-law and wary husband thwart.

A Taste for Death is, moreover, replete with convincing details of place and scene: a cold and muddy river bank, a clinically antiseptic operating room, the pleasant cottage of a writer of children's books, the tidy apartment of the upwardly mobile young Kate, the stately manor of the Tory minister, the Romanesque basilica where the murder occurs.

Summary

P. D. James's novels are realistic studies of the hidden realities of the soul that compel forbidden acts of violence and murder. Yet despite their grim, clinical detail and their cynical, uncompromising study of behavior, they postulate, in sophisticated, literate prose, the civilizing influence of daily domestic acts, of art, architecture, poetry, and song.

A sense of irony and of existential absurdity lies behind James's depiction of a civilized English façade that crumbles only slightly in the face of multiple murders by seemingly decent human beings. Her characters are three-dimensional, living and suffering in an imperfect world, one in which evil is a tangible reality and in which the diseased, the dying, and the maladjusted are simply part of what one of her characters calls the "progressive incurable disease" that is life. James's genuine curiosity about human nature and motivations is sensitive to the density of human experience and the nuances that govern lives. She coldly dissects character and act but communicates understanding and compassion for frailty. Her knowledgeable treatment of technical procedure and forensics and her meticulously detailed descriptions of place are entirely convincing. As the "Queen of Crime," James has made the crime novel an effective study of human interaction and psychology.

Bibliography

Bakerman, Jane S. "Cordelia Gray: Apprentice and Archetype." *Clues: A Journal of Detection* 5 (Spring/Summer, 1984): 101-114.

Gidez, Richard B. *P. D. James: "The New Queen of Crime."* Boston: Twayne, 1986.

Hubly, Erlene. "Adam Dalgliesh: Byronic Hero." *Clues* 3 (Fall/Winter, 1982): 40-46.

_____. "The Formula Challenged: The Novels of P. D. James." *Modern Fiction Studies* 29 (Autumn, 1983): 511-521.

James, P. D. Interview by Jane S. Bakerman. *Armchair Detective* 10 (January, 1977): 55-57, 92.

_____. "No Gore, Please—They're British: An Interview with P. D. James." Interview by Marilyn Stasio. *Writer* 53 (March, 1990): 15-16.

Siebenholler, Norma. *P. D. James.* New York: Ungar, 1981.

Gina Macdonald

SAMUEL JOHNSON

Born: Lichfield, Staffordshire, England
September 18, 1709
Died: London, England
December 13, 1784

Principal Literary Achievement

Long known principally through James Boswell's *The Life of Samuel Johnson, L.L.D.* (1791) as a talker and eccentric, Johnson is now known best for poetry and prose that make him one of the major figures of the eighteenth century.

Biography

Samuel Johnson was born to a fifty-two-year-old bookseller, Michael Johnson, and his forty-year-old wife, Sarah Johnson, on September 18, 1709, in Lichfield, Staffordshire, England. Samuel was a precocious child who soon spent much time reading widely in his father's shop. After a typical classical education at Lichfield Grammar School, Johnson entered Pembroke College, Oxford, in the fall of 1728. When his funds ran out in December of the next year, however, he returned to Lichfield to work in his father's bookshop. Johnson's first published work, a translation into Latin of Alexander Pope's "The Messiah," appeared in 1731, the year of his father's death. Johnson was soon occupied briefly as a schoolmaster in a small town in Leicestershire and afterward in Birmingham as a translator.

At the age of twenty-four he met and married a widow, Elizabeth (Jervis) Porter, called "Tetty," twenty years his senior. Tetty reportedly described the tall, rawboned, awkward Johnson as "the most sensible man that I ever saw in my life." This astonishing marriage, which was childless, lasted until Tetty's death in 1752.

After the failure of a school that Johnson opened near Lichfield, he resolved to seek his fortune as a writer in London. Leaving Tetty behind, he set off in 1737 nearly penniless on the 120-mile trek by horse and on foot with the manuscript of an unfinished tragedy, *Irene* (1749) under his arm, in the company of David Garrick, a former pupil who wanted to become an actor.

In the years that followed, Garrick became a famous and wealthy actor, while Johnson eked out a bare existence as a Grub Street hack, writing miscellaneous ill-paid pieces such as translations and biographical essays for Edward Cave's *Gentleman's Magazine*. Johnson's work for Cave also included approximations of parliamentary debates assembled from scraps of conversations overheard in coffeehouses and on

the streets (publication of the actual debates themselves was prohibited). In these versions, Johnson achieved effective anti-Robert Walpole propaganda, reasonably accurate content, and style generally far better than the originals.

In 1738, Johnson published *London: A Poem in Imitation of the Third Satire of Juvenal*, comparing corruption in London under Walpole's ministry to that in Juvenal's degenerate Rome. Praise of the poem by Pope and other literary connoisseurs did not mean financial success for Johnson. Occasionally, he was hungry. Sometimes, in the company of other unfortunates, he walked the London streets at night or slept on bulks along the Thames because he lacked the price of a cheap lodging. These experiences left him with a clear memory of real poverty and a deep sympathy for poor people. This memory and sympathy served him well in writing *An Account of the Life of Mr. Richard Savage, Son of the Earl Rivers* (1744; commonly known as *Life of Richard Savage*), a full-length biography of an indigent author and Johnson's sometime companion who had died in 1743.

Two years later, Johnson's financial condition had improved enough for him to rent a rather large three-story house at Gough Square, near Grub Street, and to send for his wife. In the top story of this house, Johnson began work on his *A Dictionary of the English Language* (1755). This project took eight years of laboriously copying more than 116,000 suitable printed quotations, filing the papers in boxes, and doing research and writing. While the work on the dictionary was being pushed forward with the help of a succession of eight amanuenses, Johnson was also active on other literary fronts.

In 1749, he published *The Vanity of Human Wishes: The Tenth Satire of Juvenal Imitated*, perhaps the most profound of all of his poems, and, with Garrick's help, he staged his tragedy *Irene*, at last. The next year, he began *The Rambler* (1750-1752), a semiweekly periodical containing his own thoughtful essays on important human concerns, which continued until 1752, the year of Tetty's death.

With the publication of *A Dictionary of the English Language*, Johnson's fame and fortune grew. Oxford awarded him an honorary M.A. degree, and he was soon able to begin another immense project, an edition of William Shakespeare, to be published by subscription, and on another periodical, *The Idler* (1758-1760), for which he wrote essays on the human condition in a generally lighter tone than those of *The Rambler*.

Johnson was still not entirely free from money troubles. When his mother died in 1759, he needed to raise money quickly for her funeral expenses. He thus completed *Rasselas, Prince of Abyssinia* (1759), a moral tale that he seems to have begun some time before her death, for which he received one hundred pounds. In 1762, an annual pension of three hundred pounds awarded by the government made Johnson financially secure, at last. By 1763, when James Boswell, Johnson's first biographer, met him for the first time, Johnson was a celebrity, feared for his acuteness, famed as a talker, and admired for his abilities, endurance, and energy.

Although Johnson suffered from depression, from which he recovered with the help of new friends, the Thrales, he was not idle after the publication of his edition of Shakespeare and the subsequent award of an honorary LL.D. by Trinity College,

Dublin, in 1765. Johnson's next major work, however, came a number of years later. In 1773, at the age of sixty-four, he undertook a strenuous journey with Boswell, who wished to show him something of his native land. This resulted in *A Journey to the Western Islands of Scotland*, published in 1775. Johnson also toured Wales with the Thrales in 1774 and accompanied them to France the next year. At this time, he received an honorary doctorate in civil law from Oxford. He continued to call himself plain "Mr. Johnson."

Johnson's last lengthy literary project, *Prefaces, Biographical and Critical, to the Works of the English Poets* (1779-1781; commonly known as *The Lives of the Poets*), occupied the years between 1777 to 1781. It consisted of biographical and critical prefaces to the reprinted works of fifty seventeenth and eighteenth century English writers. Though occasionally perfunctory, many of those prefaces featured in *The Lives of the Poets*—especially those on Abraham Cowley, John Milton, John Dryden, Isaac Watts, and Pope, among others—contain some of Johnson's most incisive criticism.

Johnson had always feared death, but in the last years of his life he decided to confront it. Among friends who died was a humble physician for whom Johnson had provided a home for many years. This man is commemorated in some of the most moving verse that Johnson ever wrote, "On the Death of Dr. Robert Levet." Johnson's own robust physical health began to break down, too, and he experienced recurrences of depression. His religious faith sustained him, but this time Mrs. Thrale was not there to nurse him through crises; a widow for a time, she had remarried against Johnson's wishes. By the fall of 1784, his sufferings from asthma and dropsy became acute. He became bedridden after returning from a trip to Oxford in late November. After praying fervently and taking leave of his friends, he died of what seems to have been complications of dropsy on December 13 in London. On December 20, Johnson's funeral took place in Westminster Abbey, where he was buried in the Poets' Corner.

Analysis

As James L. Clifford points out, critics who followed Johnson generally were not favorably impressed by his writings. They decided that his work was pompous, didactic, and even bigoted. Critics now consider Johnson a teacher, moralist, and wise man who appeals strongly to readers because of his sincerity, lucidity, and vigor. No one would claim, however, that Johnson is easy reading. His vocabulary is frequently abstract and Latinate. His sentences are often long, sonorous and muscular. They seem to demand of readers a tolerance for ample and unhurried thought. Yet although Johnson wishes his readers to understand him, he is not condescending. Rather, he tries to raise them to his own level. He provides many examples to make his points and to put them in broad moral and social context. He also makes frequent use of analogies to things that are familiar, striking, and concrete.

In all of Johnson's writings, his sympathy with weak and downtrodden people is clear. In *The Rambler*, issue 39 (1750), he sympathizes with unhappily married women. In *The Rambler*, issue 148 (August 17, 1751), he warns parents about the misuse of parental authority and cruelty toward children. In *The Rambler*, issue 114 (April 20, 1751), he speaks out against capital punishment for such crimes as robbery. In *The Rambler*, issues 170-171 (November 2 and 9, 1751), he calls for compassion toward prostitutes, many of whom were victims of circumstance. In 1777, an argument by Johnson was successful in freeing Joseph Knight, whose black skin had condemned him to slavery.

Johnson was scrupulous in his concern for the truth and did not passively accept other people's opinions. In 1762, his search for the truth made him look into the alleged appearance of the Cock Lane Ghost, and he exposed it as a fraud. In 1773, he accompanied Boswell on a strenuous journey to the Scottish Highlands to investigate the claim of James Macpherson that his publication of a long pseudoepic poem was in reality authentic folk poetry by the Gaelic poet Ossian. When Johnson wrote *The Lives of the Poets*, he did not merely rely on printed authorities for information about his subjects but tried to search for material on his own—a rare practice in his day.

Because Johnson's critical judgments on literature sometimes differ from those of mainstream received opinion, they are often assumed to be prejudiced. Indeed, Johnson says what he thinks and leaves no doubt as to why. He calls the form of Milton's "Lycidas" "easy, vulgar and therefore disgusting." Yet he gives his reasons: the inherent improbability of using pastoral imagery to talk about the activities of college friends and acquaintances, and the combinations of these pastoral fictions with "the most awful and sacred truths of Christianity." That is, Milton spoke of college students as *sheep*, of their teachers as *shepherds*, and later, impiously and irreverently, of these *shepherds* as ecclesiastical pastors and saints.

Johnson's poetry addresses the same themes as his prose: human pain and difficulty, the need for morality and truth. In "On the Death of Dr. Robert Levet," a poem of nine simple quatrains, Johnson expresses his personal grief for the loss of his "obscurely wise and coarsely kind" friend. He also makes Levet's use of his modest gifts to benefit the sick poor a model for readers. Even Johnson's humorous advice to a spendthrift young heir in "To Sir John Lade, on His Coming of Age" includes both an understanding of lighthearted youth and a serious warning of dangers that might cause Sir John to "hang or drown at last." Johnson's human sympathies and his insistence on truth and morality make readers conscious of his presence in everything that he wrote. He is a compelling guide and friendly teacher who insists that readers take him seriously.

LONDON

First published: 1738
Type of work: Poem

London, the center of British life, is so corrupt that good people must leave it and those of genius, unrewarded, cannot survive in it.

London, a poem in twenty-seven stanzas of varying lengths, is written in pointed heroic couplets. An imitation of Juvenal's third satire, it revives Juvenal's complaints against flattery, fraud, perjury, theft, and rejection of old Roman virtues and applies them to the British metropolis. Like Juvenal, Johnson is rhetorical and dramatic. He, too, presents readers with a scene: A man, injured by the viciousness and folly of the city, leaving for the peace and solitude of the country, is bidding farewell to his friend.

Johnson's poem opens with a man named Thales waiting on the banks of the Thames for the boat to take him to Wales. Thales reviews his reasons for leaving town: selfishness, greed, the absence of public and private virtue, and the disappearance of true patriotism. The greatest effects of these calamities are felt by the young and the talented. Still other evils, such as arson, random violence, and even murders committed by pampered young delinquents and mischievous drunkards, are directed against the helpless poor or unsuspecting citizens. Thales can say no more because his boat has arrived. Yet he promises to come out of solitude to renew his attack on London vice when his friend is ready to leave the city.

London presents a problem to readers: To whom is Thales addressing his grandiose monologue, which is appropriate for a large audience? Merely to the single friend who accompanied him to the boat? It is ironic that the very people who need his message are not there to hear it. It is also possible that Johnson, to show how deeply his speaker is affected by his ordeal, has him "forget" that only one person is listening to him. Of course, outside the fictional situation of the poem, Thales has as an audience all the readers of *London*.

London is, in part, a public poem, a satire attacking the corrupt, long-entrenched government of Sir Robert Walpole. A typical Tory complaint repeated several times in the poem—how much London had changed since its glorious days—parallels Juvenal's lament for the death of old Roman virtue. The speaker expresses anger and disappointment for England's losses: of the "fair Justice" of King Alfred, of the heroism and sanctity of King Edward, of the bravery of King Henry (Johnson does not specify which Henry), and of the honor and commercial ascendancy of Queen Elizabeth. Instead, under Walpole, "Worth" and "Science" are ignored, insulted, attacked, and forced by their enemies to leave the capital. These include abstract representations of evil such as "the supple Gaul," "the silken Courtier," the "fiery Fop," the "frolick Drunkard," the "midnight Murderer," *Orgolio*, and *Balbo*, as well as real people, all Whigs, such as Lords Hervey, Marlborough, and Villiers. Such evil undermines the nation and even poisons the English soil.

London is also a private poem, which expresses Johnson's personal sense of injury in the outrages committed by a vicious society on the virtuous individual. It also contains concrete details that tie it to Johnson's own experience. Johnson had seen two of his friends, Henry Hervey and Richard Savage, victimized and forced, like Thales in the poem, to leave London for Wales.

The poem's rhetorical structure allows the speaker to turn from observations to questions to exclamations, from panoramic descriptions of a society in moral chaos to mock exhortations to villains to do their worst, from condemnations of evil to prayers to be spared. The structure also permits the expression of a wide range of strong feelings—anger, loss, sorrow, rage, regret, indignation—and allows these feelings to build to an almost unbearable tension. Even so, the reader has an impression that great reserves of emotional power are being restrained by an immense effort. Thus, the famous lines in which Johnson describes his own unfortunate condition, "Slow rises worth, by Poverty deprest," sound mild and innocuous out of context. Yet within the poem, they indicate wrath and despair about to explode. These emotions and the themes with which they are associated appear repeatedly in Johnson's writings.

LIFE OF RICHARD SAVAGE

First published: 1744
Type of work: Biography

Johnson tells the story of his impoverished literary friend, Richard Savage, who asserted that he was the illegitimate son of a countess and an earl.

In *Life of Richard Savage* (the full title is *An Account of the Life of Mr. Richard Savage, Son of the Earl Rivers*), his first full-length biography, published anonymously, Johnson describes the sensational life of a Grub Street writer and poet who was his friend and sometime companion in frolic and poverty. When Savage died in 1743, Edward Cave, the publisher, hurried to make arrangements with Johnson to write Savage's notorious story. Johnson had to work quickly. He made some attempts to consult records and examine original documents, but he was less concerned with factual accuracy than with telling the truth about the character of a man who, though unfortunate, had brought most of his misfortunes on himself. Clearly, Johnson was aware of his friend's many shortcomings. He also wished to defend Savage's memory from malign attacks. Even more, however, he wanted to write an account that would be useful to readers both as an inspiration and as a warning.

According to Johnson's account, which believed Savage's claim to high birth, Savage's mother, Lady Macclesfield, who wished to escape from her marriage, stated that she had committed adultery and that the child she carried had been fathered by Earl Rivers. Her husband's application to Parliament to have the marriage dissolved was successful, and Lady Macclesfield's baby was declared illegitimate. When the baby was born, Rivers acknowledged his paternity but took no other notice of the child. The baby's mother, who remarried soon after her divorce, sent him to a poor woman to be reared as her own and paid no more attention to him. The baby came to be called Richard Savage. His maternal grandmother and his godmother took enough interest in him to pay for his care and his education, but because his mother stated that he had died, Rivers made no provision for him in his will. Thus, Richard Savage lost a legacy of six thousand pounds. Then, Savage's mother tried to have him sent to the American plantations and, failing that, had him apprenticed to a shoemaker. When his nurse died, Savage found among her papers evidence showing who he really was. He began an unsuccessful lifelong campaign, which alternated pleas and vilification, to be recognized and supported by his mother.

Savage must have had considerable charm, for he was helped by Sir Richard Steele, the actress Anne Oldfield, and the writer Aaron Hill, who were impressed by his talent for writing and conversation. A short spurt of good fortune ended when Savage was implicated in a murder, tried, found guilty, and condemned to death. His mother obstructed his friends' efforts to get him a reprieve, but eventually he received a royal pardon.

The patronage of Lord Tyrconnel, his supposed cousin, enabled Savage to return to society and made him a literary lion. Yet Savage's frequent drunkenness, outrageous behavior, and sale of a set of books that Tyrconnel had lent him caused a split between them and the end of Tyrconnel's financial support. Savage, ever resilient, addressed Queen Charlotte as her "Volunteer Laureate" in a poem on her birthday and succeeded in getting a small annual pension from her. When that, or any other money came his way, Savage spent it on wine and jollity, and soon he was without any money, and often without food or shelter. His friends proposed that he go to Wales, where he could write and live cheaply. After a year, however, he was back in London, living in dissipation and want. His friends, their funds and their patience exhausted, let him be taken to Newgate Prison, where at least he would have shelter from the elements. For six months, all went well. Savage was well treated by his jailers. He received visits from his friends and continued to write. In the summer of 1743, though, he became ill and died within a few weeks.

In the *Life of Richard Savage*, Johnson discusses briefly some of Savage's works, such as *The Wanderer* (1729) and *The Bastard* (1728), two poems concerned mainly with Savage's own life and misfortunes; *An Author to Be Let* (1729), a pamphlet that unwisely satirized nearly everyone in the literary establishment of the day; and two poems, *The Volunteer Laureate* (1732, the already-mentioned birthday poem addressed to the queen) and *London and Bristol Compared* (1744), which Johnson quotes in full. Savage's writings were striking, original, and dignified, says Johnson. They might be faulted for uniformity and occasional harshness of style, but they were nonetheless remarkable performances, considering the unfavorable circumstances under which they were written.

Johnson is more interested in discussing Savage's character than his writings. This bent is particularly obvious at the end of the account, where he points out Savage's virtues and abilities, as well as his vices and weaknesses. Savage did not look like a ruffian. His manner was dignified, his mind was strong and agile, his conversation was stimulating, his judgment of literature and people was sound. He was often compassionate and generous. Yet he was a waster of his own considerable talents, a slave to his passions, a victim of dissipation. He was unreliable. He was inordinately vain of his abilities and his writings.

Johnson does not condemn Savage or allow others, especially those "who have slumber'd away their time on the down of affluence," to speak ill of Savage or his writings. Instead, Savage's accomplishments should be an inspiration to those who also suffer deprivation or a lesson to those who do not, showing that imprudence and dissipation "make knowledge useless, wit ridiculous, and genius contemptible."

THE VANITY OF HUMAN WISHES

First published: 1749
Type of work: Poem

Human efforts can do nothing to achieve security or happiness, but heavenly wisdom can create calm and happiness that humankind cannot achieve alone.

The Vanity of Human Wishes, published eleven years after *London*, is an imitation of Juvenal's tenth satire. It, too, is a long poem. It consists of twenty-five stanzas of varying lengths, written in heroic couplets. It is also concerned with morality. Its rhetorical style is similar to that of *London*: It also has a speaker who uses the same kind of personifications, the same kind of pointed sentences, the same kind of figures of speech as Johnson's earlier poem. Yet *The Vanity of Human Wishes* is a more philosophical poem than *London*. Its scope is larger and its manner is more mature.

The poem opens with a magniloquent invitation from a speaker stationed above and beyond the earth to "Let Observation, with extensive View/ Survey Mankind, from *China* to *Peru*" to see how, in the whole inhabited world, various patterns of destruction thwart human efforts. The eye can discern the wavering of an individual who pursues a dangerous solitary course, as well as the larger movements resulting from the sinking of whole nations. The scene encompasses the entire human condition, from humble to exalted. It also takes in the whole of human history, which, from earliest times, was preoccupied with a single question: Can human beings achieve security, fortune, and happiness? Until close to the end of the poem, the answer is no.

The reader is presented with a series of portraits, arranged in what seems to be an order of increasing mischance, of splendid and ambitious persons, such as Cardinal Thomas Wolsey, Charles XII of Sweden, and Xerxes I, who meet with defeat and shame by merest accident. These alternate with vignettes of nameless and typical figures who are also undone by life. Life's anonymous victims include the scholar, like Johnson himself, whose desire for knowledge and fame is destroyed by "Toil, envy, want, the patron, and the jail." The rich old man who hopes to buy health and a fresh appetite for enjoyment instead acquires heirs who hope soon to get their hands on his estate. The ambitious mother who thought beauty, rather than virtue, would help her children to advance sees them destroyed because of it.

The multiplication of images, which is accompanied by an increasing complexity of language, also suggests rising tension. The compression of human problems in the question near the end of the poem, "Must helpless man, in ignorance sedate,/ Roll darkling down the torrent of his fate?" indicates not merely the compounded horror of the human condition but also a tension that is nearly unbearable. The distance between the speaker and the reader is diminished. Also, the distance from what the speaker and the reader see is eliminated, so that both are on the verge of the fate that they witness.

For Johnson, the only possible answer is found in resignation based on religious hope and prayer that asks for love, patience, and faith. With these three, "celestial wisdom" creates the gift of calm and happiness that the human mind cannot obtain on its own.

RASSELAS

First published: 1759
Type of work: Philosophical tale

Rasselas leaves his birthplace, the Happy Valley, to find a life that will ensure happiness, but he decides at length that he has searched in vain.

Rasselas, Prince of Abyssinia, Johnson's most famous work, was written rapidly to pay the expenses of Johnson's mother's funeral and published anonymously. It tells in forty-nine brief chapters what seems at first to be a simple story with a clear moral. A young prince, Rasselas, is imprisoned in his Abyssinian birthplace, the Happy Valley. It is a paradise surrounded by mountains, which, once left, cannot be reentered. Although his life seems perfect, Rasselas is nonetheless bored and unhappy. He manages to escape from his home together with his tutor, Imlac, his sister, Nekayah, and her maid, Pekuah. They set out for Cairo on a quest for a kind of life that will bring happiness.

Rasselas soon discovers that happiness cannot be found among pleasure-seeking young men, learned older men, Stoic philosophers, hermits, or heads of government. His sister, Nekayah, who looked for happiness in private life, found only empty-headed cheerfulness in the daughters of the families that she visited, discord between parents and children, and often discord between spouses. Imlac then proposes that they visit the Pyramids to look for the secret of happiness in the past. When they arrive, Nekayah's maid, Pekuah, afraid of being closed in forever, balks at entering and so is left outside while the others make their explorations. Yet when Rasselas, Nekayah, and Imlac emerge into daylight, Pekuah is missing. She has been kidnapped by Arab horsemen. For the first time, Rasselas, and especially Nekayah, experience real loss and genuine unhappiness.

After seven months, Pekuah is returned unharmed to her mistress. The group happily returns again to Cairo. There, Rasselas announces an intention to devote himself to the life of a scholar. Imlac tells about a scholar whom he knows, an astronomer who seems happy but, upon closer acquaintance, proves to be mad and to believe firmly that he is in control of the weather and the seasons. The astronomer, in fact, is attempting to name Imlac his successor as controller of weather and the seasons. After the young people meet the old astronomer and converse with him, however, his sanity, and also his unhappiness, returns.

What they had seen and done outside the Happy Valley had given Rasselas, Nekayah, and Pekuah a measure of experience that they had not had before and desires they knew could not be fulfilled. At the end of the tale, in "The Conclusion, in Which Nothing Is Concluded," Pekuah wishes to become prioress of an order of pious women; Nekayah, to found a college of learned women; Rasselas, to become a just ruler. None of these is immediately within grasp, so the three, together with Imlac and the old astronomer, decide to return to Abyssinia as soon as possible. They will not, however, be able to reenter the Happy Valley.

Rasselas is not a novel. It is not concerned with so-called real life, but with symbolic action. Its central problem, how and where happiness can be found, is never directly answered, but instead it is considered and reconsidered with increasing refinement from different viewpoints. Its characters, for all of their admirable goals and delicate tastes, are not rounded persons but representative types. They are aids in complicating and clarifying happiness. They show that efforts to obtain happiness are futile, but also that, as in *The Vanity of Human Wishes*, happiness can be conferred or received as a gift.

In *Rasselas*, Johnson is, of course, the teller of the tale and often, perhaps, in the figure of Imlac, the wise man. Imlac is comically enthusiastic about his learned interests and would talk forever if not stopped. Yet he is also the character in the tale best equipped to find a solution to the problem of happiness. Imlac is a quintessential teacher, tireless, and, like Johnson, generous. He donates the results of a whole lifetime of activity and thought for Rasselas' benefit. He sees to it that Rasselas and his party avoid obvious foolishness, that they experience whatever good is at hand, and that they consider all available possibilities before they make decisions.

Rasselas has often been compared with Voltaire's *Candide*, another philosophical tale dating from 1759 and concerned with the problem of finding happiness. Voltaire recommends "cultivating one's garden" as a solution to humankind's difficulties. He does not promise bliss as an outcome of this activity, but rather contentment. Yet Johnson is more pessimistic and more scrupulous than Voltaire. In *Rasselas*, humankind is in a more precarious situation than in *Candide*, more like that of "helpless Man" at the end of *The Vanity of Human Wishes*, but without the possibility of a religious solution to the problem. In *Rasselas*, nothing is entirely within human control, not even the cultivation of a small parcel of land. Impossibilities are everywhere, and trouble can lurk even in the most featureless landscape.

Summary

No longer considered as a man notable merely because of his eccentric personal mannerisms and interesting talks, Samuel Johnson at last has come into his own as one of the greatest English writers of the eighteenth century. His range is broad. He is a large-souled poet, an incisive essayist, a careful and energetic editor, a pioneer in the art of biography, and a profound moralist. His achievements also include the first *A Dictionary of the English Language* based on scientific principles and a body of literary criticism, which later critics ignore at their peril.

Johnson's special appeal lies in his psychological depth, his integrity, and his love and pity for humankind. These qualities continue to speak to the minds and hearts of readers.

Bibliography

Boswell, James. *Life of Johnson*. London: Oxford University Press, 1953.

Clifford, James L. *Dictionary Johnson*. New York: McGraw-Hill, 1979.

_____. *Young Sam Johnson*. New York: McGraw-Hill, 1955.

Greene, Donald, ed. *Samuel Johnson: A Collection of Critical Essays*. Englewood Cliffs, N.J.: Prentice-Hall, 1965.

Greene, Donald. *Samuel Johnson*. Rev. ed. Boston: Twayne, 1989.

Johnson, Samuel. *Samuel Johnson*. Edited by Donald Greene. New York: Oxford University Press, 1984

Johnson, Samuel. *The Yale Edition of the Works of Samuel Johnson*. 16 vols. New Haven, Conn.: Yale University Press, 1958-1990.

Margaret Duggan

BEN JONSON

Born: London, England
June 11, 1573
Died: London, England
August 6, 1637

Principal Literary Achievement

A celebrated playwright and poet, Jonson is best known for his satirical comedies, lucid lyrics, and incisive critical opinions.

Biography

Benjamin Jonson, posthumous son of a minister, was born in or near London, England, on June 11, 1573. He received an excellent foundation in classical letters at Westminster School under headmaster William Camden, a famous scholar. Although unable to continue his education at a university, he was an avid reader and on his own became a serious student of classical language and literature. For a time, Jonson followed his stepfather's bricklaying trade, but in 1591 he went to the Low Countries to fight in the army. According to his own account, he bravely killed a foe in view of both the English and enemy camps.

Jonson returned to London in 1592, and two years later married Anne Lewis. In the next year or two, he began a career as actor and playwright. He soon got into trouble. In 1597, he was jailed for his part in *The Isle of Dogs* (1597), a play that the authorities considered subversive, and the next year killed a fellow actor, Gabriel Spencer, in a duel. His goods were confiscated, and he was branded on the thumb and jailed. While in prison, he converted to Roman Catholicism but later returned to the Anglican faith.

By the start of the seventeenth century, Jonson's reputation as a satirical comedian was well established. He rejected the fashionable romantic comedy and, starting with *Every Man in His Humour* (1598, 1605), staged in 1598, began writing scathing attacks on human vices such as greed, lust, and envy. *Every Man in His Humour* was followed by *Every Man out of His Humour* (1599), *Cynthia's Revels* (1600-1601), and *The Poetaster* (1601), all in the new satirical vein.

Jonson wrote for both adult and children's acting companies, and from 1600 to 1602 he participated in the famous war of the theaters, a conflict involving the Elizabethan playwrights John Marston, Thomas Dekker, and Jonson. He also became well known for his courtly masques created in collaboration with the architect Inigo Jones. Al-

though best at writing satirical comedy, Jonson also wrote tragedy, producing two of significance, *Sejanus* (1603) and *Cataline* (1611), which use classical models.

In 1605, with James I on the throne, Jonson was back in jail. He voluntarily joined his collaborators on *Eastward Ho!* (1605), which had been found offensive for its ridicule of Scots. That same year, he assisted the Privy Council in its inquiries into the Gunpowder Plot, an ill-devised Catholic scheme to blow up Parliament.

The richest period of Jonson's dramatic writing was between 1606, when *Volpone* was first produced, and 1616, when his collected plays and poetry were published in *The Workes of Benjamin Jonson. Epicœne: Or, The Silent Woman* (1609), *The Alchemist* (1610), *Bartholomew Fair* (1614), and *The Devil Is an Ass* (1616) were all penned in that decade.

Jonson then abandoned writing plays for almost ten years. A royal pension allowed him some leisure time for other activities. In 1618, he took a walking tour of Scotland and visited the poet William Drummond of Hawthornden, in whom he confided some of his more biting critical opinions. The following year, recognizing Jonson as a scholar and writer of importance, Oxford granted him an honorary degree.

In 1625, two years after a fire had destroyed his library, Jonson returned to writing plays. He did not, however, regain his earlier form. His most famous dramatic works belong to the fruitful period between 1598 and 1616. His last well-known comedy, *The Staple of News*, was produced in 1626, at the very start of his return to playwriting. From then until his death, he wrote what his detractors termed his "dotages," but one fragmentary work, *The Sad Shepherd*, published posthumously in 1640, is an engaging piece.

In 1628, when he was appointed city chronologer, Jonson was struck with paralysis, probably from a stroke. Thereafter, he largely remained confined to his quarters, where dedicated followers gathered and formed the "Sons of Ben." These were mostly poets, influenced by Jonson's verse, which they imitated. The period of his later masques, written for the court of Charles I from 1625 to 1635, was marked by a strained relationship with Jones. In 1631, they quarreled bitterly and ended their collaboration for good. Jonson's reputation as an affable intellectual and arbiter of literary taste remained intact until his death on August 6, 1637, in London. He was buried in the Poets' Corner of Westminster Abbey under the epitaph, "O Rare Ben Jonson," testifying to the high esteem in which his contemporaries held him.

Analysis

One well-worn critical notion is that, although we admire Ben Jonson, we love William Shakespeare. Jonson's dramatic output in fact rivaled Shakespeare's. He wrote nineteen plays, collaborated in several others, and crafted twenty-four courtly masques and entertainments. Yet despite Jonson's great reputation among his contemporaries, his star has long been eclipsed by the phenomenal achievement of his great fellow dramatist and friend. Granted, Shakespeare's genius is unmatched by any of his contemporaries except in isolated instances, but no other lesser genius has been treated to such unfavorable comparisons with Shakespeare as Jonson has. He was to a degree responsible for this turn of events. An outspoken critic, Jonson passed on some negative assessments of his older friend's work that ultimately made him the target of unjust criticism by many admirers of Shakespeare.

In the prologue to the second version of *Every Man in His Humour*, Jonson presented a critical manifesto that has been wrongly interpreted as a personal attack on Shakespeare conceived in petty jealousy. Although Jonson does allude to Shakespeare's use of the Chorus in his *Henry V* (1589-1591) plays, his real concern is with the violation of logic characteristic of the popular chronicle play, which, complained Jonson, would often cover the entire span of a character's life in an obvious violation of classical rules. Jonson was simply rejecting the history play in general, preferring comedy, which could mirror the times and "sport with human follies, not with crimes."

Clearly, Jonson's neoclassical bias led him to rebuke the practices of the stage that went against his sense of propriety and reason. Jonson's comedy, because it is didactic, naturally gravitates toward satire. Its purpose, to make people laugh at their own foolishness, is corrective; hence, in Jonson's greatest plays, including *Volpone* and *The Alchemist*, the main characters are either tricksters who cheat fools or fools themselves. Jonson's comic mode is thus very different from that of Shakespeare, who is only satirical incidentally.

Jonson also believed that the overdrawn, exaggerated, and flowery speech of many characters was too wearisome, and he preached writing in language that people actually used, including slang heard in the street. That demand would also put him at artistic odds with Shakespeare, who framed different styles of expression for an extraordinary range of characters. Jonson, while embracing the concept of the dramatic unities of time, place, and action, did not always follow it. In contrast, Shakespeare, who either did not entertain the idea or simply rejected it on some occasions, as in *The Tempest* (1611), practiced it to perfection.

In his best dramatic work, Jonson is a brilliant craftsman. His comedies are intrigue plays with complex designs, and for sheer stage razzle-dazzle, they have few rivals. Jonson parades before the audience a succession of fools, brilliantly drawn and comically driven by some obsessive vice or "humor" that makes them fair game for crafty swindlers who prey on their weaknesses. That design becomes central in several of Jonson's comedies, but the playwright's genius was such that it never becomes merely formulaic.

Jonson's susceptibility to criticism lies not in an inability to depict characters but in his disinterest in depicting sympathetic ones. Since his purpose was satirical, he seldom moves his focus away from tricksters and fools toward the more genial types found in the festive comedies of Shakespeare. Shakespeare's comedies are triumphant and affirm life. Jonson's comedies take a sour look at it. Within that limitation, and on his own terms, Jonson is a master playwright. His best works offer comic delight in their design. Once set in motion by the tricksters and driven by their own foolishness, the victims move with increasing rapidity through successive scenes until the action gets beyond the tricksters' control. Resourceful though they may be, the overreaching tricksters end up being victimized by their own greed.

While Jonson is better known as a dramatist than lyrical poet, in the fashion of his own age, he undoubtedly viewed his poetry as his highest literary achievement. He is the primary figure in one of two major movements in poetry in the first half of the seventeenth century. The other movement, the so-called Metaphysical school, followed in the footsteps of John Donne. The "tribe" or "sons" of Ben emulated what Jonson preached and for the most part practiced.

Whereas the modern reader might have trouble reading Jonson's comedies, which suffer somewhat from their topical word use, that same reader should find much of Jonson's lyrical poetry remarkably clear. Unlike Donne and other Metaphysical poets, Jonson and his followers strove for clarity, symmetry, and simplicity in verse, which is classical in form and spirit. Except in a few pieces affecting the Metaphysical mode, Jonson's poetry is free of the strained imagery and intricate thought of Donne and his followers.

Marked by decorum and restraint, Jonson's lyrics are public and objective, cool and rational, urbane and polished. Many of his pieces are terse, notably his songs, epigrams, and epitaphs. They are also didactic, sometimes satirical, even, at times, self-mocking. Marked by understatement and irony and purged of all emotional excess, some of his lyrics achieve an objective detachment that makes them seem cold. It is their pared down, uncomplicated statement that gives many of Jonson's lyrics their modern tone.

Seconded by his critical opinions circulated among members of his group, Jonson's poetry introduced a public poetry that would for a time gain ascendancy over the more private, subjective, and obscure verse of the Metaphysical poets. An important seminal figure in the classical movement, Jonson's artistic tastes make him a parent of the neo-Augustan Age.

VOLPONE

First produced: 1606 (first published, 1607)
Type of work: Play

A Venetian "magnifico" who pretends to be dying in order to cheat greedy fortune hunters is undone by his own vanity.

No work is more firmly bound to Jonson's name than his great satirical verse comedy *Volpone*. It achieves the mastery of purpose claimed by the playwright and reflects his devotion to classical theories, but it remains a distressing comedy that defies easy interpretation.

The play's predication is, however, quite simple. Volpone and his servant Mosca pretend that Volpone is dying and encourage Venetian fortune hunters to vie for Volpone's favor in hopes of being named his heir. All visit Volpone, prompted by Mosca to bring gifts to convince Volpone of their kind concern for his health. Volpone is, of course, perfectly well, but he and Mosca put on such a good act that the legacy hunters are completely fooled. The greedy victims include Corbaccio, an old, deaf miser; Voltore, a conniving lawyer; Corvino, a rich merchant who jealously guards his young, attractive wife, Celia; and Lady Would-be, the wife of a ridiculous English knight.

Complications arise when Mosca convinces Corbaccio to claim that he is drawing up a new will disinheriting his son, Bonario, and naming Volpone his heir. After Corbaccio agrees, Mosca taunts Bonario and challenges him to go to Volpone's house to overhear Corbaccio confirm the fact. Meanwhile, Volpone, who has been scheming to seduce Corvino's wife, has Mosca talk the foolish merchant into leaving Celia alone with Volpone, who then attempts to force himself on her. Bonario catches him in the act, rescues Celia, and denounces Volpone and Mosca.

Fearful that the game is ended, Volpone throws himself down in despair, but Mosca devises a new scheme to escape trouble. He convinces Corbaccio that his son is out to kill him, tells the suspicious Voltore that Bonario has made Celia swear that Volpone had raped her, and gets Corvino to denounce Celia as a lewd woman. Celia and Bonario, totally innocent, are brought to court, and through the testimony of the legacy hunters and Voltore's cunning, are found guilty in an obvious travesty of justice.

The pair of tricksters then go too far. Determined to vex the fools further, they spread the news that Volpone has died. Each would-be heir then comes to Volpone's house to claim the magnifico's legacy, only to be told that Mosca is the heir. Mosca knows that Volpone himself is now vulnerable and quickly makes plans to cheat him.

Seeking revenge on Mosca, the would-be heirs return to the court to claim that Bonario and Celia have been falsely charged and that Mosca has practiced criminal deceptions. Mosca is called to court, and when he refuses to confirm that Volpone is actually alive, he impels Volpone, disguised as an officer of the court, to reveal himself rather than be tricked. At last discovering the truth, the judges sentence both the tricksters and the fools to appropriate but very harsh, uncomic punishments. Mosca is to be whipped and sent to the galleys. Volpone, his wealth confiscated and given to a hospital for incurables, is to be imprisoned until he does in fact become sick and lame.

Jonson's work is based on a popular beast fable of the fox that feigned death, but its complexity can be fully explained only by reference to the Roman institution of legacy hunting and such diverse works as *Aesop's Fables* (1484), the Bible, and Desiderius Erasmus' *Moriæ Encomium* (1511; *The Praise of Folly*, 1549). The comedy can also be seen as a morality play within its beast-fable guise. Volpone, like the fox pretending to be dead, traps unwary birds of prey, who are, of course, greedy men hoping to benefit from his death. Jonson's theme and real concern is the unnaturalness of sin. His strong moral intent is driven home by a constant reference to the beast fable in the speeches of Volpone and Mosca.

The dramatist's artistic purpose, as the play's prologue confirms, is to entertain and enlighten the audience while observing the unities of time, place, and action.

Strictly speaking, however, Jonson violates his own artistic rules. The action all takes place in Venice within the course of a single day, but classical symmetry is destroyed by the inclusion of a subplot involving Sir Politic Would-be and his fellow Englishman, Peregrine.

The setting of the play, Venice, was probably chosen by Jonson for its reputation as a city full of carnival-like attractions, much like Jonson's own London. Volpone's household includes abnormal human pets, and at one point he disguises himself as a mountebank or quack to catch a glimpse of Celia. It is a Venice teeming with Renaissance life, zestful and curious, a magnet for English travelers such as Peregrine and the Would-bes.

The atmosphere is right for the deceit and trickery practiced by Volpone and Mosca on the callous, hypocritical legacy hunters. Volpone is, of course, no less perverse than his victims. In fact, his opening salutation to his gold, which he venerates as a saint, grotesquely distorts normal human values. As long as his victims are greedy fools, however, Volpone's ingenuity makes him more rogue than villain. Only when Bonario and Celia become enmeshed in his intrigue does he grow ripe for the comic unmasking that marks the play's grim finale.

Volpone works through an admirable use of sustained dramatic irony, which is a powerful theatrical device. The audience, recognizing the deceptions practiced by Volpone and Mosca, delights in their clever manipulation of their victims. The irony leads to some hilarious moments, as, for example, when Mosca prompts Corvino to vilify Volpone to his face after convincing him that the fox is nearly in a coma, or the scene in which Mosca must yell at the deaf and feeble Corbaccio to get him to understand anything at all.

Threaded through the play, the farcical subplot of Sir Politic and Peregrine offers a humorous counterpoint to the fierce, unrelenting satire on compulsive greed in the main plot. In Sir Pol, Jonson pokes fun at harmless fanatics who find conspiracy afoot everywhere. Among other fantastic disclosures, Sir Pol tells Peregrine that he knows how to sell Venice to the Turks. After Peregrine becomes convinced that Sir Politic is actually a pimp for his wife, Lady Pol, he decides to get revenge on him. In the disguise of a merchant, he leads Sir Pol to believe that Peregrine is really a Venetian secret agent who now plans to arrest him. He then helps Sir Pol hide inside a ridiculous contraption made of a tortoise shell before revealing his true self and mocking the silly knight.

Sir Pol's asinine delusions and his fanciful "projects" are in the tradition of burlesque and mimicry, appropriate to the parrot, his beast-fable counterpart. Lady Pol, in the fortune hunt, is more directly related to the main plot, but she too is a mimic, aping the dress and manners of Venice and trying the Italian seduction game as if it were a mere extension of Venetian fashions. The topicality of the Sir Politic plot makes it easy to overlook its important function in the play. It contrasts English folly with Italian vice and adds texture and density to the whole. It also clarifies the relationship between vice and folly, showing how each is a species of the unnatural, which is, after all, Jonson's central, unifying theme.

THE ALCHEMIST

First produced: 1610 (first published, 1612)
Type of work: Play

A trio of London sharpers trick their greedy victims through clever manipulation and alchemical gibberish and mock rites.

Like *Volpone*, *The Alchemist*, also in verse, has a complex intrigue plot with a radial design. In both plays, there is a central place where deceit is practiced on a procession of fools. In *The Alchemist*, the setting is Lovewit's London house, where, in Lovewit's absence, his butler Jeremy has invited a cheater, Subtle, and his whore, Doll, to set up shop as tricksters on a profit-sharing basis.

At the beginning of the play, Subtle and Jeremy haggle over their respective cuts, and Doll manages to restore peace at the moment that the first of the fools, Dapper, enters. He is a clerk whom Jeremy, as Captain Face, has encouraged to consult with "Doctor" Subtle. Dapper wants a familiar spirit to help him win at gambling. After telling him that he is related to the Queen of Fairy, the tricksters whisk him out in order to welcome the next victim, Drugger, a tobacconist who wants to use magic for arranging his shop properly. After he leaves, the tricksters spot Sir Epicure Mammon approaching. Jeremy quickly changes into his disguise as Lungs, Subtle's alchemical assistant, to welcome the knight and his friend, Surly.

What Sir Epicure wants, and Jeremy and Subtle have promised to deliver, is the "philosopher's stone," the end result of the alchemical process. The stone is supposed to have great power, offering its owner eternal youth and the ability to transform base metals into gold. Sir Epicure is a believer, but Surly is not, and no amount of alchemical mumbo jumbo changes his mind. Meanwhile, Sir Epicure is led to belive that Doll is a lord's sister driven mad by scholarship.

After getting rid of Sir Epicure and Surly, the tricksters bring in the Puritan Ananias, who wants the philosopher's stone to aid his cause. Ananias refuses to pay any more money without first seeing some results, and Jeremy indignantly throws him out. Drugger then returns and tells Subtle and Jeremy about Dame Pliant, a rich widow, and her brother, Kastril, prompting Subtle and Jeremy's great interest.

After Ananias returns with Tribulation Wholesome, and they are sent off to settle an ethical point, the other clients start parading in too quickly. For a moment, Subtle and Jeremy get rid of all but Dapper, whom they prepare for a visit from the Queen of Fairy. They blindfold him, tie him to a chair, take his money, and begin pinching him as fairies. Interrupted by Sir Epicure knocking at the door, the rascals gag Dapper with gingerbread and lock him in a privy closet.

Jeremy as Lungs introduces Sir Epicure to Doll, then changes into his Captain Face uniform to welcome Kastril and Dame Pliant. Almost immediately Surly arrives, disguised as a Spanish don who speaks no English, which induces Subtle and Jeremy to insult him and openly confess their intentions to fleece him. Surly wants to see Doll, but since she is busy with Sir Epicure, they introduce him to Dame Pliant.

At this point, matters get totally out of control. Sir Epicure blunders by alluding to the philosopher's stone, which makes Doll spout passages from an obscure scholarly work. Jeremy, as Lungs, tries to quiet her, and Subtle, always feigning piety, pretends to be deeply affronted by Sir Epicure's lust. Meanwhile, Surly removes his Spanish disguise, denounces the tricksters, and proposes marriage to Dame Pliant. Jeremy, who as Face had been giving Kastril fighting lessons, tries to get him to challenge Surly, but Kastril will not fight. Ananias and Drugger arrive to add to the rout, and, as if to underscore the insanity, the alchemical project explodes.

The play draws to its complex unwinding with the return of Lovewit, who hears complaints from his neighbors. Jeremy at first tries to cover for the tricksters, but several of their victims return to confirm the neighbors' account of their going and coming. With the help of his chastised butler, Lovewit takes full advantage of the situation. Jeremy drives off Doll and Subtle, claiming their booty for his master. Lovewit then marries Dame Pliant, and when officers come to search his house, he promises that he will return the goods of any victims who certify how they lost them. Since the fools are unwilling to disclose their stupidity, Lovewit keeps everything.

As in *Volpone*, in *The Alchemist* Jonson investigates the relationship between tricksters and their victims. Yet the two plays are very different in tone. *The Alchemist* lacks the decadent atmosphere of the earlier play. The perversion of the opening scene in *Volpone* gives way in *The Alchemist* to the bawdy outfacings of Subtle and Face, and the comic thrust never succumbs so completely to the moral degeneration that marks the darker moments of the former work. Unlike *Volpone*, *The Alchemist* seems to lack an organic, unified, and complete plot. Plot implies development in character or idea, but in *The Alchemist* characters undergo no changes, and the tricksters pay no penalty except the loss of their ill-gotten gains. The play develops as a series of redundant episodes in which the same theme is implicit from start to finish. Unlike Volpone and Mosca, however, the intriguers in *The Alchemist* deceive only fools deserving of their fate, and they therefore pay no harsh penalty.

The foolish victims are not interdependent. They duplicate and mirror each other, but they do not interact. They come together only by accident, not to work in concert, as Voltore, Corbaccio, and Corvino do in the trial scenes in *Volpone*. The only concerted efforts, always unstable, are made by the tricksters—Subtle, Face, and Doll. Characters of tremendous zest, they give the play its great appeal. All three share with Volpone and Mosca one important trait; greedy themselves, they also are comic overreachers who do not know when to quit. Although deft and resourceful, they cannot prevent their scheme from running beyond their control.

The central referent of the play is alchemy and its "grand work." It is a perfect emblem for the play's action, a metaphor for the bulging confidence scheme. By design, the play is tumultuous, with quick costume swapping and breathless sleight-of-hand activity that picks up, goes amiss, and finally undoes the trio of swindlers.

Jonson's dramatic technique, duplication, is carefully patterned in the play. Each of the fools approaches Jeremy and Subtle in the same way. Variety is found only in the nature of their problems. In each case, Jeremy and Subtle promise results, then subject the victim to deliberate neglect before the final cheating. The repeated pattern is a simple but clever dramatic device. To reduce the central import of *The Alchemist* to a blunt attack on human greed is to oversimplify its theme. As in *Volpone*, Jonson is attacking a human depravity that offends against God's creation, and his target is not merely a single vice but any impiety or false idol that perverts nature.

ON MY FIRST SON

First published: 1616
Type of work: Poem

The poet addresses his deceased son in a brief elegy that includes an appropriate epitaph.

In "On My First Son," Jonson addresses his first-born son, also named Benjamin, who died of the plague in 1603. The poem is an epigram, modeled on those of the Roman poet Martial. It starts as a valediction or farewell using a poetic apostrophe, but it quickly becomes apparent that the son's departure is eternal and that the poet is lamenting his death.

Jonson's ideas in the poem reflect the influence of his models. Classical epitaphs often reiterated the idea of life as a sort of borrowing from fate. The poet claims that his son has only been "lent" to him, and with the boy's death, fate has merely exacted payment of the debt "on the just day." Also classical in origin is the implicit notion that excessive good luck could kindle the jealousy of the gods, and that knowing this, a wise man should not be too fond of what he loves.

Despite these classical underpinnings, Jonson's poem does not violate Christian orthodoxy. In attempting to console himself, the grieving father notes that death is an enviable state, free of the ravages of the world and the flesh and an escape from old age. Jonson says that his sin lay in placing too much "hope" in his son, implying that his grief arises from selfish and presumptuous expectations. The poet ends by vowing never to like too much that which he loves.

A compact poem, "On My First Son" consists of only twelve lines in the form of six rhymed couplets. It compresses its thought with great economy of statement and tightly controlled syntax. The poem even threads in a brief epitaph—"here doth lie/ Ben Jonson his best piece of poetry"—which in its simplicity and ironic understatement suggests a profound depth of feeling. Jonson's reserve at this point quickly dissolves into a sincere and poignant reflection that is the thematic center for the whole piece.

TO THE MEMORY OF MY BELOVED MASTER WILLIAM SHAKESPEARE, AND WHAT HE HATH LEFT US

First published: 1623
Type of work: Poem

The poet offers generous praise of William Shakespeare in lines commemorating his genius and his art.

Jonson's eighty-line tribute to Shakespeare, "To the Memory of My Beloved Master William Shakespeare, and What He Hath Left Us," was written to accompany that dramatist's plays in the famous 1623 edition prepared by Shakespeare's friends and fellow actors, John Heminge and Henry Condell. The poem is generous in its praise and argues that, despite whatever private reservations he might have had, Jonson wanted to go on public record as one of Shakespeare's greatest admirers.

The eulogy starts by addressing Shakespeare directly, in an apostrophe, but midway through the poem it shifts to address the English nation. The country, personified as Britain, should "triumph" in Shakespeare, a genius "not of an age, but for all time!" In this middle section, Shakespeare is spoken of in the third person, but Jonson subtly shifts once more to address his deceased friend before the poem's conclusion.

In the first half, Jonson surveys possible motives for his lavish praise and rejects "silliest ignorance," "blind affection," and "crafty malice," with the implication that his motives are pure, based on sound critical judgment. He does make the rather infamous statement that Shakespeare had "small Latin, and less Greek." Out of context, that observation may seem condemnatory, but Jonson's implication is that Shakespeare's genius is of such an order that he exceeds the greatest writers of "insolent Greece" and "haughty Rome" without being beholden to them for his art—a remarkable admission from an avowed classicist.

A central theme of the poem, one repeatedly used in Shakespeare's own sonnets, is that art offers its creator immortality. Shakespeare, claims Jonson, will live as long as "we have wits to read, and praise to give." The idea of art's transcendent capability leads to the finale of the poem, an apotheosis or poetic immortalizing, which, in the elegiac tradition, transfixes the subject in the heavens as a constellation, the "star of poets." That is high public praise from a writer whose natural bias lay against poetic excess. Jonson's great skill gives it and other lavish statements of praise a sincere ring, and the result is one of the finest poetic eulogies in the English language.

Summary

For forty years, Ben Jonson was the preeminent literary force in England. He was the leading comic dramatist of Jacobean England, the most highly esteemed creator of masques, a celebrated poet, a cultivator of new literary talent, and an arbiter of his day's literary taste.

Centuries after Jonson's death, his dramatic and poetic legacy remains significant. Such plays as *The Alchemist* and *Volpone* are still being produced. Moreover, Jonson's more ambitious poems are, along with his lyrics, now viewed as the products of an inspired genius. Among English authors, there are few whose works have weathered the passage of time as successfully as have those of Jonson.

Bibliography

Barish, Jonas A. *Ben Jonson and the Language of Prose Comedy.* Cambridge, Mass.: Harvard University Press, 1960.

Barton, Anne. *Ben Jonson, Dramatist.* New York: Cambridge University Press, 1984.

Bryant, J. A. *The Compassionate Satirist: Ben Jonson and His Imperfect World.* Athens: University of Georgia Press, 1972.

Dessen, Alan C. *Jonson's Moral Comedy.* Evanston, Ill.: Northwestern University Press, 1971.

Enck, John J. *Jonson and the Comic Truth.* Madison: University of Wisconsin Press, 1957.

Knoll, Robert E. *Ben Jonson's Plays: An Introduction.* Lincoln: University of Nebraska Press, 1964.

Leggatt, Alexander. *Ben Jonson, His Vision and His Art.* New York: Methuen, 1981.

McDonald, Russ. *Shakespeare and Jonson, Jonson and Shakespeare.* Lincoln: University of Nebraska Press, 1988.

Sweeney, John Gordon. *Jonson and the Psychology of Public Theater: To Coin the Spirit, Spend the Soul.* Princeton, N.J.: Princeton University Press, 1985.

Trimpi, Wesley. *Ben Jonson's Poems: A Study of the Plain Style.* Stanford, Calif.: Stanford University Press, 1962.

John W. Fiero

JAMES JOYCE

Born: Dublin, Ireland
February 2, 1882
Died: Zurich, Switzerland
January 13, 1941

Principal Literary Achievement

Joyce perfected the short story and the novel of education and then revolutionized fiction, especially the novel, with *Ulysses*.

Biography

James Augustine Joyce was born into a respectable, if improvident, middle-class family in Dublin, Ireland, on February 2, 1882. He was sent to Clongowes Wood College, a Jesuit boarding school, at the age of six; he entered Belvedere College in 1893. In 1898, he entered another Jesuit institution, University College, Dublin. Joyce was an excellent student but his rebellious nature was becoming clear after he published "The Day of the Rabblement," an attack on the new Irish theater, and refused to sign a petition against the heresy in William Butler Yeats's "Countess Cathlee."

Joyce went to Paris in 1902 to study medicine but had to return to Ireland in 1903 when his mother was dying. During this period, he began an autobiographical novel that later became *Stephen Hero* (1944); some early stories that he published were later revised into the collection *Dubliners* (1914). In 1904, Joyce met Nora Barnacle, the woman who was to become his wife. Nora was from Galway and was employed as a chambermaid. She lacked Joyce's education and social background, but he later claimed that she made him a man. She went abroad with him shortly after their meeting and lived with him until his death. In 1905, Joyce left Ireland for good; he went to Trieste and settled there. Over the next few years, he completed the stories that became *Dubliners*. Although it was initially refused publication because of obscene passages in a number of its stories, *Dubliners* was finally published in 1914.

In 1913, Joyce was introduced to the poet Ezra Pound. Pound put Joyce in touch with people who could give him financial support and gave him access to a number of modernist journals. During these years, Joyce had been reshaping his early autobiographical novel into the posthumously published *Stephen Hero*. It was first published in a journal with which Pound was connected, *The Egoist*, in 1914 and in book form in 1916 as *A Portrait of the Artist as a Young Man*. Joyce now had two major works in print and a growing reputation as a modernist writer, yet he would never

achieve popular success. He still had difficulties in supporting himself and his family. Language tutoring brought in little money and his books even less.

Joyce began the most important work of his career, *Ulysses* (1922), in 1914. *Ulysses* was to transform the novel and modern literature with its many innovations. The early writing of the novel was slow, but Joyce began to serialize the early chapters in another Pound-influenced journal, the *Little Review*, in 1918.

In 1915, Joyce and his family moved to Zurich to escape the problems caused by World War I. He still had great difficulty in finding enough money to keep his household going. He was also having the first serious problems with his eyesight, which would lead to his eventual blindness. After the war was over, Joyce moved to Paris at the suggestion of Pound. It was through Pound that Joyce found a benefactor, Harriet Weaver, who helped support him both before and after he had completed *Ulysses*. In 1922, *Ulysses* was published, and it was quickly recognized by discerning critics as a great—indeed, a landmark—book.

The next year, 1923, Joyce began work on *Finnegans Wake* (1939), then known as "Work in Progress." It was to be his most controversial book. Many of Joyce's most ardent supporters were dismayed at this final development in his fiction. Joyce was, however, sure of his own genius and direction and continued with the creation and serial publication of the book.

In the mid-1930's, Joyce was spending more time in Zurich than in Paris. His daughter, Lucia, was having severe mental problems, so he called on some of the noteworthy psychiatrists in Switzerland. In addition, Joyce's eyesight was failing, and he wished to consult a doctor in Zurich about this problem. In 1939, *Finnegans Wake* was finally published, and a few critics did attempt to elucidate the text, but the reception was decidedly less favorable than that of *Ulysses*. Soon after that, France fell to Germany, and Joyce was forced to take up residence in Zurich. He died there on January 13, 1941.

Analysis

Joyce is a master of style, and readers can find a different one for each of his major works. In *Dubliners*, he adopts a narrow and (for Joyce) conventional realistic approach. In addition, each story is told in the style of the protagonist; the narrator does not impose a style. *A Portrait of the Artist as a Young Man* (1914-1915, serial; 1916), however, uses a much richer and more romantic style, since it is told through the consciousness of an emerging artist. Stephen Dedalus meditates on words and finds that he is attracted not by their meaning but by their sound and rhythm. In such scenes as Stephen discovering his vocation upon the beach and his declaration of his artistic purpose, the style is raised to a very lofty plane. When Stephen creates his villanelle, both the poem and the commentary are in the vein of high Romanticism. *Ulysses* is much more varied; there is the intellectual style of Stephen and the plain style of Bloom, but readers find midway into the book that stylistic experimentation dominates the book. There is, for example, a chapter, "Sirens," done in musical prose rhythms and filled with allusions to music. There is the parody style of "Cyclops" and the history of English prose style from Anglo-Saxon to the twentieth century in "Oxen of the Sun." It seems as if plot and character are subordinated to style as the end of the book approaches.

There are a few important themes evident in the major works. One is women's betrayal. Joyce was fascinated by betrayal and returned to it many times. In *A Portrait of the Artist as a Young Man*, for example, he uses the betrayal of Stephen's beloved as a necessary prelude to his flight from Ireland in order to become an artist. Women help him find his vocation and are the subject of his art, but their betrayal is necessary for his freedom. In *Ulysses*, women are once more unfaithful. Molly Bloom betrays her husband and Stephen discusses Anne Shakespeare's betrayal of her husband, William. In addition, Stephen's mother is haunting him and preventing his growth.

Another important theme in Joyce is Dublin (or Ireland in general); it is a place that is described as a net, a trap that imprisons or restrains the characters. Nearly all of them long for some escape but none really succeeds in finding it. Even Stephen Dedalus, Joyce's alter ego, is forced to return to the Dublin he had left behind to become an artist. Others dream about a fuller life, but all such dreams are dashed. If there is a spiritual liberation of the country, it can come only through the artist, who alone has the vision to renew the people.

Joyce is unusual in that he never repeats himself. He works on a genre until he exhausts the possibilities for his art. He undertakes the genre of the short story and perfects the mode. Indeed, much of modern story technique is based on Joyce's "epiphany," a depiction of the essence of the character and the situation, and his objective narration. He then tries the novel of education and perfects the study of a sensitive individual consciousness. The growth of that consciousness from baby talk and mere sound to the villanelle and poetic prose is dazzling. Joyce then turns to a novel based on a Greek myth and re-creates that novel. Now the novel can break the plot or subordinate it to style; it also becomes a truly encyclopedic work containing theology, social commentary, and fantasy, as well as the more usual novelistic interests of plot and character.

DUBLINERS

First published: 1914
Type of work: Short stories

This collection comprises satiric pictures of life in Dublin that expose the paralysis of will of each of the protagonists in the collection.

Dubliners is not a collection of short stories that were written at various periods and with various themes. It is clearly meant to be a unified work of art. Joyce said that he chose Dublin as the setting because it was "the center of paralysis." Yet he also stated that his purpose was to depict "the eventual spiritual liberation of my country." Such a "liberation" could occur only if the Dubliners were to shed the myths about Ireland and face their true situation.

The stories of *Dubliners* are cunningly arranged. The first three stories clearly constitute a unit; they portray the life of a child in Dublin and are filled with disillusionment and a recognition of failure. "Araby" describes a failed quest as a nameless boy promises to go to a bazaar called Araby to buy a gift for a young girl. The boy is a dreamer who ignores daily life to dwell upon his beloved. It is significant that he invests her with religious imagery when he speaks of a "chalice" he is protecting. He also does not see her clearly; she is always a brown shape to him, and he worships his idea of her rather than her true self.

On the day of his planned visit to Araby, his uncle is late, and it seems that the boy will not be able to go. Finally, the uncle enters, drunk, and gives him money. It is late when the boy arrives at the bazaar, and he finds not the magic and mystery of his dreams but a woman flirting with two men at a counter. He hears a voice announce that the light is out—a metaphor for the extinguishing of his quest. The epiphany is very harsh: "Gazing up into the darkness I saw myself as a creature driven and derided by vanity; and my eyes burned with anguish and anger." The boy feels ashamed of his earlier dreams; he, like the other Dubliners, is incomplete. His dreams have been smashed and he is filled with self-loathing.

The next stories deal with young and mature people in Dublin. They suffer from a paralysis of the will as well as a failure to fulfill plans or complete escapes or projects. In "Eveline" the main character has found a beau, Frank, who wishes to take her to Buenos Aires against the opposition of her father. She sits in a dusty room and weighs the claims of both sides. Most of her meditation deals with her father and her home. It is a familiar if grim place; the father is a drunk who makes Eveline give him all the money she earns at her job. She can recall only a few positive images of her father. In contrast, Frank is "very kind, manly, open-hearted." He loves music and will give Eveline an honorable place as his wife. Eveline seems to decide between the two when she thinks of the fate of her mother: "that life of commonplace sacrifices closing in final craziness." In panic, she chooses Frank; he will save her. At the end of the story, however, she cannot answer the call of Frank to join him on the ship. She remains in a state of paralysis between Frank and her home. Her fears of being drowned and her obligations to her family overcome the freedom promised by Frank. She cannot escape Dublin and is described as being "passive, like a helpless animal." "Eveline" is a quintessential *Dubliners* story. The dream of a fuller life is betrayed by fear and paralysis of the will.

The last group of stories deals with institutions: "Ivy Day in the Committee Room" with politics, "A Mother" with the musical world of Dublin, and "Grace" with religion.

The last story in the collection, "The Dead," seems to stand alone as a kind of coda. The story itself is very detailed in its presentation of a middle-class and educated world. The protagonist, Gabriel, is Gabriel Conroy. The reader hears Gabriel's inner thoughts as he meditates on Ireland and his place in it. He is an inner exile in Dublin who takes his vacations on the Continent, writes a review of a British poet, Browning, and has little use for the Irish Literary Revival of language and culture. The structure of the story is the destruction of his aloofness and egotism.

The first of the assaults on Gabriel's egotism is with the servant Lily. Gabriel makes social conversation with Lily primarily, it seems, to enhance his own image. He pretends to be genuinely interested in Lily and manages to offend her. " 'O, then,' said Gabriel gaily, 'I suppose we'll be going to your wedding one of these fine days with your young man, eh?' " Lily is angered and complains of men who fail to meet their commitments. Gabriel is embarrassed at this outburst and later feels that he has used the wrong tone with her.

The next assault on Gabriel is made by Miss Ivors. Miss Ivors is a nationalist and criticizes Gabriel for writing his review in a pro-British journal. She also criticizes him for going to the Continent to learn foreign languages when he has his own language to learn. "O, to tell you the truth," Gabriel suddenly responds, "I'm sick of my own country, sick of it!" Gabriel is especially upset because Miss Ivors has criticized him in front of other people.

The last confrontation is the most important and is with his wife, Gretta. After the party is over, Gabriel has romantic feelings about his wife. She, however, seems to be distant and tired. He draws her to him, but she resists his advances. Finally, she reveals that she was thinking not of Gabriel but of a young man she knew in Galway. Gabriel tries to belittle this relationship but does not succeed. Instead, he suddenly begins to realize who he is and what his relationship with his wife has been. He now sees himself as a "ludicrous figure" who has idealized his "clownish lusts." When Gretta reveals that the young man, Michael Furey, died for her, Gabriel's egotism and his world are destroyed. He feels that some "impalpable and vindictive being was coming against him." Gabriel then passes through stages to reach his final state. He becomes a prophet who announces the death of his aunt, Julia Morkan. He begins to shed "generous tears" as he thinks of the death of Michael Furey. Furey had died for love, and although Gabriel has never felt love before, "he knew that such a feeling must be love."

The last movement of the story is very difficult to interpret. Gabriel recognizes that it is time "to set out on his journey westward." That journey can be interpreted as either toward life or toward death. A journey to the west is traditionally associated with death, but all of the positive characters—Gretta, Furey—come from the west. In addition, Gabriel feels his own identity and all of Ireland "fading out into a grey impalpable world." The last sentence speaks of the snow falling "like the descent of their last end, upon all the living and the dead." The ending of the story is seen in positive terms by some critics as a figurative rebirth for Gabriel. Others see it as the destruction of Gabriel and the world of Dublin, literally a last judgment. Still others see it as ambiguous, making it impossible for the reader to decide whether the ending is positive or negative. Yet another interpretation is that Gabriel is a prophet who points the way to the eventual "spiritual liberation" of Dublin through the love that he, Gabriel, recognizes but cannot feel. Thus, the ending signifies a cleansing of society in order to rebuild it on new principles.

A PORTRAIT OF THE ARTIST AS A YOUNG MAN

First published: 1914-1915 (serial), 1916
Type of work: Novel

This novel examines the growth, development, and emergence of the artist in detail.

A Portrait of the Artist as a Young Man is a *Bildungsroman*, a novel of education; in this case, it is the growth of the artist from his earliest childhood to his declaration of his proper role as an artist, a "priest of the eternal imagination." The novel begins with the earliest experience of the protagonist, Stephen Dedalus. His world is a world of sensations, especially of touch and smell. Later those sensations will be connected to words, and by the end of the book he recognizes that words have an independent existence. He also recognizes the demands that he submit, to "apologize," as his father and Aunt Dante demand. Throughout the novel, Stephen is continually evading most of the demands that are placed on him. An artist must be free.

The next section takes place at a Jesuit boarding school, Clongowes; the concluding incident in the chapter also takes place there. Stephen had lost his glasses and was, therefore, unable to do his lesson. Father Dolan, however, refuses to accept his explanation. Stephen goes to the rector, Father Conmee, to seek redress. Conmee at first suggests that Father Dolan did not know of the lost glasses, but Stephen insists that he did know. Finally, Conmee reluctantly agrees to order Dolan not to punish Stephen the next day. The chapter ends with Stephen declared a hero by his classmates; he now feels "happy and free." Each chapter of the book ends in some kind of triumph for Stephen. The beginning of the following chapters, however, shows a decline.

The second chapter continues the development of Stephen as he experiences a change in his situation. His father's finances decline and he leaves Clongowes and becomes a day student at another Jesuit school, Belvedere. He also begins to be interested in women. He is involved with the young Ellen and dreams about the fictional Mercedes, who will initiate and transform him. He imagines an encounter with Mercedes when "weakness and timidity and inexperience would fall from him." Stephen's initiation, however, is more sordid. He feels lust rather than love and wishes to fall into sin with a real woman and not an idealized figure from fiction. He goes to the red-light district of Dublin to seek that encounter. The chapter ends with Stephen and a prostitute. She embraces him, and he feels "joy and relief." He will not, however, kiss her; he wishes to retain his aloof independence but finally surrenders and submits. It is, however, a necessary fall; Joyce's artist must fall in order to create "life out of life."

The beginning of the chapter is a decided decline. Stephen does not feel transformed but degraded by his sexual encounter. He feels like a beast instead of a man. Then a retreat is announced at school; Stephen is to hear powerful sermons by a Jesuit. He is immediately affected; he feels that the words are aimed directly at him. He also thinks of a way out; the Virgin will take his hand and that of an innocent young girl, Emma, and lead him to forgiveness and an innocent love. It will not, however, be that easy for Stephen; he is forced to confront his sin and his fate by the Jesuit preacher. The preacher speaks of hell and its terrible punishments. He cites the condemnation of Lucifer, who, like Stephen, will not serve or submit. His description of hell sounds remarkably like Clongowes. The smells and companions of the preacher's hell are exactly like Stephen's memories of his first school. The effect on Stephen is immediate. He calls for help that evening in his bedroom and vomits in disgust at what he has done. He believes that he has lost his innocence and turned himself into a beast. He confesses his sin and once more submits, although this time it is to the Church rather than a prostitute. The last scene of the chapter parallels the earlier one; he takes the host as he had taken the kiss. Yet the Church is not to be Stephen's final choice; it is only a stage in his development.

There is a marked change in the beginning of the next chapter. Stephen has become religious, but his life afterward tends to be dry and mechanical. He imagines himself as a spiritual accountant adding up his devotions. He is then approached by the rector to see if he aspires to the priesthood, particularly for the Jesuit order. At first, he is attracted to the image of himself as a Jesuit, but he quickly dismisses it when he imagines himself back in the cold and smells of Clongowes. In addition, he discovers that his place is "wandering among the snares of the world."

The novel then brings Stephen back to the disorder of his home. He begins to recall a beautiful phrase he has memorized and realizes that it is not the meaning or the "colors" of the words that please him but their sound pattern or rhythm. Stephen as a developing artist has developed his relationship with words from the identification of sound and meaning to a love of syntactic patterns for their own sake.

At the end of the chapter, Stephen comes upon a young girl on the beach. She is described as "a strange and beautiful seabird." His response is one of "profane joy." Her image passes into him, and he announces his vocation. "To life, to err, to fall, to triumph, to recreate life out of life!" It is the most important of the many triumphant chapter endings. Stephen realizes that his place is in the fallen world rather than that of the priesthood. He now knows what his vocation is but has not yet actually created a work of art to certify his role as an artist. At this point, he is a potential artist, and a very young one.

The first part of chapter 6 is devoted to Stephen's discussion of the aesthetic he has developed; it is a prelude to the actual creation of a poem in the second part of the chapter. Stephen's aesthetic is rather sophisticated and can be related to many of Joyce's own works. He speaks of the stages of an artist's work: from lyric to epic to dramatic. The artist begins, as Stephen does, with self-expression and continues to "refine himself out of existence." The aim is an impersonal art that Joyce develops in *Ulysses*. He also spells out the three elements needed in a work of art: "wholeness, harmony, and radiance."

The poem that Stephen writes is a villanelle, a highly artificial form; many critics have condemned it and see Stephen as the type of artist that Joyce would reject. They see a considerable amount of distance between Joyce and his protagonist. Others, however, see Stephen as a young but genuine artist.

The last section of the chapter is filled with images of flight as Stephen prepares to leave Ireland and its "nets" of patriotism and church. The true artist needs to be independent, which is impossible for Stephen in Ireland. One other ironic note is found at the close of the chapter. Stephen sees his beloved, to whom he had just written a poem, being caressed by his friend, Davin. Joyce, obsessed with the betrayal of friends and lovers, wrote about it in nearly every one of his major works.

The last part of the book is a series of journal entries by Stephen. The narrator has disappeared. The entries speak of Stephen's beloved, the images of the road and his departure, and the type of art Stephen is to pursue. The last two entries speak of Stephen's exalted role as an artist: "I go to encounter for the millionth time the reality of experience and to forge in the smith of my soul the uncreated conscience of my race." The aim is not merely to create individual works but to bring about a "spiritual liberation."

ULYSSES

First published: 1922
Type of work: Novel

The novel re-creates the *Odyssey* in one day in the life of Dublin as the protagonists meet and complete an imperfect quest.

Ulysses is based on Homer's *Odyssey* (c. 800 B.C.) but compresses the action of the earlier epic into one day. The basic narrative of the *Odyssey* is maintained: Leopold Bloom, the modern counterpart to Ulysses, returns home to his wife and son and then overcomes the suitors and reclaims his place. Stephen Dedalus, the counterpart to Telemachus, needs to grow into a man and be united with his absent father.

The first section of the book, the "Telemachiad," deals with Stephen. Stephen has returned to Ireland from Paris to face the death of his mother and is haunted by the ghost of his mother and oppressed by the demands of his real father. He needs to purge his mother's ghost and find a new father. Stephen is oppressed, as is Telemachus, by the usurpers in the tower where he lives. Stephen's thoughts are abstruse, philosophical, and filled with guilt; he no longer seems to be a potential artist. He wanders around Dublin in search of some relief. One noteworthy episode takes place in the National Library, where Stephen expounds his theory of William Shakespeare's *Hamlet* (1600-1601), which is really a theory that is directly related to Joyce's own life and work. Stephen also goes to visit a newspaper and tells two of the editors his short story, "A Pisgah Prophecy," which is similar to early stories in *Dubliners*. The proposing of a theory and creation of a literary work by Stephen is also found in *A Portrait of the Artist as a Young Man*. Perhaps Stephen is beginning to fulfill his claim to be a true artist.

Leopold Bloom is an ordinary man with an extraordinary curiosity about everything around him. He, like Stephen, has problems within his family. His wife, Molly, is unfaithful to him and today has received a note from the notorious Blazes Boylan telling her that he will visit her. In addition, Bloom's son, Rudy, died fourteen years before, rendering Bloom impotent. If Stephen needs a father, Bloom needs a son. They will travel through Dublin and occasionally cross paths before their meeting and tenuous union in the last part of the book.

Bloom is a fairly complaisant husband; he never confronts Molly about Boylan and has his own deceits as a compensation. He has received a letter from Martha Clifford, with whom he is conducting an extended flirtation. On his travels, he observes and interacts with the Dubliners. The anti-Semitism and hostility against the Jewish Bloom is seen a number of times. The most important conflict he has about his Jewishness is depicted in the "Cyclops" episode, in which he defends himself forcefully against racial attacks.

The union between Bloom and Stephen begins in the "Circe" chapter. Bloom is humiliated and exalted in the chapter; he is abused by women for his weakness and oddities, while Stephen is drunk and is about to squander or lose his money. Bloom has followed him from a maternity hospital and acts like a father in saving Stephen's money and defending him against charges by the police. He is going to bring him home, where Stephen will teach Molly Italian pronunciation and have a place to stay. Stephen, who seems to have purged his mother's ghost by swinging his walking stick at it in "Circe," is obviously meant to replace the dead Rudy and restore Bloom's virility, but he seems unconvinced by Bloom's offer. There is a wonderful scene between Bloom and Stephen in the next chapter, "Ithaca," where they urinate together and share a cup of cocoa. Some union of father and son does take place. Stephen, however, declines Bloom's offer. He has changed since the beginning of the novel, but not completely. Bloom has also changed, but not completely. He still has his problem with impotence and Molly's adulteries. The book provides only provisional solutions for the complex problems of the two characters.

The last chapter, "Penelope," is the famous monologue of Molly Bloom. Molly does speak of some of the changes in the book. Bloom has now ordered her to make him bacon and eggs in the morning. She speaks of the sexual encounter with Boylan but asserts that Bloom had more "spunk" in him. Above all, she recalls the first sexual experience with Bloom on Howth, where she gave her "Yes." For all its incompleteness, the book ends with the affirmation by Molly and significant changes in the main characters.

Summary

James Joyce is a preeminent modernist writer and a great innovator. He altered forever the way the world thinks of fiction. He added a subtlety to the well-plotted short story, provided a richness of detail and an intensity to the central consciousness of the novel of education, and turned the novel into an epic, a form capable of including diverse materials and styles. He did nothing less than transform modern literature.

Bibliography

Ellmann, Richard. *James Joyce*. New York: Oxford University Press, 1965.

Hayman, David. *Ulysses: The Mechanics of Meaning*. Englewood Cliffs, N.J.: Prentice-Hall, 1970.

Kenner, Hugh. *Dublin's Joyce*. Bloomington: Indiana University Press, 1956.

Morse, J. Mitchell. *The Sympathetic Alien*. New York: New York University Press, 1959.

Tindall, William York. *James Joyce: His Way of Interpreting the Modern World*. New York: Charles Scribner's Sons, 1950.

James Sullivan

FRANZ KAFKA

Born: Prague, Czechoslovakia
July 3, 1883
Died: Kierling, near Vienna, Austria
June 3, 1924

Principal Literary Achievement

Notable for their spare, unadorned prose style, Kafka's short stories and three novels lead deep into the subconscious and expose the fears from which all people suffer to some extent.

Biography

Franz Kafka was born on July 3, 1883, in Prague, Czechoslovakia, the first child born to Hermann and Julie Kafka. A second son died in infancy, leaving Franz as the only son, with three younger sisters. Franz reacted negatively to his paternal forebears. His grandfather had been a butcher, something that Franz found so repugnant that he became a vegetarian. His works contain descriptions of meat and wounds that reflect this revulsion. His father was in business and owned his own shop, but Franz was permanently bothered by his gruff and insulting treatment of his employees. This recollection is perhaps reflected in "Die Verwandlung" (1915; "The Metamorphosis," 1936), in Gregor Samsa's description of the hostile and suspicious chief clerk. Kafka's mother was unable to give him the attention that he would have liked, since she also worked in the store, but Franz felt more affinity with her side of the family, particularly with his bachelor uncles, one of whom, Siegfried Löwy, was a country doctor.

Despite his childhood fears of failure, Franz progressed effortlessly through school and went on to earn his doctorate in law at the German University in Prague. After a brief placement with one firm, which he left because of the abusive language in the office, Kafka found his permanent employment with the Workers' Accident Insurance Institute, where his function was deemed so essential that he could not be drafted for active service in World War I.

The war years were among the most tumultuous and productive in Kafka's life. In Europe, there was a pervasive atmosphere of decadence and disillusionment. Five hundred years of Habsburg rule were drawing to a close, and the war would culminate in the collapse of the Austro-Hungarian Empire.

During these years, Kafka spent much time agonizing over his relationship to Fe-

lice Bauer, whom he had met in August of 1912 and to whom he had proposed in June of 1913. It was mainly an epistolary association. Felice did not live in Prague, and she and Kafka often had disagreements when they met. Reflecting the prejudices of his background, Kafka regarded marriage and a family of one's own as de rigueur in one sense, but he was also increasingly aware of his calling as a writer, and he did not see how he could find the time to combine the two. In July of 1914, he and Felice broke off their engagement, but the letters continued, and in July of 1916 they became informally engaged again. This second engagement was made official in July of 1917 and broken off again in December of the same year. It was during his preoccupation with Felice that Kafka wrote, among other things, "The Metamorphosis," *Der Prozess* (1925; *The Trial*, 1939), and *Ein Landarzt* (1919; *A Country Doctor*, 1940).

Kafka's stated reason for breaking off the second engagement was that he had been diagnosed with tuberculosis. He had suffered a severe hemorrhage, leading the cleaning lady to comment that he was not long for this world. In fact, he lived another seven years, and aside from taking several leaves of absence and then early retirement from his firm, he did not slow his pace at all.

He met other women. In 1919, he became engaged to Julie Wohryzek, who also had tuberculosis, but broke off this engagement when they did not get the lease for the apartment that they had wanted. In 1920, he had an affair with Milena Jesenká-Polak, who was translating his stories into Czech. She was intellectually and artistically compatible with him, but she broke off the relationship, saying she could not leave her husband despite his harsh treatment of her. In July of 1922, Kafka went to stay with his youngest and closest sister, Ottla, at her home in the country. It was there that he wrote the first nine chapters of *Das Schloss* (1926; *The Castle*, 1930) in a matter of a few weeks. Only in the last year of his life, in September of 1923, did Kafka finally overcome his considerable inhibitions and move in with a woman in Berlin. He was forty; Dora Dymant was nineteen.

Kafka bequeathed his literary estate to his friend and fellow-writer Max Brod, instructing him to continue the work Dora had begun of burning the manuscripts. Brod instead ensured that all of Kafka's remaining works, diaries, and letters were published. Kafka died on June 3, 1924, at the sanatorium in Kierling, near Vienna, Austria.

Analysis

Kafka is probably the only author who has treated such profound subject matter without couching it in poetic language. His unadorned style, consistently simple syntax, and workmanlike prose present the subject matter in such a lucid and accessible manner that the works speak persuasively to the inner psyche. They remain disturbing and enlightening excursions into the nature of the self that are valid for all time.

The human psyche is Kafka's main topic, not political or social commentary, and not specifically autobiography, although clearly his was the mind he knew best. While it is helpful for the reader to have some knowledge of his biography, of Prague, of the time in which Kafka lived, and of concurrent intellectual developments, it is not essential. The works transcend Kafka's immediate situation. They have been translated into numerous languages and are effortlessly understood as masterpieces by every culture in which they are read.

If one wishes to place Kafka's works in intellectual history, the two concurrent developments that show the closest similarities with his style are psychoanalysis and science fiction. Psychoanalysis, pioneered by Sigmund Freud and Carl Gustav Jung, emphasized the importance of dreams, which spring from the subconscious, for revealing the deeper reality of life. Many of Kafka's works have a dreamlike quality and, according to him, seemed to write themselves. The magnificent short story "Das Urteil" (1913, 1916; "The Sentence," 1928; better known as "The Judgment," 1945), for example, was written in one sitting during an evening in September, 1912. Although very pleased with the work, Kafka did not know what it meant. He did not consciously attempt to create symbolic works, and that is precisely why they are so rewarding to experience. Kafka intuitively knew what was right, but he left it to others to decipher his work.

Science fiction, in a more deliberate manner, imports the same departure from linear reality that characterizes dreams. Time and space may be infinitely contracted or expanded, and it is not unusual for mythical beasts to appear. A founder of science fiction, the man who invented the word "robot," was Karel Čapek, also a Czech. H. G. Wells was writing in Britain at the same time. Kafka's works do invoke the structure of fantasy. In "A Country Doctor," for example, unearthly horses transport the doctor a distance of ten miles in an instant, but the return journey is interminable. Such effects, though, are subsidiary to Kafka's main topic. Although on the verge of speculative fiction, he is not writing about the supernatural per se but about the human psyche, the utterly natural.

Kafka was also unavoidably influenced by the *spiritus mundi*, the *Zeitgeist*, or spirit of his time, but not in such a way as to date his works. As a Jew in a city where there were race riots, as the subject of a dynasty in decline, Kafka captured the prevailing feeling of uncertainty and helplessness, and he observed without judgment. No doubt his extensive legal training was also operative in forming his technique of impartially describing conflicting viewpoints. Even in Kafka's cathartic *Brief an den Vater* (1953; *Letter to His Father*, 1953)—which he delivered to his mother—he was able to understand in all fairness how his behavior must have seemed from his father's point of view. Thus, the characters in his works are seldom portrayed bluntly as either good or bad, right or wrong. They are three-dimensional and as complex as any human being. Even the antagonists may turn out to be right. Kafka's stories are not written with the interpretive wisdom of hindsight but with the urgency and uncertainty of current experience.

The omission of a clear verdict on any specific character or situation also enables Kafka's works to be understood on more than one level. Frequently, his apparent catastrophes are not catastrophes at all but liberating measures necessary for transcendence. It is always the hardworking white-collar professional who meets his demise: the businessman Georg Bendemann in "The Judgment," the banker Josef K. in *The Trial*, and the doctor in "A Country Doctor." Taken purely as story, these appear to be tragic fates. The men fall victim to forces beyond their control and either self-destruct, or allow themselves to be destroyed, or cannot prevent themselves from being destroyed. Their common type, however, indicates that they may, on another level, be representative of someone who needed to be removed, of Kafka the lawyer, who repeatedly took precious time away from Kafka the writer, who was in ascendance. As in the later Greek dramas, the tragedy of the flesh can be read as the beginning of the ascendance of the spirit, or, perhaps more appropriately to Kafka, the self. The spirit of the artist rises phoenixlike from the absurd and often contrived demise of the businessperson. Kafka often expressed the wish to dedicate himself to his writing, and it seems he portrayed its fulfillment in some of his works.

To understand the rich, multiplex statements about the reality of the self in Kafka, it is frequently necessary to see several characters as different aspects of the main protagonist. A modified psychoanalytical approach may prove useful in this context. In "The Judgment," for example, one can see a weak ego (the friend in Russia) torn between the desires of the id (Georg Bendemann) and the dictates of the superego (the father figure). Eventually, the id is suppressed (drowned), the superego may relax (collapse), and, by implication, the ego will flourish (be able to write).

All this sounds oppressively grim, and indeed, on first reading, many of Kafka's works do seem horrible and depressing. The fatalism of most of his characters, though, which Kafka only began to counter in 1922 with *The Castle*, is always offset in tone by careful choreography, by a splendid sense of humor that appreciates the ridiculous in all that humanity does. When reading his stories aloud, Kafka and his listeners were frequently overcome with laughter. It is his ethereal laughter that melts "the frost of this most unhappy of ages" ("The Country Doctor"), ensuring not only endless fascination with Kafka but also his relevance for all time.

THE TRIAL

First published: *Der Prozess*, 1925 (English translation, 1937)
Type of work: Novel

Arrested on his thirtieth birthday, Josef K. battles with an unusual court for a year before allowing himself to be executed without a proper trial.

The Trial was begun in July of 1914, when Kafka turned thirty-one. He had just broken off his first engagement to Felice Bauer. He had also been unable to write any literature for more than a year, and he was feeling simultaneously frustrated by this writer's block and guilty for having been unfair to either Felice or himself (depending on how one looked at it). Out of this inner turmoil arose *The Trial*, which was completed within six months.

Like all Kafka's writing, *The Trial* achieves a fine balance between the real and the imagistic, containing enough references to everyday life that the reader is initially tempted to confront the content of the surface story with logical argumentation. Were this a standard crime story, one would say that K., who was a banker by profession, misses three excellent opportunities to save himself. At the beginning of the novel, when arrested without being told why, K. neglects to contact his friend the public prosecutor. In the middle of the novel, when it would help to get away for a while, K. turns down his uncle's invitation to stay with him in the country. At the end of the novel, K. avoids the policeman, who clearly wants to intervene.

The premise of fantasy, though, is that it details inner reality. Kafka was involved in coming to terms with himself, and he presents the reader with strong evidence that K. and the court are one and the same. Names are always significant in Kafka's works, and one of the two warders who arrests Josef K. on his thirtieth birthday is called Franz—that is, the reader is to understand, Franz Kafka. Josef K. subsequently complains to the Examining Magistrate about the man's behavior and is surprised, on leaving the bank an evening or two later, to hear moaning coming from behind a door he has never opened. To K.'s astonishment, there are the two warders about to be flogged by a third man with a birch, and K. watches as Franz is flogged senseless. On his way home the next day, K. opens the door of the room again: "What he saw, instead of the darkness he had been expecting, destroyed his self-possession completely. Everything was exactly the same, just as he had found it the evening before when he opened the door. The old files and ink-bottles just inside the door, the Flogger with his birch, the warders still completely undressed." Clearly, it is all in K.'s mind, for he must be present for the scene to continue.

What is happening to K., then, is an inner sorting of priorities. What is on "trial" is Kafka's own lack of existential authenticity. At the time that he wrote *The Trial*, Kafka had already realized that Felice would have been more of a hindrance in his life than a help. Her counterpart in the novel is Fräulein Bürstner (same initials), who does not wish to get involved with K. The other aspect of Kafka's life that necessarily continued to interfere with his writing was his professional work as a lawyer with the Workers' Accident Insurance Institute. This situation is analogous to K.'s workaday existence in the bank. Kafka the writer must have derived great satisfaction from placing on trial and sentencing to death that aspect of his life that was guilty of wasting his time, but that he nevertheless needed.

Der Prozess is translated into English as "the trial" or "the process." In fact, no trial takes place in the novel, so the reader might do well to consider the other meaning of the title. Hegelian and post-Hegelian German philosophy, with which Kafka was familiar, made use of the Greek terms "process" and "praxis" to describe contrasting modes of existence. Process imports the notion of an implacable system wherein one is acted upon by forces one does not understand and cannot alter. Surely this is the case of Josef K. in *The Trial*. "Praxis," the opposite of "process," is an act of taking control of one's own destiny, and that is what the more mature protagonist of the same name, K., undertakes to do in Kafka's later novel *The Castle*.

THE CASTLE

First published: *Das Schloss*, 1926 (English translation, 1930)
Type of work: Novel

K. is summoned by the Castle to work as a land surveyor, but, on arrival, he is unable to determine why he was called.

The Castle is unfinished. It breaks off after the twentieth chapter, with alternative versions in the manuscript indicating that the plot could have continued in two different directions. Critics have tended to be led by Max Brod's report of how Kafka once told him the novel was to end: The Land-Surveyor was to find only partial satisfaction and die exhausted by his struggle. If this is taken as a foregone conclusion, the interpretation is necessarily partial to the dark and depressing aspects of the novel. From an impartial reading of the story, though, it seems equally possible that K., the outsider, could usher in the triumph of reason over the hopelessly entangled and inefficient bureaucracy of the Castle.

The first reading, which ends with K.'s defeat, is consistent with many of Kafka's earlier works and seems to echo the short parable "Vor dem Gesetz" (1915; "Before the Law," 1930) included in *The Trial*, in which the man from the country exhausts all of his resources and eventually dies in the futile attempt to gain admittance to the Law. An essential difference between the characters in the earlier works and the protagonist in the last novel, though, is that K. neither reveres nor is intimidated by the Castle and its agents, and he has a refreshing tendency to speak his mind. Kafka wrote *The Castle* during the last two years of his life, during which he overcame many inhibitions. It is this new spirit and confidence that seems to speak through K. in the second reading, which emphasizes his chances of success.

It is difficult for the objective reader to take the Castle seriously. Desirable apparently only because it is inaccessible to the common individual, it is a disappointment from the start, to K.'s eyes not a castle at all but "only a wretched-looking town, a huddle of village houses, whose sole merit, if any, lay in being built of stone; but the plaster had long since flaked off and the stone seemed to be crumbling away." Furthermore, there is little evidence of the Castle's having actually done anything for the people in the village. Its "gentlemen" are unprincipled and adept only at keeping the best for themselves. First the Mayor's house, then the Herrenhof are shown to be awash in paperwork, with files hopelessly outdated and no order to the system.

How, then, does the crumbling Castle manage to retain its control over the villagers, indeed command their respect, devotion, and services? First, it maintains a cloak of secrecy around its activities, if any, and tolerates no outsiders. It is a closed system whose preeminence goes unchallenged. Second, it terrorizes those who refuse to be exploited, as evidenced by Amalia's case. Third, it moves quickly to try to bring any active newcomers alongside. K. is told that no surveying will be necessary and is presented with two ridiculous assistants whose purpose is to keep him distracted. Then he is sent a letter congratulating him on the fine land surveying he and his assistants are doing, thereby tempting him to do nothing but maintain appearances, like the rest of the Castle's employees.

From the start, though, K. does not seem like the sort to surrender. In the second chapter, in a significant flashback to his childhood, K. remembers how he was one of the few boys who managed to climb the high wall around the graveyard. "The sense of that triumph had seemed to him then a victory for life." This scene establishes his personality.

In the village, K. refuses to be browbeaten and manipulated, and he persists in trying to force an interview with Klamm to get to the root of why he was summoned. In the thirteenth chapter, one of the students approaches and offers help, believing that K. in the distant future will "excel everybody." Finally, in the eighteenth chapter, K. barges in on Bürgel, one of the "gentlemen" secretaries in the Herrenhof, only to fall asleep to the drone of Bürgel's voice. Critics who subscribe to a defeatist reading of *The Castle* interpret K.'s falling asleep as a great opportunity lost, for K. could conceivably have gained access to the Castle through Bürgel, whose name is the diminutive of the German word *Burg*, or castle. By this point in the novel, though, the Castle and its representatives have been exposed as so corrupt that K.'s overwhelming desire to sleep can be seen as a natural defense mechanism. K. dreams that he has already achieved a great victory by fighting against and banishing a naked secretary built like a Greek god, and this dream seems to be prophetic. There is every indication that K. will overcome the Castle.

The main interpretive question is what the Castle represents. Surely it embodies the reality of all persons and institutions girded in cloaks of illusory authority, from the Church to the village teacher, and lampoons the tricks and devices of those whose interests are served by the perpetuation of grand fraud. Kafka was concerned with eternal verities, which was what made him a great writer. The K. in this work has identified the mysterious "Law" and its authority structures by which the K. of *The Trial* was oppressed, and he finds that it is a sham and a chimera. He laughs at it.

THE METAMORPHOSIS

First published: "Die Verwandlung," 1915 (English translation, 1936)
Type of work: Short story

Commercial salesman Gregor Samsa awakens one morning to find himself turned into a large bug, which forces his dependent family to become self-sufficient.

"The Metamorphosis" is Kafka's longest story and one of his most frequently analyzed works. Tripartite in form, it traces the months from Gregor Samsa's unique metamorphosis to his death from dehydration, injury, and general neglect. Gregor's health declines as the health of his father, mother, and sister improves. His metamorphosis from the sole breadwinner to an utterly dependent and undesirable creature prompts the metamorphosis of his sluggish family into hardworking, happier people.

The point is often made that, although it is Gregor who takes on a grotesque form, the real ugliness in the story lies in his family's attitude toward and treatment of him, in their assumption that he is responsible for the debt incurred by his father. As the parents and sister selfishly exploit the best years of Gregor's youth, any possibility he might have of marrying and establishing a family of his own is reduced to his making a fretwork frame for a magazine picture of a woman. They have used him up.

Likewise, his employer shows no appreciation for Gregor's humanity and seems bent only on getting the maximum return from his employee. After five years without missing a day, Gregor needs only to miss one train to have the chief clerk threaten him with dismissal. They, too, use him up.

The integrity of Gregor's self is under attack from all sides. Not even his bedroom is a safe retreat. It has doors in all three inside walls, enabling his mother, his father, and his sister to question him simultaneously. No wonder, then, that Gregor revolts. He takes on a form that makes his further exploitation impossible.

Kafka explicitly forbade any artistic illustration of the bug for the book cover. That would have given too mundane a form to a transformation that signifies a revolt of the subconscious, a breakthrough after a long period of self-denial. Gregor entertains the idea that the same may happen to the chief clerk himself some day.

Significantly, the title of the story is not "The Bug" but "The Metamorphosis." The emphasis is on the change itself, on exploring who one really is and what one really likes to do, on being guided by one's own urges, with no worry concerning where they will lead. Gregor discovers that he feels most comfortable squeezed under the sofa or hanging upside down from the ceiling. His voice changes, so that his speech is unintelligible to humans. He is ravenously hungry, but not for human food. He is moved as never before by his sister's violin playing. "Was he an animal, that music had such an effect upon him? He felt as if the way were opening before him to the unknown nourishment he craved." Gregor's new sensitivity to music and the new sound of his words are clear indications that the story may be read as the self-discovery of the artist.

Kafka does not downplay the risk inherent in eccentric self-expression. Part 1 of the story ends with Gregor's sustaining an injury along his side as his mulish father forces him back into his room. Part 2 ends with Gregor sustaining a more serious, perhaps fatal wound, as his father pelts him with apples. Part 3 ends with Gregor dead, covered with refuse and dust, and disposed of by the cleaning lady. The danger, clearly, of voluntary or involuntary nonconformity is that one may be misunderstood, mistreated, or entirely rejected. Before his metamorphosis, though, Gregor was no better off than after it. While the manifestation of his uniqueness was considered by some to be grotesque, it was an advance over his former routine.

A COUNTRY DOCTOR

First published: *Ein Landarzt*, 1919 (English translation, 1940)
Type of work: Short stories

These fifteen stories reflect on the human condition, on the uncertain spirit of the time during World War I, and on the nature of the artist.

A Country Doctor is a collection of stories written between 1914 and 1917. The order of the stories was determined by Kafka, who decided to withdraw the fifteenth story, "Der Kübelreiter" ("The Bucket Rider"), before publication.

The questions addressed in the stories are existential. Human society is so far removed from the natural state that it at times seems to have become lost in its own rules and bureaucracy. Old institutions no longer command respect and take up too much precious time. Behind these general observations, which were certainly true in the declining days of the Habsburg monarchy, there is in Kafka's works always the autobiographical element, the realization that his writing was the most important thing in his life, and the resentment of his professional obligations as a lawyer and of his fiancée Felice as diversions from his main objective.

Kafka's story sequence establishes a framework whereby the collection opens with a story of a horse in a law firm and ends with one in which an ape delivers "Ein Bericht für eine Akademie" ("A Report to an Academy"). This framework operates to strip away any veneer of respect one may still entertain for these institutions, and, in a masterful kind of "reverse anthropomorphism," it compares humans unfavorably with animals. What is done to animals is not to their benefit. The female chimpanzee has "the insane look of the half-broken animal in her eye." By extension, Kafka seems to be questioning the benefit of what humankind is doing to itself, of the jobs that keep people occupied through the best years of their lives, causing them to conform to hierarchical constructs that deny and suppress their inner selves.

Yet the thought of usurping civilization's rigorous and often dehumanizing controls and structures gives rise to the fear of a relapse into barbarianism. "Ein altes Blatt" ("An Old Manuscript") describes what happened when the nomads assumed power. "Schakale und Araber" ("Jackals and Arabs") cleverly portrays the logical fallacies inherent in the plans for most uprisings, and it identifies the real problem as the nature of the beast rather than the situation.

Some of the stories portray characters overcome by inertia, while others deal with the inability to overcome mortality. Offsetting these, however, are the two death stories that seem, ironically, infused with energy and a sense of purpose. In "Ein Brudermord" ("A Fratricide"), the man who is killed is the one who is a conscientious office worker. Is Kafka wishfully clearing his time-consuming professional life out of the way? In as immediate a style, "Ein Traum" ("A Dream") portrays the burial alive of Josef K., who is also the protagonist in Kafka's novel *The Trial*. While Josef is alive, the artist engraving the tomb has difficulty writing, but as soon as Josef is wafted down into a great hole, his own name races across the tombstone "in great flourishes." An autobiographical reading of these stories is that Kafka's involvement in his own life lacks authenticity for him and that aspects of his self need to be excised. The indication of where he belongs is given in the brilliant short piece "The Bucket Rider." In it, a freezing man comes to the realization that there is no help for him in this world, and he ascends by supernatural means into the "regions of the ice mountains." This image is a metaphysical removal from the world.

Kafka withdrew "The Bucket Rider" from the collection, perhaps because its message was more elaborately stated in the title story, "A Country Doctor." In this story, the most beautiful and most fantastic of all, Kafka symbolically discards both the profession and the fiancée. The doctor loses his practice and his maid. Instead, he is transported by supernatural means to the bedside of a sick boy, who has a blossom in his side, an unsightly wound that he brought into the world as his only dowry and of which he will die. That is the gift of the artist, which is of consuming magnificence, transporting its owner into the world of the spirit.

Summary

Franz Kafka is uncontestedly one of the strongest, most original literary voices of the twentieth century. His unpretentious prose, while seemingly rooted in the everyday, penetrates deeply into the reality of the human psyche. All rings true on the psychological level, bizarre though the scenes and circumstances of the narrative may be. Moral precepts shimmer in the distorting light of multiple interpretations, for the works are absolute and support many different interpretations.

Like dreams, Kafka's writing is both fantastic and vividly entertaining and evokes powerful emotional responses ranging from fear to sustained laughter. He was unique, a sovereign artist, a writer for all time.

Bibliography

Bloom, Harold, ed. *Franz Kafka*. New York: Chelsea House, 1986.

Corngold, Stanley. *The Commentators' Despair: The Interpretation of Kafka's "Metamorphosis."* Port Washington, N.Y.: Kennikat Press, 1973.

——————. *Franz Kafka: The Necessity of Form*. Ithaca, N.Y.: Cornell University Press, 1988.

Flores, Angel, ed. *The Kafka Debate: New Perspectives for Our Time*. New York: Gordian, 1977.

Heller, Erich. *Franz Kafka*. New York: Viking Press, 1974.

Marson, Eric. *Kafka's "Trial": The Case Against Josef K.* St. Lucia, Queensland: University of Queensland Press, 1975.

Politzer, Heinz. *Franz Kafka: Parable and Paradox*. Ithaca, N.Y.: Cornell University Press, 1966.

Rolleston, James. *Kafka's Narrative Theater*. University Park: Pennsylvania State University Press, 1974.

————————, ed. *Twentieth Century Interpretations of "The Trial."* Englewood Cliffs, N.J.: Prentice-Hall, 1976.

Spann, Meno. *Franz Kafka*. Boston: Twayne, 1976.

Jean M. Snook

YASUNARI KAWABATA

Born: Osaka, Japan
June 11, 1899
Died: Zushi, Japan
April 16, 1972

Principal Literary Achievement

Long recognized in Japan as a literary innovator, Kawabata was awarded the Nobel Prize in Literature in 1968, the first Japanese writer to be so honored.

Biography

Yasunari Kawabata was born in Osaka, Japan, on June 11, 1899. When Kawabata was two years old, his father died. His mother died the following year, and Kawabata and his sister went to live with his maternal grandparents. Kawabata's grandmother's death in 1906 was followed two years later by the death of his sister (his only sibling), leaving him alone with his grandfather. Following his grandfather's death in 1914, Kawabata moved into a middle-school dormitory in Osaka, where he stayed until moving in with relatives to attend high school in Tokyo.

In 1920, Kawabata entered Tokyo Imperial University to study English literature. In his second year, however, he decided to major in Japanese literature. While still in college, Kawabata came to the attention of Kan Kikuchi, a noted editor and author. Kikuchi was so taken with the younger man that he secured a position for Kawabata on the staff of the literary journal *Bungei shunju* (literature of the times) and provided Kawabata with the use of his home. After graduating from Tokyo University in 1924, Kawabata and several other young writers who had been associated with *Bungei shunju* founded their own literary journal, *Bungei jidai* (literary age). The new journal was seen as the official publication of the Shinkankakuha (Neo-Perceptionist) movement. Writers of the Neo-Perceptionist movement were heavily influenced by such Western writers as James Joyce and Gertrude Stein.

Following some early publications in college, Kawabata's first literary breakthrough came with the publication of *Izu no Odoriko* (1926; *The Izu Dancer*, 1955). This story would provide a model for much of Kawabata's later fiction: an autobiographical protagonist and an unattainable, virginal love.

In the early 1930's, Kawabata began to experiment in his short fiction with the stream-of-consciousness technique developed by Joyce. Kawabata also experimented with Surrealism in his short fiction and poetry. During this period, Kawabata worked

on several literary magazines, including the influential *Bungakkai* (literary world). He also began to develop many of his "palm-of-the-hand stories." He started writing these very short stories during the 1920's and published 146 of them over the course of his literary career. Kawabata married in 1931, but he and his wife (Hideko) remained childless until adopting a daughter in 1943. In 1932, Kawabata began publishing the autobiographical series *Fubo e no Tegami* (1932-1934; letters to my parents). In one of the letters, he explains that he made the decision to remain childless to avoid the possibility of subjecting a child to the orphan's life that he had known.

In 1934, Kawabata began work on *Yukiguni* (serial, 1935-1937, 1947; 1948; *Snow Country*, 1956). Between 1934 and 1937, Kawabata published various chapters of *Snow Country* in a series of magazines. He added a chapter in 1939, another in 1940, and a final chapter in 1947 when the novel was published. That each of the early chapters can stand on its own merit is a testament to both Kawabata's skill as a writer and his belief that the novel could end at any point.

During World War II, Kawabata spent much of his time writing self-reflexive childhood reminiscences and studying *Genji monogatari* (c. 1004; *The Tale of Genji*, 1925-1933), Murasaki Shikibu's classic insider's view of the eleventh century Japanese royal court. While Kawabata was able to retain his apolitical beliefs during the war, he did travel extensively in occupied Manchuria and served on several government-sponsored literary projects.

Kawabata became president of the Japanese chapter of the International Association of Poets, Playwrights, Editors, Essayists, and Novelists (PEN) in 1948 and served in that capacity for seventeen years. The late 1940's and early 1950's were productive years for him. He completed two novels, *Sembazuru* (serial, 1949-1951; 1952; *Thousand Cranes*, 1958) and *Yama no Oto* (1957; *The Sound of the Mountain*, 1970) and found time to assist a new generation of Japanese authors, most notably Yukio Mishima. Kawabata was also beginning to gain an international following during this time through English and German translations of his fiction.

The 1960's provided an equally busy time for Kawabata as he toured American universities and campaigned at home for conservative political candidates. He was also, of course, still writing. Upon the publication of *Kyoto* (*The Old Capital*, 1987) in 1962, Kawabata checked himself into a hospital to recover from a drug dependency developed over the course of writing the novel. In 1968, Kawabata (who had already received every major Japanese award for literature) was awarded the Nobel Prize in Literature. The Nobel Committee cited *Snow Country*, *Thousand Cranes*, and *The Old Capital* as being the basis for their decision.

On April 16, 1972, in Zushi, Japan, Kawabata took his life, leaving no note.

Analysis

When Kawabata was awarded the Nobel Prize, many Japanese readers reacted with the same confusion expressed by American readers when William Faulkner was awarded the same prize in 1949. The native audiences for both writers were surprised that an author whom they found so difficult to understand could be appreciated by foreign audiences. Kawabata earned his reputation for being inaccessible through his early experiments with Western-based literary techniques such as stream-of-consciousness and Surrealism. Even after he moved beyond his flirtation with Western literary styles, he confounded Japanese writers with his fondness for plotless, open-ended stories and his fragmentary, anecdotal "palm-of-the-hand stories."

The characteristic open-endedness and incompleteness of Kawabata's fiction, combined with the failure of many of his major characters to attain their goals, led some critics to label him a nihilist. Kawabata complained that such critics missed the point of his fiction: "I have never written a story that has . . . nihilism as its main theme. What seems so is in truth a kind of longing for vitality." Makoto Ueda, a critic and scholar of Japanese literature, has suggested that Kawabata's fondness for incomplete endings and open-ended stories is the result of Kawabata's desire to capture the free-flowing nature of life, not a desire to suggest a lack of meaning or completeness for life.

Ueda has noted that the chief characteristics of Kawabata's fiction are beauty, sincerity, and sadness. These three characteristics are not, however, separate entities. Rather, they are intertwined. For example, in *Snow Country*, Yoko's voice is described several times as being so beautiful that it is sad, and even her nose is described as being beautiful with an element of sadness. Beauty also incorporates an element of sincerity, for one who is sincere and pure of heart has a spiritual beauty. Certainly, Kawabata was interested in the outward beauty of landscapes and people, but he was more concerned with the beauty of tradition and emotions.

Kawabata believed that three groups were best prepared to recognize pure beauty. First, little children, because of their innocence, inexperience, and purity of soul, were incapable of seeing ugliness in the world. Second, young women who had not yet experienced life or physical love, who still believed in spiritual, asexual love, were capable of recognizing pure beauty. Finally, dying men were capable of recognizing pure beauty because their closeness to death helped them to transcend the desire for sexual love.

Kawabata's conception of the beauty of pure love can be seen in his first major literary work, *The Izu Dancer*. *The Izu Dancer* is structured around a female dancer and a young student who comes upon the traveling troupe to which the dancer belongs and is immediately attracted to the girl. The young man happens to see the dancer emerge from a bath in a stream, and he is relieved to discover that she is actually a child. His relief is the result of being released from the sexual tension implied by a male/female relationship. Now he will be able to enjoy love in its purest, most unattainable form and travel freely with the dancers until it is time for him to return to school.

The beauty of tradition is also apparent in Kawabata's fiction. The ancient tea ceremony and the equally historic game of Go figure prominently in two of Kawabata's major novels, *Meijin* (1954; *The Master of Go*, 1972) and *Thousand Cranes*. Kawabata was as much concerned with the beauty, purity, and simplicity of these Japanese traditions as he was with the characters of the novels for which the traditions provide the structure.

Kawabata believed that the writer's goal should be to create in literature a life of unusual beauty, simplicity, and truth. He recognized that this would be an artificial world, an ideal world, yet he also believed that it was a world that needed to be created. Kawabata believed that a "pure life" was one devoted to the pursuit of an ideal. Recognizing that few dreams are ever realized, Kawabata believed that attaining the ideal (whatever form it may take) was not as important as the pursuit itself. For him, the ideal often took the form of a pure, virginal love, a love that, by its very nature, was unattainable because humankind's desire for physical love ultimately results in the destruction of virginity. Kawabata's use of the unattainable virgin has been linked to his engagement to a fifteen-year-old in the early 1920's.

Death is also present in much of Kawabata's fiction, for anyone who seeks the essence (purity) of life must be willing to risk everything, even death, in pursuit of the ideal. Also, death that occurs before spiritual love can be breached, as in the case of the young man who is the center of Yoko and Komako's lives in *Snow Country*, assures the continuation of the spiritual love. Yoko, for example, states that she will never be able to nurse or mourn another man as she has nursed and mourned the music teacher's son. *The Sound of the Mountain* is reflective of Kawabata's concern with his own mortality. Although he was only in his early fifties while he was writing the novel, death had been an important part of his life from the earliest days.

SNOW COUNTRY

First published: *Yukiguni*, 1935-1937, 1947 (serial), 1948 (English translation, 1956)
Type of work: Novel

An independently wealthy man makes three visits to his mistress in the mountain country of Japan in search of an illusive dream that remains unfulfilled.

"The train came out of the long tunnel into the snow country." Through the opening line of *Snow Country*, the central character, Shimamura, and the reader are transported back in time. The snow country of the novel has only recently been linked to modern Japan by the railroad. Indeed, as Shimamura notes as he returns to Tokyo after his second visit, "the train . . . was not from the same world as the trains one finds on the main lines."

Shimamura's world, represented by Tokyo, is a world being invaded by Western influences in architecture and life-styles. The world on the other side of the mountains from Tokyo is a world of rice harvests, winter carnivals, houses built in the style of the old regime, and Chijimi linen that can be traced back to antiquity. Clearly, when Shimamura travels to the snow country, he is leaving behind the decadence of modern Japan and returning to a Japan of the past, a Japan that values simplicity and purity. Shimamura himself acknowledges that he must return to the mountains to regain some of the honesty that is lost by living in Tokyo. Despite his professed desire for honesty, however, Shimamura is more concerned with illusion than with reality. In the opening section of the novel, he views Yoko through her reflection in the mirrorlike window of the train car, but what he sees is an image "floating" in the glass, not Yoko herself.

Shimamura's fascination with occidental ballet is also representative of his desire to maintain a distance between reality and illusion, as if closeness to a dream destroys the dream. In fact, that is exactly what has happened to him with his earlier fascination with the dance-drama of Kabuki theater. As he researched and studied Kabuki dance and became acquainted with individual dancers, he became dissatisfied with the object of his obsession and turned his attentions to ballet. In this new study, he is determined to maintain the distance between illusion and reality by never watching a ballet performance. He will content himself with studying ballet through books and photographs, assuring that the new dream cannot be destroyed.

Shimamura's relationship with Komako is also built around the pursuit of a dream, a spiritual relationship with a woman. This dream is nearly realized during their first meeting, related through a flashback as Shimamura is traveling toward a second meeting in the mountains. Shimamura and Komako's first meeting is in the spring, a time of hope and promise. When Shimamura first meets Komako, he is attracted to her physically, but he moves quickly to separate her in his mind from a woman to be used for physical pleasure. He sees a purity in her that creates a feeling of revulsion for his physical desires. Komako also recognizes that they may be on the verge of something pure and magical and points out to him that relationships between men and women last longer if they remain "just friends." Physical desire (aided by some *sake*) overpowers the couple's good intentions, however, and the possibility of a purely spiritual relationship is destroyed. The remaining sections of the novel center around Komako's "fall from grace" and Shimamura's interest in the "unspoiled" Yoko.

Shimamura's second visit to the mountain village begins with an air of optimism, for, while he has been away from Komako, he has felt closer to her and hopes to recapture something from their first encounter. Once again, he is attracted more to possibilities than to realities. The openness of that first meeting, however, cannot be recaptured; it has been destroyed by the physical relationship. This meeting takes place in the winter, symbolizing the arrested state of their relationship.

Komako is presented in a different light during the second meeting. She is no longer the young woman whom Shimamura met six months earlier; she is now a geisha in the full sense of the word. Nevertheless, Shimamura still finds a purity in her because she has become a geisha to help pay the medical bills of her former fiancé, who is dying, and to avoid being trapped in a loveless marriage to an old man who has proposed to her. Komako, however, recognizes that there is no longer the possibility for anything but a sexual relationship between Shimamura and herself. Consequently, she drinks heavily when she is engaged to attend parties in her role as a geisha.

When Shimamura returns to the snow country for his third visit, it is autumn, a foreshadowing of the end of the relationship. During the third visit, Komako is drinking even more heavily and strikes out verbally against Yoko, telling Shimamura that the younger girl is insane. Komako is aware of Shimamura's attraction to Yoko and the possibility of pure love that the younger girl represents.

Yoko, ironically, is the character who comes closest to realizing the dream of a pure, asexual love. Yoko served as a nurse for Komako's former fiancé and has spent every day since his death tending his grave. Now she tells Shimamura she is ready to go to Tokyo; she knows she will never love another man in the same way. She has captured the purity of love that Shimamura and Komako had been seeking. Her apparent death at the end of the novel assures that there will be no other men in her life.

The novel ends, characteristically for Kawabata, with nothing resolved for the main characters. It is not even certain that Yoko has died from her leap off the burning warehouse.

THOUSAND CRANES

First published: *Sembazuru*, 1949-1951 (serial), 1952 (English translation, 1958)
Type of work: Novel

A young Tokyo bachelor attempts to reconcile his life to the realities of postwar Japan and the traditions of the past.

The ancient Japanese tea ceremony, which provides the backdrop of *Thousand Cranes*, is as important as the two motifs intertwined throughout the novel: the loss of values in postwar Japan and the elusive search for love.

The tea ceremony itself is symbolic of Japan's drift away from tradition and historical values. Kikuji Mitani, the protagonist, seems indifferent to his father's collection of antique tea bowls and the tea ceremony itself. His office mates share his lack of interest in the ceremony. Chikako Kurimoto, a former mistress of Kikuji's late father and a teacher of the tea ceremony, wistfully tells Kikuji that fewer and fewer young girls seem to be interested in learning the ways of the tea ceremony. Chikako also notes that the tea ceremony has also been tainted by foreign observers, such as some Americans who visited recently.

The two young women who are of interest to Kikuji in the novel have close ties to the tea ceremony. Chikako is trying to arrange a marriage between Kikuji and Yukiko Inamura. Yukiko, as a student of Chikako's, is tied to the past. Fumiko Ota, a former student of the tea ceremony who is often seen in European dress, is linked to the present. Consequently, as Chikako tries to pressure Kikuji to accept an arranged marriage to Yukiko, and as he tries to define his feelings for Fumiko, he is not merely choosing between two women—he is choosing between the Japan of the past and modern Japan.

Kikuji lives alone in his father's house, both his parents having died. It is a house of the past, in architecture and furnishings—even the maid is a remnant from his father's days. Kikuji continually talks of selling the house and allows it to fall into disrepair. The house represents the traditions of the past, and Kikuji is unsure of the validity of these traditions in postwar Japan. He works in a modern building and leaves his house in Western-style suits, only changing into a kimono when he returns home.

When Chikako arranges a tea ceremony to bring Kikuji and Yukiko together, he is attracted by the latter's beauty. Yet he is also offended by the tradition of arranged marriages and the role that Chikako is trying to play in his life. Despite his attraction to Yukiko, Kikuji realizes that there will always be a distance between them because of her ties to the past and because of his ambivalent feelings for the past.

Chikako's tea ceremony also brings Kikuji together with Mrs. Ota and her daughter Fumiko. Fumiko, like Kikuji, is torn between the past and present. She has avoided learning the tea ceremony and is often found wearing European clothes. After her mother's suicide, she makes a formal break with the past by selling her mother's house.

Kikuji's growing alienation from the past can be seen in his use of the antique water pitcher that Fumiko gives him after her mother's death. The pitcher was created for use in the tea ceremony, but Kikuji uses it to hold Western flowers. Near the end of the novel, Chikako, frustrated with her inability to control Kikuji's life, accuses him of being ignorant of Japanese thinking—the worst insult that she can think of making.

Kikuji's dissatisfaction in the novel is not limited to his search for a cultural identity; his dissatisfaction is also related to an inability to find love. When Kikuji was eight years old, his father took him on a visit to Chikako's—his father's mistress at the time. Kikuji saw an ugly birthmark on Chikako's breast and now associates ugliness with sex. He sees Chikako's venomous behavior toward Mrs. Ota and Fumiko as an ugliness derived from her sexual relationship with his father. Even as an adult bachelor, Kikuji feels "soiled" after sexual encounters.

Fumiko also sees ugliness in sex. She blames her mother's adulterous relationship with Kikuji's father for the early deaths of Kikuji's father and mother. She even believes her mother's suicide is the result of her mother not being able "to stand her own ugliness," an ugliness that stems both from her mother's relationship with Kikuji and from her mother's seduction of Kikuji. Fumiko's own suicide at the end of the novel is linked by Kikuji to guilt that she may be feeling over her sexual surrender to him.

Ironically, Fumiko's death comes after she has symbolically broken with the past by selling her mother's house and by shattering a three-hundred-year-old tea bowl that her mother had owned. Her death is also ironic because, through his sexual encounter with Fumiko, Kikuji has "escaped the curse and paralysis" that have dominated his life. Unfortunately, he fails to explain this freedom to Fumiko. When he goes to tell her the next morning, he discovers that it is too late. His indecisiveness the night before has allowed true happiness to escape him.

Summary

Yasunari Kawabata's true gift as a writer, the gift recognized and cited by the Nobel Prize Committee, was his appreciation of Japanese traditions and his ability to explore the interrelationships between the past, present, and future through the language and literary traditions of the twentieth century. While similar themes ran through much of Kawabata's works, each piece of his fiction has its own unique character and style, be it the attention paid to a physical description of a black water lily or a psychological study of human indifference.

Bibliography

Gessel, Van C., and Tomone Matsumoto, eds. *The Showa Anthology: Modern Japanese Short Stories*. 2 vols. Tokyo: Kodansha International, 1985.

Hibbett, Howard, ed. *Contemporary Japanese Literature*. New York: Alfred A. Knopf, 1977.

Keene, Donald. *Dawn to the West: Japanese Literature of the Modern Era*. New York: Holt, Rinehart and Winston, 1984.

_____. *Modern Japanese Literature*. New York: Grove Press, 1960.

Rimer, J. Thomas. *A Reader's Guide to Japanese Literature*. Tokyo: Kodansha International, 1988.

Ueda, Makoto. *Modern Japanese Writers*. Stanford, Calif.: Stanford University Press, 1976.

Ronald E. Smith

NIKOS KAZANTZAKIS

Born: Heraklion, Crete
February 18, 1883
Died: Freiburg, West Germany
October 26, 1957

Principal Literary Achievement

Kazantzakis, through his examination of the nature of human freedom and the concept of God in a variety of literary works and forms, is the most important Greek writer of the twentieth century and a formidable figure on the world literary stage.

Biography

Nikos Kazantzakis was born in Heraklion on the Greek island of Crete on February 18, 1883, at a time when that island was under the control of the Ottoman Turks. Rebels fought against the Turks during Kazantzakis' childhood, and they were finally successful in 1898. Once Kazantzakis' family fled to Greece for safety in the midst of the violence of revolution, and as a teenager Kazantzakis was sent to the island of Naxos for the purposes of both schooling and personal safety. Thus, Kazantzakis was born into a world of struggle and movement; struggle became the dominant theme of his writing and movement the theme of his life.

In 1902, young Kazantzakis moved from Crete to Athens to study law, but by 1906 his literary career had also begun with his first novel, *Ofis ke kríno* (1906; *Serpent and Lily*, 1980), and the political play *Ksimerónei* (1907; day is breaking), which was produced the next year and which won acclaim for Kazantzakis. In 1907, Kazantzakis moved to Paris to begin graduate study in philosophy. While there, he encountered the works of two philosophers whose ideas were to influence greatly the rest of his career: the German Friedrich Wilhelm Nietzsche, who believed that human beings must violate the rules and conventions of the past in order to break through to a new consciousness; and the Frenchman Henri Bergson, who thought that time is relative to the human condition and not measured by an abstract standard and that the life force (*élan vital*) is constantly fighting to assert itself through a resistant matter. By 1909, Kazantzakis had finished his dissertation on Nietzsche and returned to Crete, where he became one of the leaders of a literary group that championed the use of the ordinary (demotic) Greek spoken by common people in place of the more formal Greek favored by older literary artists. Kazantzakis and his colleagues hoped thereby

to revive the literature of Greece.

Kazantzakis spent the next fifteen years traveling all over Greece and central Europe, becoming involved with many political schemes designed to overthrow the old capitalistic and imperial order, jumping from one philosophical viewpoint to the next, having many experiences that would inform his later works, but writing comparatively little. In 1911, he married Galatea Alexíou, whom he had met while living in Athens. In 1912, war broke out in the Balkans, and Kazantzakis volunteered for duty but wound up assisting the prime minister. Then, in a complete reversal of the path that he had been following, in 1914 and 1915 Kazantzakis toured Greece with a friend, poet Angelos Sikelianós. A highlight of their trip was a visit to Mount Athos, a famous monastery that was one of many where they stayed. Kazantzakis lived alone in a bare monk's cell for months. As a result of this journey and his reading of Dante Alighieri, Leo Tolstoy, and Western and Eastern religious scriptures, Kazantzakis decided that political change was not the answer to humankind's problems and began to think instead in religious terms, even considering starting a new religion. In 1917, Kazantzakis failed in an effort to mine lignite coal, but during the effort he met a life-affirming worker, George Zorbas. This adventure was to serve as the basis for his most famous novel, *Vios Kai politela tou Alexe Zormpa* (1946; *Zorba the Greek*, 1953). In 1917, Kazantzakis traveled to Switzerland, and he stayed there for the next two years.

Kazantzakis was brought back to political struggle in 1919, when the Greek government assigned him to help repatriate thousands of Greeks who were being persecuted by the Bolsheviks in the Russian Caucasus region. He also took part in the meetings of the World War I peace conference at Versailles and worked in northern Greece resettling refugees from the Caucasus, an experience that he used in the novel *Ho Christos Xanastauronetai* (1951; *The Greek Passion*, 1954; also known as *Christ Recrucified*). Disillusioned again by strife in Greece, Kazantzakis left the country in 1920 and spent the decade moving about Europe, visiting or living and working in Paris, Germany, Vienna, Italy, the Soviet Union, Palestine, Cyprus, Egypt, and Czechoslovakia, frequently returning to Greece while writing articles, translations, and reference works for a living. During this period, he divorced his first wife, met Eléni Samfou, who was to become his companion and second wife, and suffered several painful and debilitating attacks of the facial eczema that was to plague him for the rest of his life. He also became enamored of communism (the reason for his visits to Russia), became involved in more political turmoil in Greece, and began work on the volume that he regarded as his most important, his continuation of Homer's epic, *Odysseia* (1938; *The Odyssey: A Modern Sequel*, 1958).

Kazantzakis' wanderlust continued into the 1930's, including a trip to Japan and China, but he finally established a home on the Greek island of Aegina. During this period, he became known to a wider reading audience through his travel articles and books. During World War II, he was confined to Greece because of the German occupation, and in 1945 he returned to politics as a socialist and married Eléni Samfou. Civil war broke out in Greece at the end of World War II, and in 1946, because of controversy generated by both his politics and his writings, he left Greece for England and later Paris, where he worked as a translator for the United Nations Educational, Scientific, and Cultural Organization (UNESCO). Later, he and his wife moved to Antibes, France, where he lived for the rest of his life, since opposition to his politics and literary works prevented his return to Greece. This time was also a period of intense creative activity, during which Kazantzakis wrote and translated several plays and wrote the novels *The Greek Passion, Hoi aderphophades* (1963; *The Fratricides*, 1964), *Ho Kapetan Michales* (1953; *Freedom or Death*, 1956; also known as *Freedom and Death*), and *Ho teleutaios peirasmos* (1955; *The Last Temptation of Christ*, 1960; also known as *The Last Temptation*). The last novel is his most controversial because it presents Jesus Christ as beset by sexual and psychological problems and incurred the censure of both the Greek Orthodox and Roman Catholic churches.

Meanwhile, Kazantzakis' health was failing as his reputation continued to grow. The facial eczema attacked him again, and in 1953 an infection led to the loss of an eye, but doctors also pinpointed the source of the eczema as a lymphatic disorder, which, during a hospitalization in Germany the next year, was diagnosed as benign lymphatic leukemia. In 1956, he received the Peace Prize in Vienna and narrowly lost the Nobel Prize in Literature to Juan Ramón Jiménez. The next year, Kazantzakis had an adverse reaction to a vaccination during a trip to the Far East and was rushed to the hospital in Germany where his leukemia had been diagnosed. He died of Asiatic influenza in Freiburg, West Germany, on October 26, 1957. He was buried in his native Crete in spite of the opposition of the Greek Orthodox church. Still working to the end, the last books that he completed were the novel *Ho phtochoules too Theou* (1956; *Saint Francis*, 1962; also known as *God's Pauper: St Francis of Assisi*) and the autobiography *Anafora ston Greko: Myhistorema* (1961; *Report to Greco*, 1965).

Analysis

There is no more typical event in Kazantzakis' life than his attempt, while living in Vladimir Ilych Lenin's Russia in 1922, to unite and reconcile the political activism and materialism of communism with the asceticism and spirituality of Buddhism (an effort discussed in his philosophical book *Salvatores Dei: Asketike* (1927; *The Saviors of God: Spiritual Exercises*, 1960). Judged from outside Kazantzakis' worldview, such an endeavor seems hopeless, pointless, and doomed to failure from the outset. Yet the effort to yoke the extremes of human experience appears over and over in Kazantzakis' work. Odysseus in his *The Odyssey* is both a sacker of cities and a seeker after spiritual peace. The protagonist of *The Greek Passion*, chosen to portray Jesus in a Passion play, begins to assume that role in life and becomes not a man of peace but a revolutionary. Finally, Christ himself in *The Last Temptation of Christ* is unsure whether he should lead a religious revolt or abandon the struggle for an ordinary life with a home and family; beset by doubts, he is still trying to understand the nature of his mission even as he hangs on the Cross.

The inversion of everyday logic and human behavior that is basic to Kazantzakis' thinking appears even in the titles of his books. God is not the Savior of humanity, men and women are the saviors of God (in *The Saviors of God*). Kazantzakis thought of all creation, all existence, as a divine project in which the Holy Spirit, residing in the hearts and minds of humanity, must fight to overcome the resistance of the flesh, which always wants to take the easy way out, surrender to its appetites, and surrender in the face of egotistic greed and oppression. God cannot save humankind, for it is the embodiment, the incarnation, of the Spirit of God. It is for humanity to speak and act in terms of that Spirit and thereby save God. The British title of Kazantzakis' novel about Cretan rebellion against the Turks, *Freedom or Death*, is *Freedom and Death*, a pairing more appropriate for the writer's viewpoint. The doomed Cretans fight against impossible odds because that is the only way to assert the divine spirit of freedom and the unity of all life. Few are willing to undertake such a struggle, so their effort is bound to end in death. In that death, they reach the zenith of their exercise of freedom, so the appropriate title is not freedom *or* death, which implies that humanity has a choice between these conditions, but freedom *and* death, which grimly acknowledges the inevitable conclusion of such an attempt. For Kazantzakis, relationships are never stated in "either/or" terms, such as "either politics or religion" or "either the world or God," but in "and/and" terms. In order to understand, for example, politics or religion, the modern human must try to act upon the truths of each at the same time. To act as if only one side of the pair exists is to act on only partial knowledge and therefore really to be blind. The true answer is not "politics or religion" but "politics and religion," and, one should add, everything else, too. Kazantzakis tried to include as much experience in his life and literary works as he could possibly gather. To those who disagree with his philosophy, Kazantzakis was a madman racing over the globe in search of impossible fulfillment; to his admirers, he lived and wrote a quest for a new definition of the relationships between humans and fellow humans and between humankind and God.

ZORBA THE GREEK

First published: *Vios kai politela tou Alexe Zormpa*, 1946 (English
translation, 1953)
Type of work: Novel

A shy and unassertive scholar meets a lusty peasant who renews the scholar's faith in humanity and transforms his life.

Zorba the Greek is based on Kazantzakis' friendship with a real person, George Zorba, who helped the author in an ill-fated scheme to mine lignite in Greece. In the novel, the first-person narrator, known as "The Boss" (a title that Zorba gives him), who is a slightly changed version of Kazantzakis himself, journeys not to Greece but to Crete to mine the coal. Zorba, who fascinates and captivates The Boss the moment that they meet, keeps urging his employer to cast aside convention and live life more fully. He demonstrates how to do this by dancing, playing his guitarlike *santuri*, and spouting life-affirming philosophy and declarations about the nature of God, which are usually jokes and riddles. For example, Zorba explains the chaos of the physical world by pointing out that fishers pray to God to make fish blind so that they will swim into the nets; the fish pray to God to make the fishers blind so that they will cast their nets in the wrong places. Since God is the God of both fishers and fish, sometimes God listens to the prayers of the fish and sometimes to the prayers of the fishers, so sometimes fish are caught and sometimes they are not.

Zorba is also a confidence man, but a goodhearted one; the tables are turned on him by women, for part of the way in which he affirms life is to romance every one who seems a likely partner, sometimes getting fooled himself and in the process losing much of The Boss's money. The most poignant episode in the book stems from Zorba's sexual appetite. Zorba had befriended an old widow who had once been a coquette, and when she is about to die, The Boss tries to get Zorba to marry her to give her a sense of fulfillment.

At the end of the novel, Zorba's get-rich scheme for transporting coal—a trestle system down the side of a mountain—literally collapses, and The Boss prepares to return to the mainland. Zorba says farewell to The Boss by telling him that he has a good heart but that he lacks one thing to be totally his own man—folly. One must, in other words, be a little crazy to be free.

The novel was adapted for film in 1964, with Anthony Quinn as Zorba and Alan Bates as The Boss, and directed by Michael Cacoyannis. The success of this film helped bring Kazantzakis' work to a wider audience.

THE LAST TEMPTATION OF CHRIST

First published: *Ho teleutaios peirasmos*, 1955 (English translation, 1960)
Type of work: Novel

Jesus Christ resists his most powerful temptation, the desire to lead a normal human life, and dies on the Cross, fulfilling his destiny of spiritually uniting humanity and God.

The Last Temptation of Christ starts near the end of the life of Jesus of Nazareth and recounts the main events of the familiar Gospel story: Jesus assumes his mission, preaches, gathers disciples, is baptized by John the Baptist, goes to Jerusalem at Passover, is betrayed by Judas, is tried, condemned, and crucified, and finally dies on the Cross. Other details are presented either unconventionally or ambiguously. Pontius Pilate's interview with Jesus is in two parts, one before Passover and not in connection with Jesus' trial; Jesus apparently raises Lazarus from the dead, but Jesus' involvement in this event is reported by the characters rather than described authorially by Kazantzakis. Peter dreams that he walked on the waves at Jesus' command and tells Matthew, who includes the story as a real event in his account of Christ's life. Jesus is enraged at this and other inaccuracies in Matthew's manuscript, which the publican is writing so that the details of Jesus' life will correspond with the predictions of the Old Testament prophets, but Matthew says that he is directed by an angel. Although the tone of the novel is serious, this method of reporting the story of Jesus may be a reminder that, in his other works, Kazantzakis describes God as sometimes inconsistent and possessing a sense of humor. Kazantzakis may have de-emphasized Jesus' connection with Judaic tradition in order to underscore the point that, as a human being as well as God, he would have to have had the doubts that any human would have about his or her path in life.

These doubts are the source of the "last temptation" of the title. While enduring the agony of the Cross, Jesus swoons and dreams that he has awakened into a life in which he escaped the torment of the religious zealot, married, and fathered children. This "life" turns out to be a fantasy placed in his mind by Satan; his disciples return and accuse him of being a traitor by denying his mission, rejecting the Cross, and negating the truth of the power of the divine Spirit, which they wish to spread throughout the world. Summoning his strength, Jesus awakens from his dream, dies, and in that death brings freedom to himself and humankind. The novel ends at this point rather than with the Resurrection because Kazantzakis thought that Christ's death fulfilled both prophecy and his spiritual role; nothing more was needed.

Few novels have caused more outrage; religious figures of several faiths condemned the book as both blasphemous and heretical, and literary critics found the wild swings in Jesus' character and in the attitudes of others toward him either baffling or rendering the novel flawed and episodic. Kazantzakis clearly regards Jesus as the Son of God and Savior of humankind, but his presentation of Christ does not fit any conventional religious view. In 1989, Martin Scorsese directed a film version that was faithful to the novel and even more controversial than the book on which it was based.

Summary

Nikos Kazantzakis created works of art not as a sterile aesthetic exercise but as part of a lifelong effort to unify God, humanity, and the physical world. His works are important for those seeking to find a new viewpoint that will free humanity from the greed and selfishness that have characterized past centuries.

Bibliography

Bien, Peter. *Kazantzakis: The Politics of the Spirit*. Princeton, N.J.: Princeton University Press, 1989.

_____. *Nikos Kazantzakis*: New York: Columbia University Press, 1972.

_____. *Tempted by Happiness: Kazantzakis, Post-Christian Christ*. Wallingford, Pa.: Pendle Hill, 1984.

Kazantzakis, Helen. *Nikos Kazantzakis*. Translated by Amy Mims. New York: Simon & Schuster, 1968.

Levitt, Morton P. *The Cretan Glance: The World and Art of Nikos Kazantzakis*. Columbus: Ohio State University Press, 1980.

Prevelakis, Pandelis. *Nikos Kazantzakis and His Odyssey: A Study of the Poet and the Poem*. Translated by Philip Sherrard. New York: Simon & Schuster, 1961.

Jim Baird

JOHN KEATS

Born: London, England
October 31, 1795

Died: Rome, Italy
February 23, 1821

Principal Literary Achievement

One of the second generation of Romantic poets, Keats elevated the ode form to a new level of lyrical expression and came to symbolize the supreme literary craftsman.

Biography

Born in London, England, on October 31, 1795, John Keats was the son of Frances and Thomas Keats, the manager of a livery stable in the north of London. The oldest of four children, two brothers and a sister, John was eight years old when his father fell from a horse and suddenly died. The death of John's father and his mother's sudden decision to remarry had a dramatic effect on the poet's life. When Alice Jennings, John's maternal grandmother, heard of her daughter's decision to marry again, she arranged to have the Keats children come live with her and her husband, John Jennings. This move eventually resulted in the children moving to a different suburb of the city, Enfield, where John and George began school. This development was a key moment in Keats's early life.

The Enfield school, which was run by the Reverend John Clarke, not only introduced Keats to the various pleasures of literature, which of course was to become the consuming passion of his life, but also brought the young poet into contact with the Reverend Clarke's precocious and well-read son, Charles Cowden Clarke. Charles Clarke, who was eight years older than John and who eventually became an important writer, too, quickly established himself as John's mentor and friend. It was through his new friend that Keats encountered many of the books that were to play an important role in his poetry.

In March of 1810, John Keats's mother died of tuberculosis. This event was not the sudden blow that his father's earlier death had been, but it was no less traumatic. It is difficult to know precisely how this loss shaped the young man's character, but it is quite likely that this event, combined with the earlier death of his father, deepened the poet's sense of the tragic nature of human existence. As a result, the transitoriness and pain of life are themes that run throughout his poems and letters. Indeed,

he would eventually develop the belief that suffering and death are essential to the growth of the human soul, for it is death and suffering that awakens one to the intense beauty of life. People only come to feel the glory of life and the wonder of existence when it is suddenly taken from them, Keats concluded.

At the age of fourteen, John Keats became the head of the Keats family. He might have remained in school and gone on to receive a university education, since there was a provision in a trust fund set up by his grandmother that would cover those costs. Yet because of legal complications and the incompetency of Richard Abbey, a London tea merchant who was assigned as guardian for the children upon the death of their mother, John was denied his inheritance and, instead, apprenticed to Thomas Hammond, a local apothecary-surgeon. For the next four years, Keats studied medicine with Hammond. This intense training in medicine was relieved only by occasional visits to the nearby Charles Clarke to borrow books and discuss literature.

In 1815, at the age of nineteen, Keats moved to London proper to do his student internship at Guy's Hospital, where he lived and worked for the next two years. It is difficult to overestimate the impression that Guy's must have made on the young poet, whose first responsibility at the hospital was dressing surgical wounds. The sights and sounds of the operating and recovery rooms must have been extremely poignant, particularly since these rooms were filled with patients who had been surgically treated without the benefit of anesthetics. Keats had already experienced the deep emotions of suffering and loss through the death of both parents; now, he was to see that same agony and death displayed on a much larger scale and on a more regular basis in his daily rounds at the hospital.

During his two years at Guy's, Keats became increasingly convinced that poetry was to be his life's work. Life and death were the dominant concerns of his days, but reading and writing were the governing passions of his nights. Long days at the hospital were regularly followed by evenings of writing verse, reading books borrowed from Clarke, and discussing literature with friends and fellow medical students. It is important to note, however, that art was not a refuge for Keats from the agony of life, although he did look to poetry as a way of escaping the unpleasantness of his daily existence. To the contrary, poetry was the supreme expression of the intense experience of living in a world of pain and sorrow, pleasure and joy, the passing and the permanent. It is during this period that Keats produced his first significant poem, "On First Looking into Chapman's Homer." It is also during this time that Clarke introduced Keats to Leigh Hunt, a popular essayist of the day, to John Reynolds, a poet, and to Benjamin Haydon, an increasingly important painter. These contacts further persuaded Keats that his true vocation was literature, not surgery. Keats left Guy's Hospital in 1817 to dedicate himself exclusively to the writing of poetry. This year also marks the publication of his first book of poetry, *Poems* (1817).

That same year, Keats moved in with his brothers, George and Tom, who now lived in the London suburb of Hampstead. There he finished his second volume of poetry, *Endymion: A Poetic Romance* (1818), the mythological story of a mortal shepherd's love for the immortal goddess Diana. Having finished this project, Keats spent the summer of 1818 on a walking tour through the Lake District and Scotland. His return brought with it three painful discoveries. First, he was diagnosed to be in the early stages of tuberculosis, which was the same disease that had killed his mother and would, in less than three years, claim his own life. Second, and even more jarring, he found that the critics had not liked the two volumes of poetry that he had recently published. Although the impact of these negative criticisms has been overstated, it is probably true that Keats's conviction that his fame as a poet would never last can be traced to these early reviews of his work. Third, in the same year that Keats was diagnosed with tuberculosis, he would watch his youngest brother, Tom, also die of the same disease. Shaken but determined to continue writing, Keats moved to Wentworth Place in 1819. There he met Fanny Brawne, his first love, to whom he was engaged in October of that year.

In 1819, Keats wrote all of his greatest poetry. In that single year, he wrote *Lamia*, "The Eve of St. Agnes," all the great odes ("Ode on Indolence," "Ode on a Grecian Urn," "Ode to Psyche," "Ode to a Nightingale," "Ode on Melancholy," and "To Autumn"), as well as the Miltonic fragment "Hyperion," which he would later rework as *The Fall of Hyperion: A Dream* (1856). No other single year in literary history has seen such an outpouring of poetic genius, particularly by such a young poet.

The results of this great year were published in 1819 and on into 1820, the year that both marks the extraordinary heights of Keats's artistic career and foretells the imminent end of his short but remarkable life. The worsening tuberculosis made it almost impossible to continue working. When the doctors finally ordered the poet to seek a warmer climate (a common prescription in that day for sufferers of this disease), Joseph Severn, Keats's close friend, accompanied him to Rome. They sailed on September 18, 1820. A few weeks after arriving in Rome, Keats suffered a serious relapse. On February 23, 1821, he died, in Rome, at the age of twenty-five. Buried in the Protestant Cemetery in Rome, he had arranged to have the following words inscribed upon his tombstone: "Here lies one whose name was writ in water."

Analysis

Keats was a poet, and it is in his poetry that he gave the fullest expression to his genius. Yet before turning to the poetry, it may be useful first to address some of the central concerns of the poet, as expressed in his various letters to family and friends. It is in these letters, for example, that he tried to articulate his philosophies of art and life, asking and answering such questions as, What is the true character of a poet? What is the proper role of the poet in society? What is the relationship between art and life? and What is the function of the imagination?

In his letter of October 27, 1818, to Richard Woodhouse, a friend and supporter, Keats offers one of his earliest attempts to define what a poet is. Keats begins by declaring that a poet has no self or identity. A poet, like a chameleon, absorbs the colorations of the outside world, becoming one with the things seen, heard, and touched. Keats's point is that, for poets to comprehend their subjects fully, to enter into the life of things around them, they must free themselves from their own limited experiences of the world—their own biases, emotions, and points of view—and merge with that which they hope to understand and describe. This sympathetic understanding, as opposed to a reasoned understanding, depends not upon logic or even intellect but rather upon imagination. Through the imagination, then, the poet is projected into the subject and lives according to its essential qualities. From this notion of the poet comes one of Keats's most significant contributions to poetic theory, the idea of Negative Capability. This idea extends the above beliefs about escaping the self to form a philosophy about the poetic character and its proper relationship to the world. In his December 21, 1817, letter to his brothers, George and Tom, Keats defined Negative Capability quite simply as "when a man is capable of being in uncertainties, mysteries, doubts, without any irritable reaching after fact and reason." For Keats, in other words, poetic knowledge comes from accepting the inexplicable mysteries of the world. The poet should not force the world to make sense, for to do that is to reduce and simplify the world and to equate that reduction and simplification with a true understanding. A more profound understanding comes when the poet lives in conjunction with doubt and uncertainty. Again, Keats rejects reason and logic as suitable agents of truth, preferring instead to rely upon imagination and feeling. This preference may help to explain what Keats means when he writes at the end of his important poem "Ode on a Grecian Urn" that " 'Beauty is truth, truth beauty,'—that is all/ Ye know on earth, and all ye need to know." The truth that Keats finds in beauty is not the truth that the scientist or historian seeks to discover and document. For Keats, the essential truth of something, a sunset, for example, can be grasped only through a full appreciation of its beauty. As Keats explains in his letter to George and Tom, December 21, 1817: "with a great poet the sense of Beauty overcomes every other consideration, or rather obliterates all consideration."

This notion of the poet and what constitutes true knowledge goes a long way toward explaining why Keats wrote the kind of poetry that he did. Keats's purpose as a poet is not to teach the reader the so-called truths of this world, in any conventional sense of that word. Nor, Keats argues, is it the poet's business to bully the reader into accepting a ready-made set of conclusions. Poetry, in other words, should "proclaim" nothing. Instead, the ambition of the poet is to arouse the readers' imaginative faculties so that they may participate in the larger existence of creation. As exercises in imagination, Keats's poems seek to lift their readers out of their contracted worlds and to raise them to a level of awareness and understanding that is at peace with complexity, ambiguity, contradiction, and mystery. That is the stuff of life; or at least it was the stuff of Keats's difficult life. All attempts to escape that condition through "an irritable reaching after fact and reason" can only result in a sorry self-deception and a diminishment of human experience.

ENDYMION: A POETIC ROMANCE

First published: 1818
Type of work: Poem

Taken from Greek mythology, this poem is the story of a mortal shepherd's
quest for immortality through his ideal love, the goddess Diana.

Endymion: A Poetic Romance, Keats's first major work, represents the poet's first
sustained attempt to explore the relationship between the real world of human experience and the ethereal world of an idealized existence. Divided into four books, the
poem traces Endymion's progress from his initial desire to rise above his earthly
existence by cultivating his love for Diana, the goddess of the moon, who represents
ideal love, to his gradual reconciliation, in the end, to his mortal condition and the
love that he feels for an Indian maiden whom he meets during his quest. Upon realizing the dangers of trying to deny his own human nature, Endymion suddenly discovers that the Indian maiden, his mortal counterpart, is really Diana, his immortal
desire, in disguise. In the end, Endymion learns that he can only rise above his mortal
nature and achieve some kind of idealized existence if he first accepts "his natural
sphere." Keats's point, as in other poems, is that any attempt to achieve an abstract
ideal must begin with an acceptance of concrete human experience.

Book 1, which opens with the often-quoted line, "A thing of beauty is a joy for
ever," describes the source of Endymion's discontent with his life as a local chieftain.
His life as a man of action and worldly concerns is disrupted by a dream in which he
imagines himself carried through the skies by a goddess. When she finally returns
him to earth, he suddenly finds that his surroundings no longer seem beautiful or
satisfying. Having experienced the ethereal world of abstract beauty, Endymion is
unable to appreciate the physical beauty of the world around him.

Books 2, 3, and 4, which take place under the earth, at the bottom of the sea, and
in the sky, trace Endymion's quest for the goddess of his dream. During his journey,
he encounters various characters, the last of whom is Glaucus, who is chained to the
bottom of the sea. Glaucus, like Endymion, had once been satisfied with his existence as a mortal, but, aroused by "distemper'd longings," he had transformed himself into a sea-god. When he rejected the seductions of the sea witch, Circe, she
chained him to the bottom of the sea for a thousand years. One condition of Glaucus'
release is that he and Endymion must locate the bodies of all the lovers who have
drowned at sea and restore them to life. Only by engaging once again in the world of
mortal actions can Glaucus escape the dreadful consequences of trying to escape his
own mortality.

In book 4, Endymion reenacts the lesson of Glaucus. Having met an Indian maiden,
Endymion is torn between his love for this mortal woman and his idealized love for

his immortal goddess. Eventually, he admonishes himself for rejecting his own concrete humanity in favor of "his first soft poppy dream." In the end, he learns the essential lesson of his life—that to reject his own humanity is to reject all humanity and the things of this earth.

When Endymion discovers in the end that the Indian maiden is really Diana in disguise, he achieves through this synthesis of these two figures the final wisdom of his life and of Keats's poem: that any desire to achieve the ideal must begin not with a rejection of the mortal world but rather with an acceptance of the human condition. It is through an intense appreciation for the concrete and common things of this world that one penetrates the ethereal and idealized world within and beyond.

ODE TO A NIGHTINGALE

First published: 1819
Type of work: Poem

In this meditation on the song of the nightingale, Keats explores the power of the imagination to free him from the human condition.

"Ode to a Nightingale," along with "Ode on Indolence," "Ode on a Grecian Urn," "Ode on Melancholy," and "To Autumn," all of which were written between March and September of 1819, documents Keats's ongoing struggle to reconcile himself to his own mortality. The deaths of his father (1804) and mother (1810), combined with the imminent death of his brother, Tom, who was in the last stages of tuberculosis, as well as the recent diagnosis of his own contraction of tuberculosis, brought the poet to consider the transient nature of human existence and to search for some form of permanence in nature or in art. The song of the nightingale, which is seen as a kind of natural poet, offers Keats such a symbol of permanence. The poem records Keats's struggle to merge his life with the immortal song of that bird and thereby escape, at least temporarily, his own mortality.

The poem can be divided into three movements or parts. The first part, stanzas 1 to 3, describes the narrator's anguish upon hearing the immortal song of the bird in the distance. The "full-throated ease" with which it sings completely captures the poet's attention, causing him to forget, temporarily, his own mortality. That happiness, however, is short lived, for it quickly becomes the occasion for the poet to remember his own temporary existence.

The pain of that recognition is what generates the desire for escape through wine in the second stanza. Through wine, the poet may find some release from the pain invoked by the bird's song. Clearly, the poet sees the wine as an agent of nature, which further suggests that he sees nature as a source of escape from his own mortality, a common notion among many Romantic poets. The poet reasons that if he can forget his impending death, he will be able to join the bird and subsequently escape what the bird has never known: "The weariness, the fever, and the fret/ Here, where men sit and hear each other groan."

In stanza 4, which begins the second movement, the poet rejects wine and turns instead to "the viewless wings of Poesy." Wine enables him to forget, but it dulls the senses and obstructs vision. Poetry, on the other hand, engages the imagination, enlivens the senses, and empowers the poet to transcend himself and become one with the bird. "Already with thee!" the poet announces his imaginative oneness with the bird.

Stanzas 5, 6, and 7 describe the poet's close union with the bird. The poet "cannot see" what flowers are at his feet, but his imagination can create the scene unavailable to his eyes, including such minute and hidden details as the "Fast fading violets cover'd up in leaves." As his imagination works to re-create the bird's world, the poet's attention is temporarily diverted from "The weariness, the fever, and the fret" of human existence.

Vision gives way to sound in stanza 6, where the poet reveals that he has long been "half in love with easeful Death." The transcendental experience of the previous stanza leads him to recall past times when he had wanted to escape his mortal condition. "To cease upon the midnight with no pain" now seems particularly inviting. Yet, as the poet notes at the end of stanza 6, were he to die, he would be surrendering to the very thing that he hopes to escape—mortality. Moreover, to die is to become deaf to the song of the bird, "To thy high requiem become a sod." There the poet discovers the painful paradox of human existence: Life is a source of great pain and anguish, and yet, oddly enough, to escape the pain and anguish through death is to lose the very thing that makes death desirable. To die is to forfeit all access to beauty and joy.

The final turn comes in the last stanza where the spell is broken, the poet is imaginatively disengaged from the bird, and he returns to the mortal world "Where palsy shakes a few, sad, last gray hairs,/ Where youth grows pale, and spectre-thin, and dies." The poet concedes that "the fancy cannot cheat so well/ As she is fam'd to do" and is left to wonder if what he has experienced was in fact a visionary moment of transcendence or only a "waking dream." In either case, the poem ends on the ironic note that, although the poet believes that he is trapped within the mortal world of death and change, in fact, like the nightingale whose immortal song is heard by succeeding generations, the poet, through his poetry, has achieved a kind of immortality after all. The poem, like the bird's song, will be heard by future generations, and with each hearing or reading, the spirit of John Keats will live again.

ODE ON A GRECIAN URN

First published: 1820
Type of work: Poem

In a world of change and uncertainty, art offers the poet a symbol of permanence and timeless truth.

"Ode on a Grecian Urn" addresses many of the same concerns that occupied Keats in "Ode to a Nightingale," except that in this poem he turns his attention from the natural poetry of the bird to the human artistry of the urn. Unable to escape his sense of life's transience through the immortal song of the bird, Keats looks to the timeless truth embodied in the urn. Keats once again encounters the paradox that is central to all of his art: To achieve immortality is to rid oneself of change, but it is change, not stasis, that produces the contrasts necessary for all that is good.

In the first stanza, the poet contemplates first the urn as a whole, which he characterizes as a "historian," and then turns his attention to the detailed scene engraved onto the side of the urn. The urn first is described as an "unravish'd bride of quietness," calling attention to the fact that it is only when the poet begins to think about the urn that it begins to tell its story. The urn cannot speak, in other words, until it is spoken to. That is a significant point, for it leads to the conclusion that the immortal urn exists in any meaningful way only when it comes into contact with, and is activated by, the inquiring intelligence of a mortal observer. Immortality, the poet again seems to be saying, depends in some fundamental way upon its opposite.

He then begins asking the urn questions about the people portrayed on the side of the urn. He wonders who they are, "deities or mortals, or of both," and speculates about the location of the engraved scene, "In Tempe or the dales of Arcady?" The setting is obviously ancient Greece, a time when mortals and gods often interacted. From the very beginning, therefore, the poet is concerned with the issue of immortality, both as it is represented by the immortal urn and by the godlike characters whose "legend" is engraved on the side.

Stanza 2 shifts from questions to observations. The first observation stems from the experience of the first stanza. Having tried to experience imaginatively the scene before him, the poet reaches the conclusion that the imagination, when engaged by art, produces an experience that is superior to reality. The sounds of the pipes are sweet, to be sure, but the sounds supplied by the imagination "Are sweeter," because the imagination can alter and improve upon actual experience. Not bound by the material world, the imagination is capable of conjuring up sights, sounds, and emotions far beyond one's physical human capabilities. It would seem, therefore, that Keats is suggesting that the world of the imagination, which is the world of art, is preferable to the world of actuality. In the ideal world of art, where life need not conform to the limitations of flesh and blood, everything is as it should be; there the leaves never fall from the trees, no one ever dies, youth never fades, and lovers are forever young and forever in love. Keats comes to that realization through the scene before him: Although the lover, poised to kill his beloved, will never actually complete the act, nevertheless it is not a loss, since his beloved "cannot fade, though thou hast not thy bliss,/ For ever wilt thou love, and she be fair!"

This praise for the perfection and permanence of art continues through stanzas 3 and most of 4 until the poet pauses to wonder about the "little town by river or sea shore" that has been vacated by the people portrayed on the urn. In attending this celebration of life, they have left their village forever, never to return. In this detail the poet discovers a complication in his admiration for permanence, for even as the lovers will always be young and in love, so in turn will the village always be empty and silent with "not a soul to tell/ Why thou art desolate." There is a shift in tone from the celebratory mood of the previous two stanzas to a somber, almost sad picture of the deserted town and its eternal silence. The celebration of life on the urn has its counterpart in the unspoken death of the village. Again Keats brings life and death together, but in this case both are made immortal through art. Keats's point is that if there is much that is desirable in the immortality of his lovers and their eternal celebration of love and life, there is also much that is undesirable in this idealized world; not only will the lover never actually kiss his beloved (they will always remain right on the verge of touching each other's lips) but also everything that surrounds this event likewise will be frozen in time, including the abandoned village.

In the end, the poet sees the urn as a friend to humanity, but that friendship resides less in the particular truth that the urn has to teach humankind and more in the fact that the message is truth, and truth (whether joyful or painful) is beautiful. The questions of whether the permanence of art is good or bad, whether immortality is better than mortality, or whether stasis is preferable to change are all set aside in the end in favor of a statement about the lasting importance of truth—all truth—and the capacity of art to convey that truth from one generation to the next. Whether or not one agrees with Keats's poem is ultimately unimportant; what is important is that his poem discloses a truth, the great and enduring gift of art.

Summary

Although John Keats died believing that he would be forgotten by future generations of readers, he is now regarded as one of the great poets of the English language. The felicitousness of his phrasing, the sensuality of his diction, and the richness of his imagery, combined with his profound understanding of the intimate relationship between life and art, make Keats, like William Shakespeare before him, a model to those who look to poetry for an aesthetic apprehension of human experience.

Bibliography

Abrams, M. H., ed. *English Romantic Poets*. New York: Oxford University Press, 1975.

Bate, Walter Jackson. *John Keats*. Cambridge, Mass.: Harvard University Press, 1963.

Bloom, Harold. *The Visionary Company*. Rev. ed. Ithaca, N.Y.: Cornell University Press, 1971.

Bush, Douglas. *John Keats*. New York: Macmillan, 1966.

Wasserman, Earl R. *The Finer Tone*. Baltimore: The Johns Hopkins University Press, 1953.

Jack Siemsen

RUDYARD KIPLING

Born: Bombay, India
December 30, 1865
Died: London, England
January 18, 1936

Principal Literary Achievement

One of the most controversial British writers by the beginning of the twentieth century, Kipling is loved for his romantic treatment of India and hated for his imperialistic view of the Indian people.

Biography

Rudyard Kipling was born in Bombay, India, on December 30, 1865. His father, John Kipling, was a middle-class craftsman and designer who had received a post at a school of art in Bombay, probably with the help of his wife's brother-in-law, the Pre-Raphaelite painter Sir Edward Coley Burne-Jones. Kipling's mother's name was Alice Macdonald. By all reports, the young Kipling was spoiled by his parents and their Indian servants. When he was five years old, however, his parents began to fear that he was growing more Indian than English, so they brought him and his younger sister back to England, where they were boarded with a Captain Holloway and his wife, who were strangers to the Kiplings.

According to Kipling's own account, in his autobiography as well as in fictional accounts in his works, he was not happy during this period, particularly after the death of Captain Holloway. For whatever reason, Mrs. Holloway did not like him and frequently punished him for what she saw as his headstrong and spoiled behavior. Because of her Calvinist threats of hellfire and damnation, Kipling called the house in the little seaside town the House of Desolation. His life was made even more miserable by his worsening eyesight, which caused his schoolwork to suffer.

In 1878, his mother returned to England to spend some time with her children, but once again she left for India, this time leaving Kipling in the United Services College boarding school in North Devon, where he stayed until 1882. Because the school had been recently founded primarily for the sons of military officers who could not afford to send them anywhere else, however, it quickly developed a reputation for being a place for bullies and toughs, as Kipling's fictional *Stalky & Co.* (1899) makes abundantly, sometimes obnoxiously, clear.

Since the school was primarily established to get boys past the military examina-

tions rather than into Oxford or Cambridge, Kipling, an omnivorous reader but not the best of students, did not continue his education but left England at the age of seventeen to rejoin his parents in India and to take a position on the staff of an English newspaper, *The Civil and Military Gazette*, in Lahore. Kipling wrote news articles as well as topical fiction for the paper until 1887, when he was transferred to a larger paper, *The Pioneer*, in Allahabad. His job there was to edit the weekly magazine supplement, in which one of his own stories usually appeared. He published his first collection of stories written for the Lahore newspaper, *Plain Tales from the Hills*, in 1888. Also during this time, he wrote a number of other stories, such as *Wee Willie Winkie* (1888) and *The Phantom Rickshaw and Other Tales* (1888), which were published in what was called the Railway Series.

In 1889, Kipling went back to London by way of America, and the following year British magazine editors began publishing the Railway Series, which was well received. Kipling enjoyed great success and was very prolific during this London period. He published *Barrack-Room Ballads and Other Verses* (1892), a collection of poems that includes such well-known works as "Gunga Din" and "Mandalay," as well as his first novel, the autobiographical *The Light That Failed* (1890), and some of his most highly respected short stories, such as "Without Benefit of Clergy."

In 1892, Kipling married Caroline Balestier, sister of Wolcott Balestier, with whom he had collaborated on the romance *The Naulahka: A Story of East and West* (1892). When their honeymoon was cut short by the failure of Kipling's bank, they went to stay with Caroline's family in Brattleboro, Vermont, where they lived for four years and where Kipling wrote *The Jungle Book* (1894), *Captains Courageous* (1897), and the first draft of *Kim* (1901). When Kipling became involved in a bitter squabble over money with Caroline's younger brother Beatty, he had to return to England in 1896. In 1907, he became the first English writer to win the Nobel Prize in Literature.

Kipling and his family lived for five years near Rottingdean, not far from Brighton, and then moved to a mansion in rural Sussex. They spent each winter in South Africa, where Kipling met influential British political figures and became even more convinced of the god-given mission of the British to govern over "blacks" and "browns" (as the people of color were called there). After the Boer War, during which he helped edit a newspaper for the British troops, Kipling became more vocal about his imperialism and consequently more alienated from many of his compatriots, who did not share his views. After losing his son in battle during World War I, his hatred of the Germans gave rise to one of his most memorable short stories, "Mary Postgate." Suffering ill health during his final years, particularly because of an ulcer that he feared was cancer, Kipling remained the conservative reactionary until his death on January 18, 1936, in London, not long after he had turned seventy. He was buried in Poet's Corner in Westminster Abbey.

Analysis

Although Robert Louis Stevenson was the first British writer to build his career on the short-story form, Kipling was the first to stimulate a considerable amount of criticism, much of it adverse, because of his short fiction. In fact, much of the negative criticism that Kipling received is precisely the same kind of criticism that has often been lodged against the short-story form in general—for example, that it focuses only on episodes, that it is too concerned with technique, that it is too dependent on tricks, and that it often lacks a moral force.

Henry James was perhaps the first to note that the young Kipling realized very early the uniqueness of the short story, seeing what chances the form offered for "touching life in a thousand different pieces . . . each a specimen and an illustration." Yet it is just this appreciation for the episode, according to Edmund Wilson, that prevented Kipling from becoming a great novelist:

> You can make an effective short story, as Kipling so often does, about somebody's scoring off somebody else; but this is not enough for a great novelist, who must show us large social forces, or uncontrollable lines of destiny, or antagonistic impulses of the human spirit, struggling with one another.

Moreover, it is not simply because Kipling could not "graduate," as it were, to the novel that critics have found fault with him. Critic Randall Jarrell says that Kipling lacks a "dispassionate moral understanding," that his morality is too one-sided, and that he does not have the ability both to understand things and to understand that there is nothing to be done about them. Short-story writer Frank O'Connor confesses his embarrassment in discussing Kipling's stories in comparison with those of storytellers such as Anton Chekhov and Guy de Maupassant, for he believes that Kipling is too conscious of the individual reader as an audience who must be affected.

C. S. Lewis also recoiled from Kipling for similar reasons. Complaining about what he calls the excess of Kipling's art, he complains that Kipling constantly shortened and honed his stories by blotting out passages with Indian ink. Ultimately, says Lewis, the story is often shortened too much, and, as a result, "the style tends to be too continuously and obtrusively brilliant" with no "leisureliness." Similarly, Wilson says that it is the paradox of Kipling's career that he "should have extended the conquests of his craftsmanship in proportion to the shrinking of the range of his dramatic imagination. As his responses to human beings become duller, his sensitivity to his medium increased."

Such remarks either ignore or fail to take seriously the fact that the short tale practiced by Kipling is not designed to focus on character but rather on fable, on the meaning of an episode in an ideal form. Bonamy Dobrée, in one of the best-known critical efforts to revive interest in Kipling as an artist, has noted this fabular aspect of Kipling's stories, suggesting that as Kipling's mastery of the short-story form increased, he became more and more inclined to introduce an element of fable. "Great realist as he was, it is impossible to see what he was really saying unless the fabular element is at least glimpsed."

Yet the fabular element, so common to the short-story form, often is criticized as being limiting in Kipling, as indeed over the years such an element has been a central source of adverse criticism of short fiction generally. It has been suggested that while Kipling's desire to have complete control of his form and medium can lead to impressive achievements in fantasy and fable, it can also lead to a simplification and distortion. In the short story, it is the fable that is the focus; characters exist for the sake of the story. Kipling was perhaps the first English writer to embrace these characteristics of the short-story form wholeheartedly; thus, his stories are perfect representations of the transition point between the old-fashioned tale of the nineteenth century and the modern British short story.

THE STRANGE RIDE OF MORROWBIE JUKES

First published: 1885
Type of work: Short story

This work is a combination adventure story and social parable in which a man finds himself trapped in an otherworldly realm somewhere between life and death.

"The Strange Ride of Morrowbie Jukes" is based on a conventional type of gothic story popular during the early part of the nineteenth century. It is a form that Edgar Allan Poe adapted for his own use and thus made part of the foundation of the short-story form. Kipling's treatment of this genre begins with the familiar literary convention of being presented as a true story; the central character and storyteller Jukes was a civil engineer and thus not a man to take the trouble to invent imaginary tales. When Jukes's story begins, the motivation for his journey to the mysterious realm is supplied in a typically ambiguous gothic way: Jukes has a fever and is light-headed and hallucinatory. Madly chasing a dog into the desert, his horse stumbles and falls. When Jukes regains consciousness, he finds himself in a horseshoe-shaped crater of sand so steep that he cannot climb out. The only way out is across the river where the horseshoe opens out, but that way is guarded by an invisible sentry with a rifle and by a bed of quicksand.

Jukes discovers that he is not alone in the crater; a small band of ragged natives appear, one of whom he recognizes as a telegraph master, Gunga Dass. It is from Gunga Dass that he learns where he is—a sort of wasteland holding place where those who have been in a cataleptic trance are taken until they die in actuality. In existence for at least a century, the hidden village is legendary; no one ever escapes except by death. Thus, the unfortunates who end up there are examples of the "living dead," for even though they live, they are as good as dead and buried. It is part of Kipling's parable pattern that the unfortunates are primarily native Indians of the lower caste.

Much of the story centers on Jukes's helpless situation and his sense of humiliation that, although he is a Sahib, a representative of the dominant race, in this place he is like a child completely at the mercy of the natives. Ironically, it is by means of death that Jukes discovers a way to save his life. Finding the body of another Sahib who has died there before, Jukes discovers a notebook with directions for bypassing the quicksand. Although he knows that the white man was killed by Gunga Dass, he has not counted on the treachery of the Indian toward himself. Gunga Dass knocks him unconscious and leaves him there to die. Immediately thereafter, Jukes's escape, much like the escape of a character in a story by Poe, is abruptly effected when one of his servants finds him and pulls him out of his sandy trap.

On the one hand, the story seems little more than a gothic adventure story of a strange journey, a dreamlike experience with no real meaning. On the other hand, the situation of the white Sahib caught between two worlds, the world of life and the world of death, and at the mercy of Gunga Dass, has symbolic significance even though its surface plot is pure action-adventure. It turns the usual Kipling story of the white man's dominance over the brown man on its head and suggests that, in the world of the living dead, it is the scavenger who survives. Jukes does not earn his escape as Gunga Dass does, but he is pulled out of the hidden valley as if he were abruptly awakened from a bad dream.

THE MAN WHO WOULD BE KING

First published: 1888
Type of work: Short story

Two white men set themselves up as rulers of a hidden country, but their own pride brings about their downfall.

One of Kipling's most Conrad-like stories is one of his earliest pieces, "The Man Who Would Be King," which Henry James called an "extraordinary tale" and which many critics have suggested is a typical Kipling social parable about British imperialism in India. One critic, Walter Allen, calls it a "great and heroic story," but he says that Kipling evades the metaphysical issues implicit in the story and refuses to venture on the profound generalizations forced upon Conrad in *Heart of Darkness* (1902). Although "The Man Who Would Be King" does not contain the philosophic generalizations of Conrad's tale, and is perhaps not as subtle a piece of symbolist fiction, it is nonetheless a coherent piece of fabular fiction carefully constructed and thematically significant.

The secret of the story is its tone; indeed, tone and style are everything in the work. The story focuses primarily on the crucial difference between a tale told by a narrator who merely reports a story and a narrator who has lived the story he tells. The first-person, primary narrator is a journalist whose job it is to report the doings of "real kings," whereas Peachey Carnehan, the inner narrator, has as his task the reporting of the events of a "pretend king." The primary narrator (Kipling) tells the story of Peachey and Daniel Davrot, which, although it is fiction, is presented as if it were reality. The secondary narrator (Peachey) tells a story of Peachey and Davrot in which the two characters project themselves out of the "as-if" real world of the story into the purely projected and fictional world of their adventure.

The tone of the tale reflects the journalist-narrator's bemused attitude toward the pair of unlikely heroes and his incredulity about their "idiotic adventure." "The beginning of everything," he says, is his meeting with Peachey in a railway train, where he learns that the two are posing as correspondents for the newspaper for which the narrator is indeed a real correspondent. Role-playing is an important motif in the story, for indeed Peachey and Davrot are always playing roles; they are essentially vagabonds and loafers with no real identity of their own. After the narrator returns to his office and becomes "respectable," Peachey and Davrot interrupt this respectability to tell him of their fantastic plan and to try to obtain from him a factual framework for the country where they hope to become kings. "We have come to you to know about this country, to read a book about it, and to be shown maps," says Carnehan. "We want you to tell us that we are fools and to show us your books." The mythic proportions of the two men—or rather their storybook proportions, for "mythic" is too serious a word here for the grotesque adventurers—are indicated by the narrator's amused awareness that Davrot's red beard seems to fill half the room and Carnehan's huge shoulders the other half.

The actual adventure begins with more role-playing as Davrot pretends to be a mad priest (an ironic image that he indeed is to fulfill later) marching forward with whirligigs (playful crosses) to sell as charms to the savages. The narrator again becomes "respectable" and turns his attention to the obituaries of real kings in Europe until three years later, when Peachey returns, a "whining cripple," to confront the narrator with his story that he and Davrot have been crowned kings in Kafiristan, exclaiming, "you've been sitting here ever since—oh, Lord!" Peachey's inserted story thus stands in contrast to the pedestrian story of the narrator's situation and is contrasted with it by its fantastic, storylike nature in which Peachey and Davrot have indeed set themselves up as fictional kings in a real country.

The storylike nature of the adventure is indicated first of all by Peachey's frequent confusing of himself with Davrot and by his frequent reference to himself in the third person:

> There was a party called Peachey Taliaferro Carnehan that was with Davrot. Shall I tell you about him? He died out there in the cold. Slap from the bridge fell old Peachey, turning and twisting in the air like a penny whirligig.

Moreover, Peachey and Davrot often speak to the people Davrot calls the "lost tribe" in biblical language. The purpose of these biblical allusions is to give Peachey's tale an authoritative story framework, indeed the most basic and dignified story framework in Western culture. Davrot becomes king by moving from fighting to craft via masonic ritual, a ritual that reaffirms Davrot's superior position and controls his followers. Since Davrot has projected himself into the role of god as king, however, and thus assumes a position in the kingdom as the fulfillment of prophecy and legend, he is bound to this particular role. It is only when he wishes to escape the preestablished role and marry a native girl that his world falls apart. When he is bitten by his frightened intended bride, the cry of the people, "Neither God nor Devil, but a man," breaks the spell and propels Davrot and Peachey back into reality again.

The fact that Peachey and Davrot are really double figures is indicated not only by Peachey's reference to himself as suffering Davrot's fate but also by the fact that, if Davrot is the ambiguous god-man, then it is Peachey who must be crucified. Kipling finds it necessary of course to make this split, for the god-man must not only die but also be resurrected. Peachey is the resurrected figure who brings the head of Davrot, still with its crown, back to tell the tale to the narrator. Peachey's final madness and death, and the mysterious disappearance of the crowned head, are the ironic fulfillment of a final escape from external reality.

It seems clear from the seriocomic tone and the parodic use of biblical story and language that what Kipling is attempting in "The Man Who Would be King" is a burlesque version of a basic dichotomy in the nature of story itself. The narrator, who deals with real events in the world, tells a story of one who in turn tells a story of fantastic events in which the real world is transformed into the fabular nature of story. Davrot and Peachey project themselves into a purely story world, but once they are accepted there, they cannot break the code of the roles that they have assumed. When they do make such an effort, the story they have created, and thus the roles they have played, become apparent as fictional roles only and crumble like a pack of cards. The man who would be a king can be a king only in the pretend world of story itself, and then only as long as story-world or story-reality is maintained. A story character cannot be human, for when he or she attempts to become real—when the character begins to take his or her story status as true reality—the story ends. It is little wonder that "The Man Who Would be King" has such a comic tone, for truly what Kipling is playing with here is not the nature of empires but the nature of story. If one wishes to read this tale as a parable of the tenuous and fictionally imposed nature of British imperialism, then such a reading is possible, but only because the story is primarily about the essentially tenuous nature of the fable world itself.

MRS. BATHURST

First published: 1904
Type of work: Short story

Four men are baffled by the relationship between a sailor who deserts the navy and the widowed keeper of a New Zealand hotel who follows him to England.

"Mrs. Bathurst" is one of the most cryptic and puzzling of all Kipling's stories. Part of what makes the story such a mystery is the method by which it is told, for it is presented almost completely as a dialogue among four men. Furthermore, the dialogue is so clipped and cryptic that it is often difficult to follow. The principle characters are Petty Officer Pyecroft, his friend Sergeant Pritchard of the marines, the narrator, and his friend Inspector Hooper of the South African railways. Pyecroft and Pritchard tell the other two men the story about Warrant Officer Vickery, who deserted the service with only eighteen months left before his discharge, and his mysterious relationship with Mrs. Bathurst, a young widow who managed a hotel in New Zealand.

The central story of Vickery and Mrs. Bathurst is prefaced by a brief account about the officer Boy Niven, who lured a small group of sailors and marines into the woods for no other reason than for personal publicity. At the end of this inconclusive and seemingly irrelevant little tale, the conversation moves to Vickery and his mysterious desertion so close to his discharge. The first ambiguous reference to Vickery is to his nickname "Click," in reference to the four false teeth on his lower left jaw that were not set properly and thus made a clicking sound when he talked fast. At the reference to the false teeth, Inspector Hooper is meaningfully described with his hand in his waistcoat pocket, although at this point it is certainly not clear why Hooper should have Vickery's false teeth on his person.

When Mrs. Bathurst is introduced, most of the conversation is between Pyecroft, who is telling the tale, and Pritchard, who knows the lady and vouches for her kindness and integrity. He cannot believe that she is the cause of a married man and father like Vickery deserting the service. In a key phrase in the story, however, Hooper, after hearing of Mrs. Bathurst's ladylike behavior, says, "I don't see her somehow." To see Mrs. Bathurst becomes the challenge of the story. Even though both Pyecroft and Pritchard say they have seen her only once or twice, they can remember her vividly. Pyecroft says, "That's the secret. 'Tisn't beauty, so to speak, nor good talk necessarily. It's just It. Some women'll stay in a man's memory if they once walk down a street."

Kipling's puzzling story is, in some ways, about this kind of fascination, for all four of the men can remember having met one or two women of that nature, and all agree that if a man gets struck with that kind of woman, he goes crazy. What gives the story its particular turn of the screw is the "dark and bloody mystery" of Vickery's own vision of Mrs. Bathurst. Pyecroft tells of Vickery's insisting that he accompany him to a showing of an early motion picture, the cinematograph, in Cape Town, South Africa. Pyecroft knows that something strange is involved, for he says the look of Vickery's face reminded him of "those things in bottles in those herbalistic shops at Plymouth—preserved in spirits of wine. White an' crumply things—previous to birth as you might say."

What makes Pyecroft's description of the experience at the cinematograph so crucial to the story is the particular nature of early audience response to the new film technology. While watching a film, early viewers often mistook it momentarily for reality. In the particular film scene that Vickery wants Pyecroft to see, the London Mail train is shown arriving at the station and the passengers getting out "just like life." As they walk toward the camera, and thus seemingly toward the film viewers, they walk right out of the picture. Pyecroft sees Mrs. Bathurst come straight toward them, looking at them in a blind way without seeing and then melting out of the picture "like a shadow jumpin' over a candle." Vickery says, "it's the woman herself," and he urges Pyecroft to come with him to see her again the next night. For five consecutive nights, they go to see the film to watch Mrs. Bathurst make her forty-five-second walk toward them with that blind look in her eyes.

Although Pyecroft declares that Vickery is insane, he says that Vickery told him that Mrs. Bathurst was in England looking for him. Vickery tells Pyecroft that, whereas he only had to watch, "I'm it." Moreover, he tells Pyecroft to remember that he is not a murderer, that his wife died in childbirth six weeks after he left England on his last voyage. When the listeners to Pyecroft's story ask for the rest of it, he replies, "the rest is silence." All that is known for sure is that Vickery deserted and disappeared.

The story ends with the men considering the possible meaning of Vickery's experience. Hooper says, "I wonder what it was," and Pyecroft replies, "I've made my 'ead ache in that direction many a long night." Once again, when Pyecroft mentions hearing Vickery's clicking teeth, Hooper's hand goes significantly to his waistcoat pocket. It is Hooper who ends the story with a grisly little tale of his own about two tramps he saw standing by the railway in the interior. Having been struck by lightning, the two were burned to charcoal and fell to bits when Hooper touched them. The man who was standing up had the false teeth, says Hooper; the other was squatting down and watching him. Both of them fell to pieces when he touched them, Hooper explains. The story ends with Pyecroft saying that after having seen Vickery's face for five consecutive nights, he thanks God that he is dead.

Critics have long puzzled over this story, complaining that Kipling cut too much out of it and thus left it stripped of any explanatory detail. Although one knows that the standing pile of ashes is Vickery, one can only guess that the other one is Mrs. Bathurst herself, since no other character has been introduced in the story. "Mrs. Bathurst" focuses on the unexplainable mystery of human fascination, but it is the mystery of the cinema that serves as the central metaphor, for as Vickery watches the film night after night, he is in that curious situation experienced by all filmgoers of being a viewer who cannot himself be seen. Moreover, as he tells Pyecroft, he is not merely a viewer but is the missing character in the film, for he insists that Mrs. Bathurst has gone to England to find him. Instead of playing a told story over and over again, as is the usual short-story convention, the film creates the illusion of the actual event being repeated. What is so unbearable to Vickery is that Mrs. Bathurst's search for him seems to be repeated over and over again. Although it obviously took place in the past, every time he sees it, it seems to be taking place in the present. Making the story depend on dialogue rather than on narration, Kipling not only makes the cinema scene the central metaphor of the story but also makes cinema technique the means by which the story is told.

Summary

Rudyard Kipling was one of the most popular British authors at the start of the twentieth century, the most widely read author since Charles Dickens. His position as an artist, however, is not as assured as his popular success. He has been criticized for his jingoistic imperialism that smacks of later fascism, and he has been soundly criticized for being more concerned with fictional technique than with the human emotions of his characters. He has been compared, perhaps unfairly, with the great writer Joseph Conrad; both men were writing at roughly the same time. Although there are surface similarities between the two, in that both focus on strange and exotic realms either at sea or on other continents, Conrad, with his ambiguities and subtleties and his profound exploration of human evil and isolation, seems a true symbolist genius, whereas Kipling often seems merely a good storyteller.

To take a negative approach to the work of Kipling because he is a storyteller rather than a philosophic novelist, however, is to be guilty of the pervasive bias against short fiction as not being as important as the novel. A large number of Kipling's stories, such as "Without Benefit of Clergy," "Mary Postgate," "The Gardener," and "Baa Baa, Black Sheep," as well as "Mrs. Bathurst" and "The Man Who Would Be King," are significant transition works that signal the beginnings of the modern short story.

Bibliography

Carrington, Charles. *The Life of Rudyard Kipling*. Garden City, N.Y.: Doubleday, 1955.

Dobrée, Bonamy. *Rudyard Kipling: Realist and Fabulist*. London: Oxford University Press, 1972.

Gilbert, Elliot L. *The Good Kipling*. Athens: Ohio University Press, 1972.

_____, ed. *Kipling and the Critics*. New York: New York University Press, 1965.

Rutherford, Angus, ed. *Kipling's Mind and Art*. Stanford, Calif.: Stanford University Press, 1964.

Stewart, J. I. M. *Rudyard Kipling*. New York: Dodd, Mead, 1966.

Tomkins, J. M. S. *The Art of Rudyard Kipling*. London: Methuen, 1959.

Wilson, Angus. *The Strange Ride of Rudyard Kipling*. New York: Viking Press, 1978.

Charles E. May

MAGILL'S
SURVEY
OF
WORLD
LITERATURE

GLOSSARY

Aesthetics: The branch of philosophy that studies the beautiful in nature and art, including how beauty is recognized in a work of art and how people respond to it. In literature, the aesthetic approach can be distinguished from the moral or utilitarian approach; it was most fully embodied in the movement known as aestheticism in the late nineteenth century.

Alienation: The German dramatist Bertolt Brecht developed the theory of alienation in his epic theater. Brecht sought to create an audience that was intellectually alert rather than emotionally involved in a play by using alienating techniques such as minimizing the illusion of reality onstage and interrupting the action with songs and visual aids.

Allegory: A literary mode in which characters in a narrative personify abstract ideas or qualities and so give a second level of meaning to the work, in addition to the surface narrative. Two famous examples of allegory are Edmund Spenser's *The Faerie Queene* (1590, 1596) and John Bunyan's *The Pilgrim's Progress* (1678). For modern examples, see the stories and novels of Franz Kafka.

Alliteration: A poetic technique in which consonant repetition is focused at the beginning of syllables, as in "Large mannered motions of his mythy mind." Alliteration is used when the poet wishes to focus on the details of a sequence of words and to show the relationships between words in a line.

Angry young men: The term used to describe a group of English novelists and playwrights in the 1950's and 1960's, whose work stridently attacked what it saw as the outmoded political and social structures (particularly the class structure) of post-World War II Britain. John Osborne's play *Look Back in Anger* (1956) and Kingsley Amis' *Lucky Jim* (1954) are typical examples.

Angst: A pervasive feeling of anxiety and depression often associated with the moral and spiritual uncertainties of the twentieth century, as expressed in the existentialism of writers such as Jean-Paul Sartre and Albert Camus.

Antagonist: A character in fiction who stands in opposition or rivalry to the protagonist. In William Shakespeare's *Hamlet* (c. 1600-1601), for example, King Claudius is the antagonist of Hamlet.

Anthropomorphism: The ascription of human characteristics and feelings to animals, inanimate objects, or gods. The gods of Homer's epics are anthropomorphic, for example. Anthropomorphism occurs in beast fables, such as George Orwell's *Animal Farm* (1945). The term "pathetic fallacy" carries the same meaning: Natural objects are invested with human feelings. *See also* Pathetic fallacy.

Antihero: A modern fictional figure who tries to define himself and establish his own codes, or a protagonist who simply lacks traditional heroic qualities, such as Jim Dixon in Kingsley Amis' *Lucky Jim* (1954).

Aphorism: A short, concise statement that states an opinion, precept, or general truth, such as Alexander Pope's "Hope springs eternal in the human breast."

Apostrophe: A direct address to a person (usually absent), inanimate entity, or abstract quality.

Archetype: The term was used by psychologist Carl Jung to describe what he called "primordial images" that exist in the "collective unconscious" of humankind and are manifested in myths, religion, literature, and dreams. Now used broadly in literary criticism to refer to character types, motifs, images, symbols, and plot patterns recurring in many different literary forms and works. The embodiment of archetypes in a work of literature can make a powerful impression on the reader.

Aristotelian unities: A set of rules for proper dramatic construction formulated by Italian and French critics during the Renaissance, purported to be derived from the *De poetica* (c. 334-323 B.C.; *Poetics*) of Aristotle. According to the "three unities," a play should have no scenes irrelevant to the main action, should not cover a period of more than twenty-four hours, and should not occur in more than one place or locale. In fact, Aristotle insists only on unity of action in a tragedy.

Assonance: A term for the association of words with identical vowel sounds but different consonants: "stars," "arms," and "park," for example, all contain identical *a* (and *ar*) sounds.

***Auto sacramental*:** A Renaissance development of the medieval open-air Corpus Christi pageant in Spain. A dramatic, allegorical depiction of a sinful soul wavering and transgressing until the intervention of Divine Grace restores order. During a period of prohibition of all secular drama in Spain, from 1598 to 1600, even Lope de Vega Carpio adopted this form.

Autobiography: A form of nonfiction writing in which the author narrates events of his or her own life. Autobiography differs from memoir in that the latter focuses on prominent people the author has known and great events that he has witnessed, rather than on his own life.

Ballad: Popular ballads are songs or verse that tell dramatic, usually impersonal, tales. Supernatural events, courage, and love are frequent themes, but any experience that appeals to ordinary people is acceptable material. Literary ballads—narrative poems based on the popular ballads—have frequently been in vogue in English literature, particularly during the Romantic period. One of the most famous is Samuel Taylor Coleridge's *The Rime of the Ancient Mariner* (1798).

Baroque: The term was first used in the eighteenth century to describe an elaborate and grandiose type of architecture. It is now also used to refer to certain stylistic features of Metaphysical poetry, particularly the poetry of Richard Crashaw. The term can also refer to post-Renaissance literature, 1580-1680.

***Bildungsroman*:** Sometimes called the "novel of education," or "apprenticeship novel," the *Bildungsroman* focuses on the growth of a young protagonist who is learning about the world and finding his place in life; a typical example is James Joyce's *A Portrait of the Artist as a Young Man* (1916).

GLOSSARY

Blank verse: A term for unrhymed iambic pentameter, blank verse first appeared in drama in Thomas Norton and Thomas Sackville's *Gorboduc*, performed in 1561, and later became the standard form of Elizabethan drama. It has also commonly been used in long narrative or philosophical poems, such as John Milton's *Paradise Lost* (1667, 1674).

Bourgeois novel: A novel in which the values, the preoccupations, and the accoutrements of middle-class or bourgeois life are given particular prominence. The heyday of the genre was the nineteenth century, when novelists as varied as Jane Austen, Honoré de Balzac, and Anthony Trollope both criticized and unreflectingly transmitted the assumptions of the rising middle class.

Burlesque: A work that by imitating attitudes, styles, institutions, and people aims to amuse. Burlesque differs from satire in that it aims to ridicule simply for the sake of amusement rather than for political or social change.

Capa y espada: Spanish for "cloak and sword." A term referring to the Spanish theater of the sixteenth and seventeenth centuries dealing with love and intrigue among the aristocracy. The greatest practitioners were Lope de Vega Carpio and Pedro Calderón de la Barca. The term *comedia de ingenio* is also used.

Catharsis: A term from Aristotle's *De poetica* (c. 334-323 B.C.; *Poetics*) referring to the purgation of the emotions of pity and fear in the spectator aroused by the actions of the tragic hero. The meaning and the operation of the concept have been a source of great, and unresolved, critical debate.

Celtic romance: Gaelic Celts invaded Ireland in about 350 B.C.; their epic stories and romances date from this period until about A.D. 450. The romances are marked by a strong sense of the Otherworld and of supernatural happenings. The Celtic romance tradition influenced the poetry of William Butler Yeats.

Celtic Twilight: Sometimes used synonymously with the term Irish Renaissance, which was a movement beginning in the late nineteenth century which attempted to build a national literature by drawing on Ireland's literary and cultural history. The term, however, which is taken from a book by William Butler Yeats titled *The Celtic Twilight* (1893), sometimes has a negative connotation. It is used to refer to some early volumes by Yeats, which have been called self-indulgent. The poet Algernon Charles Swinburne said that the Celtic Twilight manner "puts fever and fancy in the place of reason and imagination."

Chamber plays: Refers to four plays written in 1907 by the Swedish dramatist August Strindberg. The plays are modeled on the form of chamber music, consisting of motif and variations, to evoke a mood or atmosphere (in these cases, a very sombre one). There is no protagonist but a small group of equally important characters.

Character: A personage appearing in any literary or dramatic work. Characters can be presented with the depth and complexity of real people (sometimes called "round" characters) or as stylized functions of the plot ("flat" characters).

Chorus: Originally a group of singers and dancers in religious festivals, the chorus evolved into the dramatic element that reflected the opinions of the masses or commented on the action in Greek drama. In its most developed form, the chorus consisted of fifteen members: seven reciting the strophe, seven reciting the antistrophe, and the leader interacting with the actors. The chorus has been used in all periods of drama, including the modern period.

Classicism: A literary stance or value system consciously based on the example of classical Greek and Roman literature. While the term is applied to an enormous diversity of artists in many different periods and in many different national literatures, it generally denotes a cluster of values including formal discipline, restrained expression, reverence of tradition, and an objective, rather than subjective, orientation. Often contrasted with Romanticism. *See also* Romanticism.

***Comédie-Française*:** The first state theater of France, composed of the company of actors established by Molière in 1658. The company took the name *Comédie-Française* in 1680. Today, it is officially known as the *Theatre Français* (*Salle Richelieu*).

Comedy: Generally, a lighter form of drama (as contrasted with tragedy) that aims chiefly to amuse and ends happily. The comic effect typically arises from the recognition of some incongruity of speech, action, or character development. The comic range extends from coarse, physical humor (called low comedy) to a more subtle, intellectual humor (called high comedy).

Comedy of manners: A form of comedy that arose during the seventeenth century, dealing with the intrigues (particularly the amorous intrigues) of sophisticated, witty members of the upper classes. The appeal of these plays is primarily intellectual, depending as they do on quick-witted dialogue and clever language. For examples, see the plays of Restoration dramatists William Congreve, Sir George Etherege, and William Wycherley. *See also* Restoration comedy/drama.

***Commedia dell'arte*:** Dramatic comedy performed by troupes of professional actors, which became popular in the mid-sixteenth century in Italy. The troupes were rather small, consisting of perhaps a dozen actors who performed stock roles in mask and improvised on skeletal scenarios. The tradition of the *commedia*, or masked comedy, was influential into the seventeenth century and still exerts some influence.

Conceit: A type of metaphor, the conceit is used for comparisons that are highly intellectualized. When T. S. Eliot, for example, says that winding streets are like a tedious argument of insidious intent, there is no clear connection between the two, so the reader must apply abstract logic to fill in the missing links.

Conversation poem: Conversation poems are chiefly associated with the poetry of Samuel Taylor Coleridge. These poems all display a relaxed, informal style, quiet settings, and a circular structure—the poem returns to where it began, after an intervening meditation has yielded some insight into the speaker's situation.

Cubism: A term borrowed from Cubist painters. In literature, cubism is a style of poetry, such as that of E. E. Cummings, Kenneth Rexroth, and Archibald MacLeish, which first fragments an experience, then rearranges its elements into some new artistic entity.

Dactyl: The dactylic foot, or dactyl, is formed of a stress followed by two unstressed syllables, as in the words "Washington" and "manikin." "After the pangs of a desperate lover" is an example of a dactylic line.

Dadaism: Dadaism arose in France during World War I as a radical protest in art and literature against traditional institutions and values. Part of its strategy was the use of infantile, nonsensical language. After World War I, when Dadaism was combined with the ideas of Sigmund Freud, it gave rise to the Surrealist movement.

Decadence: The period of decline that heralds the ending of a great age. The period in English dramatic history immediately following William Shakespeare is said to be decadent, and the term "Decadents" is applied to a group of late-nineteenth and early twentieth century writers who searched for new literary and artistic forms as the Victorian Age came to a close.

Detective story: The "classic" detective story (or "mystery") is a highly formalized and logically structured mode of fiction in which the focus is on a crime solved by a detective through interpretation of evidence and clever reasoning. Many modern practitioners of the genre, however, such as Raymond Chandler, Patricia Highsmith, and Ross Macdonald, have placed less emphasis on the puzzlelike qualities of the detective story and have focused instead on characterization, theme, and other elements of mainstream fiction. The form was first developed in short fiction by Edgar Allan Poe; Jorge Luis Borges has also used the convention in short stories.

Dialectic: A philosophical term meaning the art of examining opinions or ideas logically. The dialectic method of Georg Wilhelm Friedrich Hegel and Karl Marx was based on a contradiction of opposites (thesis and antithesis) and their resolution (synthesis). In literary criticism, the term has sometimes been used by Marxist critics to refer to the structure and dynamics of a literary work in its sociological context.

Dialogue: Speech exchanged between characters, or even, in a looser sense, the thoughts of a single character. Dialogue serves to characterize, to further the plot, to establish conflict, and to express thematic ideas.

***Doppelgänger*:** A double or counterpart of a person, sometimes endowed with ghostly qualities. A fictional *Doppelgänger* often reflects a suppressed side of his personality, as in Fyodor Dostoevski's novella *Dvoynik* (1846; *The Double*, 1917) and the short stories of E. T. A. Hoffmann. Isaac Bashevis Singer and Jorge Luis Borges, among other modern writers, have also employed the *Doppelgänger* with striking effect.

Drama: Generally speaking, any work designed to be represented on a stage by actors (Aristotle defined drama as "the imitation of an action"). More specifically, the term has come to signify a play of a serious nature and intent that may end either happily (comedy) or unhappily (tragedy).

Dramatic irony: A situation in a play or a narrative in which the audience knows something that the character does not. The irony lies in the different meaning that the character's words or actions have for himself and for the audience. A common device in classical Greek drama. Sophocles' *Oidipous Tyrannos* (429 B.C.; *Oedipus Tyrannus*) is an example of extended dramatic irony.

Dramatic monologue: In dramatic monologue, the narrator addresses a persona who never speaks but whose presence greatly influences what the narrator tells the reader. The principal reason for writing in dramatic monologue is to control the speech of the major persona by the implied reaction of the silent one. The effect is one of continuing change and often surprise. The technique is especially useful for revealing characters slowly and for involving the reader as another silent participant.

Dramatic verse: Poetry that employs dramatic form or technique, such as dialogue or conflict, to achieve its effects. The term is used to refer to dramatic monologue, drama written in verse, and closet dramas.

Dramatis personae: The characters in a play. Often, a printed listing defining the characters and specifying their relationships.

Dream vision: An allegorical form common in the Middle Ages, in which the narrator or a character falls asleep and dreams a dream that becomes the actual framed story.

Dystopian/Utopian novel: A dystopian novel takes some existing trend or theory in present-day society and extends it into a fictional world of the future, where the trend has become more fully manifested, with unpleasant results. Aldous Huxley's *Brave New World* (1932) is an example. The utopian novel is the opposite: It presents an ideal society. The first utopian novel was Sir Thomas More's *Utopia* (1516).

Elegy: A long, rhymed, formal poem whose subject is meditation upon death or a lamentable theme. The pastoral elegy uses a pastoral scene to express grief at the loss of a friend or important person. *See also* Pastoral.

Elizabethan Age: Of or referring to the reign of Queen Elizabeth I of England, lasting from 1558 to 1603, a period of important developments and achievements in the arts in England, particularly in poetry and drama. The era included such literary figures as Edmund Spenser, Christopher Marlowe, William Shakespeare, and Ben Jonson. Sometimes referred to as the English Renaissance.

English novel: The first fully realized English novel was Samuel Richardson's *Pamela* (1740-1741). The genre took firm hold in the second half of the eighteenth century, with the work of Daniel Defoe, Henry Fielding, and Tobias Smollett, and reached its full flowering in the nineteenth century, in which great novelists such as Jane Austen, Charles Dickens, William Makepeace Thackeray, Anthony

Trollope, Thomas Hardy, and George Eliot produced sweeping portraits of the whole range of English life in the period.

Enlightenment: A period in Western European cultural history that began in the seventeenth century and culminated in the eighteenth. The chief characteristic of Enlightenment thinkers was their belief in the virtue of human reason, which they believed was banishing former superstitious and ignorant ways and leading to an ideal condition of human life. The Enlightenment coincides with the rise of the scientific method.

Epic: Although this term usually refers to a long narrative poem that presents the exploits of a central figure of high position, the term is also used to designate a long novel that has the style or structure usually associated with an epic. In this sense, for example, Herman Melville's *Moby Dick* (1851) and James Joyce's *Ulysses* (1922) may be called epics.

Epigram: Originally meaning an inscription, an epigram is a short, pointed poem, often expressing humor and satire. In English literature, the form flourished from the Renaissance through the eighteenth century, in the work of poets such as John Donne, Ben Jonson, and Alexander Pope. The term also refers to a concise and witty expression in prose, as in the plays of Oscar Wilde.

Epiphany: Literally, an epiphany is an appearance of a god or supernatural being. The term is used in literary criticism to signify any moment of heightened awareness, or flash of transcendental insight, when an ordinary object or scene is suddenly transformed into something that possesses eternal significance. Especially noteworthy examples are found in the works of James Joyce.

Epistle: The word means "letter," but epistle is used to refer to a literary form rather than a private composition, usually written in dignified style and addressed to a group. The most famous examples are the epistles in the New Testament.

Epistolary novel: A work of fiction in which the narrative is carried forward by means of letters written by the characters. Epistolary novels were especially popular in the eighteenth century. Examples include Samuel Richardson's *Pamela* (1740-1741) and *Clarissa* (1747-1748).

Epithet: An adjective or adjectival phrase that expresses a special characteristic of a person or thing. "Hideous night," "devouring time," and "sweet silent thought" are epithets that appear in William Shakespeare's sonnets.

Essay: A brief prose work, usually on a single topic, that expresses the personal point of view of the author. The essay is usually addressed to a general audience and attempts to persuade the reader to accept the author's ideas.

Everyman: The central character in the work by the same name, the most famous of the English medieval morality plays. It tells of how Everyman is summoned by Death and of the parts played in his journey by characters named Fellowship, Cousin, Kindred, Goods, Knowledge, Confession, Beauty, Strength, Discretion, Five Wits, and Good Deeds. Everyman has proved lastingly popular; there have been many productions even in the twentieth century. More generally, the term means the typical, ordinary person.

Existentialism: A philosophy or attitude of mind that has gained wide currency in religious and artistic thought since the end of World War II. Typical concerns of existential writers are humankind's estrangement from society, its awareness that the world is meaningless, and its recognition that one must turn from external props to the self. The works of Jean-Paul Sartre and Franz Kafka provide examples of existentialist beliefs.

Experimental novel: The term is associated with novelists such as Dorothy Richardson, Virginia Woolf, and James Joyce in England, who experimented with the form of the novel, using in particular the stream-of-consciousness technique.

Expressionism: Beginning in German theater at the start of the twentieth century, expressionism became the dominant movement in the decade following World War I. It abandoned realism and relied on a conscious distortion of external reality in order to portray the world as it is "viewed emotionally." The movement spread to fiction and poetry. Expressionism influenced the novels of Franz Kafka and James Joyce.

Fable: One of the oldest narrative forms, usually taking the form of an analogy in which animals or inanimate objects speak to illustrate a moral lesson. The most famous examples are the fables of Aesop, who used the form orally in 600 B.C.

Fabliau: A short narrative poem, popular in medieval French literature and during the English Middle Ages. Fabliaux were usually realistic in subject matter and bawdy; they made a point of satirizing the weaknesses and foibles of human beings. Perhaps the most famous are Geoffrey Chaucer's "The Miller's Tale" and "The Reeve's Tale."

Fairy tale: A form of folktale in which supernatural events or characters are prominent. Fairy tales usually depict a realm of reality beyond that of the natural world in which the laws of the natural world are suspended.

Fantasy: A literary form that makes a deliberate break with reality. Fantasy literature may use supernatural or fairy-tale events in which the ordinary commonsense laws of the everyday world do not operate. The setting may be unreal. J. R. R. Tolkien's fantasy trilogy, *The Lord of the Rings* (1955), is one of the best-known examples of the genre.

Farce: From the Latin *farcire*, meaning "to stuff." Originally an insertion into established Church liturgy in the Middle Ages, farce later became the term for specifically comic scenes inserted into early liturgical drama. The term has come to refer to any play that evokes laughter by such low-comedy devices as physical humor, rough wit, and ridiculous and improbable situations and characters.

Femme fatale: The "fatal woman" is an archetype that appears in myth, folklore, religion, and literature. Often she is presented as a temptress or a witch who ensnares, and attempts to destroy, her male victim. A very common figure in Romanticism, the fatal woman often appears in twentieth century American literature.

Figurative language: Any use of language that departs from the usual or ordinary meaning to gain a poetic or otherwise special effect. Figurative language embodies various figures of speech, such as irony, metaphor, simile.

First person: A point of view in which the narrator of a story or poem addresses the reader directly, often using the pronoun "I," thereby allowing the reader direct access to the narrator's thoughts.

Folklore: The traditions, customs, and beliefs of a people expressed in nonliterary form. Folklore includes myths, legends, fairy tales, riddles, proverbs, charms, spells, and ballads and is usually transmitted through word of mouth. Many literary works contain motifs that can be traced to folklore.

Foreshadowing: A device used to create suspense or dramatic irony by indicating through suggestion what will take place in the future. The aim is to prepare the reader for the action that follows.

Frame story: A story that provides a framework for another story (or stories) told within it. The form is ancient and is used by Geoffrey Chaucer in *The Canterbury Tales* (1387-1400). In modern literature, the technique has been used by Henry James in *The Turn of the Screw* (1898), Joseph Conrad in *Heart of Darkness* (serial, 1899; book, 1902), and John Barth in *Lost in the Funhouse* (1968).

Free verse: Verse that does not conform to any traditional convention, such as meter, rhyme, or form. All poetry must have some pattern of some kind, however, and there is rhythm in free verse, but it does not follow the strict rules of meter. Often the pattern relies on repetition and parallel construction.

Genre: A type or category of literature, such as tragedy, novel, memoir, poem, or essay; a genre has a particular set of conventions and expectations.

German Romanticism: Germany was the first European country in which the Romantic movement took firm grip. Poets Novalis and Ludwig Tieck, philosopher Friedrich Wilhelm Joseph Schelling, and literary theorists Friedrich and August Wilhelm Schlegel were well established in Jena from about 1797, and they were followed, in the second decade of the nineteenth century, by the Heidelberg group, including novelist and short-story writer E. T. A. Hoffmann and poet Heinrich Heine.

Gnomic: Aphoristic poetry, such as the wisdom literature of the Bible, which deals with ethical questions. The term "gnomic poets" is applied to a group of Greek poets of the sixth and seventh century B.C.

Gothic novel: A form of fiction developed in the late eighteenth century that focuses on horror and the supernatural. An example is Mary Shelley's *Frankenstein* (1818). In modern literature, the gothic genre can be found in the fiction of Truman Capote.

Grand Tour: Fashionable during the eighteenth century in England, the Grand Tour was a two- to three-year journey through Europe during which the young aristocracy and prosperous, educated middle classes of England deepened their knowledge of the origins and centers of Western civilization. The tour took a standard route; Rome and Naples were usually considered the highlights.

Grotesque: Characterized by a breakup of the everyday world by mysterious forces, the form differs from fantasy in that the reader is not sure whether to react with humor or with horror. Examples include the stories of E. T. A. Hoffmann and Franz Kafka.

Hagiography: Strictly defined, hagiography refers to the lives of the saints (the Greek word *hagios* means "sacred"), but the term is also used in a more popular sense, to describe any biography that grossly overpraises its subject and ignores his or her faults.

Heroic couplet: A pair of rhyming iambic pentameter lines traditionally used in epic poetry; heroic couplet often serves as a self-contained witticism or pithy observation.

Historical fiction: A novel that depicts past historical events, usually public in nature, and that features real, as well as fictional, people. Sir Walter Scott's Waverley novels established the basic type, but the relationship between fiction and history in the form varies greatly depending on the practitioner.

Hubris: Greek term for "insolence" or "pride," the characteristic or emotion in the tragic hero of ancient Greek drama that causes the reversal of his fortune, leading him to transgress moral codes or ignore warnings.

Humanism: A human-centered, rather than God-centered, view of the universe. In the Renaissance, Humanism devoted itself to the revival of classical culture. A reaction against medieval Scholasticism, Humanism oriented itself toward secular concerns and applied classical ideas to theology, government, literature, and education. In literature, the main virtues were seen to be restraint, form, and imitation of the classics. *See also* Renaissance.

Iambic pentameter: A metrical line consisting of five feet, each foot consisting of one unstressed syllable followed by one stressed syllable: "So long as men can breathe or eyes can see." Iambic pentameter is one of the commonest forms of English poetry.

Imagery: Often defined as the verbal stimulation of sensory perception. Although the word betrays a visual bias, imagery, in fact, calls on all five senses. In its simplest form, imagery re-creates a physical sensation in a clear, literal manner; it becomes more complex when a poet employs metaphor and other figures of speech to re-create experience.

Impressionism: A late nineteenth century movement composed of a group of painters including Paul Cézanne, Édouard Manet, Claude Monet, and Pierre-Auguste Renoir, who aimed in their work to suggest the impression made on the artist by a scene rather than to reproduce it objectively. The term has also been applied to French Symbolist poets such as Paul Verlaine and Stéphane Mallarmé, and to writers who use the stream-of-consciousness technique, such as James Joyce and Virginia Woolf.

Irony: Recognition of the difference between real and apparent meaning. Verbal irony is a rhetorical trope wherein *x* is uttered and "not *x*" is meant. In the New Criticism, irony, the poet's recognition of incongruities, was thought to be the master trope in that it was essential to the production of paradox, complexity, and ambiguity.

Jacobean: Of or pertaining to the reign of James I of England, who ruled from 1603 to 1623, the period immediately following the death of Elizabeth I, which saw tremendous literary activity in poetry and drama. Many writers who achieved fame during the Elizabethan Age, such as William Shakespeare, Ben Jonson, and John Donne, were still active. Other dramatists, such as John Webster and Cyril Tourneur, achieved success almost entirely during the Jacobean era.

Jungian psychoanalysis: Refers to the analytical psychology of the Swiss psychiatrist Carl Jung. Jung's significance for literature is that, through his concept of the collective unconscious, he identified many archetypes and archetypal patterns that recur in myth, fairy tale, and literature and are also experienced in dreams.

Kafkaesque: Refers to any grotesque or nightmare world in which an isolated individual, surrounded by an unfeeling and alien world, feels himself to be caught up in an endless maze that is dragging him down to destruction. The term is a reference to the works of Austrian novelist and short-story writer Franz Kafka.

Leitmotif: From the German, meaning "leading motif." Any repetition—of a word, phrase, situation, or idea—that occurs within a single work or group of related works.

Limerick: A comic five-line poem employing an anapestic base and rhyming *aabba*, in which the third and fourth lines are shorter (usually five syllables each) than the first, second, and last lines, which are usually eight syllables each.

Linear plot: A plot that has unity of action and proceeds from beginning to middle to end without flashbacks or subplots, thus satisfying Aristotle's criterion that a plot should be a continuous sequence.

Literary criticism: The study and evaluation of works of literature. Theoretical criticism sets forth general principles for interpretation. Practical criticism offers interpretations of particular works or authors.

Lyric poetry: Lyric poetry developed when music was accompanied by words, and although the "lyrics" were later separated from the music, the characteristics of lyric poetry have been shaped by the constraints of music. Lyric poems are short, more adaptable to metrical variation, and usually personal compared with the cultural functions of narrative poetry. Lyric poetry sings of the self; it explores deeply personal feelings about life.

Magical Realism: Imaginary or fantastic scenes and occurrences presented in a meticulously realistic style. The term has been applied to the fiction of Gabriel

García Márquez, Jorge Luis Borges, Günter Grass, John Fowles, and Salman Rushdie.

Masque: A courtly entertainment popular during the first half of the seventeenth century in England. It was a sumptuous spectacle including music, dance, and lavish costumes and scenery. Masques often dealt with mythological or pastoral subjects, and the dramatic action often took second place to pure spectacle.

Melodrama: Originally a drama with music (*melos* is Greek for "song"). By the early nineteenth century, it had come to mean a play in which characters are clearly either virtuous or evil and are pitted against one another in suspenseful, often sensational situations. The term took on a pejorative meaning, which it retains: any dramatic work characterized by stereotyped characters and sensational, improbable situations.

Metafiction: Refers to fiction that manifests a reflexive tendency, such as Vladimir Nabokov's *Pale Fire* (1962), and John Fowles's *The French Lieutenant's Woman* (1969). The emphasis is on the loosening of the work's illusion of reality to expose the reality of its illusion. Such terms as "irrealism," "postmodernist fiction," and "antifiction" are also used to refer to this type of fiction. *See also* Postmodernism.

Metaphor: A figure of speech in which two dissimilar objects are imaginatively identified (rather than merely compared) on the assumption that they share one or more qualities. The term is often used in modern criticism in a wider sense, to identify analogies of all kinds in literature, painting, and film.

Metaphysical poetry: A type of poetry that stresses the intellectual over the emotional; it is marked by irony, paradox, and striking comparisons of dissimilar things, the latter frequently being farfetched to the point of eccentricity. Usually used to designate a group of seventeenth century English poets, including John Donne, George Herbert, Andrew Marvell, and Thomas Traherne.

Meter: Meter is the pattern of language when it is forced into a line of poetry. All language has rhythm, but when that rhythm is organized and regulated in the line so as to affect the meaning and emotional response to the words, then the rhythm has been refined into meter. The meter is determined by the number of syllables in a line and by the relationship between them.

Mock epic: A literary form that burlesques the epic by taking a trivial subject and treating it in a grand style, using all the conventions of epic, such as invocation to the deity, long and boastful speeches of the heroes, and supernatural machinery. Alexander Pope's *The Rape of the Lock* (1712, 1714) is probably the finest example in English literature. The term is synonymous with mock heroic. *See also* Mock hero.

Mock hero: The hero of a mock epic. *See also* Mock epic.

Modernism: A term used to describe the characteristic aspects of literature and art between World War I and World War II. Influenced by Friedrich Nietzsche, Karl Marx, and Sigmund Freud, modernism embodied a lack of faith in Western civilization and culture. In poetry, fragmentation, discontinuity, and irony were common; in fiction, chronological disruption, linguistic innovation, and the stream-of-consciousness technique; in theater, expressionism and Surrealism.

Morality play: A dramatic form in the late Middle Ages and the Renaissance containing allegorical figures (most often virtues and vices) that are typically involved in the struggle over a person's soul. The anonymously written *Everyman* (1508) is one of the most famous medieval examples of this form.

Motif: An incident, situation, or device that occurs frequently in literature. Motif can also refer to particular words, images, and phrases that are repeated frequently in a single work. In this sense, motif is the same as leitmotif. Motif is similar to theme, although the latter is usually more abstract.

Myth: An anonymous traditional story, often involving supernatural beings, or the interaction between gods and humans, and dealing with the basic questions of how the world and human society came to be. Myth is an important term in contemporary literary criticism. The critic Northrop Frye, for example, has said that "the typical forms of myth become the conventions and genres of literature." He means that the genres of comedy, romance, tragedy, and irony (satire) correspond to seasonal myths of spring, summer, autumn, and winter.

Narrative: An account in prose or verse of an event or series of events, whether real or imagined.

Narrator: The character who recounts the narrative. There are many different types of narrator. The first-person narrator is a character in the story and can be recognized by his use of "I"; third-person narrators may be limited or omniscient. In the former, the narrator confines himself to knowledge of the minds and emotions of one or at most a few characters. In the latter, the narrator knows everything, seeing into the minds of all the characters. Rarely, second-person narration may be used (an example can be found in Edna O'Brien's *A Pagan Place*, published in 1970).

Naturalism: The application of the principles of scientific determinism to fiction. Although it usually refers more to the choice of subject matter than to technical conventions, conventions associated with the movement center on the author's attempt to be precise and objective in description and detail, regardless of whether the events described are sordid or shocking. Naturalism flourished in England, France, and America in the late nineteenth and early twentieth centuries.

Neoclassicism: A term used to describe the classicism that dominated English literature from the Restoration to the late eighteenth century. Modeling itself on the literature of ancient Greece and Rome, neoclassicism exalted the virtues of proportion, unity, harmony, grace, decorum, taste, manners, and restraint. It valued realism and reason over imagination and emotion. *See also* Rationalism, Realism.

Neorealism: A movement in modern Italian literature, extending from about 1930 to 1955. Neorealism was shaped by opposition to Fascism, and by World War II and the Resistance. Neorealist literature therefore exhibited a strong concern with social issues and was marked by pessimism regarding the human condition. Its practitioners sought to overcome the gap between literature and the masses, and its subject matter was frequently drawn from lower-class life. Neorealism is associated preeminently with the work of Italo Calvino.

Nonsense literature/verse: Nonsense verse, such as that written by Edward Lear and Lewis Carroll, makes use of invented words that have no meaning, portmanteau words, and so-called macaroni verse, in which words from different languages are mingled. The verse holds the attention because of its strong rhythms, appealing sounds, and, occasionally, the mysterious atmosphere that it creates.

Novel of education: See *Bildungsroman.*

Novel of ideas: A novel in which the characters, plot, and dialogue serve to develop some controlling idea or to present the clash of ideas. Aldous Huxley's *Eyeless in Gaza* (1936) is a good example.

Novel of manners: The classic example of the form might be the novels of Jane Austen, wherein the customs and conventions of a social group of a particular time and place are realistically, and often satirically, portrayed.

Novella: An Italian term meaning "a little new thing" that now refers to that form of fiction longer than a short story and shorter than a novel.

Objective correlative: A key concept in modern formalist criticism, coined by T. S. Eliot in *The Sacred Wood* (1920). An objective correlative is a situation, an event, or an object that, when presented or described in a literary work, expresses a particular emotion and serves as a precise formula by which the same emotion can be evoked in the reader.

Ode: The ode is a lyric poem that treats a unified subject with elevated emotion, usually ending with a satisfactory resolution. There is no set form for the ode, but it must be long enough to build intense emotional response. Often the ode will address itself to some omnipotent source and will assume a spiritual hue.

Oxford Movement: A reform movement in the Church of England that began in 1833, led by John Henry (later Cardinal) Newman. The Oxford Movement aimed to combat liberalism and the decline of the role of faith in the Church and to restore it to its former ideals. It was attacked for advocating what some saw as Catholic doctrines; as a result, Newman left the Church of England and became a Roman Catholic in 1845.

Panegyric: A formal speech or writing in praise of a particular person or achievement; a eulogy. The form dates back to classical times; the term is now often used in a derogatory sense.

Parable: A short, simple, and usually allegorical story that teaches a moral lesson. In the West, the most famous parables are those told in the Gospels by Christ.

Parody: A literary work that imitates or burlesques another work or author, for

GLOSSARY

the purpose of ridicule. Twentieth century parodists include E. B. White and James Thurber.

Pastoral: The term derives from the Latin "pastor," meaning "shepherd." Pastoral is a literary mode that depicts the country life in an idealized way; it originated in classical literature and was a popular form in English literature from 1550 to 1750. Notable pastoral poems include John Milton's "Lycidas" and Percy Bysshe Shelley's *Adonais.*

Pathetic fallacy: The ascribing of human characteristics or feelings to inanimate objects. The term was coined by John Ruskin in 1856, who disapproved of it, but it is now used without any pejorative sense.

Persona: *Persona* means literally "mask": It is the self created by the author and through whom the narrative is told. The persona is not to be identified with the author, even when the two may seem to resemble each other. The narrative persona in Lord Byron's *Don Juan* (1819-1824, 1826), for example, may express many sentiments of which Byron would have approved, but he is nonetheless a fictional creation who is distinct from the author.

Personification: A figure of speech that ascribes human qualities to abstractions or inanimate objects.

Petrarchan sonnet: Named after Petrarch, a fourteenth century Italian poet, who perfected the form, which is also known as the Italian sonnet. It is divided into an octave, in which the subject matter, which may be a problem, a doubt, a reflection, or some other issue, is raised and elaborated, and a sestet, in which the problem is resolved. The rhyme scheme is usually *abba abba ced cde, cdc cdc,* or *cde dce.*

Philosophical dualism: A theory that the universe is explicable in terms of two basic, conflicting entities, such as good and evil, mind and matter, or the physical and the spiritual.

Picaresque: A form of fiction that revolves around a central rogue figure, or picaro, who usually tells his own story. The plot structure of a picaresque novel is usually episodic, and the episodes usually focus on how the picaro lives by his wits. The classic example is Henry Fielding's *The History of Tom Jones, a Foundling* (1749).

Pindaric ode: Odes that imitate the form of those composed by the ancient Greek poet Pindar. A Pindaric ode consists of a strophe, followed by an antistrophe of the same structure, followed by an epode. This pattern may be repeated several times in the ode. In English poetry, Thomas Gray's "The Bard" is an example of a Pindaric ode.

Play: A literary work that is written to be performed by actors who speak the dialogue, impersonate the characters, and perform the appropriate actions. Usually, a play is performed on a stage, and an audience witnesses it.

Play-within-the-play: A play or dramatic fragment performed as a scene or scenes within a larger drama, typically performed or viewed by the characters of the larger drama.

Plot: Plot refers to how the author arranges the material not only to create the sequence of events in a play or story but also to suggest how those events are connected in a cause-and-effect relationship. There are a great variety of plot patterns, each of which is designed to create a particular effect.

Poem: A unified composition that uses the rhythms and sounds of language, as well as devices such as metaphor, to communicate emotions and experiences to the reader.

Poet laureate: The official poet of England, appointed for life by the English sovereign and expected to compose poems for various public occasions. The first official laureate was John Dryden in the seventeenth century. In the eighteenth century, the laureateship was given to a succession of mediocrities, but since the appointment of William Wordsworth in 1843, the office has generally been regarded as a substantial honor.

Polemic: A work that forcefully argues an opinion, usually on a controversial religious, political, or economic issue, in opposition to other opinions. John Milton's *Areopagitica* (1644) is one of the best known examples in English literature.

Postmodernism: The term is loosely applied to various artistic movements that have succeeded modernism, particularly since 1965. Postmodernist literature is experimental in form and reflects a fragmented world in which order and meaning are absent.

Pre-Raphaelitism: Refers to a group of nineteenth century English painters and writers, including Dante Gabriel Rossetti, Christina Rossetti, and William Morris. The Pre-Raphaelites were so called because they rebelled against conventional methods of painting and wanted to revert to what they regarded as the simple spirit of painting that existed before Raphael, particularly in its adherence to nature; they rejected all artificial embellishments. Pre-Raphaelite poetry made much use of symbolism and sensuousness, and showed an interest in the medieval and the supernatural.

Prose poem: A type of poem ranging in length from a few lines to three or four pages; most occupy a page or less. The distinguishing feature of the prose poem is its typography: it appears on the page like prose, with no line breaks. Many prose poems employ rhythmic repetition and other poetic devices not found in prose, but others do not; there is enormous variety in the genre.

Protagonist: Originally, in the Greek drama, the "first actor," who played the leading role. The term has come to signify the most important character in a drama or story. It is not unusual for there to be more than one protagonist in a work.

Proverb: A wise and pithy saying, authorship unknown, that reflects some observation about life. Proverbs are usually passed on through word of mouth, although they may also be written, as for example, the Book of Proverbs in the Bible.

Psychological novel: Once described as an interpretation of "the invisible life," the psychological novel is a form of fiction in which character, especially the inner life of characters, is the primary focus, rather than action. The form has characterized much of the work of Henry James, James Joyce, Virginia Woolf, and William Faulkner. *See also* Psychological realism.

Psychological realism: A type of realism that tries to reproduce the complex psychological motivations behind human behavior; writers in the late nineteenth century and early twentieth century were particularly influenced by Sigmund Freud's theories. *See also* Psychological novel.

Pun: A pun occurs when words with similar pronunciations have entirely different meanings. The result may be a surprise recognition of an unusual or striking connection, or, more often, a humorously accidental connection.

Quest: An archetypal theme identified by mythologist Joseph Campbell and found in many literary works. Campbell describes the heroic quest in three fundamental stages: departure (leaving the familiar world), initiation (encountering adventures and obstacles), and return (bringing home a boon to transform society).

Rabelaisian: The term is a reference to the sixteenth century French satirist and humorist François Rabelais. "Rabelaisian" is now used to refer to any humorous or satirical writing that is bawdy, coarse, or very down to earth.

Rationalism: A system of thought that seeks truth through the exercise of reason rather than by means of emotional response or revelation, or traditional authority. In literature, rationalism is associated with eighteenth century neoclassicism. *See also* Neoclassicism.

Realism: A literary technique in which the primary convention is to render an illusion of fidelity to external reality. Realism is often identified as the primary method of the novel form; the realist movement in the late nineteenth century coincided with the full development of the novel form.

Renaissance: The term means "rebirth" and refers to a period in European cultural history from the fourteenth to the early seventeenth century, although dates differ widely from country to country. The Renaissance produced an unprecedented flowering of the arts of painting, sculpture, architecture, and literature. The period is often said to mark the transition from the Middle Ages to the modern world. The questing, individualistic spirit that characterized the age was stimulated by an increase in classical learning by scholars known as Humanists, by the Protestant Reformation, by the development of printing, which created a wide market for books, by new theories of astronomy, and by the development of other sciences that saw natural laws at work where the Middle Ages had seen occult forces. *See also* Humanism.

Restoration comedy/drama: The restoration of the Stuart dynasty brought Charles II to the English throne in 1660. In literature, the Restoration period extends from 1660 to 1700. Restoration comedy is a comedy of manners, which centers around complicated plots full of the amorous intrigues of the fashionable upper classes. The humor is witty, but the view of human nature is cynical. Restoration dramatists include William Congreve, Sir George Etherege, and William Wycherley. In serious, or heroic, drama, the leading playwright was John Dryden. *See also* Comedy of manners.

Roman à clef: A fiction wherein actual persons, often celebrities of some sort, are thinly disguised. Lady Caroline Lamb's *Glenarvon* (1816), for example, contains a thinly veiled portrait of Lord Byron, and the character Mark Rampion in Aldous Huxley's *Point Counter Point* (1928) strongly resembles D. H. Lawrence.

Romance: Originally, any work written in Old French. In the Middle Ages, romances were about knights and their adventures. In modern times, the term has also been used to describe a type of prose fiction in which, unlike the novel, realism plays little part. Prose romances often give expression to the quest for transcendent truths.

Romanticism: A movement of the late eighteenth century and the nineteenth century that exalted individualism over collectivism, revolution over conservatism, innovation over tradition, imagination over reason, and spontaneity over restraint. Romanticism regarded art as self-expression; it strove to heal the cleavage between object and subject and expressed a longing for the infinite in all things. It stressed the innate goodness of human beings and the evils of the institutions that would stultify human creativity. The major English Romantic poets are William Blake, Lord Byron, Samuel Taylor Coleridge, John Keats, Percy Bysshe Shelley, and William Wordsworth.

Satire: A form of literature that employs the comedic devices of wit, irony, and exaggeration to expose, ridicule, and condemn human folly, vice, and stupidity. Justifying satire, Alexander Pope wrote that "nothing moves strongly but satire, and those who are ashamed of nothing else are so of being ridiculous."

Scene: A division of action within an act (some plays are divided only into scenes instead of acts). Sometimes, scene division indicates a change of setting or locale; sometimes, it simply indicates the entrances and exits of characters.

Science fiction: Fiction in which real or imagined scientific developments or certain givens (such as physical laws, psychological principles, or social conditions) form the basis of an imaginative projection, frequently into the future. Classic examples are the works of H. G. Wells and Jules Verne.

Sentimental novel: A form of fiction popular in the eighteenth century in which emotionalism and optimism are the primary characteristics. The best-known examples are Samuel Richardson's *Pamela* (1740-1741) and Oliver Goldsmith's *The Vicar of Wakefield* (1766).

Shakespearean sonnet: So named because William Shakespeare was the greatest English sonneteer, whose ranks also included the earl of Surrey and Thomas Wyatt. The Shakespearean sonnet consists of three quatrains and a concluding couplet, rhyming *abab cdcd efef gg*. The beginning of the third quatrain marks a turn in the argument.

Short story: A concise work of fiction, shorter than a novella, that is usually more concerned with mood, effect, or a single event than with plot or extensive characterization.

Simile: A type of metaphor in which two things are compared. It can usually be recognized by the use of the words "like," "as," "appears," or "seems."

Skaz: A term used in Russian criticism to describe a narrative technique that presents an oral narrative of a lowbrow speaker.

Soliloquy: An extended speech delivered by a character alone on stage, unheard by other characters. Soliloquy is a form of monologue, and it typically reveals the intimate thoughts and emotions of the speaker.

Song: A lyric poem, usually short, simple, and with rhymed stanzas, set to music.

Sonnet: A traditional poetic form that is almost always composed of fourteen lines of rhymed iambic pentameter; a turning point usually divides the poem into two parts, with the first part (octave) presenting a situation and the second part (sestet) reflecting on it. The main sonnet forms are the Petrarchan sonnet and the English (sometimes called Shakespearean) sonnet.

Stanza: When lines of poetry are meant to be taken as a unit, and the unit recurs throughout the poem, that unit is called a stanza; a four-line unit, a quatrain, is one common stanza. Others include couplet, *ottava rima*, and the Spenserian stanza.

Story line: The story line of a work of fiction differs from the plot. Story is merely the events that happen; plot is how those events are arranged by the author to suggest a cause-and-effect relationship. *See also* Plot.

Stream of consciousness: A narrative technique used in modern fiction by which an author tries to embody the total range of consciousness of a character, without any authorial comment or explanation. Sensations, thoughts, memories, and associations pour forth in an uninterrupted, prerational, and prelogical flow. For examples, see James Joyce's *Ulysses* (1922), Virginia Woolf's *To the Lighthouse* (1927), and William Faulkner's *The Sound and the Fury* (1929).

Sturm und Drang: A dramatic and literary movement in Germany during the late eighteenth century. Translated as "Storm and Stress," the movement was a reaction against classicism and a forerunner of Romanticism, characterized by extravagantly emotional language and sensational subject matter.

Surrealism: A revolutionary approach to artistic and literary creation, Surrealism argued for complete artistic freedom: The artist should relinquish all conscious control, responding to the irrational urges of the unconscious mind. Hence the bizarre, dreamlike, and nightmarish quality of Surrealistic writing. In the 1920's and 1930's, Surrealism flourished in France, Spain, and Latin America. (After World War II, it influenced such American writers as Frank O'Hara, John Ashberry, and Nathanael West.)

Symbol: A literary symbol is an image that stands for something else; it may evoke a cluster of meanings rather than a single specific meaning.

Symbolism: A literary movement encompassing the work of a group of French writers in the latter half of the nineteenth century, a group that included Charles Baudelaire, Stéphane Mallarmé, and Paul Verlaine. According to Symbolism, there is a mystical correspondence between the natural and spiritual worlds.

Theater of Cruelty: A term, coined by French playwright Antonin Artaud, which signifies a vision in which theater becomes an arena for shock therapy. The characters undergo such intense physical and psychic extremities that the audience cannot ignore the cathartic effect in which its preconceptions, fears, and hostilities are brought to the surface and, ideally, purged.

Theater of the Absurd: Refers to a group of plays that share a basic belief that life is illogical, irrational, formless, and contradictory, and that humanity is without meaning or purpose. Practitioners, who include Eugène Ionesco, Samuel Beckett, Jean Genet, Harold Pinter, Edward Albee, and Arthur Kopit, abandoned traditional theatrical forms and coherent dialogue.

Théâtre d'avant-garde: A movement in late nineteenth century drama in France, which challenged the conventions of realistic drama by using Symbolist poetry and nonobjective scenery.

Third person: Third-person narration occurs when the narrator has not been part of the event or affected it and is not probing his own relationship to it but is only describing what happened. He does not allow the intrusion of the word *I.* Third-person narration establishes a distance between reader and subject, gives credibility to a large expanse of narration that would be impossible for one person to experience, and allows the narrative to include a number of characters who can comment on one another as well as be the subjects of commentary by the participating narrator.

Tragedy: A form of drama that is serious in action and intent and that involves disastrous events and death; classical Greek drama observed specific guidelines for tragedy, but the term is now sometimes applied to a range of dramatic or fictional situations.

Travel literature: Writing that emphasizes the author's subjective response to places visited, especially faraway, exotic, and culturally different locales.

Trilogy: A novel or play written in three parts, each of which is a self-contained work, such as William Shakespeare's *Henry VI* (*Part I*, 1592; *Part II*, c. 1590-1591; *Part III*, c. 1590-1591). Modern examples include C. S. Lewis' Space Trilogy (1938-1945) and William Golding's Sea Trilogy (1980-1989).

Trope: Trope means literally "turn" or "conversion"; it is a figure of speech in which a word or phrase is used in a way that deviates from the normal or literal sense.

Verismo: Refers to a type of Italian literature that deals with the lower classes and presents them realistically using language that they would use. Called *verismo* because it is true to life, and, from the writer's point of view, impersonal.

Verse: Verse is a generic name for poetry. Verse also refers in a narrower sense to poetry that is humorous or merely superficial, as in "greeting-card verse." Finally, English critics sometimes use "verse" to mean "stanza," or, more often, to mean "line."

Verse drama: Verse drama was the prevailing form for Western drama throughout most of its history, comprising all the drama of classical Greece and continuing to dominate the stage through the Renaissance, when it was best exemplified by the blank verse of Elizabethan drama. In the seventeenth century, however, prose comedies became popular, and in the nineteenth and twentieth centuries verse drama became the exception rather than the rule.

Victorian novel: Although the Victorian period extended from 1837 to 1901, the term "Victorian novel" does not include works from the later decades of Queen Victoria's reign. The term loosely refers to the sprawling works of novelists such as Charles Dickens and William Makepeace Thackeray, which are characterized by a broad social canvas.

Villanelle: A French verse form assimilated by English prosody. It is usually composed of nineteen lines divided into five tercets and a quatrain, rhyming *aba*, *bba*, *aba*, *aba*, *abaa*. The third line is repeated in the ninth and fifteenth lines. Dylan Thomas' "Do Not Go Gentle into That Good Night" is a modern example of a successful villanelle.

Well-made play: From the French term *pièce bien faite*, a type of play constructed according to a "formula" that originated in nineteenth century France. The plot often revolves around a secret known only to some of the characters, which is revealed at the climax and leads to catastrophe for the villain and vindication or triumph for the hero. The well-made play influenced later dramatists such as Henrik Ibsen and George Bernard Shaw.

***Weltanschauung*:** A German term translated as "worldview," by which is meant a comprehensive set of beliefs or assumptions by means of which one interprets what goes on in the world.

Zeitgeist: A German term meaning the spirit of the times, the moral or intellectual atmosphere of any age or period. The *Zeitgeist* of the Romantic Age, for example, might be described as revolutionary, restless, individualistic, and innovative.

LIST OF AUTHORS